Mexico

A Culinary Quest

Ana Karen Cruz Casiano
in her kitchen near San
Felipe del Progreso,
Estado de México

Mexico
A Culinary Quest

Hossein Amirsadeghi
Ana Paula Gerard

Photography
Adam Wiseman

Additional Photography
Hossein Amirsadeghi
Carlos Alvarez Montero
Maryam Eisler

Consulting Editor
Andrea Belloli

Chief Project Director
Anne Field

Culture & Planning, Mexico
Sonia Gonzalez

Coordination & Logistics, Mexico
Miriam Tato

Project Director, Mexico
Venetia Thompson

Thames & Hudson

Baja California
232

Sonora
222

Chihuahua
480

Baja California Sur
214

Sinaloa
200

Durango
186

Zacatecas
312

Nayarit
492

Jalisco
346

Colima
504

First published by TransGlobe Publishing Ltd
in conjunction with Thames & Hudson Ltd

First published in the United Kingdom in 2017 by
Thames & Hudson Ltd
181A High Holborn
London WC1V 7QX
www.thamesandhudson.com

First published in 2017
in the United States of America by
Thames & Hudson Inc.
500 Fifth Avenue, New York
New York 10110
www.thamesandhudsonusa.com

© 2017 TransGlobe Publishing

Text and captions
© 2017 Hossein Amirsadeghi
Photography by Adam Wiseman, Hossein Amirsadeghi,
Carlos Alvarez Montero, Maryam Eisler

TransGlobe Publishing Limited
5 Fleet Place
London EC4M 7RD
United Kingdom
www.tgpublishingltd.com
info@tgpublishingltd.com

British Library Cataloguing-in-Publication Data
A catalogue record for this book is available from
the British Library

Library of Congress Catalog Control Number 2016955398

ISBN: 978-0-500-97082-9

Designed by Struktur Design Limited
Printed and bound in China

Contents

The Land of Moctezuma
Hossein Amirsadeghi

To tell it like it is, Mexico is a land of passions and paradoxes, the real deal in the Americas as far as culture, history, nation-building and political drama go, stretching back three thousand years. No other continental American country's history can match the magical exuberance and cacophony of experiences, the turmoil and periods of violence that Mexicans have endured since the conquistadors arrived to upend millennia of Aztec, Maya, Toltec, Zapotec and Olmec civilisation. Meanwhile North America did not even merit a mention.

And not just in the New World. Maya astronomy and mathematics were at various stages ahead of European, Near Eastern and Chinese knowledge and expertise. From the mighty stone cities of the Maya to the Aztecs' military prowess, from its conquest by Spain to its tortuous rise as a modern nation, Mexico can boast a rich history and culture whose roots have been traced back ten millennia. A quick look at this historical timeline reveals the impact of early civilisations on the region's landscape and society, followed by three hundred years of colonial rule, the struggle for independence in the early 1800s and the country's rebuilding in the twentieth century.

This book is in no shape or form intended as historical narrative, though I've woven in enough ancient, modern and contemporary history in short, sharp bursts to bring together the diverse, colourful threads that informed my own Mexican experience. The thirty-two breakers that divide the book into sequential sections help outline the narratives that become revelatory within the profile texts and pictorial journey that *Mexico: A Culinary Quest* has realised in order to delight *all* the senses. Not targeting a Mexican audience as such, though the book is a unique affirmation of the Mexican people's achievements. Instead, the target is more a global audience whose knowledge and experience of the country have for the most part been unhappily tuned to focus on its negative perceptions – its social dissonance, political dysfunction, populist dystopianism and economic distortion. Not forgetting governmental and judicial corruption and the violence of the drug cartels, compounded by forceful militarisation of the security forces as an inevitable response.

It may also surprise the reader to hear that the book is not strictly speaking focused on the culinary arts of Mexico. It is more of a quest for the heart and soul of the country and its people through the medium of food. Goodness knows there have been enough Mexican cookbooks, even some good ones, to fill multiple shelves. No – this tome is an adventure and a quest, inspired by a whim and engineered though sheer pizzazz and chutzpah, made possible by the support of worthy people at many levels of society, some of whose names are noted in the acknowledgements on the very last turn of this six-hundred-page wanderlust-document. A book that began life at a measured trot but that was soon in full-throated canter just to keep up with people and places as Mexico began to reveal itself in all its splendour. There's simply too much country to cover in one book, frankly, even in such an ambitious one as this is. Too many beautiful places: landscapes, countryside, cities, small towns, villages and the lonely hamlet perched at 3,000 metres next to an eagle's nest in the Sierra Tarahumara. Not forgetting the *Pueblos Mágicos*, so many jewels in the golden crown that sits atop this land of mountains, lush valleys, arid deserts and incomparable coastlines.

Mexico is the quintessential land of mountains, with more than half the country over 1,000 metres above sea level. Mountains clad in pine forests, valleys adorned with nature's bounties, even the arid desert alive with the sounds and smells of nature. The country is one of the world's three richest in terms of flora and fauna, with thirty thousand species of plants, a thousand different birds and five hundred species of mammals, many of them unique to Mexico. Verily I say unto thee: The country's a naturalist's paradise from its snow-capped peaks to its deserts, its tropical forests to its mangrove swamps. It's even got the world's second-largest barrier reef, and contains 12 per cent of the world's biodiversity.

Mexico has given humanity such vital staples as maize, squash, beans, chillies, avocados, papayas and cacao (chocolate). Not to mention Diego Rivera, Frida Kahlo, Octavio Paz and Carlos Fuentes. I don't mean to sound clichéd, but scratch the surface and you'll

(far left) **Ana Paula Gerard and Hossein Amirsadeghi in Guanajuato City, Guanajuato;** (left) **Breakfast of local cheese, cream and tamales cooked in green banana leaves by Maru Toledo at Rancho El Teuchiteco, Ahualulco de Mercado, Jalisco; and** (facing page) **The desert at dusk: Rancho Santa Marta, Baja California Sur**

discover hidden treasures, more than just the gold and silver that glitters. Full disclosure: I like Mexico. Didn't know the country before and, I daresay, won't have much to do with it in the future. But this Mexican quest turned into something profoundly moving and a very special experience indeed, as I followed the country's seasons during 2016 and learned to comprehend its history and geography and appreciate its people.

The ordinary Mexican is the embodiment of passion and paradox. One in ten Mexicans is from an indigenous group, with sixty-two different Indian languages still spoken across the country's time zones. Nahuatl (the language of the Aztecs) is most commonly used, with Mayan, Zapotec, Mixtec and Otomí used as other indigenous tongues. Pride and prejudice, consequentially, play equal parts in national mind-sets.

The familial bond is key in Mexico across all races, creeds and social strata; then comes loyalty to community, neighbourhood, village, town, state and country in order of priority. Rarely have I come across a people as collectively patriotic as Mexicans, though. Not always in a constructive manner, mind, as some folk express unwavering certitude in the face of other people's faults; many Mexicans are prone to blame other people and nations for their own shortcomings.

These are some of the attributes of the people I was privileged to meet on this journey, guiding me to define an agenda-free take on the country. Shaping a vision heightened by sensory perceptions of Mexico *de tous horizons*. My exposure to, and experience of, the country were not lacking. I'd published *Contemporary Art Mexico* not two years before starting out on this quest, visited Mexico City on several occasions in the process, got to know people of all backgrounds and artistic temperaments. Always volatile, the artistic temperament. Not entirely reflective of grass-roots socio-psychology. Gets you into trouble in extrapolation, and then there's the writer's worst sin: generalisation. Then again, I'm drawn to the flame when it comes to creative dissonance.

The earlier book's success, and my exploration of Mexico's contemporary art scene, opened a window onto the country's kaleidoscopic perspectives, revealing a trap-door on a desire to get to know more about Mexico, outside the rarefied élites of the art world. What of the people, their politics and purpose? I'd merely scratched the surface, and felt a strong need to speak to the soil, to learn of the toil of the land. I was intrigued by the people, mildly fascinated by their uncommon history, sensually aroused by the food, titillated by the colours of the place and the daily passion plays of individuals.

Art, as important as it is in the scheme of contemporary civil society (and élite politics), was not going to satisfy this sense of arousal. My Mexico City-centric experience (apart from a Sunday bus trip to Puebla and back) left me panting for more. But how was I to scratch this itch and produce a worthwhile exercise in global publishing at the same time? To see every aspect of the country and judge for myself, find proof of adulation, and abuse, commonly heard inside and outside the country? Leaving aside the colourful travel guides, glimpsing a random novel of experience, perusing a worthy book or two on someone's coffee table, plus all the column-inches of journalism on Mexico I could find did not satisfy my curiosity. Hence a desire to hit the road. But how? I was pretty much done with the arts, and I've no interest in crafts. Architecture could be a possible entry point in the Mexican context, but the subject had never brought me to smell the ink on a press. I'd done impulsive book-making journeys before, chasing the Arabian horse around the world, tracking the falcon across thirty countries, hunting down some of America's and Britain's finest artists in their sanctuaries.

The answer hit me during a lunch break in the Polanco area of Mexico City, tanking up in anticipation of the gruelling task of picking apart the psyche of a famous contemporary artist (who shall remain famously nameless). I'm as befuddled by the names of dishes and restaurants as I am by artists and their keepers, so I must confess to a lack of memory in regard to what I ate (or where) that inspired my take on Mexican cuisine, of which I knew *nada*. If you can do art, why not food, I thought. Hence *Mexico on a Plate*, an idea hatched into hibernation until a chance dinner with Carlos Salinas and Ana Paula Gerard on a cold, depressing February night in London. Between the hors d'oeuvres and dessert was this monumental enterprise befittingly born.

It's remarkable how great journeys take shape, on a whim and a wing and a prayer. *Mexico: A Culinary Quest* has proven a joy-ride, a journey conceived and concluded within twelve months, covering a country of nearly 2 million square kilometres and a population approaching 130 million with a GDP of nearly US$1.5 trillion (eleventh largest in the world) and twenty-six UNESCO World Heritage Sites, with places and locations that are simply out of this world and, incidentally, some of the best food that can be found anywhere.

Why food? Let Octavio Paz, Mexico's literary giant, answer that one: 'Eroticism is the most intense passion and gastronomy the most extensive!' UNESCO's 2010 declaration of traditional Mexican cuisine as an intangible form of cultural heritage quoted the writer Alberto Ruy Sánchez describing the exuberance of Mexican cuisine displayed against well-laid and overflowing tables resplendent with offerings of every colour and aroma. Served in handcrafted dishes, evoking endless abundance for the enjoyment of the eye and the pleasure of the palate. These bountiful tables create close bonds among people, the declaration continued. 'Excess becomes another form of transcendence. It carries us beyond the dish, palate, or belly to the sense of what life has in common.'

That last sentence was the seed corn for this project, the *metate* in which I prepared this dish of a book by searching out the life and soul of the people of Mexico through their culinary traditions and epicurean tastes. By chronicling a journey of close observation across the country's picturesque canvas via the medium of more than a hundred entertaining, informative characters from all backgrounds and lifestyles across the country's thirty-two states, *Mexico: A Culinary Quest* attempts to capture the essence and spirit of Mexican food history as well as a wide range of contemporary cooking styles. The book seeks out cultural idiosyncrasies within the realm of food to become a sketch of the country's personality and character, achieved by burrowing under its skin.

And what burrowing there has been, with penetrating one-on-one interviews marinated into profile dishes which concentrate less on the classic recipe formula than on presenting the reader with specially commissioned photography captioned to background the text. The lively images create a filmic journey intended to position the reader with access to often stupendous landscapes while placing

(facing page, left) **A street-food vendor in Camino Verde, Tijuana, Baja California;** (facing page, right) **A girl and her brother busking at the Saturday street market in Plaza San Jacinto, San Ángel, Mexico City;** and (right) **Chef Ricardo Muñoz Zurita, Hossein Amirsadeghi and some sumptuous bougainvillea in San Ángel, Mexico City**

people's daily lives into context; always dramatic, these landscapes are a painter's delight, for each canvas tells a different story. Essentially, I took Virginia Woolf's quote to heart ('One cannot think well, love well, sleep well, if one has not dined well') and turned it into a quest. Having started out with the theory that *Homo sapiens* began to evolve around the kitchen table (or variations thereof through time), this book was fashioned as an experiential test, exploring the singular relationship between mind and stomach.

Did culture or agriculture come first in the human drama? That pertinent, if not teasing, question was asked repeatedly in the development of this book. We've come to recognise that culture consists of learned experiences, transmittable behavioural patterns which often defy natural selection or logic. Food and cooking were the most elemental experiences of humankind. Therefore, it would follow that the first learned cultural experience was the hunting, gathering and preparation of food. The socialisation engendered by group interaction among humans needing to collaborate in the hunt; the long-winded experimental process of breeding and cross-breeding, cultivating the seeds and grasses that allowed humanity's growth. The act of sharing and caring by the family unit seated round the fire cooking a meal. These were the primary acculturations in shared and learned experience that transformed themselves into elective practices which then locked in human behaviour over hundreds or thousands of years. All this was apparent in its

contemporary context as I journeyed across the land, shaping my experiences into a visual and editorial handshake across time, cultures, disciplines, beliefs and the essence of Mexico today. The project turned into a search for truth, knowledge and experience in understanding a country I barely knew.

That's what questing is all about. Not just a word in a book's title, more a directional lead to its readership. This book's intention is to showcase the extraordinary mix that amplifies Mexico's regional ethos, allowing the differing culinary tastes and their attendant social aesthetics to become manifest without too much editorial interference. It is a capture of the moment, a portal to all things Mexican with a view to platforming the country's offerings to a wide audience set against the busy canvas of people, places, terrain, architecture, and life lived in urban and rural settings. It is, I hope, a unique interplay between visual, textual and symbolic narratives. Symbols, after all, are everything to nations, races and peoples. Even the book's dust jacket was chosen symbolically, an oblique reference to food in combination with history, religion, society and culture. An image of ceremonial tortillas cooking on an ancient *comal*, the social and political motifs as old as Mexico itself. One painterly tortilla shows an eagle devouring a serpent perched atop a cactus – an Aztec prophecy that guided the *ancestors* (a word Mexicans love) to Lake Texcoco and the building of Tenochtitlán, the Aztec Empire's capital city built on an island in a marshy lake that is today's Mexico City.

This was no Homeric odyssey by any stretch of the imagination. Things were just too well organised and operationally cosy. Nevertheless, it turned out to be a cultural tracking exercise tracing the elements that have brought Mexico to its present state. I had chosen the title to reflect some form of odyssey but quickly came up against its pretentious ramifications. The word *odyssey* was then replaced by *quest*, and Homer by Tolkien, but in the realm of the real. The taxonomy of the word *quest* conjures up matters mythical, physical and metaphysical, reflecting fictional characterisations with symbolic or allegorical connotations. It demands of the writer a journey with an end-goal, yet our journey had more purpose than goal, and I was determined to complete the whole with a flourish. Obstacles there were aplenty (read about some of them in the breaker texts, if you're interested in how the onion was skinned), but we managed to showcase exotic locations and different cultures within a national culture, just as the word *quest*'s antonym demands. As to any supernatural requirements of the classical interpretation of the word, I must confess that on several occasions I felt a force beyond the ordinary, whether in human, spiritual or natural encounters. The moral force of a quest also demands protagonists changing character, or at the very least reformulating perspectives along the journey, a revised *Weltanschauung*. All these literary or semi-philosophical sentiments are therefore reflected in some form or measure within the book.

'Everything you possess of skill, and wealth, and handicraft, wasn't it first merely a thought and a quest?' Jalaluddin Rumi ruminated seven centuries ago as he continued his lifelong quest in search of the Beloved. Yes, I confess to some reformulation in spirit, certainly a different take on the country, its people, customs, culture and natural temper. The Mexican people moved beyond stereotypes, leading to a questioning of what makes and breaks a nation. Given the tumult of present-day border politics with its northern neighbour, this quest has taught me to view Mexican people and culture in a better light, and to decry those who would condemn the country without cause or warrant.

It is not uncommon for one's own people to have a monopoly on virtue. Mexicans are no exception. A religious and superstitious people prone to expressions of victimhood in their observation of festivals and such, they have, through generations of oppression, grown an emotional tendency to assert and reassert their independence at every turn. A people with natural grace and characterful beauty, Mexicans are geniuses at stringing words together in the most elaborate formulations without committing to their consequences. With laughter and smiles, or the ultimate kiss-off (the Mexican shrug), there's a tendency to get nowhere. But a Mexican's word, I've generally found, is his or her badge of honour. If you can get the word to be spoken, that is. The surface *politesse* can become tortured at times, given the richness of the Spanish language … *Es la costumbre del pais* is often the default refrain.

Mexicans are an intensely pictorial people, living their history and traditions in their daily lives. You have a country with huge potential, dramatic nature and landscapes continuously painted into practice, whether on the exteriors of towns and villages or in colourful vestments and simple artefacts. The realities of life for most Mexicans are hard (53 per cent of the population lives below the poverty line), but the silent nobility with which the *campesino* faces existence never fails to inspire. 'Everybody talks but nobody listens!' was how one grizzled old-timer explained his compatriots' shortcomings.

As for my culinary quest, it began and finished with Laura Esquivel. Hers was the first book (and film) I searched out to gain inspiration when setting off on my journey. How fitting, as she was the last person I interviewed at her home in Coyoacán, Mexico City. Esquivel spoke of revelations in the national ethos through the possibilities of cuisine. Of Granny's *muy antiguas* recipes, showing off the family scrapbook that led to her writing *Like Water for Chocolate*, an international bestseller. Esquivel spoke in nostalgic terms of old-fashioned Mexican hospitality, of the goodness of the people and the injustices of an industrialising society losing touch with the heritage of the land. She sighed at the inequities of cross-border political

conflict but delighted in the prospect of her country becoming more self-reliant and independent of industrial blackmail. Mexico, she lamented, has become a giant *maquiladora* servicing US and international industry, polluting its social and political climates, and damaging the environment beyond the point of sustainable renewal.

Noble thoughts, these, but the harsh realities of modern life cannot (unlike the Magical Realism of Juan Rulfo and Esquivel) turn the clock back, or return to a pastoral ideal that decries the spread of industry and agri-business. The working population continues to grow with increasing demands on national resources, while government has to deal with myriad problems born not only of its own inadequacies but of constraints imposed by the social, economic and political order. In the end, all societies are forced into a Faustian embrace of policies and ideas intended for the common good yet always leading to some degree of dysfunction and, at times, dystopian outcomes.

This book is intended as a memory trail, the capture of the Mexican moment in time, for all time. I challenge anyone to do better, and foreswear any aim beyond wonderment at nature and the possibilities of cultural renewal. Perhaps it is best to leave the last words to Faust himself:

You'll sit forever, gluing things together,
Cooking up a stew from others' scraps,
Blowing on a miserable fire,
Made from your heap of dying ash.
Let apes and children praise your art,
If their admiration's to your taste,
But you'll never speak from heart to heart,
Unless it rises up from your heart's space.

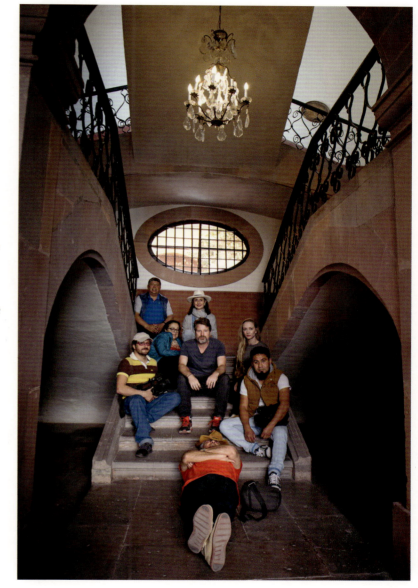

(facing page, left) **Restaurante La Tequila in Guadalajara, Jalisco, where more than two hundred different tequilas are on offer;** and (right) **Xkeken** *cenote* **(sinkhole) near Valladolid, Yucatán**

(left) **Dunas de Yeso in Cuatro Ciénegas, Coahuila, a biosphere preserve whose brilliant white sandy landscapes stretch into the distant horizon**

(above) **The Mexico project team on the staircase of an impeccably restored sixteenth-century mansion in Querétaro:** (from top left) **Francisco Mendoza (logistics), Ana Paula Gerard (executive editor), Sonia Gonzalez (project director), Venetia Thompson (project director), Adam Wiseman (photographer), Homero Jiménez (cameraman), Donato López (assistant cameraman), Hossein Amirsadeghi (editor/publisher)**

(following spread, left) **Maite Flores García learning to prepare tortillas in San Pablo del Monte, Tlaxcala; and** (right) **Bullfighter César Montes ready for the** *corrida* **in Zacatecas city**

Food & Culture in Mexico: An Historical Narrative
Margarita de Orellana

We Mexicans are rather demanding of our food. And we know how to eat well. The story of our taste is that of a unique cuisine. How to decipher it? How to explain the tenacity of a taste acquired by some, inherited by others? It is said that we have a discriminating palate. We quickly discard food that is generic or of poor quality. And we know how to detect good seasoning, a vital skill when it comes to obtaining the desired flavour. The history of our unusual culinary taste is both ancient and contemporary, and cannot be understood without considering the preeminence of maize.

In maize we were born, in maize we die

To see maize dough take the shape of a perfect disc between the expert hands of a woman, hands that convey it to the *comal* (griddle) for cooking and from there to our mouths, is a joy that doubtless unites all Mexicans. The tortilla is not only bitten into: it wraps, accommodates and stores other food, acting as both napkin and spoon. Once the plate has been wiped clean, even the spoon is eaten.

Not so long ago, the art of *tortear* (making tortillas by hand) had almost disappeared, especially in urban areas. Nowadays, machines provide us with most of our tortillas. The ritual of bringing that first morsel, plain or salted, to our mouths, even if it is a warm tortilla recently expelled by a mechanical device, is something we treasure. That everyday gesture performed by all Mexicans while enjoying maize tortillas, or any of the dishes that unfurl from that same plant, carries with it a history that stretches back over five thousand years. The ancient inhabitants of Mexico domesticated maize along with many other plants, among them squash, beans, avocados, chilli peppers, tomatoes, and maguey and *nopal* cacti. The myriad ways of preparing maize, from tortillas of different sizes and colours to tamales that range from small to half a metre in length (*sacahuil*), not to mention beverages and soups – *atoles*, *champurrados*, *pozoles* – have endured for centuries without interruption. After the Spanish conquest, the ways in which maize was consumed were enriched by the arrival of culinary contributions from other lands. Without maize, there would be no Mexican cuisine as we know it today. Nor, perhaps, would there be any Mexico at all.

Maize enjoyed a powerful mythical reputation among the ancient Mexicans. It was considered to be a sacred plant. From the Olmecs to the Mexica, the plant was associated with many divinities. According to the Maya and other cultures of Mesoamerica, human beings are made out of maize. Moreover, since it is a plant that cannot reproduce on its own, thus requiring the hands of farmers, it is said that we are both the origin and creation of maize. Somehow, we take in a mouthful of ourselves with each bite. The great historian of Nahuatl culture Miguel León Portilla noted that one of the names the Aztecs had for maize was Tonacayo, which means 'our flesh', 'our sustenance', suggesting a sort of autophagy.

Among the Maya, the god of maize was considered an ideal of beauty. Since the fields where the plants are cultivated are in constant movement due to the wind as well as slash-and-burn farming, they also compared it to a tireless dancer. The religious conduct of the Maya revolved around maize. Even ceremonies celebrating the birth of a child were (and continue to be, in some villages) conjoined. As people prayed, the newborn's umbilical cord was cut above a maize plant, which, stained with blood until it steamed, was stored until the next planting, when the kernels were removed and sown in hopes of a prosperous harvest. Thus, metaphorically, the Maya ate of their own blood.

According to the Mexica, the goddesses of maize were associated with the maize-cob god Cintéotl, son of the Earth and Sun. Tender maize was personified by Xilonen – hence in all likelihood the word *jilote*, or 'green maize'. Chicomeacóatl personified the growth of the plant but was also that which could be eaten and drunk, while Xilomanaliztli represented the start of the growing season because he made offerings of green maize to the soil. During the entire sowing process, rituals were practised that sought to ensure a successful harvest. Tribute was paid to all of the gods.

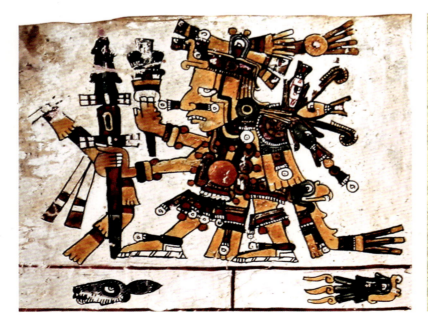

(far left) **Centéotl, the Aztec maize god, from the Borgia Codex. Photo courtesy of Biblioteca Apostolica Vaticana, Vatican City;** (left) **Xilonen, the Aztec goddess of young maize, whose name is related to *jilote*, the Mexican word for an unripe ear of maize, from the Florentine Codex. Photo courtesy of Biblioteca Medicea Laurenziana, Florence; and** (facing page) ***Market Stall*, 1766. Museo Nacional de Historia, 'Castillo de Chapultepec', Mexico City. Photo courtesy of Secretaría de Cultura.INAH.SINAFO. FN.MÉXICO**

In Mexico today, maize rituals continue to exist in many indigenous cultures. It would seem that the Spaniards failed to eradicate these practices, although they were modified by the presence and imposition of new gods. The myths and rites dedicated to maize continue to be passed down from one generation to the next, providing continuity and identity to each of our diverse original cultures. The Spaniards adapted their own ritual calendar to the pagan agricultural cycles of the peoples they conquered. Despite our myriad tongues, customs and cultures, year after year the people of Mexico share their fervour for this sacred plant. Some communities build altars with offerings. Special dishes are served, permission is asked before sowing, then thanks are given for every harvest. The fields of maize are adorned with flowers, and home altars are decorated with candles, gourds, seeds, liquor and tobacco.

León Portilla listed some of the dishes mentioned in codices or by chroniclers during the early years of the Viceroyalty. The Florentine Codex, perhaps the most complete register of that era, was composed as a collaboration between Friar Bernardino de Sahagún and his indigenous informants, one of whom spoke Nahuatl, Spanish and Latin. It mentions that the Aztec nobility consumed coloured tortillas in a range of sizes. (In Mexico there are over sixty varieties of maize, and their cobs boast many colours.) The tortillas were followed by tamales made out of maize kernels and turkey meat. Other game was consumed (boar, deer, iguana and quail), as well as frogs, axolotls, winged ants, grasshoppers, stink bugs and maguey worms. Aromatic plants such as epazote (*Dysphania ambrosioides*), herbs and greens like *pápalo* (similar to coriander), *quintoniles*, *chaya* (tree spinach) and *achiote* (annatto) featured in Aztec cuisine, not to mention fruit such as the tricoloured *zapote*, *chirimoyas*, *tejocotes* and *mameyes*. Beverages like cacao water were prepared with vanilla, flowers and honey, while *atoles* were made with maize dough, beans, honey and a variety of chilli peppers. In contrast, the diet of Aztec peasants was reduced to just a few ingredients: maize tortillas, roasted maguey and *nopal* cactus pads, insects, worm tamales and a limited range of *atoles*. León Portilla concluded that the prehispanic diet was fairly balanced and did not include many carbohydrates, given that lard or oil for frying had not yet been introduced. Nearly all the dishes described by him continue to be consumed today.

Nopal, maguey, cacao

Despite the omnipresence of maize in Mexican gastronomy, there are other emblematic fruits and plants that have long histories. Some of the more visible ones are *nopal*, maguey and cacao.

The *nopal* cactus is key to our landscape and the emblem of Mexico City, formerly known as Tenochtitlán. Sixteenth-century chroniclers maintained that the *nopal* was born out of the heart of the first man sacrificed to the god of the Sun, Huitzilopochtli. This happened at the start of the Aztec Empire, which would later encompass a great deal of Mesoamerica. The national seal on the Mexican flag features an eagle perched on a *nopal*, holding its fruit, a prickly pear, in its claws. Aside from the outstanding flavour of its leaves and fruit, various parts of the *nopal* plant were used as curative remedies. It has been said that it also provided Mexican culture with colour, given that the parasite that feeds off it, the

Grana cochinilla, gave us the carmine hue that sustained the vibrant economy of New Spain for several centuries, above all that of Oaxaca.

The maguey's visual richness has influenced artists and poets alike. The plant has also offered Mexicans many gifts. Garments, rope and paper are made from its fibres; instruments of sacrifice and needles from its tips; and its long leaves are used for thatching roofs. Delicious honey is manufactured from its sap. Mayahuel, the prehispanic maguey goddess, was represented with four hundred breasts from which the white milk of pulque flowed without end. We might say that pulque was, for centuries, the national beverage, more so than mezcal or tequila. Before the arrival of the Spaniards, we are told by historians of Mesoamerica, pulque was consumed by the elderly, the adventurous and those destined for sacrifice. For the most part, inebriation was a punishable offence. All of this changed after the conquest because, as it became popular, pulque brought with it many calamities.

Save few exceptions, *nopal* and maguey did not travel the world. On the other hand, cacao – the name comes from the Mayan *kakau* – was cultivated from the Olmec to the Nahua. All of these people knew how to extract its nutritious, medicinal and spiritual essence. No-one imagined at the time that this plant and its *xocolatl*, or chocolate, would travel the *world*, giving pleasure to so many. Unfortunately, it plays a minor role in Mexico today. Crops are scanty and chocolate production is depleted. However, efforts have begun to improve production and replenish seeds on the verge of extinction.

Room for flavour

Also characteristic of Mexican cuisine are the areas where food is prepared. Certain elements from the past endure there. León Portilla noted that the Mexica called this space *tenamaztli*, considering it to be sacred, because they believed that the powerful force of fire resided there. Predictions were made around the hearth. A great many kitchen utensils from the prehispanic era are still in use today: *metates* (grinding stones), *molcajetes* (large mortars), *cazuelas* (casseroles), clay jars, *chiquihuites* (baskets) and *comales*. These necessities could bring good or bad fortune. For example, when a *metate* cracked, it meant that someone in the household would die. We know how important the same utensils are to Mexican cooking today. A sauce elaborated in a stone *molcajete* will never be surpassed by one made in a blender. Industrial blends cannot compare with the dough forged on a *metate*; the stone adds an incomparable supplementary flavour. A broad jug with a narrow spout is the best receptacle for an *atole* or *champurrado*. The beating of hot chocolate in a jar with a wooden mill increases the flavour of the drink and produces its foamy consistency.

For centuries, kitchens were places of tiresome labour. One had to carry in the firewood and water, and each meal demanded hours of preparation. Even though cooking spaces have been modernised, some of the utensils of prehispanic cooking continue to be indispensable.

Mestizo cuisine

Starting with the conquest, the *caciques* (cultural leaders) would offer their women to the Spaniards. Thus, the *cacique* of Tabasco gave La Malinche to Hernán Cortés. This gesture constituted a pledge on the part of the warrior alliance against the Aztec Empire, a new social order created to destroy it. That is why Cortés prohibited his soldiers from bringing women over from Spain. In fact he was reviving a weapon of Arab origin: intermarriage with new allies. La Malinche learned Spanish and became Cortés' companion and translator. One might say that with this emblematic couple, *mestizaje*, or racial blending, was born.

Mestizaje, in addition to arising in other walks of life, also took place in gastronomy. Mexican cuisine is a combination of Mesoamerican, Mediterranean, Arab and African elements, and it adapted various Asian cuisines as well. With outsiders came wheat, rice, grapevines, sugarcane, citrus fruit and other produce unknown to the New World, not to mention condiments such as cinnamon, sesame, onion and garlic, and animals such as the pig (baptised *cochi* or *cochino*, 'one who sleeps'), cattle and horses. The blending of foodstuffs and culinary techniques resulted in a colonial cuisine that may also be defined as *mestizo*, and therefore Mexican. At first, it was as Baroque as those who prepared and consumed it. It diversified by incorporating fried foods – hence our delicious snacks involving maize as a base or wrapper: tostadas, *chalupas*, *garnachas*, enchiladas, *gorditas* and so on. Moreover, thanks to the arrival of sugarcane, desserts proliferated, as did a variety of sweets.

At first it was the friars who taught the indigenous people their culinary techniques. Soon convents were built for nuns and monasteries for priests, both in Mexico City and elsewhere. Starting in the seventeenth century, the kitchens of convents became privileged places where culinary *mestizaje* was born, resulting in such sophisticated dishes as many-coloured *moles* and the famous *chiles en nogada*, a chilli-based dish with walnut sauce. Spanish-born nuns and those of Spanish heritage coexisted with the Indian, black and *mestiza* women who served them. Together they contributed their culinary knowledge to the daily diet of Mexicans. The historian Manuel Ramos Medina noted, not without a touch of irony, that it may be no accident that the creation of *mole* is attributed to the religious orders of Puebla. The word probably derives from a question asked by a servant woman: 'Mother, what should I do with these chilli peppers, chocolate and herbs I've ground on the *metate*? Shall I keep grinding them?' (*Molli* in Nahuatl means 'to grind'.) Moreover, Nahua women prepared a festival dish called *chilmolli*, comprised of chilli peppers, maize dough and cacao in which tortillas were soaked. It could be accompanied by meat and vegetables during special festivities, but for the most part it was a vegetarian dish. The nuns cooked similar dishes, introducing lard and spices from abroad such as sesame seeds. Finally, they achieved a semblance of the famous *mole* of Puebla. For Alfonso Reyes, a great poet and glutton, the nuns' colonial *mole* is the cornerstone of our gastronomy, and refusing that dish opens one to accusations of treason.

Before the arrival of sugar, many sweets were made out of maize and honey from bees or maguey. *Amaranto*, a grain that was cultivated five thousand years ago, was blended with maguey honey to form dough used to fashion figurines of the gods to use as offerings. They were then consumed with relish. Considering this practice to be heretical, the Spaniards prohibited the preparation or consumption of such dough. The prohibition contributed to a drastic reduction in the cultivation of this nutritious sweet, widely considered today to be a marvellous food source with a major market presence. In all likelihood, the nuns from the sixteenth century ate a frugal diet and fasted regularly. However, during the festivals of patron saints (which continue to be important today), they would break their fasts, giving rise to the abundance of sugary sweets prepared by pious hands. These desserts were, and are, an invitation to gluttony.

Little is known of the tables of the sixteenth century. There were no dining rooms in homes, according to some historians, only refectories in convents. Everyone else ate in kitchens or wherever they came to rest. Excavations in Mexico City unearthed crude clay platters on which monks served the poor what they called 'fool's soup'. It is easy to imagine what it consisted of. On the other hand, in the seventeenth century, as is clear from still-life paintings of the time, dishes were made of clay, *talavera* pottery or glass as well as silver. By the eighteenth century, paintings document a greater abundance of silver on tables in what may be dining rooms.

Public food

In the late eighteenth century, Mexico City witnessed a proliferation of eateries, among them *fondas*, *fogones*, *almuercerías*, *tepacherías*, wine shops and ice cream parlours. During festivals that featured specific dishes such as the Day of the Dead or Christmas, celebrations were held of course. The arches of buildings were filled with *alfeñiques* (sweets) in the shapes of animals, coffins and mermaids. People would give these to each other as offerings for the dead. Over the Christmas holidays, even more sweets, nuts, almonds, pine nuts and peanuts were sold, as well as seasonal fruit like *perones*, lemons and *tejocotes* (a species of hawthorn), either soaked

(facing page) *Wool loader in a food stall*, circa 1915–20. Casasola Archive, Fototeca Nacional (inventory number 161879). Photo courtesy of Secretaría de Cultura.INAH.SINAFO. FN.MÉXICO; and (left) Winfield Scott, *Market Sellers*, c 1930. Fototeca Nacional (inventory number 459804). Photo courtesy of Secretaría de Cultura.INAH.SINAFO. FN.MÉXICO

in sugar or dried. Similar celebrations took place in other cities and continue today, in both urban and rural areas.

Mexican independence sparked the arrival of French immigrants. By 1830, the first *fondas galas* – more elaborate than simple taverns – were open for business. Regarding the French cuisine so highly prized by the upper and middle classes, author José Iturriaga noted, 'We received not only dishes and techniques, but also words, such as restaurant, menu, chef, buffet, mayonnaise, omelet, *volován* or *vol-au-vent*, croquette, canapé, mousse, and soufflé, among others.' In the mid-nineteenth century, the famous 'pastry war', the first French intervention in Mexican affairs, began when a French baker demanded compensation from Mexico when rioters destroyed his shop. Once the conflict had ended, French influence was felt more strongly in many walks of daily life among the upper and middle classes. According to the guide *El Viajero en México*, in 1864 there were in the capital 111 pastry and chocolate shops, fourteen hotels with restaurants, twenty-three *fondas*, eleven cantinas, and nearly eighty-four cafés and ice cream parlours. Writer Salvador Novo described how Indians who came to the city to sell their wares remained unaffected by these changes; their frugal diet was the same as always. Mme Calderón de la Barca, who lived in Mexico at the time, describes the Indians as 'very plain, with a humble, mild expression of countenance, very gentle, and wonderfully polite in their manners to each other'. She also tells us that the middle classes ingested plenty of meat, while the Indians did not. Street vendors would hawk their wares, crying, 'Lard! Lard! One and a half reals!', 'Plump little cakes fresh from the oven!' or 'Ducks! Oh my soul, hot ducks!'

Novo confirmed that in the early twentieth century there were, above all in the cities, three social classes: the *pelados*, or 'shorn ones', including the indigenous people who continued to sustain their traditional diet (maize, beans, squash, chilli peppers); the middle classes, who had added many dishes to the culinary repertoire; and

the wealthy. Extreme poverty was occasionally recorded by reporters and photographers in the capital. One of them, José Frías, who signed his work as Juan de Sena, called the most impoverished the 'honourable brotherhood of beggars' in 1921. The poor were served by cooks whom they called '*las escamocheras*'. These were to be found near Tepito, still one of the city's most marginalised and dangerous neighbourhoods. On great trays filled with grease, the cooks would serve up *escamochas* – that is to say, the scrambled leftovers from restaurants. According to Juan de Sena, this was food for the suicidal. A serving cost 5 centavos instead of 1.5 pesos, which was the lowest price one could find in any cafeteria. It would seem that this custom had also been common in the 1800s, when cooks from wealthy homes would do the same with their mistresses' leftovers. It was a good strategy to avoid wasting food. Other members of the 'brotherhood' would meet at *los agachados*, or 'bowed head', stalls, where they ate squatting on their haunches. One of these *locales* was called Sanborncito, a parody of the aristocracy of the era who frequented the coveted Sanborns (today, a vast cafeteria chain).

Decades after the revolutionary clashes that lasted roughly from 1910 to 1920, a new influence became perceptible in gastronomy, one that arrived from across Mexico's northern border. In the central part of the country, the aforementioned Sanborns, aside from serving Mexican dishes, began to offer corned beef, roast beef, cottage cheese and cornflakes. During World War II, Mexicans felt the North American influence even more strongly when another item was added to the culinary mix: fast food. Today, of course, sandwiches, hamburgers, hot dogs and pancakes continue to be served everywhere. Meanwhile, Mexico City began to grow at a dizzying pace starting in the 1940s, and its restaurants and *fondas* followed suit. Some Spanish restaurants made names for themselves, others featured Mexican food, and many specialised in the food of China, Lebanon, France and elsewhere. The city offered, and continues to offer, an enormous variety of food for all tastes and budgets.

(left) *Street vendors offering their products*, circa 1910. Fototeca Nacional (inventory number 459812). Photo courtesy of Secretaría de Cultura.INAH.SINAFO. FN.MÉXICO. (facing page, top) San Pascual Bailón, patron saint of cooks, looks down on Guillermo Olguín's kitchen in Oaxaca; and (facing page, bottom) The seventeenth-century kitchen of the Ex Convento de Santa Rosa de Lima in Puebla. It is claimed that *mole poblano* was invented there

(Following spread) Iztaccíhuatl and Popocatépetl volcanoes overlooking the sprawl of Mexico City at dawn. Iztaccíhuatl ('white woman' in Nahuatl) has a glacier, while Popocatépetl has been active in recent years

Markets

Another culinary arena catering to Mexican taste is the *mercado*, or market. From a young age, Mexicans are fascinated by this display of colours, aromas and varieties of food blending together with the cries of vendors and loaders and a flurry of incessant movement. In Mexico City, certain classic markets remain standing today, for example the Mercado de San Juan, which continues to enjoy fame as a purveyor of high-quality products that are otherwise hard to find. Since the days of President Porfirio Díaz, other markets have also become important, such as La Merced, Sonora, La Viga and Jamaica; moreover, every district has a smaller market that is very well stocked. In these same neighbourhoods, once a week, the *tianguis*, or street markets, appear, where one is supposedly able to find the same products, only fresher and cheaper. Why do Mexicans prefer these cluttered spaces to any other kind of commerce? Sources from the past tell us how the Spaniards were stupefied by the abundance they encountered in the Indians' markets. There, they saw for the first time thousands of unfamiliar products, from vegetables, fruit and medicinal plants to utensils, blankets, metalwork and slaves. Could it be that we are loathe to let go of this cultural legacy?

In every corner of Mexico, markets exist where one can appreciate regional foods and styles of preparation. On many stalls, great tables are set up where delicious simple food can be enjoyed. Each one offers a multitude of dishes no single menu would be large enough to list. Anyone who wants to truly understand Mexico's culinary richness must visit them all, north to south, in order to sample the full range of our gastronomy. Regional dishes change a lot from one location to another. A specialist who has actually done this sort of detailed exploration has become the strongest spokesperson for traditional Mexican cuisine: Diana Kennedy. Kennedy toured hundreds of markets by automobile for years, on her own, recovering on our behalf flavours that could easily have been forgotten. Her cookbooks are small treasures that every Mexican and foreigner should use. It is vital that we preserve these kitchens, taking care

that their traditional flavours and produce do not disappear. The expansion of monoculture and industrial agriculture has contributed to the abandoning of many ancient farming practices, their knowledge minimised, sometimes gone forever.

Aside from the markets, there are street vendors across Mexico who set up shop (as they have for centuries) on strategic corners where, if their seasoning is good enough, they become very popular until, with a little luck, they are able to open a *fonda* or even a restaurant. Today, these street vendors form part of what economists call the 'informal economy'.

Shared tables

Meals to celebrate any event or special occasion within a community or extended family have not changed much over time in terms of their profound significance. If we consider many of the celebratory meals we frequently attend, religious or otherwise, such as weddings, first communions, baptisms or feasts dedicated to patron saints, where hundreds of people share the same table, what becomes glaringly obvious are the excess and economic waste. As writer Alberto Ruy Sánchez has indicated, exuberance is a fundamental trait of Mexican cuisine. Well-laid tables decorated with flowers bear a variety of dishes of every colour imaginable, their luminous textures and enveloping aromas served in and on handcrafted objects made especially for the occasion. The sense of endless abundance is there to be appreciated. To the enjoyment of the eye are added the pleasures of the palate. These exuberant tables create close bonds among the guests. 'Sharing a table in Mexico has a transcendental application: a commitment of reciprocity. Excess becomes another form of transcendence. It carries us beyond the dish, palate, or belly to the sense of what life has in common. This implies recognizing that Mexican cuisine forms part of a complete lifestyle that, when manifested in a community, lends meaning to life' – so stated UNESCO's 2010 declaration of traditional Mexican cuisine as an intangible form of cultural heritage.

The present day

Gastronomy has been in vogue in many countries for several years now, and Mexico has not remained on the sidelines. Many foreign chefs, especially from France, have experimented here with singular creativity. In the late nineteenth century, a French cook called Jacques Paire arrived to seek his fortune. His intention to blend French dishes with Mexican ingredients was seen by his colleagues as heresy. The way he told it, 'A chef ought to be open to his surroundings and rescue whatever is of value from every country. My own nature incited me to experiment with combinations born out of my contact with Mexico, taking advantage of the capacity of French cuisine to absorb elements without compromising their essence.' It is no coincidence that Paire's memoirs are entitled *Of Escargot and Escamoles*. Some Mexican chefs have delved deeper into this area over the past few decades, while others focus more on Mexican cuisine, studying it in order to invent new dishes, making maximum use of traditional ingredients. Others prefer to recreate ancient recipe books or those that belonged to their grandmothers.

Creativity in cooking is huge in Mexico right now. Over the past several decades, hundreds of chefs have attained national and international recognition. Many have opened restaurants in other countries, something that was unknown only a few years ago. There is a need to write a history of Mexican gastronomy of the past thirty years, one that follows in detail the modulations of our taste. In this regard, UNESCO's 2010 declaration was of enormous importance. It is our hope that the UN's recognition will contribute to protecting this legacy under an international code. In these difficult times, our traditional diet and myriad associated traditions and customs may be depleted, even lost. We are heirs to a great gastronomic culture. We must not let a day go by without remembering this.

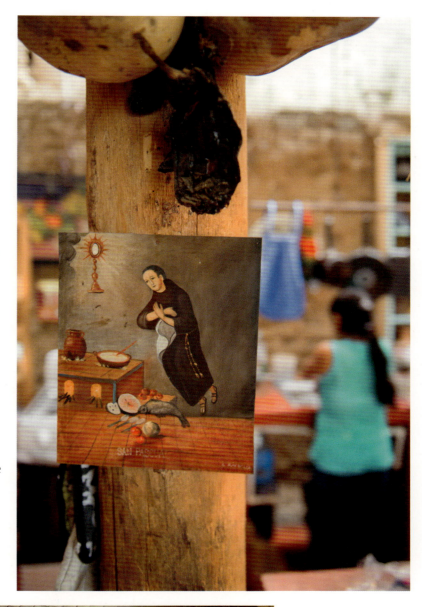

Essay sources include: Mme Calderón de la Barca, *Life in Mexico* (London, 1843); Sonia Corcuera, *Entre Gula y Templanza* (Mexico City, 1970); Diana Kennedy, *Las cocinas de México* (Mexico City, 1990); Salvador Novo, *Cocina Mexicana: Historia gastronómica de la Ciudad de México* (Mexico City, 2013); and numerous essays published in the periodical *Artes de México*.

Ciudad de México:
The Valley of Anáhuac

What can one say about Ciudad de México – Mexico City – a conurbation spanning 1,500 square kilometres and home to nine million people, extending to twenty-two million if you include Greater Mexico City? One of the ten largest conurbations on the planet, it contributes over a fifth of the country's GDP. The financial and industrial centre of Mexico, the capital city is the fifth-largest economy in Latin America.

Situated high in the mountains (2,250 metres) and at the very centre of the country, Ciudad de México is the oldest continually inhabited city on the American continent (and one of just two founded by Amerindians). It was built on Lake Texcoco by the Aztecs in 1325; Tenochtitlán (as it was called) became the centre of the Aztec Empire until its destruction by the conquistadors in 1521. The Spaniards started to rebuild the city in their own image, referring to it as Temistitán while setting about demolishing the Templo Mayor. In 1548, the city became known as Ciudad de México by royal decree, and after gaining independence from Spain, the Distrito Federal (Federal District, DF) was created in 1824. The DF has now become Mexico's thirty-second state but as an autonomous community without sovereignty.

It does not take long for the arriving visitor to come up against the capital's best and worst aspects, starting (if they are flying in) with the plane's surprisingly steep descent. Even seasoned travellers are challenged by the traffic and pollution, the road system, elevated highways and threadbare infrastructure. But Mexico City has a heart and a soul that beat to their own tempo. First there are the immediate contrasts between rich and poor. Then there are the colonial façades and modern architecture, classy vs rundown neighbourhoods, and of course the vast barrios clinging to the slopes surrounding the city and randomly placed, often alongside high-end blocks of flats. The super-modern Santa Fe financial and residential district, for instance, sits cheek by jowl with the Santa Lucia barrio (or *colonia popular*, as the barrios are quaintly called).

What is charming about the place is that every district has its distinct flavours and colours, while the colonial-era districts like the Centro Historico, San Ángel and Coyoacán have maintained their original charm. The nightmare of governance, security and provisioning of a city of this size is ongoing, not least because of the environmental chaos caused by industrial and vehicular pollution and the new global bogeyman, climate change. Mexico City is actually sinking, the ancient clay beds on which the Aztecs built it crumbling as ever-deeper wells are dug to satisfy its insatiable thirst. The water supply is predicted to run out in the next few decades. For a city built on a lake in the Valley of Anáhuac ('surrounded by waters'), this is a disturbing indictment. The cumulative consequences of some of these factors pose an existential threat to global linchpins like Mexico City, and the potential political dynamics make today's immigration and border problems pale into insignificance. As ever, you need to remember the *Mexicano*'s favourite word: *podemos* (we can).

Ricardo Rodríguez
Environmentalist, Xochimilco, Mexico City

Xochimilco Ecological Park and Plant Market was inaugurated in 1993 on *chinampas* (artificial islands) in Lake Xochimilco which had been previously declared a World Heritage Site. While much of the wetlands have been recharged, pollution and illegal settlement threaten the project's success. The district is characterised by a system of canals, the destruction of which began in the 1950s when fresh water was systematically pumped away to supply the city, and polluted water pumped back into the system, destroying aquatic and plant life.

In 2007, together with a group of friends, Ricardo Rodríguez created a company called De la Chinampa to restore the islands' ecology through the commercialisation of local products. A small group of farmers grew organic broccoli, spinach, beetroot, radishes and other vegetables which were then sold to a group of registered customers. The company provided such high-end restaurants as Pujol and Quintonil but ceased trading due to financial problems.

Rodríguez explains the artificial islands' creation in Toltec times this way: 'They placed mud over the *chinampa* and with their hands made small holes for planting. They would cover the seeds with straw [to generate heat] so that they would germinate ... What happened in antiquity is that the roots grew and took in water. Not any more.' It was the Aztecs who created a barter market with people from areas surrounding the lake who cultivated maize, beans, squashes and chillies on their *milpas*, or small fields. Other products that were traded included cattle, chickens and seeds. The Aztecs also built aqueducts and other ambitious infrastructure projects. 'But ... when the Spanish arrived, evidently they started to lose everything they had created,' Rodríguez notes. 'The Spanish began to evangelise the Aztecs, and at that time they lost two very important crops: chia and amaranth' – apparently because these seeds (ironically considered super-foods today) were associated with human sacrifice.

Rodríguez studied finance at his mother's insistence even though his passion 'has always been ecology, the ocean, animals'. After graduating and working in a bank, he 'started to investigate Xochimilco because of the axolotl', a salamander-like amphibian traditionally found in the canals and which used to keep them free of parasites. 'Currently there are no axolotls in Xochimilco; they

have been declared an endangered species,' the ecologist laments. Attempts at repopulation have been hampered by the overwhelming presence of artificially introduced tilapia, an African fish that preys on the axolotl. The importance of these attempts at cleaning up ancient waterways and wildlife cannot be overstated, Rodríguez adds. 'It is very important that Xochimilco is preserved because Xochimilco and the city are in balance. If Xochimilco disappears, the city disappears.' The area's characteristic *ahuejotes*, or willow trees, 'release so much oxygen for the city' that the zone around the *chinampas* can be thought of as 'a third lung' for the district. 'In independent Mexico, once the Spanish Crown left, Mexico City was *chinampas*,' he adds. 'If Xochimilco disappears, we will lose a part of our culture as Mexicans.'

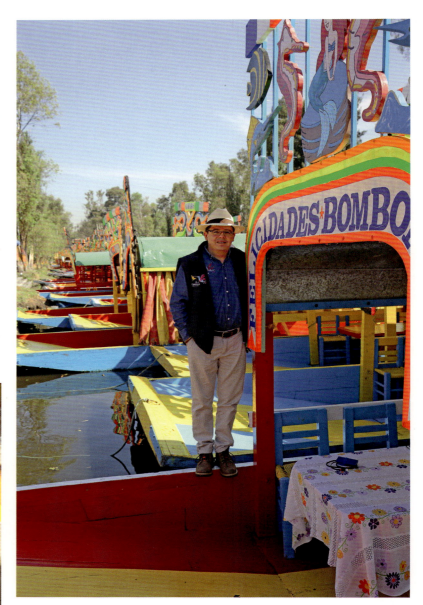

(facing page, left) **Picnic lunch afloat a** *trajinera*. **These barges, modelled on prehispanic boats, function as tourist attractions in Xochimilco today; and** (facing page, right) **Ricardo Rodríguez on board a** *trajinera*

(left) **Rodríguez holding an** *axolotl*, **or salamander. Thought to be an incarnation of the god Xolotl, the** *axolotl* **was used as medicine and in Aztec ceremonies. An endangered species, it is essential for balancing Xochimilco's ecosystem;** (above) **Rodríguez and Felipe Caputilla on a** *chinampa*, **a type of artificial agricultural plot used by prehispanic peoples nearly a thousand years ago. Fashioned from willow roots, these floating islands are passed down within families for generations; and** (top) **Caputilla holding a** *chapine*, **a type of sprout grown in the canal mud**

(above) **José Bacilio Hernández rowing on the canal in Xochimilco. Rowers inherit their jobs from their parents and grandparents; and** (right) **A typical plot along the canal in Xochimilco. Many** *chinampas* **have been abandoned as young people are increasingly unwilling to maintain them**

(left & below) **Rodríguez delivering produce from his** *chinampa* **to Quinta San Diego, a restaurant in Milpa Alta, and** (bottom) **enjoying a meal there**

(following spread) **Many parts of Xochimilco are still semi-rural, with some communities specialising in the construction and repair of** *trajinera* **barges**

Alejandro Escalante
Researcher & Author of *La Tacopedia*, Polanco & Coyoacán, Mexico City

'There are three elements to a taco: the tortilla, the filling and the salsa or garnish. When one of them is good, you have a taco.' So says contributor to online food journal Animal Gourmet, radio-show host and author Alejandro Escalante, whose wildly popular *La Tacopedia* was named the best cookbook published in Mexico by the international magazine *Gourmand* in 2013.

The history of the taco is as old as Mexico itself and is linked to the Aztecs' use of omelettes rather than implements to hold food for eating. For Escalante, eating with tortillas constitutes an art form. Proper tortillas are made from *nixtamal* – maize boiled in limewater (calcium hydroxide) – left overnight and then ground before being made into dough. Remains of maize from 10,000 BC have been found in the state of Guerrero, while *masa* – maize flour – was first recorded in 700 BC. 'Once you have *masa*, you can make tortillas,' Escalante explains. 'This is the beginning of civilisation on the American continent.' People were eating with tortillas as early as the Maya period; sculptures from that time show women making *nixtamal* on *metates*, or grinding stones. (Sauces were, and still are, made by the same process.) The word *taco*, however, dates from the beginning of the twentieth century and refers to something rolled – in fact, at least to begin with, the food of the poor. '*Tacos de canastas* was what peasants took with them from home to the fields,' Escalante explains. 'They make them really warm and then wrap them so they cook from the steam. When you eat them hours later, they are still warm, and they have a new texture.' The transformation of maize, he believes, represented a technological discovery 'that absolutely changed [American] civilisation ... because it's so nutritious that if you have a taco with beans and chilli, you can live off that'.

Mexico's wide range of chillies is key to the preparation and enjoyment of tacos. 'They are so different, the flavours and the uses, because not every chilli goes with everything,' Escalante explains. 'Everything has its purpose and its sense ... Not only that, all the *antojitos* [traditional corn-based delicacies similar to tapas] are also related ... There are so many different *antojitos*, and they are all made with *masa* in different shapes and different circumstances.' Nowadays tacos are Mexico's basic foodstuff. 'When I was young, it was a not-so-important thing,' he says. 'When I was writing about this five years ago, people would say, "What? Are you crazy? Why do you want to write about this!?" Nobody was thinking or theorising about it.' Today, tacos are being made using 'a very modern, revolutionising approach', though the choice and presence of chilli remain of critical importance: 'In New York or Los Angeles and here in Mexico City, they are doing fantastic things.' Mistakenly described as fast food, tacos are, Escalante points out, only 'fast at the end': 'Because of the preparation and the different styles, there are some that take days [to make], but they are eaten in just a couple of bites.' He cites a few noteworthy varieties, including one based on *cecina* (cured meat), *longaniza* (sausage) and *chicharrón* (pork crackling) – 'three elements that go together really well'. *Tacos al pastor* 'involve Middle East immigrants who came [to Mexico and use a] vertical grill, like the one used for *shawarma*, the kebab from Iraq ... There are many houses which make really good *pastor*; it's typical for Mexico City. There's *tacos de cabeza*, which I also like a lot and which is steamed beef. There are so many different styles, it's hard to say which one is the best, or which one you like most. Insects are also really tasty'. His favourite is the *chinicuil*, the red agave worm.

For Escalante, the proof that people can live on tacos alone is incontrovertible. 'There have been centuries where the peasants of Mexico have lived from bean tacos and fresh chillies, because the combination of *masa nixtamal* with beans creates certain proteins, all the vitamins, the amino acids, so it's a very nutritious mixture ... There's also the culture of the *milpa*, which is the field where they grow the maize, and it's associated with beans and courgettes, or *calabacín*. And also with tender cactus, all different kinds of chillies and what is called "*quelites*", which are all kinds of edible herbs ... So the notion of the *milpa* as a field that a family can live from was a very wise cultural improvement, an intelligent way of living.'

(facing page) **Alejandro Escalante discusses tacos as haute cuisine with chef Iván Díaz at The Palm in Polanco, one of the country's most expensive** *taquerías*; (left, above & following spread) **Escalante out on a** *taquería* **crawl, and** (top) **at La Casa de los Tacos in Coyoacán, which he co-owns with photographer Héctor Ramos**

Armando Ramírez
Author & Historian, Tepito, Mexico City

'I am from the barrio of Tepito, the barrio of tradition and violence,' proclaims the writer Armando Ramírez. 'Burglars, gunshots and characters from the gutter press – it is a boxer's canvas.' Ramírez was at university studying economics and just nineteen when his prize-winning novel *Chin Chin el teporocho* was published (1971). The book sold a million copies, and Ramírez dropped out of uni. Even today, *Chin Chin el teporocho* continues to enjoy brisk sales.

Ramírez's father was a boxer, his mother a housewife. Although he had no formal academic training in literature, for more than thirty years he has been creating a mosaic of iconic urban characters, his stories inspired by oral tradition and focusing on the pickpockets and other ne'er-do-wells in his neighbourhood. He has been a scriptwriter, a news reporter, and a creator and producer of television series, and in 1974 founded a collective called Tepito Arte Acá together with artists Daniel Manrique, Julián Ceballos Casco, Virgilio Carrillo and Felipe Ehrenberg. The group devised productions, activities and publications related to the visual arts, literature, theatre and sociology. Meanwhile Ramírez continued to write more novels.

Ramírez describes himself as a man 'from the 'hood', a 'man of the people', and Tepito, where he was born, as 'violent, illegal, rich in cultural identity, ancient, from the times of Tlatelolco [an Aztec city-state], prehispanic, mischievous, folkloric … People from this neighbourhood are skilled orators and are mentally agile … They play a lot with the meanings of words'. He portrays daily life in Tepito as being 'a party every day. We dance in the streets every day; we take the mickey every day; we eat, have fun, drink every day … In Tepito, people wake up late, around 10.00 or 11.00 in the morning … The marketplace opens at noon and closes at 10.00, 11.00 at night, even midnight … At 1.00 or 2.00 in the morning, people chat, drink and hang out'. Actual work is done 'while chatting by making deals *mano a mano*'; illegal businesses range from porn to drugs and prostitution, but there is plenty of legal commerce as well, based in 'workshops that produce plastic, clothes, sneakers, knickers, shirts, T-shirts, sweaters … We sell a lot of clothes for Mexico City, and we export to countries in Central America'.

Ramírez comments with insight and humour on the physical proximity of Tepito to the historic centres of Mexican identity: 'Near Tepito we have the symbolic powers: the National Palace, the [Aztec] Templo Mayor and the Cathedral. Every presidential candidate, every candidate or political force, has to come here and lick everyone's boots because it is a sounding board. We joke that the Virgin of Guadalupe appeared here; this is the place where they founded the city; this is where the eagle came to devour the snake.' On the culinary side, the area's typical menu items include tripe and other offal as well as *migas*, 'a broth that has pigs' bones, a bit of chilli and loads of stale bread' in it – per Ramírez, the perfect morning-after cure for a hangover.

(left) **Armando Ramírez visiting the Iglesia de Regina Coeli in the Centro Histórico.** (facing page) **Inside the Mercado Abelardo L. Rodríguez in Tepito are murals by students of Diego Rivera, as well as Isamu Noguchi's 20-metre-long** *History as Seen from Mexico in 1936*

(facing page) **A *vecindad* (housing estate) in Tepito, similar to the one Ramírez grew up in;** (above) **Ramírez in front of a mural depicting *La Familia Burrón* – a comic strip about a typical working-class family in Mexico City, created by Gabriel Vargas in 1948 – and** (right) **at Café Regina, his favourite haunt in the Centro Histórico**

(above) *Chapulines* (grasshoppers) prepared with chilli, salt and lime, and commonly found around market streets; and (facing page) *Mole* being made in the Mercado de Coyoacán

(left) **Soumaya Slim near ARCHIVO Diseño y Arquitectura in San Miguel Chapultepec. Her jacket, designed by Jorge Ayala de Riberolles, pays tribute to** *torta* **street food.** (right) **Slim outside the Mercado El Chorrito in San Miguel Chapultepec buying an** *esquite* **of maize with chillies, mayonnaise and lime, an ubiquitous street snack**

Soumaya Slim, scion of a wealthy family, has become a leading figure in Mexican philanthropy, specifically in the areas of medicine, the arts and design. Slim and her husband, architect Fernando Romero, live in Lomas de Chapultepec. 'Mexico City,' she says, 'is neighbourly, unruly and special... I wouldn't live anywhere else.' Educated in Mexico, Slim received a BA in Art/Art History from Universidad Anahuác and is active in the family foundation, Fundación Carlos Slim, as well as being Vice-president of the Museo Soumaya and curator of its collection, which is housed in a building dedicated to her mother. The collection includes seventy thousand works ranging in date from the fifteenth to the mid-twentieth centuries, among them the largest private collection of sculptures by Auguste Rodin. Together with her husband, Slim founded ARCHIVO Diseño y Arquitectura in 2012 as a space dedicated to collecting, exhibition and rethinking design. The centre boasts a programme of exhibitions and activities and has a collection of fifteen hundred design objects from the early twentieth century to the present day, including both Mexican designs and international classics. The Slim Foundation, with which Slim is also involved, has funded over seven thousand organ transplants in the last decade.

Although she does not cook herself, Slim is a keen proponent of Mexican cuisine. Her earliest culinary memories centre around tacos and her favourite dish, *mole*. 'When my mother wanted to make me happy or console me, she would give me *mole*,' she says. The version she prefers is 'traditional black *mole* from Oaxaca', which contains 'chopped chicken, many different kinds of chilli, some maize ... I don't know how to cook it so I don't know the ingredients. I just know what it tastes like!' Slim sees the recent explosion of interest in Mexican cooking as signalling 'a revolution', saying, 'It's very interesting to see what new chefs are doing with these ancestral ingredients, having new interpretations and new textures ... The flavours are very close to the traditional [ones], even though there's some experimentation ... In most cases, you find the spirit, the flavours, the memories that come with flavour.' And she believes in the importance of contemporary Mexican cuisine as an ambassador for Mexican culture. 'Design is the subject of use in a very intimate way, and the kitchen and food are the same. Eating is very personal because you do it in relation to your own body, and also in relation to the people around you. [When it comes to] the ritual of eating, sometimes with friends, Mexico is like Mediterranean and Latin American cultures ... It's so important culturally, food and mealtimes ... In food you can see the generosity of the Mexican spirit.'

Juan José Zezatti, 'Super Astro Jr'
Lucha Libre Wrestler, Cuauhtémoc, Centro, Mexico City

Professional masked wrestler Juan José Zezatti goes by the *luchístico* name of Super Astro Jr. Zezatti is named after his father, who had an illustrious wrestling career, making his debut in 1974 and becoming world champion in 1984.

Mexico's version of professional wrestling is a huge spectator sport, eclipsed only by soccer. Characterised by colourful masks, plenty of bling and oceans of spandex, the sport is free-style in nature and dates back to 1863. In the early 1900s its popularity started to grow after two businessmen began promoting no-holds-barred fights without weapons or protection. In 1933 the Empresa Mexicana de Lucha Libre (Mexican Wrestling Organisation) was established, and within a year, matches were being sold out. Today the EMLL is known as the Consejo Mundial de Lucha Libre (World Wrestling Council);

its home, the Arena México, is professional wrestling's mecca. A typical match involves dropkicks, backflips and leg locks. Both male and female wrestlers take part, as do wrestlers in drag known as *exóticos*. In the biggest matches, *luchadores* bet their masks; the losers must remove theirs, thereby revealing their identities.

The wrestling-themed *fonda* known as El Cuadrilátero, founded by Zezatti's parents, boasts of serving the largest sandwich 'ever seen', *El Gladiador*. Its ingredients include eggs, chorizo, sausage, bacon, chicken, steak, ham and cheese – a true protein-fest. The sandwich is so large that it can barely be held with both hands. Anyone able to eat it in fifteen minutes does not have to pay for their meal. The *fonda* claims that approximately ninety people have achieved this.

(above) **Juan José Zezatti attempts the famous *El Gladiador* sandwich challenge;** (right) **Victor Manuel Zamarillo, the café's cook, prepares a sandwich for *lucha libre* fans. El Cuadrilátero was named after the wrestling ring dominated by Super Astro Sr; and** (facing page) **Zezatti, a *luchador*-in-training, beneath a portrait of his father and the family's growing collection of *lucha libre* memorabilia**

(following spread, left) **A *quinceañera* marks the transition to womanhood at the Parroquia de San Jacinto in San Ángel. This Aztec coming-of-age tradition, continued by the Catholic Church, is celebrated by families from all social strata; and** (following spread, right) **San Ángel Inn, a seventeenth-century hacienda and monastery that is now one of Mexico City's most famous restaurants, claims to serve the best margaritas in town**

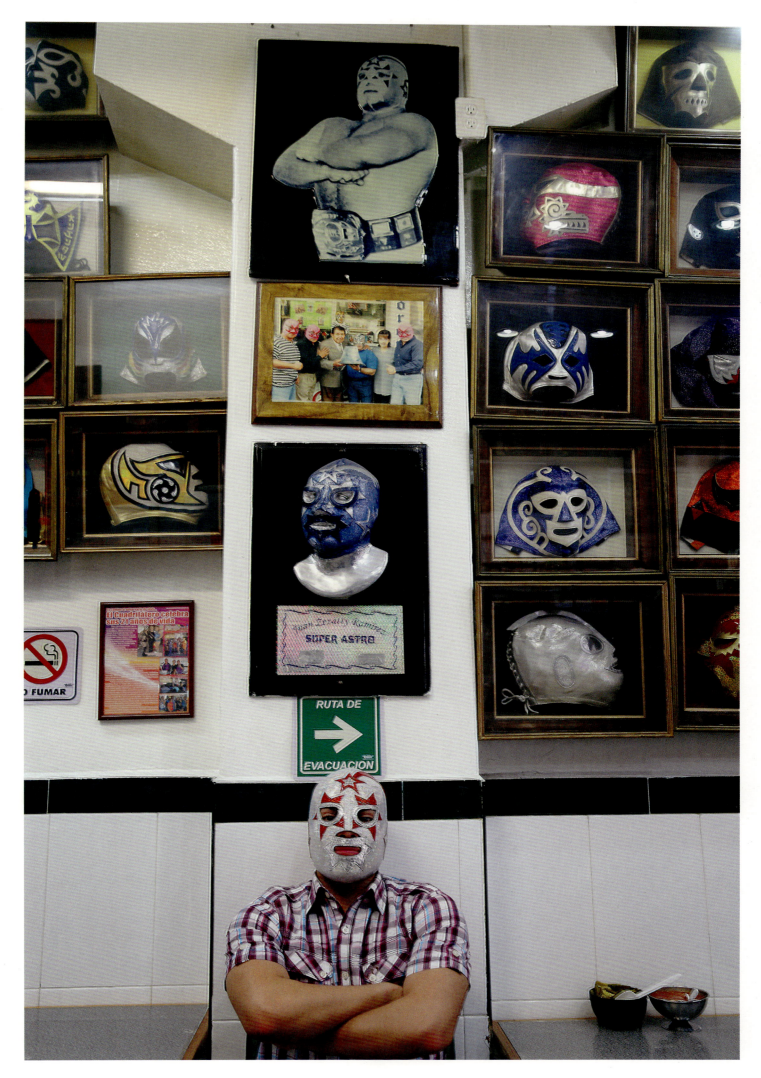

Ricardo Muñoz Zurita
Chef & Author, Azul y Oro, Coyoacán, Mexico City

'I am a chef who has dedicated himself to researching traditional Mexican food for thirty years,' states Ricardo Muñoz Zurita. 'I have been all over Mexico … meeting people on beaches, in big cities, in coastal towns, in the mountains, beside rivers, because Mexican gastronomy is very diverse. In order to accomplish the eleven books I have written and the fifty I am planning on writing, I have to travel throughout [the country].' Known as 'the anthropologist of Mexican cuisine', Muñoz never thought he would become an author. 'But one day I said to myself, "Who is going to write all of the books that need to be written?" … I opened several restaurants, which also serve the purpose of showcasing a lot – obviously not all – of the food that's mentioned in my books.' His most notable work to date: *Larousse Diccionario Enciclopédico de la Gastronomía Mexicana*, first published in 2013.

Named a 'prophet and preserver of a culinary tradition' by *Time* magazine in 2001 and the recipient of endless culinary awards, Muñoz had to go abroad to study as there were no cooking schools in Mexico in the 1980s. In 2002 he established his restaurant chain Azul, where the focus is on traditional gastronomy. His parents were from Tabasco. 'The people in Tabasco have a lot of water around them and also a lot of sunlight,' he notes. 'It's hard to get a cloudy day … In Tabasco you have a lot of things prepared with coconut … We used to eat different types of turtles … fish … and duck.' In Xalapa, Veracruz, where his family lived during his childhood, 'they love to stuff chillies … with shrimp or fish, but in the winter they use chicken, beef or pork.' Smoked jalapeños are a seasonal speciality. While such wide regional differences still exist today, they are less apparent because the Mexican lifestyle has changed; with many women working outside the home, there is less time for cooking. 'So all those precious dishes that were part of normal, everyday life changed a great deal,' Muñoz observes. '[Women] cook special food for a particular gathering, particular celebration or a weekend, especially on Sundays, when the whole family gathers.'

In an ideal world, Muñoz would not mind returning to earlier times because 'the food was better than what we eat now. No jars, no cans, no packets, no frozen food; that came … very recently. In those days, when you went to the supermarket, it would be very hard to find something frozen … I do like the fact that now you are able to get food from all over the world and … maybe things are presented better than in a traditional market.' But the downsides are obvious. 'Something that really bothers me is that now, a lot of people eat out of a packet or a can … It's part of our life, and I like to embrace it, but I don't want my life just to be about that … Cooking is more than just cooking.' In fact, good food makes you a better human being, claims the chef. 'Physically, spiritually and mentally, when somebody has eaten good food and it was done from the heart, the flavours are different to something that you might buy from somewhere else. So all that gets into your system and makes you happier, and when you are happier, you become a better person. But there is more to it than that, because when you eat well, you have a clear idea of what life is all about … You cannot think properly on an empty stomach … If all you eat is food that came out of cans or jars, I truly believe that your mentality is going to be like that … All your ideas are going to be sealed up somehow.'

As a child, Muñoz was served both Tabascan and Veracruz-style dishes by his mother. For example, he recalls, 'we would have (which I love) big chunks of duck, which was cooked by a long process with garlic and onion. They would drop a lot of red colouring and rice into it, so that was a main-course soup. Another day we would have [a fish dish] with fresh red-tomato sauce, capers, olives, raisins and chilli. The dish looks rather Italian … because [of] the tomato sauce, but it's actually very ancient because the tomato is from this country.' Before the advent of air transport, Veracruz was Mexico's most important port, 'so it was the first place to use capers and olives and raisins, and of course they already had tomato sauce so they brought it all together.'

Muñoz emphasises the importance of Mexico's weather in defining both the availability of ingredients and the ways in which they are prepared: 'We don't have this winter situation, for example. Traditionally we don't make jams or marmalades … because we don't need to preserve fruit … Also, the cheeses are white and not aged. We don't need to age them because we have milk all year round.' Each state has its particular culinary masterpieces, and Muñoz is happy to share his favourites. 'If I go to the peninsula of Yucatán, there is … an ancient dish that was developed by the Mayans,' he says. Originally a whole peccary cooked in a hole in the ground filled with charcoal for up to fifteen hours, it became pork-based once pigs were introduced

into Mexico. 'The magic of the dish,' the chef explains, 'is that they use seeds that give the whole preparation a reddish colour.' In Veracruz, a dish he finds 'very joyful' is *arroz a la tumbada*. '*Tumbada* is actually a word that has African influence and means "to put something into the pot".' The ingredients include rice, a range of seafood, garlic, onion, red tomatoes and herbs, among them one from the Caribbean 'that tastes half of coriander and half of parsley'.

'The way of thinking, the way of life and the way to eat in Mexico go from day to night, from night to day,' muses Muñoz. 'We are all governed by the same language, law, maybe the same customs or traditions, but when you get down to the local level, the food is entirely different.' The importance of ancient ingredients cannot be overemphasised. 'Let's put this into perspective,' the lively chef concludes. 'In the sixteenth century, when we were connected to the European world and the Americas, in Mexico we developed a very complex approach to cooking that we were only able to develop due to being in this part of the world. When we encountered Europe, they were already doing a little bit of everything due to their connection with China, Africa and the Mediterranean, and the spices they were using were not necessarily European. So somehow European cooking has a connection to Chinese and African cooking, but Mexico developed by itself. That's what makes it unique.'

(previous spread) **Ricardo Muñoz Zurita passing the library on UNAM's city campus. Designed by Juan O'Gorman in 1952, the carvings depict prehispanic motifs. The library and campus were designated a UNESCO World Heritage Site in 2007**

(facing page) **Muñoz often visits the Espacio Escultórico on UNAM's city campus for inspiration and even based a dessert on one of the sculptures. He is standing within a volcanic-stone work by Federico Silva and other artists, the centre of which functions as an eco-reserve; and** (above, left to right) **Green pork *pipián* with squash seeds, *tlacoyos* with vegetables from Tlaxcala, and *indios al balcon* (a tower of gratin potatoes under *nopal* cactus with a tomato *caldo*) served at Azul y Oro on the UNAM campus**

Elena Reygadas
Chef, Rosetta, Colonia Roma, Mexico City

'Cooking doesn't have to have a flag,' says Elena Reygadas, whose restaurant Rosetta offers Italian-style pasta alongside local specialities. Reygadas studied English Literature at UNAM before going to New York to attend the French Culinary Institute. She always loved to cook but became particularly interested in nutrition when her father had a stroke. Her first catering job was for her brother, a film-maker. 'It was quite complicated,' she recalls, 'because it was in the middle of nowhere … with people who were used to beans and maize. The rest of the team were European, and they didn't like maize and beans, so I had to do two menus – one with pasta and vegetables, and one with maize, beans and chilli. It was nice to see how we get used to certain flavours and that your taste develops from what is available. It was also the first time I cooked with responsibility, and it's when I realised that I really enjoyed cooking.' While living in London, Reygadas (recipient of the 2014 Veuve Clicquot prize for Latin America's Best Woman Chef) worked for Giorgio Locatelli. She founded Rosetta in 2010. The pasta is handmade, and the menu features ultra-fresh seafood and fish. Meanwhile Panadería Rosetta provides bread for restaurants across Mexico City. In both settings, artisanal technique is the rule.

'At my parents' house, there were always people, there was always food, always conviviality around the table,' Reygadas remembers. 'So I saw cooking as a way of getting together, as a way of community, as a way of love.' At Rosetta, she explains, 'what I cook is something really intimate … I don't cook anything that I don't like. In that sense I don't just cook for money. If I just cooked for money, I would sell … hamburgers. But I don't like hamburgers so I will never do a hamburger even if it is a good seller.' Her job with Locatelli grew out of a desire to learn Italian but evolved into an awareness of culinary changes occurring in London at that time, especially the growing popularity of gastro-pubs and nose-to-tail cuisine. Seasonality also became a preoccupation. In Mexico, she points out, 'seasons are not marked as they are in Europe. We have asparagus all year around. Living in London made me really understand seasons … When I came back, I started using Mexican ingredients but not in a Mexican traditional way … More in a … contemporary way … but of course not ignoring Mexican tradition.' Her fascination with herbs also developed in London, where she became aware of natural remedies. The Mexican 'science of curing with herbs … is mainly practised by women,' she notes. 'They can help you in childbirth; they can help with your blues and your mood swings, and also help with digestive problems.' She sources hers from a friend who grows them organically.

'Cooking now is not only about traditional Mexico; Mexican food is about Mexicans,' Reygadas observes when asked to speculate about her country's culinary future. 'We are more conscious about our products, our food, our herbs. We are more proud of them so we are happy to use them with a more contemporary approach.' While most Mexicans cannot afford to go to London to live, they can experience contemporary international cuisine via Instagram and other media, 'so they are closer to what is happening in other places. There is an openness to techniques and to ways of doing [things] that was like a taboo before. It was much more guarded, much more closed.'

(facing page) **Elena Reygadas outside the Colonia Roma townhouse that is home to Rosetta;** (above) *Ensalada de hinojo* **(fennel, orange and rocket); and** (above right) *Entrada de sardinas encurtidas en jugo de cítricos* **(sardine salad with lemon juice)**

(left) **The display that greets visitors to Rosetta includes artisan bread made with natural yeast;** (below) **Diners at Rosetta; and** (facing page) **Confit of suckling pig in pink** *mole*

(following spread) **A vegetable stall at the Mercado de Coyoacán**

Walther Boesterly Urrutia
Director General, Museo de Arte Popular, Mexico City

Mexico City's Museo de Arte Popular, located in an old firehouse, preserves and promotes Mexican folk art and handicrafts, including textiles, pottery, glass, furniture and *alebrijes* (sculptures of fantastical creatures). Each year it sponsors the *Noche de Alebrijes* parade in which such monumental sculptures compete for prizes.

The museum is overseen by Walther Boesterly Urrutia, a food enthusiast who, among many other things, is concerned about the sustainability of Mexico City's growing population, now numbering twenty-two million. 'For us,' he observes, 'food supplies, water supplies, energy supplies – they will give up in a few years.' As an example of what he calls 'the broken communion between nature and the human race', he cites the destruction over the last twenty-five years of 75 per cent of Mexico's coastal mangroves, an essential screen to protect human populations from maritime storms. 'We need to change capitalism, we cannot sustain it,' he asserts.

For Boesterly, the heart of the problem is the way food is produced and consumed. 'We eat to feed ourselves. Only a few people eat to really taste the food,' he says. People who buy tacos in the museum's courtyard, for example, 'don't have money to buy other things ... Give them something that tastes the same and the cost is five times less than the taco. To provide the taco, you need fields of corn, many slaughterhouses to kill the beef ... We need to find other answers, other ways to understand that if we can have an equilibrium with the earth, and nature, and the products that they give us, then we will stay alive'.

Boesterly is passionate and hugely knowledgeable about Mexico's numerous regional cuisines, and of course the museum he directs shines a spotlight on everyday utensils and crafts meant for the table. The country's biodiversity provides 'the chance to invent different tools, different handicrafts in different materials', he observes. 'For example, the north is very dry. The chromatic palette is poor, if you compare it with the south-west, and you need to decorate your tools with those colours and models that you have in nature. If you go south, you have many more possibilities, many more sources ... If you go to Oaxaca, you find many different ethnicities [while] in Sonora you have only three. Each ethnicity had their own way to build their culture, their way of life, the way they dress, cook, make music, dances.' In the realm of handicrafts, he adds, 'only India can come close. In terms of dyes and pigments, India and Mexico are the richest in the world. But in Mexico right now, we have only a few dyes and pigments that we are cultivating. The rest are lost.'

Mexico's seemingly paradoxical high levels of obesity are directly related, Boesterly believes, to the inexpensiveness of poor-quality ingredients and the fact that people do not drink sugar-heavy sodas because they want to but because they don't have access to potable water. He lays the blame squarely on multinational corporations in pursuit of easy profits. Set against this somewhat bleak backdrop is the rich variety of the country's underused ingredients, from ants' eggs (an excellent protein source) in the Hildago desert to cactus, fruits, vegetables and underused forest plants. Boesterly's own favourite dishes cover a huge range: 'Baja California: fish. Ensenada ... beans and lobster taco in a flour tortilla – one of the best dishes in the world ... Sonora: wonderful seafood on the coast. Monterrey: goat, *cabrito* ... There are other things you can eat, but that is the famous one. Tamaulipas: a lot of deer, but wild ... In Sonora, cactus leaves in different forms. *Camarón* with chilli: shrimp cut in very thin slices with water, Mexican lemon juice and chilli ... Acapulco: *ceviche vuelve a la vida* – 'come back to life' ... it's a cocktail of raw fish, with raw shrimps, octopus, a few oysters, lemon, ketchup, chilli and a lot of onion, tomato and coriander on top. If you go further south along the coast, to Tabasco, you find *pejelagarto*. It's a very special fish, a prehistoric animal, a step between fish and reptiles. It's delicious meat, and in this case, even though it's a living fossil, we don't have a problem ... it's not a threatened species'. Other wonders include the tamales (one of their ingredients being prunes, for sweetness) of jungly Chiapas; Yucatán's pork dishes cooked in an earth oven; and pulque from Puebla, made from the maguey, a plant whose parasitic worms are edible. Pulque 'smells very strong', the enthusiast admits, 'but it's delicious. And in terms of nutrition it is very good.'

(facing page) **Walther Boesterly Urrutia was involved in the restoration of Diego Rivera's murals covering the cement water tank at the 1950s pumping station (seen here) in the Bosque de Chapultepec**

(left) **Boesterly taking the air in front of the Museo de Antropología, with Mexico City's trademark jacaranda trees in full bloom, and** (below) **in front of Diego Rivera's giant tiled Fuente de Tláloc, dedicated to the Aztec rain god**

(above) **Boesterly reviewing the day's 'catch' (rattlesnake) with Chon owner Eduardo Guadarrama Briseño, whose father founded the restaurant; and** (right) **Rattlesnake cooked in** *pasilla chile* **sauce, a delicacy served at Chon. The restaurant also serves** *escamoles* **(ants' eggs),** *chinicuil* **(red maguey worms) and grilled crocodile**

(following spread, left to right) *Chile de árbol* and *chile guajillo* are found in markets throughout Mexico

Sofía Aspe
Interior Designer, Lomas de Chapultepec, Miguel Hidalgo, Mexico City

Designer Sofía Aspe's father, Pedro Aspe Armella, served as Mexico's Secretary of Finance and Public Credit in the 1990s, while her maternal grandfather, Ignacio Bernal, was an anthropologist. Perhaps Aspe's own mixture of practicality and passion can be traced back to this combination of genetic characteristics. In 2005 she was invited to join the board of Childfund México; she is now the organisation's director. To help with Childfund's fundraising efforts, she has organised sales of clothing by such designers as Pink Magnolia, Etro, Marc Jacobs and Rapsodia, and has also conducted auctions of contemporary art.

As with many Mexicans, food has been a passion of Aspe's since she was very young and is closely associated with the idea of family. 'Especially on my father's side, it's pretty much all we talk about,' she laughs. 'My grandfather used to say museums existed in Europe so that you could entertain yourself between meals. He was a really fat, funny guy who thought 24/7 about eating and about drinking French wine … My grandmother … is still an amazing cook at ninety years old.' Aspe continued her culinary studies in Chicago after taking a business degree and courses in Mexico at 'smaller schools' because her father would not hear of her going to college to study cooking. While in Chicago she learned classical French techniques, after which she worked at the Ritz Carlton and then, having moved back to Mexico, on the line at Four Seasons. 'It's really tough, especially in Mexico, because it's a guy's world both

here and in Chicago,' she says of her time in hotel kitchens. 'In my classroom I was the only woman. [In Chicago] it was fun, in Mexico I had a harder time … Also, there is so much more to cooking than just the fun and the passion; it's so much hard work with very small earnings. You work when people are vacationing or celebrating; it's long hours; there isn't much remuneration in the sense that people aren't telling you, "Wow, that dish was great!"' The experience was enough to make her realise that while she loved cooking, she did not love cooking professionally. Hence the shift to interior design.

Aspe believes that the careful presentation of food is critically important to the enjoyment of it. 'It doesn't have to be a matter of money,' she insists. 'It's a matter of living surrounded by nice things, maybe natural flowers, maybe linen on the tray. It's the small things whose importance I try to transmit to my clients. It's a matter of wanting it to be pretty … I would say that you love things through your eyes, so [presentation is] a big issue. Of course, compared with taste I would say it's secondary, but you like someone when you see them. It's a big thing. I do put a lot of time into it.' She credits her grandmother with inspiring her elegant sensibility: 'Yes, I learned it from her, absolutely, from her porcelains, and her mixing and matching, maybe some antique silverware … Those are the most interesting things. So I learned it from her, but then I learned it big-time in Chicago. When you start doing that [type of work], you realise just how talented chefs are. It really takes art to get art on a plate.'

(left) **Sofía Aspe with her grandmother, art historian Virginia Armella de Aspe, in Armella's dining room in San Ángel; and** (above) **Aspe with her decorator Daniela Celis on the seventeenth floor of a building she is working on in Polanco**

(facing page) **Placing the last chocolate** *concha* **on her breakfast table at home in Las Lomas**

Francisco (Paco) Calderón
Cartoonist, Colonia Roma, Mexico City

Born in Mexico City in 1959, political cartoonist Francisco (Paco) Calderón studied Communications at Universidad Iberoamericana and did a summer language course at the University of Cambridge. He was only seventeen when he began publishing his cartoons in *El Heraldo de México*. In 1990 Calderón received the Constantino Escalante Award, in 1992 the National Journalism Award, and, twelve years later, the Maria Moors Cabot Prize (honouring journalistic excellence in the Western Hemisphere). Often called the 'caricaturist of the Right', he currently writes for *Reforma*, Mexico's largest newspaper.

Calderón, who describes himself as a glutton, believes that openness is the key to success when it comes to appreciating food in what he calls his 'strange country'. When asked to define what he means by strangeness, he replies, 'We ... have been ruled for the last century in a system designed by the Aztecs; you tell me that's not strange. We are a Belgian inside an African, we are a modern country and a very old country, and we are not only door-to-door but deck-to-deck.' Interestingly, though, he also believes that Mexico is 'the most multicultural society you will ever find, and yet it is not diverse but homogenous' – a fact that may have to do with the dominance of the Roman Catholic Church. The country's food reflects this 'unified diversity' via its 'myriad of flavours', which are influenced by what Calderón describes as 'a love–hate relationship' with both Europe and the US. The latter obsession is rooted in a 'craving for the American way of life', yet his fellow citizens 'feel despised, they feel resentful, they feel like they are not invited guests'.

'I try to be a global cartoonist, I try to see both sides of the matter,' Calderón says of his profession. 'It's quite difficult, but again, being Mexican, I think that enhances your sensitivity, so you try and see both ways.' While in Cambridge studying English, he had his Damascene moment when he saw an exhibition of cartoons by Gerald Scarfe. 'That day was fantastic; that guy was like a superstar,' he recalls. He decided that he wanted to be 'the Mexican version of Gerald Scarfe, the man who really rocks society, the man who can make a change or steer a politician. I saw that, whatever dream you have, it can be done'. And when his Cambridge landlady introduced him to the work of the British master cartoonist Giles, the aspiring young Calderón exclaimed, 'This is cartooning heaven!'

Of Mexico's complex relationship with its northern neighbour, Calderón observes, 'We have to be the mature partner. We have to survive, and in order to survive we have to know the gringos. The gringos don't have to know us, which in fact they do by the way – they have a great foreign service, we do not – but we have to know the Americans, and we have to learn from them in order not to be in the same position as we were in the nineteenth century ever again.' While acknowledging the huge influence of American fast food, Calderón champions Mexican cooking, whose main ingredients – maize, beans, chilli, squash, cactus – are identical to those used by the Aztecs a thousand years ago. In Mexico, he observes, 'You can right now have an Aztec dish ... you can eat worms, you can eat bugs, you can eat frogs.' On the other hand, he adds, 'the best place to have Spanish food outside of Spain is Mexico City ... perhaps the best paella you will find ... And, contrary to Madrid or Paris, you have every international cuisine done fairly well if not very well.'

'I believe that if Mexico wants to make its imprint on the world, it won't be through industry, it won't be through demography, it won't be through religion; it will be through its cuisine,' Calderón insists. 'Mexican cuisine will conquer, maybe not today, maybe not tomorrow, but soon ... Look at the Spaniards. When I was a kid, no-one had even heard of Spanish cuisine: "Spanish *what*?! Spaniards don't cook! They live under Franco; they barely eat!" You went to Spain and the only Spanish food you [could find] was ... roasted pig. Now everyone says, "Ahhh, the Spaniards!" It's a foodie powerhouse, it's a foodie mecca. Well, Mexico is about to become that.'

(facing page) **Francisco Calderón enjoying his own cartoon in** *Reforma* **over a pre-lunch** *clamato* **(Bloody Mary) at his favourite restaurant, Contramar in Colonia Roma; and** (left) **Lunch at Contramar includes their signature dish,** *pescado a la talla***, butterflied red snapper half marinated in red-chilli** *adobo* **and half rubbed with parsley, then cooked over hot coals**

(left) **Calderón enjoys his favourite beer at a** *cervecería* **overlooking the Fuente de la Cibeles.** (above) **Graffiti, as here in Colonia Roma, are common on most city streets;** (top) **Calderón often grabs an** *elote*, **a street snack consisting of maize on the cob, lime, chilli powder and mayonnaise; and** (facing page) **A locksmith in La Condesa side by side with a mango stall in Colonia Roma**

Tatiana Bilbao & Sandro Landucci Lerdo de Tejada
Architect & Restaurateur, Polanco, Mexico City

Tatiana Bilbao studied Architecture and Urban Planning at Universidad Iberoamericana. Her practice (founded in 2004) aims to regenerate spaces in order to humanise them as a reaction against global capitalism. The recipient of numerous international prizes, Bilbao has been a visiting professor at Yale School of Architecture in New Haven and an advisor on housing and urban projects to the Mexican government. Her studio is currently working on projects in China and Europe as well as in Mexico.

'All my relatives are architects; I think it runs in the family,' says Bilbao, who grew up in the centre of Mexico City at a time when children played in the streets in complete safety. She fondly remembers her father sending her to fetch his daily newspaper. From those early experiences she retains a love for 'the richness of things'. 'I like to include a lot of different things and people [in my projects], because that is what real life consists of,' she explains. 'Diversity, organic elements, things that happen by accident – I allow those things in my work, and I promote them in collaborations … because of that sense of a neighbourhood that was a community.' Another key element or process in her work is evolution. 'Architecture needs the passage of time,' she notes. 'The architect only proposes the start of the conversation … and you never know where it's going to end.' Neighbourhoods that are eco-friendly and people-friendly are the future, she believes. 'Architecture has so many tools to enhance life that we're wasting time if we don't do that.'

Bilbao's husband Sandro Landucci Lerdo de Tejada, a publisher-turned-chef (the result of a mid-life lifestyle switch), is the cook in the house. He currently owns Bésame Mucho, a Mexican restaurant in Milan, and is set to open eateries in Denmark and Germany in 2017. 'Food started as a hobby for me,' he explains. 'I come from a family that loves to cook. My grandmother, my Italian *nonna*, used to be a great cook. She would come to Mexico and I would always be in the kitchen with her.' His twin loves for Mexico and for cooking came together, he says, 'by mere accident. It was before the Milan Expo in 2015, and we were working with the Mexican government to create the concept for the Mexican Pavilion. I asked them what was going to happen in the restaurant, because Milan was all about food. The title of the Expo was "Feed the Planet" … We told the Mexican government, "This is a really great opportunity for us to go to Italy, where we will have millions of visitors during the Expo, not only from Italy but from … the entire world. We [will be able] to do a real Mexican restaurant which will not be limited to one region or one guy. Let's invite real contemporary chefs!"'

Both husband and wife are enthusiastic advocates of everything Mexican, and agree that Mexican food is the best, most immediate way to promote the country. 'Architecture takes so much time to build, and so much money, and food is so rich, that projects that can bring Mexican food to the world can also change things,' enthuses Bilbao. 'Mexican food is not known in the world at all. When people discover it, when people come to Mexico, they go home and say, "Wow, the food was amazing!"' Both she and her husband are also tireless supporters of Mexico's younger population, for example enabling thirty students to go to Milan 'to draw on the practices and experiences of our restaurant', as Landucci explains. Bilbao adds, 'Those guys come back to Mexico and have a new world inside their heads.'

(left) **Tatiana Bilbao and Sandro Landucci Lerdo de Tejada cooking at home in Polanco; and** (facing page) **Bilbao at the Camino Real Polanco, which was designed by architect Ricardo Legorreta**

Gerardo Vázquez Lugo
Chef, Nicos, Azcapotzalco, Mexico City

In 2016, architect-turned-chef Gerardo Vázquez Lugo's restaurant Nicos was named one of San Pellegrino's World's 50 Best Restaurants in Latin America. A keen supporter of the slow food movement, Vázquez is a passionate advocate of local sourcing and traditional cooking styles. It was his mother who opened Nicos in 1957; when Vázquez took over the kitchen in 2006, the place was transformed into a high-end establishment featuring a progressive menu. One standout dish is *sopa seca de natas*, a savoury mille-feuille with tomato, cream and chicken. Nicos is also known for the range of mezcals on offer.

'I like seeing people enjoy what I've made for them,' says Vázquez simply. 'I please the people that eat the food that I prepare, and they please me if they like the food and come back.' How apparently effortless an equation! In terms of the larger questions of world poverty and poor nutrition, he believes that 'having good food is a basic right' and notes that countries where 'there are no human rights' are countries where 'the right to have good food' is also ignored. 'The premise of having good, clean and just food on every table in the world' is, he explains, 'all about political will. Agriculture has become a political matter.'

Putting his money where his mouth is, Vázquez tries to source all of his ingredients direct from farmers. 'I could get a food service company to supply the restaurant,' he notes. 'It would be easier, cheaper. I would get a very good standard of quality and it would be easier for me … I earn money from having a restaurant, I live from that, but if I take my money and pay a huge mega-corporation for food, I will be supporting that mega-corporation. I prefer to support a simple farmer.' Despite Vázquez's breadth of understanding of both cuisine and world politics, he is realistic about the influence he can have as a single restaurateur. 'I have the power to change myself, I don't have the power to change the world,' he says eloquently. His critical values? 'My body and my soul and my family.' Tellingly, he concludes, 'I decide what to do with my money.'

(left) **Gerardo Vázquez Lugo relaxing in Plaza Hidalgo outside his restaurant, where bands often play** *danzón*, **and** (facing page) **in his neighbourhood**

(top right) **Vázquez and his team at work at Nicos.** Many of his recipes have not changed since the restaurant opened in 1957, among them (above) *gusanos de maguey* (cactus worms) served in a tortilla, and (right) *escamoles* (ants' eggs) – sometimes likened to insect caviar and a speciality since Aztec times. (facing page) **Yolanda Pimentel Franco's hands** preparing Nicos' famous salsa in a *molcajete*

Restaurante Monte Cristo
Tepeyac, Mexico City

(left) **Restaurante Monte Cristo's waiter, Dionisio, bringing drinks for customers;** (below) **Grasshoppers and dried chillies;** (facing page, top left) ***Nopal* (prickly-pear cactus) salad with *acociles*, tiny red freshwater crayfish, a common dish since prehispanic times;** (facing page, top right) **Lamb tamale slow-cooked in a banana leaf;** (facing page, bottom left) ***Guanábana* tart with *zapote negro* sauce; and** (facing page, bottom right) ***Xoconostle* (prickly-pear fruit) dessert**

Restaurante Monte Cristo, housed in a nineteenth-century *mesón* (inn), is a family-run eatery known especially for its salsa trolley on which fresh salsas featuring numerous types of chillies and insects are made to order in a *molcajete*. Owned by Fernando Ramírez, the establishment has remained true in both its decor and its culinary offerings to its origin as a hostelry that welcomed travellers. The menu features traditional Mexican cuisine, for example *nopal* salad with crayfish, a pork dish with crackling, and an array of desserts, among them cheese custard drizzled with caramel and prickly-pear sorbet. Duck *sopes* and courgette-flower fritters feature as well.

Ramírez's daughter María Ramírez Fernández, a designer, was a museum professional before becoming the manager at Restaurante Monte Cristo. Although she does not do any cooking at work (because, she jokes, the inn's chefs 'do a really good job'), she enjoys preparing meals at home. Describing the restaurant's specialities in greater detail, she references a wide range of ingredients including *chile ancho* (the poblano pepper, which she insists is 'not that hot'), habanero peppers, *chile de árbol* (the small but potent tree chilli), *chapulines* (grasshoppers) and the dried black *pasilla chile*. 'Our bestselling dish,' she notes, 'is *huachinango* and *chicharrón* (fish cooked with a pork-crackling-style skin) ... We slice the *huachinango* and put in the fryer.' She describes the mouthwatering result as tasting 'crunchy on the outside and really nice in the inside'.

Basílica de Santa María de Guadalupe
Cerro de Tepeyac, Mexico City

(below) **Pilgrims visiting Mexico's primary place of worship, the Basílica de Santa María de Guadalupe in La Villa;** and (right) **Votive candles in the shape of the Virgin of Guadalupe for sale outside the national shrine. The Virgin appeared to Juan Diego Cuauhtlatoatzin in 1531; his cloak, miraculously emblazoned with her image, hangs behind the basilica's altar. He was the first Mexican to be canonised**

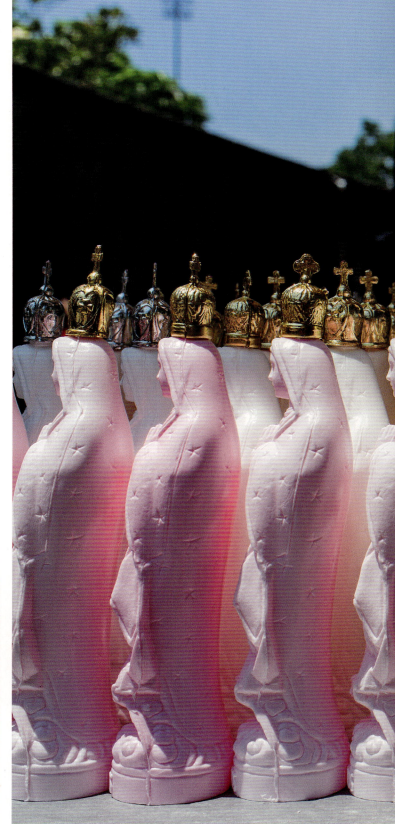

Carmen (Titita) Ramírez Degollado
Chef & Author, El Bajío, Azcapozalco, Mexico City

Chef Carmen (Titita) Ramírez Degollado was born in 1940 in Xalapa, a colonial mountain city surrounded by coffee fields. As a teenager, she was selected to represent her hometown in the Miss Red Cross pageant. Many of her childhood memories involve food; she recalls being fascinated by the fresh produce she saw at the local markets, as well as by the women vendors in indigenous dress.

Ramírez had no intention of becoming a restaurateur. However, when her husband died in 1981, she took over and expanded his restaurant, adding dishes from her native Veracruz and other Mexican states to the *carnitas* and *barbacoa* that had been his menu standards. Now an internationally recognised expert on traditional Mexican food, Ramírez heads up the El Bajío chain of sixteen restaurants in Mexico City. Her 2001 book *Alquimias y atmósferas del sabor*, a combination of recipes and autobiography, was named the Best Chef Book in Spanish as an honorary mention in the Best Chef Book in the World category at the Gourmand World Cookbook Awards (2002). Other accolades have included a Five Star Diamond Award from the American Academy of Hospitality Sciences (1998), regular invitations to participate in the Festival Anual de Centro Histórico de la Ciudad de Mexico, and the CANIRAC entrepreneur prize (2009).

Ramírez started out with fifteen employees, learning the restaurant business, long dominated by men in Mexico, on her own. In addition to the food, another hallmark she established was the restaurant's decor. Ramírez is an enthusiastic supporter of Mexican art and crafts, both of which she has used to decorate the Azcapotzalco restaurant as well as other, later locations. There is also a condiment that is unique to El Bajío: *salsa negra de chipotle meco* (black sauce with *meco chipotle* pepper), a speciality of her late nanny. The restaurant has been visited by some of the world's greatest chefs and enthusiastically reviewed by Guillermo González de Pangela and Ferrán Adrià, among many others.

'I remember everything my mother gave me ... soups and everything,' Ramírez says, 'and my grandmother ... and my nanny.' She attributes her success to hard work and to cooking every dish the same way every time. The culinary personality she most admires is chef and author Diana Kennedy, another champion of traditional Mexican cooking. Ramírez describes her fiercely purist approach this way: 'Maintaining the cooking tradition, how to make the dishes, not switching to a modern [method], which is just a little piece like this and a little thing over here'. And of course she insists on using fresh ingredients. About contemporary fusion food, she jokes, 'Yes, yes, fusion and confusion! ... Everything [looks] beautiful, but when you taste it, you say, "What happened here??!" ... Of course, I respect the young kids and their modern food, but sometimes you have to say, "This doesn't taste like anything!" And that's the truth. But when it is elaborate and the food is fresh, then it tastes like what it is.'

(above) **Carmen Ramírez Degollado and her daughter María Teresa enjoying *champurado*, a hot drink combining cocoa, maize and sugar in a wooden mixer; and** (right) **A spread at Ramírez's El Bajío, Polanco restaurant**

(facing page) **Ramírez in the kitchen of her original restaurant, with a Nativity scene from Metepec in Estado de México. Every Christmas she displays her collection of these scenes in her original restaurant in Azcapotzalco, a traditional working-class area**

Ignacio (Nacho) Urquiza
Food Photographer, Nezahualcóyotl, Mexico City

(above) **Ignacio Urquiza outside one of his favourite restaurants, El Canto de las Sirenas in Miguel Hidalgo,** (facing page, left) **inspecting fish frying and** (facing page, right) **contemplating his choices**

Ignacio (Nacho) Urquiza, whose career spans thirty years, studied film, journalism and photography; his passions are food and travel. Since 1978 he has published multiple books about Mexico, gastronomy, architecture and other subjects; he also teaches a digital-photography workshop at Estudio Urquiza. Among his numerous accolades have been Best Local Cookery Book in Mexico (Gourmand World Cookbook Awards, 2008) and Best Photography Cookbook (Gourmand World Cookbook Awards, 2013).

The authors and editors with whom Urquiza normally works give him a lot of freedom. 'I just have an approach to follow that we agree at the beginning,' he explains. A recent book about the various approaches to grilling food, for example, grew out of a conversation concerning problems he was having at home with his own cooking equipment. Whatever the angle, his love of Mexico's cuisine is a given, and he recognises the power that culinary tourism can confer. 'If our food is more and more communicated to other countries, visitors, tourists and people who are interested in food and travelling, they will come to this country much more often and in greater quantities,' he points out. 'Our economy will be affected in a very positive way. This would make the country more stable, with no need to cross the border [with the US] to find work.'

Urquiza was just five years old when his father gave him his first camera, a Kodak Brownie. His parents wanted him to be a doctor, but a gig doing aerial photography of plantations and factories convinced him that he should devote his life to the medium. Food was always a family passion. 'We used to travel a lot with my parents in Mexico,' he remembers. 'My father was an obsessive photographer. His hobby, his passion, was the darkroom, filming with Super 8 cameras ... We used to look at the map to see what time we should arrive to have the [best light] ... but also with food [in mind].'

Urquiza spent time working in Venice in the 1970s, a period he describes as being 'like a dream'. He moved on to Milan, where he found employment as an assistant to a food photographer before returning to Mexico, where he began styling food himself 'completely intuitively'. Invited by chef Patricia Quintana to pitch for a big book venture, he found that they 'had a very good connection'. The book, *Taste of Mexico*, published by Stewart, Tabori & Chang, represented 'the first time that we put a face on Mexican cuisine, from chillies to enchiladas ... That was when the story started for Patricia and for me; it was a very good, important moment. And for Mexican cuisine also'. Other books followed, about both food and architecture, two subjects which, Urquiza feels, have a range of shapes and colours in common.

When photographing food, says Urquiza, 'there are two stories: if I have to eat it, or if I have to communicate it ... If I have to eat something, it's so internal and old and Neanderthal to see something that is appealing or repelling.' (One of the things he most enjoys is eating with his hands.) Ancient needs and desires to one side, the second 'story' has to do with communicating a dish to somebody 'who has no idea about' it. 'How can I teach them what it is about? It has tortilla, it has *mole*, it has poultry, and every single part of this "architecture" has to be well identified. I cannot have something covered with sauce and just shoot it ... So I put a fork in there, and maybe that fork will let me see what's inside. Then I can show it ... One principle which I have discovered over time, and by shooting plates and dishes and desserts and beverages and everything, is that the eye can only see one point. There's only one point of desire in a dish ... I can just take you to one point, I cannot focus craving on the whole plate. There's just one point, yes or no ... So I get my camera and look for the angle, because it's like a face: every person has their best angle. I focus my lens, then intuitively I look for where the eye is going to stop.' If intuition offers the key, composition is Urquiza's obsession – 'the composition of this frame that we see the world through as photographers'. Placing every detail properly so the viewer's eye will fall on it immediately is the secret. 'As with a painting by Caravaggio, our client or spectator is looking at [an image], but if they don't find a reason to be there, they are going to go away.'

Mercedes Barcha de García Márquez
Muse, Pedregal, Mexico City

The eldest child of a pharmacist, Colombian-born Mercedes Barcha Pardo met the future Nobel Prize-winning novelist Gabriel García Márquez while she was still in high school. The two finally married in Barranquilla in 1958. On their honeymoon, García Márquez revealed his plan for what would become his two greatest novels to his new wife. Thereafter, she made it her business to anticipate whatever he needed to work in peace, for example making sure he had five hundred blank sheets of paper to write on each day. Barcha was always the first person to read her husband's manuscripts and remains an avid reader to this day.

A woman of few words, Barcha is known for her strong opinions. She and Gabo had many friends, among them Fidel Castro, who is reputed to have trusted Barcha more than her husband. Gabo's British biographer Gerald Martin singled out Barcha's intelligence, discretion and elegance as especially noteworthy. She enjoys a glass of good wine and smokes constantly. Although García Márquez is said to have fallen instantly in love with her, Barcha says she did not reciprocate immediately, adding, 'He had to work for it!' 'We were at a mutual friend's house,' she remembers. 'I think I was tricked into going there. When he walked me home, he said, "I'm going to marry you."' She was just eighteen. 'Today everything is straightforward: bed and that's that,' Barcha jokes. 'Back then it wasn't like that. You would be watched over and wouldn't be let out.' She kept all of her husband's letters in the order in which she received them, referencing them if something he did contradicted something he had written to her. Eventually he offered to buy the letters from her to prevent them falling into the wrong hands. Barcha does not remember how much she charged her husband but does remember that US dollars were the currency of choice for the transaction. Letters aside, her father 'was very happy [about the marriage] because he said Gabo [the novelist's nickname] was very intelligent. That's all he cared about'. Apparently Gabo knew he would be 'very famous' in due course.

There seems to have been an unusual mutuality in the marriage. 'He knew I was there,' Barcha says of her husband. 'He was there and I was there. That's why I say that men just need to marry a smart woman ... The thing is, we never argued, never ever. We consulted with each other about everything, and with the kids. I consult with the kids to this day.' She felt it was important for her to keep the household running smoothly, observing that 'if a man is writing, he cannot come home to trouble, because that's terrible. Especially if he comes home with that entire tangle in his mind. He was ... what did we call it? ... encompassed.' Cooking was a pastime the couple shared. Gabo learned to cook in Europe and taught his wife to prepare Italian food, later buying her a book about French cuisine that she still has. As to Mexican food, she is a fan 'but without spice': 'The best thing about Mexican food is tacos. They're delicious.'

(left) **Busts of Mercedes Barcha de García Márquez and her late husband, writer Gabriel García Márquez, at their home in Pedregal; and** (above) **Barcha cooking** *carré* **of pork, white rice, courgette flowers and a beef** *estofado* **(goulash). She enjoys experimenting with food, often cooking Italian, Spanish and French dishes**

(facing page) **Barcha in El Gabo's study, contemplating the papier-mâché model of a skeleton with monarch butterfly wings reading** *The General in His Labyrinth*

Jorge Vallejo
Chef, Quintonil, Polanco, Mexico City

The menu at Jorge Vallejo's elegant restaurant Quintonil (opened in 2012) pays homage to traditional Mexican cuisine within the framework of contemporary gastronomy. After finishing secondary school, Vallejo enrolled at the Centro Culinario de México, going on to become one of a number of talented young chefs including Mario Espinosa, Pablo Salas, Edgar Nuñez and Diego Hernández Baquedano. A protégé of Pujol's Enrique Olvera, Vallejo runs Quintonil together with his wife Alejandra Flores, who oversees the dining room.

Vallejo, considered by many to be Mexico's greatest living chef, spent a month at Noma in Copenhagen in 2011 as well as time at Madrid's Michelin-starred Santceloni and on cruise ships. Vegetables and greens take centre stage at Quintonil (the name refers to a Mexican herb), many of them from his nearby garden. He and his team keep their carbon footprint so low that many of their ingredients travel just 30 metres to his customers' plates. An advocate of products from Mexico's small agricultural suppliers, Vallejo's contemporary take on home cooking features such dishes as *salbute* with *cuitlacoche* (a high-protein fungus that grows on maize) and chilli powder; sardines in green sauce with purslane, fennel and guacamole; and *mamey* panna cotta, a sweetened corn crumble with *mamey*-seed ice cream. He prides himself on transforming inexpensive, locally available ingredients into special dishes, saying, 'It can be as delicious and innovative and avant-garde with these kinds of ingredients that cost maybe 2 or 3 pesos a kilo, for instance 5 pesos for a bunch of *quintonil* that you can get in the market. You can serve it and see what ingredients can be as delicious and innovative as an ingredient that costs a lot of money.'

Vallejo enjoys bringing his suppliers in to sample his menu and offer suggestions for adjusting it. 'Last week we had a guy who brought us mushrooms,' he says. 'We're working with these guys that work together as a community ... bringing all the mushrooms they can from the woods, and we serve them here in the restaurant. I invite them ... so they can try the food that we're doing with the ingredients that we get from them ... Sometimes they say, "We eat this mushroom this way," and it's very interesting to have this opportunity to share because they can tell you the way they eat it every day ... What we try and do with these ideas is to transform them into something we can serve at the restaurant so people ... can feel the real flavour of Mexico, not in terms of the tradition but in terms of the people, what the ordinary people of Mexico, the poorest guys, eat – something that is good because the ingredients are super-nice ... The rural people that we bring to the restaurant can see the other side of the coin with the same ingredients.'

Vallejo believes that the purpose of having his restaurant 'is not to become rich. I don't mind if I have a brand new car; I live for the way I eat'. He is committed to working with young people, observing that 'if you don't try to make your community better and become a better person and work with people that can do great things, it doesn't matter if they come from wherever they come from. I think you're doing something that is good ... What I'm trying to do is ... to encourage young people and young cooks, [to give them] the opportunity to work in a good restaurant.' He even arranges language lessons for his waiting staff so they are easily able to communicate with the numerous foreigners who come into the restaurant, especially in the evening. 'When they finish here,' he notes of his staff, 'they will have learned something to help them get a better job.'

(previous spread, left page) **Quintonil's staff and management team outside the restaurant during their daily morning meeting; and a courgette flower stuffed with deep-sea prawn; and** (previous spread, right page) **Jorge Vallejo checking fresh ingredients from Xochimilco: kale,** *huazontle* **(used like spinach),** *pleurotus de amor* **mushrooms (also known locally as** *seta piñón* **or** *seta rosa***),** *quelites* **(edible wild herbs) and** *chile de aqua* **from Oaxaca, which is cooked for twenty-four hours, blended with olive oil and served with prawns**

Quintonil specialities: (above) **fresh** *flor de calabaza***,** (middle) **avocado** *tatemado* **and** (right) **tartar of avocado** *tatemado* **with** *escamoles* **(ants' eggs). Eighty per cent of Quintonil's ingredients come from small producers.** (facing page) **Meringue with berries**

Santiago Sota
Olga Café, Polanco, Mexico City

Santiago Sota and his two siblings launched the Olga Café with help from their family in 2015. Sota, who has a degree in marketing, acts as barista and chief toaster. His brother and sister both trained as engineers. The trio's objective is to support small producers so they can improve their businesses and increase quality. The coffee sold at Olga comes from several different locations, including Chiapas, Oaxaca, Guerrero and Veracruz. The café also sells cakes made by the trio's grandmother Olga, after whom it is named, and their mother.

'Team Olga finds good-quality coffee producers and buys straight from them,' Sota explains. 'We don't go through a company because that's a real problem when you want quality coffee. You have to work with the producers … The idea is that if we believe in the coffee, everyone can win. Everyone deserves perfect compensation for what they do. We select producers because they're producing perfectly.' Trustworthy suppliers are key to Olga's success, making it possible for the café to offer a range of flavour profiles. 'Wines from Chile, or Argentina, or … France are not the same,' notes Sota. 'That's where we want to take coffee: to that point where you get the flavour of the land.' Massive price differences reflect the scale of rarity of beans, with some from Oaxaca (favoured in Japan) fetching up to six or seven times as much as 'normal' ones.

Mexico is the eighth-largest coffee producer in the world and as such stands to benefit from the current fascination with different roasts and tastes. 'Coffee is a really good way to have a new experience every day without spending too much,' Sota observes. In this sense coffee drinking is becoming like pairing certain wines with certain foods. 'I recently worked with a couple of restaurants as a roaster,' he says, 'and what I always tell the chefs is, "You take care of what kind of tomatoes you buy, what kind of water, every little detail, to make sure that my food is perfect. Why won't you serve the perfect coffee for me to drink so I can say this was the best experience I've ever had in my life?"'

Working with family members every day has its challenges. 'It's tough!' laughs Santiago's sister. 'You know each other so well, too much! We have had some big fights, but we always figure it out somehow.' The trio enjoy a decent financial turnover, but 'not as much as we could; it's going to take time'. They are in the coffee business for the long haul. 'We started this project in the field, where everything starts,' notes Santiago. 'Then the roaster, then the coffee shops, and in the end people will understand what it takes to have a cup of coffee.' It clearly takes a lot of work. 'That's because we choose to work according to a model where fair trade is the main ingredient. At the end of the day we understand that this is not a sprint, this is a marathon. If we want to get somewhere, we have to work and work. And our work starts by buying the coffee, helping the producers, helping them live in a better reality … When we started visiting coffee plantations, we found that the producers were not getting paid what they deserved for a proper job. So we decided to invite them to work in the way that we wanted to work … paying what they deserved … We are then able to offer their coffee here at a reasonable price, for everyone to buy.' This explains why the Sotas' mantra is: 'Quality is not negotiable.'

(far left) **Siblings and co-owners Constanza and Patricio Sota outside Olga Café; and** (facing page) **Santiago Sota preparing his famous brew**

Martha Ortiz
Chef, Dulce Patria, Polanco, Mexico City

Named by Ferran Adrià as one of his all-time favourite chefs, Martha Ortiz opened Dulce Patria in Mexico City in 2011 in the luxury hotel Las Alcobas. One of the first Mexican female chefs to establish herself at the forefront of gastronomy, Ortiz's dishes all have abstract names deriving from her love of literature and the arts. Fine local ingredients and plenty of colour combine to enhance the overall effect; the restaurant boasts an avant-garde interior as colourful, exuberant and idiosyncratic as the food Ortiz serves. The bar serves cocktails, mezcal, tequila, flavoured *raspados* and other *pequeñas delicias frías*, while the menu offers *ceviche*, tostadas, *guisados colorados* and *aguas frescas* crowned with flowers. Mexican wines are also featured. The chairs, textiles and crockery are all made by Mexican artisans.

As a little girl, Ortiz aspired to be either Maria Callas or a museum curator. Because her mother was an artist, she grew up surrounded by creatives, among them the diplomat, poet and Nobel Laureate Octavio Paz and the painter Rufino Tamayo. Her menus draw inspiration from a wide range of sources: opera; the visual arts; an insatiable reading habit; and Mexican women whose lives have influenced her, among them the poet Sor Juana Inés de la Cruz, the artist Frida Kahlo and the many home cooks of Michoacán. The author of eight cookbooks, Ortiz plans to open a new restaurant in London in 2017, in a hotel on Park Lane.

About her daily routine, Ortiz says, 'I love to walk, I need the market, and I love to see people. And I love to say hello ... I like people ... I like to live.' The sensual side of Mexican cuisine is important to her, born as it was out of a blending of cultures and culinary habits. 'In Mexico,' she observes, 'part of the libido comes through cooking. We are such a guilty culture that the food has to be sensual ... We have a very sophisticated culture, very mystical and magical and energetic ... We are very "body-present", but we are food-present.' She cites *mole* as a perfect example of this theory: 'When you try a *mole*, you feel the ecstasy of fifty ingredients ... When you try these fifty ingredients, you feel the spirit of love, you feel the sensuality of love, you feel the kiss of burning chillies in your mouth. So you say, "Ahhhhh, I am Mexican!"'

With her mother's artistic personality balanced by her father's profession as a doctor, Ortiz came to believe that 'cuisine is science and art at the same time.' Her parents loved to read, as she does, and she believes that the importance of this life habit cannot be overemphasised 'because when you read you think, and when you think you can invent'. The novel she best remembers reading while still at school (where it was banned) was *Captain Pantoja and the Special Service* by Mario Vargas Llosa, whom she saw on television when she was nine and recalls as being 'so handsome'. The book, she says, was a 'hidden love and guilty pleasure'. She recalls Octavio Paz coming to dinner with 'Marie-José, his beautiful and amazing wife ... She looked like Brigitte Bardot or something, a very sensual and beautiful woman. And he had wonderful, wonderful eyes ... I'd just read '*Piedra de Sol*', which I think is one of the best poems of the twentieth century, and I had to come downstairs and try to see this man'. And she was taught about literature by Sergio Fernández, a Proust expert. 'In the end, I really enjoyed it,' Ortiz remembers. 'Because when you have these stories, they are fantastic, and you have your imagination. For a day you can be maybe Ophelia, and for another day Madame Bovary, and for another day Anna Karenina.' She admits to being a 'frustrated writer' herself, and she enjoys drawing, even if her work is 'horrible'. 'I don't go to the market to see dead fish,' she jokes. 'I get inspired. I get inspired by stories. I say, "I want this [dish] to taste like blackness." And what does black taste like?'

(previous spread, left page) **Dulce Patria's colourful façade mixed with** *aguas frescas*; **and** (previous spread, right page) **Martha Ortiz taking a break**

(above) *Papalotes de atún* **(tuna butterflies). Ortiz's dishes all have abstract names deriving from her love of the arts and literature. She insists on using local ingredients and plenty of colour**

(top left) *María va a la florería*, a favourite dish of Ortiz's – cheesecake with *guanabana* and *tuna*; (top right) **Loin of pork with yellow *mole*;** (bottom left) ***Pan de elote*** **(cornbread); and** (bottom right) **Trout**

(following spread) **Tamarind and red *mole* paste for sale in Milpa Alta market**

Margarita de Orellana
Editor & Publisher, Colonia Roma, Mexico City

Daughter of Cuban immigrants and wife of writer Alberto Ruy Sánchez, Margarita de Orellana studied at Universidad Iberoamericana, going on to pursue graduate degrees in France, where she lived for a decade. Orellana sees culture as an interweaving of symbols and practices whose most refined expression is art. Her main concern as Editorial Director of *Artes de México* magazine is that Mexico's younger generation 'hardly know what their culture is ... You cannot imagine how many are forgetting. And that is very sad'. She lays the blame for this lack of interest in, and connection with, the past firmly at the door of 'modernity and the tendency to look at the United States as a role model ... Of course we have a huge migration going there, but what is paradoxical is that when they get there, they want to come back and at least remember where they come from ... So what we try to do is make them proud of what they are and what we have'.

Where food is concerned, Orellana's knowledge is both broad and deep. Referring back to the past, she notes that when the Spaniards arrived, 'they never imagined they would find twenty thousand species that were unknown to the world,' among them turkeys and the cacao plant. Mexico also hosted 150 languages in prehispanic times (of which fewer than half have survived), though these were actively repressed by the Aztecs. 'Every single part of the country had their own culture, their own language, but what we shared – what we still share – is the love of maize. Maize was a god. Even the Maya said that Mexicans are made out of maize.' She cites an Aztec practice that still survives in the Huasteca Potosina: 'They have these rituals before they start [planting] the crops. They make little altars like on the Day of the Dead ... They dress up the maize cob ... and they put it on an altar and worship it, and they sing certain songs and follow certain practices until the maize is ready. Then they put a lot of flowers in the maize field and sing to it. The aim is to have good crops.'

Despite the huge reduction in indigenous populations, Orellana stresses that the Spaniards intermarried with native people rather than isolating them on reservations, as happened in the US. The resulting syncretism is still apparent in all areas of Mexican life, most especially in cuisine, although she fears that a rigid class structure has caused the less well-off to witness nutritious traditional fare being swept away by 'transnational companies that have brought us so much trash food', which is 'cheaper and easier to make ... That has been very harmful for the country'. There is good news, however. 'It doesn't mean you can't eat well if you want to. A good tortilla is something that you cherish. And good beans ... the beans are incredible. We had about a hundred types of beans before the Spaniards arrived.'

As Mexican food gains in quality in the US, the process of deteriorating nutritional quality may be reversed, at least in part. 'Twenty years ago, I would go to any little town in the US and I would find very bad Mexican food,' Orellana remembers. 'But little by little, since [the scale of] emigration is so huge, you can have good breakfasts like you do here in any little town ... That is amazing ... It's such a rich cuisine that it's very curious that it hasn't travelled anywhere else. The fruit and vegetables did, but the dishes didn't.' That, Orellana says with some pride, is changing too, despite the current political climate.

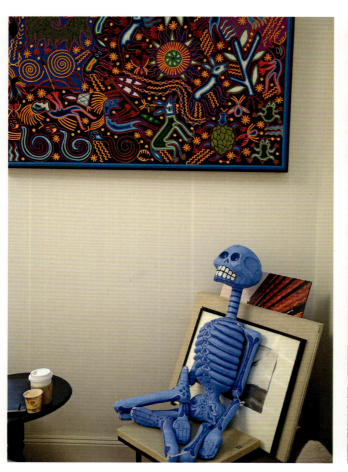

(left) **Books on Mexican cuisine and Day of the Dead mementos dot Margarita de Orellana's office; and** (facing page) **Orellana, founder and editor of** ***Artes de México***, **in her office, surrounded by publications she helped produce on Mexican food and culture**

Eduardo (Lalo) García
Chef, Máximo Bistrot, Colonia Roma, Mexico City

Born in Guanajuato, chef Lalo García had no formal education. His family emigrated to the US when he was a child to find agricultural work. While still a teenager in Atlanta, he became a restaurant dishwasher 'because as a child I was part of the economy that supported my family'. When a cook failed to turn up at work, García was given the opportunity to make salads and cold dishes. Later he moved to New York, where he met Mexican chef Enrique Olvera, owner of Pujol in Mexico City. García returned to Mexico to work with Olvera for three years. He now has three restaurants of his own.

'I love my job, but we live in a shameful political society, and that involves us restaurants,' García observes. 'There is no way to open a business legally in Mexico ... That's why I do not want to open restaurants anymore. In the near future, I would like to have a sustainable *ranchito* with a small restaurant near Mexico City, where people keep searching for me to feed them but on another level: with me raising animals and butchering them, harvesting vegetables and making cheese ... It is the strangest thing – the life that I had in childhood – to grow up with the earth, little animals and wood-burning stoves – I want to go back to how I lived before.'

Like many Mexicans, García's father began crossing the border into the US in the 1970s. 'Most of the time he crossed by himself, walking through the desert,' the chef explains. 'But for us, as kids, I don't think he wanted us to go to that much trouble, so he paid *coyotes* – *coyotes* are people that get you across. I crossed the border illegally five times; the first time was at two [years old]. I remember

the hole in the fence, I remember the smells: very desert-like, dry, the smell of wood, mesquite. I remember the stars and the moon. It was very bright because we crossed through San Diego. In the 1980s, Tijuana and San Diego were not that big. I remember my mum carrying me and us lying down in the back of a truck, and a big gate. And I remember the aeroplane. We flew from Los Angeles to Tampa.' He was deported a couple of times but found ways to return.

García blames a lack of education for the infernal complexity of Mexico's politics but is hopeful that things will change. Of the new US administration, he says, 'I think [Trump's] a loudmouth, but I also think we have a big opportunity here in Mexico to not rely on the US ... By 2018 we are going to be the biggest car manufacturer in the world, but we don't make a single Mexican brand [and] we don't process our own petroleum.' Meanwhile he is doing his bit to support the local economy. 'I employ 110 people across three restaurants,' he notes. 'I don't need 110 people. I could do it with fifty or sixty. The idea ... is to help other people rise up ... I try not to get involved in politics. I have too much to do for my businesses to think about it. I tell my employees, "This restaurant belongs to all of you. Maybe I have the title of 'owner', and maybe I make more money than you, but this restaurant belongs to all of us."' He believes that his 'little restaurant' has changed things for the better 'in the way people think about restaurants and dining and treatment towards employees. Not because of what I do, but I think it has had a very small impact on society.'

(facing page) **Eduardo García next door to Máximo Bistrot, the restaurant named after his son; and** (left) **Some ingredients with which he likes to work**

(above left) *Lechón*,
or suckling pig with
mashed potatoes, a dish
on Máximo Bistrot's
menu since it opened;
(above) *Kanpachi*, a type
of amberjack, with
soya vinegar, ginger
and avocado; and
(facing page) **Octopus
on the grill**

Zélika García
Founder, Zona Maco México Arte Contemporaneo, Granada, Mexico City

'I love to eat, I love food,' enthuses Zélika García, founder (and now Director) of Zona Maco, Latin America's most important art fair. Listed as one of the 'World's Most Creative Mexicans' by *Forbes Mexico* in 2015, García started organising art fairs straight out of university. Zona Maco, which takes place twice annually, now includes three sectors: Zona Maco Arte Contemporáneo, Zona Maco Foto and Salón del Anticuario. In addition, the fairs offer programmes of lectures and activities in museums and galleries and at exhibition sites.

García's mother was one of thirteen children, and García herself is one of almost eighty grandchildren. 'I grew up in Monterrey, and every Sunday we had all sorts of traditional Mexican dishes,' she remembers. 'It could be rice, it could be meat made in the *metate*, which was my favourite … All of the tortillas were handmade … I still bring them from my grandmother's house in Monterrey to Mexico City. And *mole* too … I love bone marrow, and she also made corn soup … Sometimes she made dishes from different states, like *chiles en nogada*, or from Puebla, because part of my family is from Puebla … So every Sunday I ate very different dishes … Of course sometimes she made some French or other things, food that was not Mexican.' Monterrey is famous for *cabrito*, or goat, another favourite of García's, as is *carne asada*, 'when they do meat on the grill outside'. Other much-loved dishes include '*fideo seco*, regular beans, and then *frijoles a la charra*, and in Monterrey *frijoles con veneno*, which are done with pork fat … Now I'm getting hungry!'

Quizzed about the relationship between food and art, García responds that 'to be a very good chef or cook is an art' in itself. 'It takes a lot of experience, of course, but also patience and time to learn, and it's a form of expression. So I think they can be related, because cooking gives you different feelings and art gives you different feelings.' Presentation is critical: 'The colours on the plate are very important. How it looks is important also because maybe you don't like it as much if it doesn't look nice on the plate. And the taste is sort of – when you see art with the eyes, the same thing happens in your mouth when you have something very special.' Painter Frida Kahlo comes instantly to mind as someone whose form of expression, fiery temperament and contrarian character evoke certain tastes. 'I can only think of Frida Kahlo in terms of colours and fruits and things like that,' muses García. 'Maybe it would be *sopa de tortilla*, tortilla soup with a lot of spice.' And then, having been put in mind of exotic flavours, she adds with enthusiasm, 'Oh, and I also love ants and worms and everything!'

(left) **Zélika García in front of Museo Soumaya and La Fundación Jumex Arte Contemporáneo (right) in the Granada district. The giant inflatable pills are by the twentieth-century Canadian art collective General Idea**

Ivonne Madrid
Head of Corporate Responsibility, Fundación Alsea, Colonia Golondrinas, Alvaro Obregón, Mexico City

'Fundación Alsea was founded in 2004,' explains Ivonne Madrid. 'Our principal objective is to secure food for vulnerable communities … In 2012, we launched our most important product, *Va por mi cuenta* (It's on Me), which promotes social consciousness about food poverty in our country. We build and operate dining centres for people in food poverty in urban areas.' The seven dining centres serve about twenty-seven hundred children daily, as well as pregnant and nursing mothers. To be eligible for free lunches, the children's parents must be earning less than 25 pesos a day; they work mainly as domestics or on building sites. The foundation also promotes environmental awareness through a programme of sustainable operation. Its goals in 2016 were to supply 80 per cent of its facilities in Mexico with renewable energy and to maintain standards of efficiency for lighting, heating and the pumping of water.

The foundation's parent company, Alsea, is a multi-brand restaurant operator based in Mexico City. Its portfolio stretches across fast-food outlets, casual dining venues and cafeteria chains in Mexico, Spain and South America. One of Mexico's largest food-service companies, Alsea's Mexican food franchises include the Vips and El Portón chains, the former with 285 outlets across the country catering to local tastes. Alsea also has franchises with a number of major American companies, among them Starbucks, Burger King, Domino's Pizza, P. F. Chang's and The Cheesecake Factory. Social responsibility is one of Alsea's five strategic areas, representing one of the company's core values. Thus the foundation strives for food safety in vulnerable communities and promotes human development by supporting initiatives that favour education.

Alsea's employees are able to participate in these programmes in two ways. The first one involves making regular donations out of their salaries. The other way to participate is by volunteering to do community service. 'We have two principal events,' Madrid explains. 'One is the global month of service with Starbucks in April and also a casual dining event in June … [There is] also a Christmas celebration with all of the beneficiaries in all the dining centres on 24 December. All of the employees come with their families, and we serve the families at the dining centres their evening meal.' Madrid describes the foundation's association with Comedor Santa María, 'a civil association that has been working for many years impacting communities that live in extreme poverty. Alsea selects the most important projects to run in the countries where we operate – Mexico, Chile, Brazil, Colombia, Argentina and Spain – so we asked Comedor Santa María to make this alliance with us. Fundación Alsea is a vehicle for social responsibility. We coordinate all of our partners and all of our efforts in order to have the funds to operate and build the dining centres, and they – with their know-how (they have been doing this for many years) and their experience – help us to operate the dining centres. It's not just about food; we are not a food factory or a china factory. We are very conscious of the nutrition that these kids need; we have standards to ensure that the children have sufficient nutrition to develop and to learn and to be different. So we do not just give them food but also nutrition, not just impacting the physical body but also the kids' minds and spirits.'

(left) **Ivonne Madrid visiting Alsea HQ in Reforma. The corporation set up Nuestro Comedor, its partnership with Comedor Santa María, to run dining halls for impoverished children**

(above) **Children having lunch at Nuestro Comedor in the Las Golondrinas barrio, where the most popular menu item is *tacos dorados* (fried-chicken tacos) with salad and lime pie for pudding; and** (facing page) **Madrid at work at the Nuestro Comedor facility in Las Golondrinas**

(following spread)
Views of the barrio of Las Golondrinas

Rodrigo Rivero Lake
Antiquarian, Polanco, Mexico City

Rodrigo Rivero Lake studied Law at UNAM. An incurable collector, he has spent a lifetime hunting for rare, intriguing items at flea markets in Mexico, at European auction houses and in India. As a young man, he made innumerable trips through Indochina and India buying Buddhist art and Chinese export porcelain. Later on, he became interested in Oriental influences on the art of Mexico, as well as Mexican manifestations in Asia. His 2006 book *Namban: Art in Viceregal Mexico* focuses on Oriental influences apparent in New Spain. Rivero is the only Mexican antiquarian who has been a member of the Oriental Ceramic Society of London and is also a patron of several museums.

'I love my country, I'm absolutely crazy for it,' enthuses Rivero. 'It's … a fantastic and bizarre and unusual country that is at the same time full of magic and full of greatness.' His early collecting years were framed by his belief that 'there was a huge period of political destruction going on around the world in a political way, in a natural way or in a religious way.' In response to this apparent storm of international ruin, he has saved, among other things, a complete church (now stored in a warehouse). His passion for collecting has, he says, made him rich in his heart if not 'in his pocket' – and in this sense he embodies the spirit of his father, 'a fantastic man full of joy and full of spirit … He had the most fantastic chances to become very rich and he didn't take them because he didn't fall for [wealth as such]'.

A true *bon viveur*, Rivero enjoys eating out. One of his favourite Mexico City restaurants is La Poblanita in Tacubaya. La Poblanita used to be a tiny *fonda*-style kitchen at the end of a dark alley; still run by the same family, it is much larger now. Rivero always downs a shot of lime juice before his mezcal and beer, claiming that it acts as 'flooring' and protects his stomach. He drinks beer to rehydrate, pointing out that 'if water destroys the roads, imagine what it does to the intestines!'

Aware of the vast economic, educational and other discrepancies among Mexico's population, Rivero believes there is nothing he himself can do to remedy them. His lack of patience with the self-regard of some members of the middle and upper classes is obvious when he cites, by way of a metaphor, the work of the Spanish Surrealist artist and anarchist Remedios Varo, who 'used to paint people walking with wooden boxes with a very small open door. That's how you look if you are like that … Maybe there are people who have to look completely camouflaged or to be kept from having to breathe the air outside'. In contrast, he adds, there are people like himself, who love life and savour every experience, no matter how mundane. 'I can go out into the street at noon,' he notes, 'and find somebody who would like to tell me something. I speak in slang to them – and they enjoy it – in order to have a conversation.'

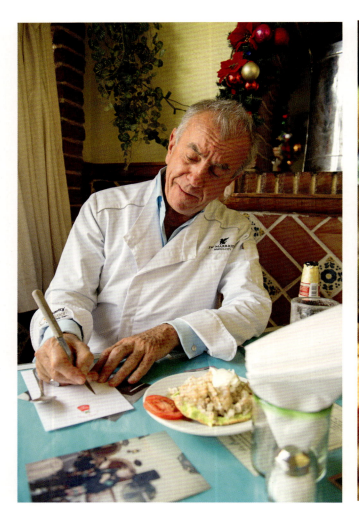

(far left) **Rodrigo Rivero Lake at La Poblanita, one of his favourite Mexico City restaurants;** (left) *Chalupas* **(small thick tortillas fried and topped with red and green chilli sauce); and** (facing page) **Rivero hamming it up for the camera at his home in Polanco – his nineteenth-century** *sarape* **is threaded with silver**

Homero Aridjis & Chloe Aridjis
Writers, Lomas de Chapultepec, Miguel Hidalgo, Mexico City

Homero Aridjis grew up in Michoacán, the son of a Greek who fought the Turks in 1922 and was exiled to Mexico four years later. When Aridjis was ten, he nearly died in a shotgun accident. Losing interest in hunting, he became a passionate advocate for the environment. The author of more than forty books of poetry and prose, Aridjis has raised public awareness on everything from sea turtles to grey whales to Mexico City's near-lethal air pollution. In 1985, he founded the Group of 100, an association of artists and intellectuals devoted to environmental protection and biodiversity. He has served as Mexico's ambassador to the Netherlands, Switzerland and UNESCO, and was twice elected President of International PEN.

Chloe Aridjis, who lives in London and Mexico City, grew up in Mexico and the Netherlands. From an early age she was surrounded by writers since her parents organised poetry festivals. She has published a collection of essays as well as two novels, one of which won France's Prix du Premier Roman. 'Culturally I feel Mexican when I'm in Europe, but when I return I realise I feel quite foreign,' she says. She describes the essence of the Mexican character as 'an attraction to exuberance and tension', a Baroque 'synchronism of prehispanic and European cultures'. Her father, on the other hand, says he feels 'like the child of two mythologies: Greek mythology and Mexican mythology ... Mexican mythology was architectonic, whereas the Greek was humanistic. Mexican [mythology] was not human. There were human sacrifices, and it was very violent ... When I was young, I felt Greek mythology the most. Later I also understood the Mexican version'.

Homero Aridjis references the documented prehispanic predilection of high-ranking people for 'squash or courgette flowers in a soup' that included human flesh, as well as the sacrifice of dozens of people when the Temple Mayor was built in Mexico City. 'The start of a building had to have this human blood,' he explains. 'For us [today], it's very mysterious, the cult of death ... It's a mystery how a country's people can be attached to human sacrifice.' He explains the highly spiced quality of much Mexican food this way: 'There's something in the culture that always strives towards intensity and extremes, and ... exuberance ... Even in the food, it has to be this experience. Even when it's pleasurable, it makes you suffer somehow. Like a slightly melodramatic – I'm not sure if that's the right word ... martyrdom that's enveloped in every authentic experience.' Chloe adds, 'I think there's always an element of the transformative and [of] surprise. Growing up eating Mexican food, one takes a lot for granted, but then when one observes the experience of foreigners who come and taste it for the first time, they're always surprised.'

Despite huge changes in other cultural areas, both father and daughter believe that when it comes to Mexicans and their food, as Homero says, 'It's always the same. For example, bureaucrats leave the office at 1.00, and in these areas there's a lot of people eating tacos in the street.' Chloe adds, 'I don't know if you've seen the stalls where bodyguards go? Sometimes their wealthy patrons are eating in restaurants ... and outside there are stalls set up specifically for their bodyguards, who are stood around eating their tacos.' Her father echoes this observation: 'Sometimes when I take a taxi, the driver says, "I am going to eat tacos in the street later." It's [a] cultural [thing.] Mexican food is very powerful ... I was in Los Angeles, San Diego – you go to places where they are making tortillas, and they are dominating the American food tradition. They prefer tacos.' For Homero Aridjis, food and celebration go hand in hand. 'Mexican food is a ceremony,' he emphasises. 'To eat is a ceremony.'

(far left) **Chloe Aridjis helping out in the kitchen at home in Las Lomas;** (left) **Maize** *sopes* **bases; and** (facing page) **The two writers in Homero's study**

Jair Téllez
Chef, Amaya, Colonia Juárez, Mexico City

'I ate sushi before I ate *mole*, jokes chef Jair Téllez, who grew up in Tijuana and the US. Téllez studied law and anthropology before becoming a professional cook. Having opened Laja ('a hyper-local food and wine place') in 1999 in the Valle de Guadalupe, Baja California, in 2008 he opened MeroToro in Mexico City. Seven years later came Amaya.

'People who want to do independent projects are able to do them here because here we can pay the rent,' the chef says of Colonia Juárez. 'I like opening restaurants in places where there's not much happening yet.' He describes himself as 'a gypsy', adding, 'I'm from nowhere, and I love that.' His first summer job, at a racetrack kitchen, led to other short-term kitchen gigs. Discussing his own education, he says, 'In your conventional Western way of looking at things, you'll be a student, then you will have money for a scholarship if you're a great student or you'll go to work. Here, things happen in a different way. You have two options. You ... regret that you live here, or you figure out a way to have that make sense.' It was in 1972 that he went to New York to attend the French Culinary Institute. 'The French were the first to make an encyclopaedic register of techniques,' he points out. 'It's like if you studied singing, they would give you an Italian method to start with. It's not that they're better singers but that they wrote the method ... If you contextualise it in the early 1800s, it makes sense ... They were categorising everything; they were into epistemology and knowledge and systems.'

Téllez feels that, as he puts it, 'many people get into the restaurant business for reasons other than making good business ... I don't do it for the money. I mean, I think about it, because I need to make it work.' Amaya has family backing so the pressure is on the chef to pursue a practical financial scenario. His approach is that of a captain surrounded by a like-minded crew. 'I see restaurants as an exercise in people; it's a group thing,' he explains. 'I empower people ... The risk of empowering people is worth more than what it would be if they weren't empowered ... I try to take myself out of the equation. It has to be a team endeavour.' The team must, of course, be entirely in sync with Téllez's programme: 'The only way that they can make the right decisions is if they internalise the way I perceive things and make decisions.'

Téllez is sensitive to the significance of Mexico's range of formative cultures and influences, as well as to the contrast between life in the cities and in the countryside. 'I'm very convinced that whatever "modernity" means, and whatever "cosmopolitan" means, it needs to be inclusive of all the nuances and differences,' he says. 'Because that's what makes this country what it is, rich and diverse ... There's this long tradition of portraying what's Mexican and what's not, what's authentic and what's not ... We have this post-colonial baggage, this thing about who we are and who those guys are who are challenging our authenticity. First it was the Spanish, then it was the French, then the Americans. That's pretty much the story of Mexican culinary identity: always feeling challenged by something external.' He is optimistic about the growing appeal of Mexican cuisine outside the country. 'Right now, all over the world they're trying to make tacos,' he notes. 'So perhaps we're at the point where Mexican food has the conditions to be self-assured in a way that it doesn't feel challenged by external influences. That also works inside. Mexican food can also be inclusive of difference, even the non-romantic manifestations of Mexican food, like me ... The good news and the bad news is that there is a lot of richness in the little nuances of why a community does this and why they do that ... It's easy to portray Mexico as a country of chillies and maize and beans, and of descendants of the Aztecs ... I respect the Aztecs, but I have no emotional relation[ship] to them. I love saying that because it's an unpopular position.'

(facing page) **Jair Téllez at his new restaurant, Amaya, and** (right) **preparing braised rabbit with wild mushrooms**

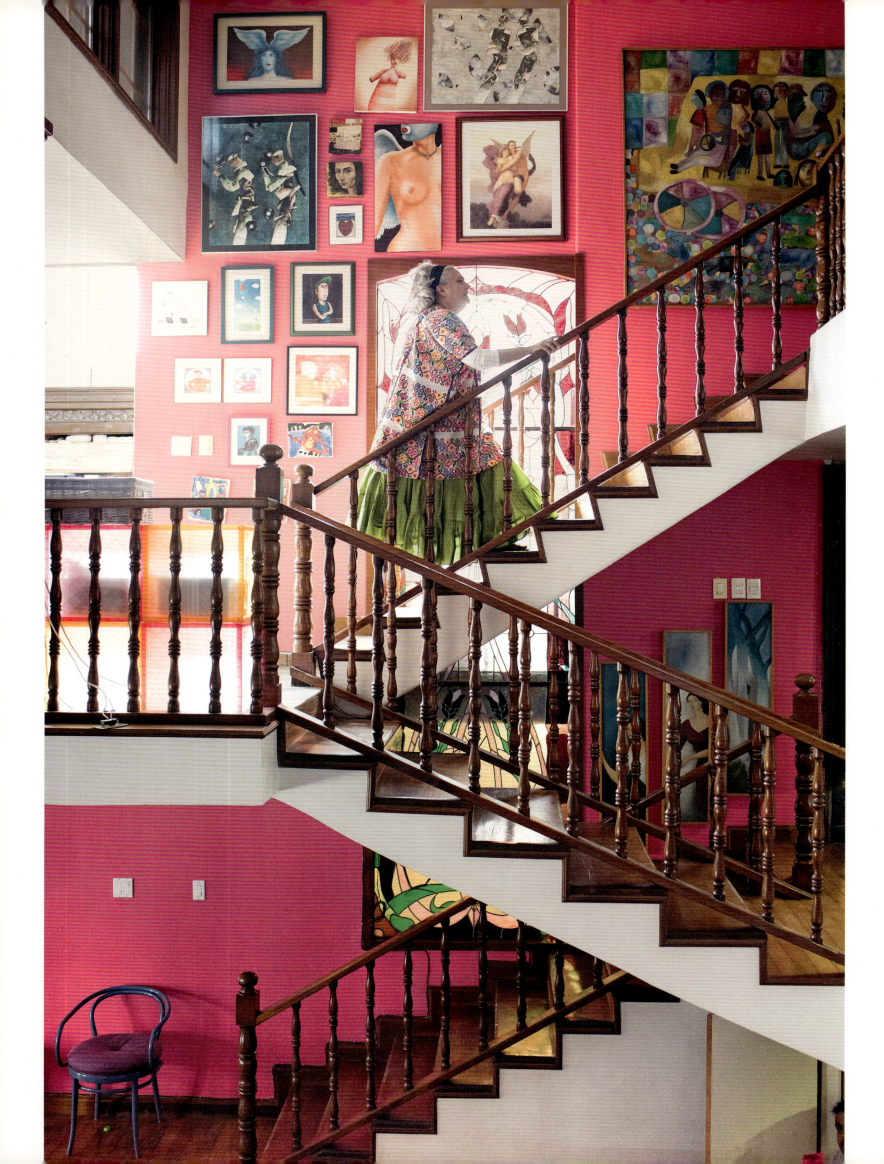

Laura Esquivel
Author, Coyoacán, Mexico City

As a teenager, Laura Esquivel became interested in Eastern spirituality, committing to a vegetarian diet and becoming a spokeswoman for what she calls 'the law of love'. Esquivel trained as a teacher, founding a children's theatre workshop and writing and producing dramas for children in the 1970s and '80s. She collaborated with her first husband, actor, producer and director Alfonso Arau, on several films. In light of these interests and activities, she came to believe that life's most important lessons cannot necessarily be taught in a classroom, and so she advocates for non-traditional learning environments and the pursuit of higher truth through rebellion against social norms. She currently serves in Mexico's Chamber of Deputies on behalf of the left-wing National Regeneration Movement (Morena) Party.

Esquivel's international bestseller *Like Water for Chocolate* (1990), a combination of novel and cookbook, was made into an award-winning film in 1994. She accepts that she has been described as a Magic Realist but points out that what she writes about is real, not magic, referencing a scene in *Like Water* 'where they have problems cooking beans, so they sing to the beans and they cook. That is not Magical Realism ... Once I was in a party where we were going to eat tamales and ... somebody said the cook was really upset when she cooked them, so to reverse that bad emotion we needed to sing to the tamales, and we did. In a few minutes they were ready! We have a lot of those kinds of stories [in Mexico] because there is something that people don't know and don't have the eyes to see: energy. We don't see energy, but we feel the impact of energy ... You don't see love, but you can feel love and you can give love, and ... in itself the act of cooking is an act of love. You are mixing the four elements of the world – air, water, fire, earth – and through the alchemy of the kitchen you do one dish in which everything is made with love'.

Most of today's politicians, says Esquivel, 'want you to believe that you are separated [from everyone else] ... that the decisions you make or your feelings are your problem, not my problem. No. It's everyone's problem when somebody is suffering, when somebody's dying of hunger; it affects the whole world'. In this context especially, she insists, the kitchen is 'a magic space in which you are not only creating life, you are recovering knowledge'. She admires contemporary scientists whose discoveries 'are helping us to understand the world of the spirit', pointing out that even the predecessors of the Mayans and the Aztecs believed that everything has a heart, that 'the thought and the word mixed together start the heartbeat. So everything – every plant, every human being, every stone, every animal – everything has a frequency.' Human beings, she adds, 'are something that is changing all the time, again through ... the energy of love. That is the energy that [permits us] to find more information, another cell, another organised form of matter'.

(facing page) **Laura Esquivel, author of** *Like Water for Chocolate*, **in her art-filled home in Coyoacán;** (far left) **Esquivel's original** *El Diario de Tita*. **The protagonist of** *Like Water for Chocolate* **keeps a diary in which the ingredients for a great novel blend with the author's spirituality through old photos, letters and dried flowers; and** (left) **Esquivel, a vegetarian, in her kitchen**

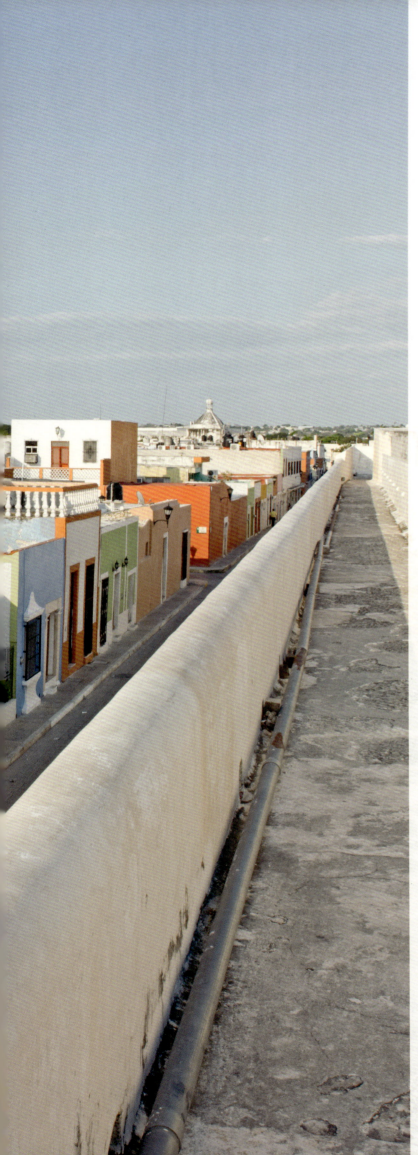

Campeche: *Reflected Glories*

Leaving Mexico City en route to 'beyond the Valley of Mexico' marks a welcome break from the capital city's pollution and crazy traffic. A great deal has been written about how chaotic Mexico City is, so arriving in one of the country's safest, most sedate states throws one into momentary culture shock. Things follow their own measured pace in Campeche. Life is unhurried, and people take long breakfast, coffee and lunch breaks.

Bounded to the south-east by Belize, Campeche's coastline faces the Gulf of Mexico, where the discovery of oil in the 1970s brought the state out of a long economic decline that had begun at the end of the colonial period. Campeche's relatively flat expanse is blanketed by inland rainforest interspersed with savanna. Its tropical climate is mixed, and the soil is not productive. The name Campeche derives from *Ah-kin-Pech*, the Maya name for the first settlements in the area, which translates as 'the place of snakes and ticks'. Established in around the seventh century as the Maya moved north from present-day Guatemala, the province is well endowed with archaeological remains.

Coming face to face with the state's history at Hacienda Blanca Flor in Hecelchakán was like turning back time, the sprawling ruins testament to glories past when the owners became rich processing sisal. The collapsed roof of the estate's private church allowed the late afternoon sun to colour its pink walls as if with an Impressionist's brush. Walls separating long-forgotten spaces now opened onto orchards and fields of maize or sorghum. A peacock strutting his stuff near the huge open-air oven used for several hundred years by nuns, mothers, daughters and aunts evoked lives long forgotten. Built in the seventeenth century, the hacienda became a fortress during the Caste War of Yucatán (1847–1901), when the native Maya rose up against the Yucatecos, people of European descent who controlled the region's economy and politics. The legal caste system during Spain's colonial imperium had placed the *peninsulares* (officials born in Spain) at the very top, while the *criollos* (those of Spanish descent) were next in the pecking order, followed by native collaborators and, finally, the *indios*, indigenous peoples with no political or social protection even by the Catholic Church, which followed the swings of power. Outnumbering the Yucatecos by five to one, the Maya *indios* chafed at the slave-like conditions in which they lived. The war lasted for half a century, and it was not until after the Revolution that peace and reconciliation allowed the region to boom once again. This prosperity was based on the production of sisal, *henequén* – a member of the agave family used for centuries to make rope – and sugar. Rich landlords coveted native communal lands, hence the old merry-go-round of displacing the dispossessed. The drama does not end there, for the Hacienda was the site of a major battle between federal and revolutionary forces in 1915.

The new owners of Hacienda Blanca Flor have long since settled into a more peaceable existence, reversing their ancestors' behaviour towards their employees, most of whom now live with them on the property, which has been lovingly restored. Lorena Casillas, whose father bought the rundown estate in the 1980s, is a lawyer by training and a vivid storyteller when it comes to the history of the place. 'We sell the experience of being in an authentic hacienda at the heart of Maya culture,' she enthuses about the estate's rebirth as a hostelry.

Doña Irma & Lorena Casillas
Traditional Cook & Owner, Hacienda Blanca Flor, Hecelchakán, Campeche

Built in the seventeenth century and now lovingly restored, Hacienda Blanca Flor's most noteworthy features are its main arch, its central courtyard and its beautiful garden. In the nineteenth century, during the lengthy Caste War of Yucatán, the building was used as a fortress while raids and intense fighting unfolded between the native Maya people and the Yucatecos of European descent (the latter had long controlled the region's politics and economy). Like other such establishments in Campeche, Hacienda Blanca Flor was dedicated to the processing of sisal, a member of the agave family cultivated on plantations and made into rope, twine and other products.

Casillas' father purchased Hacienda Blanca Flor in a state of ruin in the 1980s. 'It was like a ranch originally,' she explains. 'Then when the boom of the haciendas came, we established the hotel. We like people to understand that what we sell is the experience of being in an authentic hacienda at the centre of the Mayan heart.' *Doña* Irma is the hotel's traditional cook; her speciality is *tortitas de chaya*, *chaya* being a type of tree spinach. The most important thing about Maya culture, *Doña* Irma believes, is the language, which is in danger of disappearing. For the annual Washing of the Bones (one of the rituals celebrated each autumn on the Day of the Dead), she prepares *pibipollo* – a dish made with chicken, pork, maize flour and other ingredients – to feed the spirits of the dead. She describes the arrival of the spirits as being the moment when 'the dogs start to bark and the wind starts to blow stronger'; they depart a month later.

Casillas, who lives in Mexico City, is a lawyer specialising in reinsurance who gave up her career – which included a long professional spell in London – to run Hacienda Blanca Flor. 'I really love this place,' she explains. 'It's a must for me, for my family. We have to be here; I don't know why.' In addition to maintaining the hacienda just as it is, she would like to open a boutique on site in the future. Most of all, she wants her sons to work together to ensure that the hacienda continues to thrive.

(previous spread) **The historic fortification walls surrounding the old city of Campeche, which was one of the country's most important seaports in the 1500s and played a major role in the Spanish conquest**

(above) **Lorena and Liliana Casillas speaking with *Doña* Irma and her sister Maria Antonia in the ruins of the chapel at Hacienda Blanca Flor; and** (right) **The chapel's exterior (the hacienda dates back to 1588)**

(above left) *Doña* Irma preparing a traditional Day of the Dead tamale, or *pibipollo*; these are used as offerings on family altars commemorating the dead. *Doña* Irma's mother taught her the recipe, which she is now teaching to her grandchildren. (top) According to the sacred *Popol Vuh*, the Maya people were made out of maize. The tamale's crust therefore represents the outer body, and the chicken and filling the inner body. (right) *Doña* Irma burying the *pibipollo*, which is cooked underground with hot coals as part of the annual Day of the Dead celebrations

(above) *Don* Venancio Tuz Chi cleaning his father's bones at Pomuch graveyard in Hecelchakán. Pomuch is the only town that continues to honour the Maya tradition of ancestral bone-cleaning. Relatives are buried for three years, then dug up on the Day of the Dead to have their bones cleaned and displayed. The ritual is said to aid in healing the pain of death and preventing deceased relatives from becoming angry and wandering the streets

Mateo García Ríos
Fisherman, Port of Campeche, Campeche

Born in Campeche, Mateo García Ríos had no formal schooling; he started working at the age of six following the death of his parents. Each day he would go down to the beach with his benefactor Alejandro Cajun to salt, turn and dry fish. Soon he was fishing on his own for the 'catch of the day', using a net given to him by the Cajun family and receiving 500 pesos each time. Alcoholism was García Ríos' nemesis in his younger years, but he was saved by the offer of steady work and access to his own boat. 'They would leave me with my net and then came back to pick me up,' he explains. 'That is how I started. I went back to the colonia [where he was born], but I did not like it because there was no food. I would work as an albañil [builder] and I would take my lunch, and soon I had nothing left. So it was better to be at sea, to be working and eating.' García Ríos is hoping to secure a four-year permit for fishing with a net from SAGARPA, the Secretariat of Agriculture, Livestock, Rural Development, Fisheries and Food, a unit of the Mexican government tasked with supporting and improving local food production.

A single father for several years, García Ríos remarried and has several grandchildren now. His current permit allows him to fish for octopus, but he needs permission to fish for other species such as sea bass, which sells for 30 pesos per kilo. Fishermen are members of a cooperative that meets every day; it is essential to be a member in order to sell fish from your boat in the harbour market. 'I eat what I fish,' García Ríos says. 'I have fried pargo, but before that, I fish to sell the produce so I can take money home. My daughter Silvia and my son-in-law are helping.' Pargo (red snapper) is the fish that provides the best income, selling for 50 pesos per kilo. García Ríos cannot fish for school shark because his net is not fine enough.

'I like to be at sea because you are working and making a living out of that,' García Ríos observes. 'If we fish, we earn. If we don't fish, we do not earn. There is a lot of uncertainty so I commend myself to God and to the Virgin of Guadalupe and to the saints [especially St Roman, patron of fishermen] to have good weather and to have good pesca.' He claims to have seen St Roman in a vision on one occasion: 'We were fishing on a boat and we were sleeping, and it started to rain heavily. The boy who was with me brought the framed picture of San Román and told me that because it was raining the picture was getting wet. I got hold of it and I wrapped it in nylon and put it back in its place. It was continuing to rain very strongly when a shadow passed by. I heard it clearly; it asked me, "Where are you going?" I replied that I was going to make sure the picture would not get wet. It replied, "It will not get wet." When I turned away and looked behind me again, the boat was halfway into the sea and the boy was overboard. I went back and rescued him. Then the boat turned back again and we were safe. That is why I am telling you that San Román takes care of fishermen.'

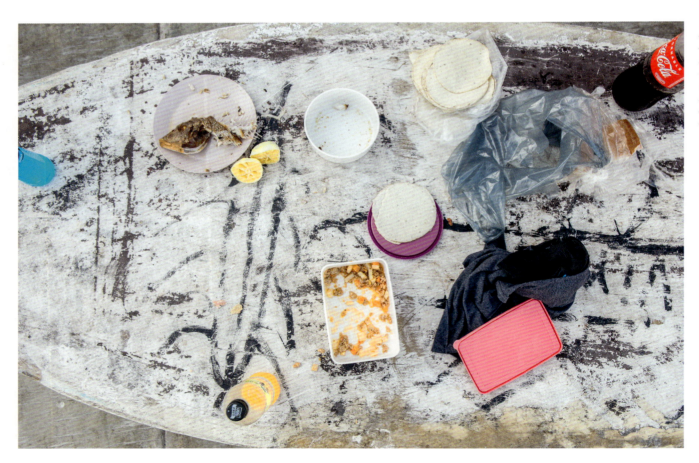

(left) **Remains of a fisherman's lunch at the port in Campeche city.** (facing page) **Mateo García Ríos, who left the land to work at the docks and became a member of the Campeche fishing cooperative by chance**

(above) **García Ríos bringing in the day's catch on his boat Lupita, almost lost in the hustle and bustle of Campeche's port**

(far left) **Fried *pargo rubia* and *cananea* prepared by** (above) **José Guadalupe Gomez at the port in Campeche city for himself and his son, eaten** (left) **with habanero chilli and bitter orange salsa**

Fishing boats in Puerto de Ciudad del Carmen, Campeche

Sara Uc García
Owner, Coctelería Cajún, Ciudad del Carmen, Campeche

Sara Uc García, born in Palizada in 1936, comes from a humble background; her father was a fisherman, her mother a domestic cleaner. After two years of primary school, Uc García's parents sent her to work as a cleaner for the family of Fernando Raful, then Secretary of Maritime Fishing; she remained in that job until she married at the age of eighteen. Her husband worked on a boat, and Uc García had to work long hours just to keep her family afloat.

Coctelería Cajún features a simple menu based on fresh, local seafood. The restaurant is known for its seafood cocktail containing shrimp, octopus, crab and oysters, as well as different kinds of fish; it is open from 9:00 a.m. to 7:30 p.m. daily. Signature dishes are based on the oysters and shrimp native to the region. The breakfast menu features sandwiches containing turkey, chicken, pork and shellfish, while *campechano*, a seafood taco, is a perennial favourite. The restaurant serves its own specially made ketchup as well as hot sauce made on the premises out of pure chilli (roasted and chopped) and lime. Conch (kept frozen as it can only be fished in season), octopus and blue crab are also available.

Uc García remembers a time when Ciudad del Carmen, where she has lived her entire life, was a peaceful town, with the markets where she shopped opening at 4.00 or 5.00 a.m. The presence of Pemex, the state-owned petroleum company, in the area has resulted in benefits (in terms of growth and greater financial stability) as well as problems (among them, rising prices). Uc García believes that there are fewer jobs to go round than there used to be, also that fishing has become more difficult, as drilling for oil has caused the fish to move further out to sea. Despite these challenges, young people continue to fish for shrimp. Another change has seen people from Mexico City and tourists from around the world visiting the area en route to Mérida.

Through all of the changes, Uc García has overseen Coctelería Cajún with the help and professional support of her numerous relatives. She is proud of their achievement. 'People who are still alive that knew me when we began come here and congratulate me because I was able to change my life,' she says.

(facing page) **Sara Uc García outside Coctelería Cajun. The restaurant she founded in 1983 supports her family and sixty other families in the area;** (right) **Soft-shell crab frying in the kitchen at Coctelería Cajun;** (below) **Soft-shell crab,** *moro* **crab claws and** *vuelve a la vida* **(return to life) cocktails, which contain a mixture of seafood; and** (bottom) **A very busy lunch service**

Doña Concepción Uribe Reyes
& *Doña* Ana Josefa Vásquez Uribe
Owners & Chefs, Las Brisas, Champotón, Campeche

Restaurant owners *Doña* Concepción Uribe Reyes and *Doña* Ana Josefa Vásquez Uribe, born in 1939 and 1965 respectively, trained with *Doña* Concepción's mother at Champotón's first restaurant, El Popular. Their approach to cooking represents the distillation of four generations' worth of experience. The cuisine of Champotón, this mother-and-daughter team believes, is unique for its choice of produce, freshness, flavour and seasoning. The two chefs describe themselves as cooking with *gusto* – that is, enjoyment and enthusiasm. 'Everything in life,' *Doña* Ana observes, 'if you do it with *gusto*, that's where the difference is. My daughter once said to me, "Mum, I am never going to be able to finish this assignment!" I said, "If you start off with saying 'I can't', you will never be able to say 'I can, and I will do it and with high spirits as well!' And you will see: it will become easier."'

Champotón is a coastal town on the Gulf of Mexico; its main industry is fishing. *Doña* Ana and *Doña* Concepción are proud that the type of food they serve has remained unchanged for many decades. 'Sometimes,' *Doña* Ana jokes, 'my mother will come and tell

me off, saying, "But that is not the right way to make it!"' Both chefs acknowledge that their family has been 'ruled' by women, with *Doña* Concepción describing the two of them as 'chatter-boxes'. 'We talk a lot,' she laughs, 'and we interrupt a lot in conversation ... That's bad manners! That's how we are.'

The two chefs remember the kitchen at El Popular as having charcoal stoves. 'My grandmother,' *Doña* Ana recalls, 'was known for her flavours, and when ministers and presidents came, even though she no longer worked at the restaurant, they turned to her to cook for their banquets ... She was not only a cook, she made cakes, meringues, everything – and everything by hand, not with an egg beater or mixer. With those wire spoons she would also make jam.' 'None of this going to the shop to get a jar of jam,' *Doña* Concepción chimes in. 'Everything made at home with elbow grease and no measurements. She would do it all by eye. Why was that? Necessity. My mother would say, "Necessity is the mother of invention." It was necessity that made me learn ... I had nine brothers.' All of the children grew up in poverty. *Doña* Concepción describes how they made coffee: 'We would put a tortilla on the fire to burn it – very burnt – and then we got a pot of water and made "coffee" with the crumbled tortilla.' The only groceries they purchased weekly were rice, sugar, beans and oil – 'the most indispensable things'. *Doña* Ana quotes her father telling the children to work 'like a circus. And you have to sell the popcorn!'

Both women agree that, as hard as life was back then, they miss those times and the fact that a delicious plate of food represented the tangible result of hard work. 'I think that my mother and father did this with a lot of sacrifices,' says *Doña* Ana. 'Like when the restaurant burned down, a lot of people asked me why I didn't rebuild it on the Malecón, because here we are not on a main road. If a bus comes in, the police come and fine it, because they aren't supposed to enter the city, they are supposed to pass by the coastline. Do you know what it gave me, not going to the coast where the main road is? The love of this place, this place that they [her parents], with great sacrifice ... started from nothing.' *Doña* Ana, who has travelled outside Champotón, is unenthusiastic about the food she has encountered elsewhere. 'Chinese food doesn't suit me,' she observes. 'I went to Tenerife, and to be honest, for me there is nothing like Mexican food ... If you go to hotels in Cancún and everything is included, the food is horrible ... What I do when I go is dedicate myself to eating French fries and burgers because everything else is horrible, truth be told.' She adds, 'Everyone says to us, "Why don't you set up a restaurant in Ciudad del Carmen or Campeche?" I personally think that places that aren't looked after by their owners on a daily basis stop being what they first set out to be. They grow and start to become a chain and get handed over to other people.' Plus, she says, 'There is no better Las Brisas than this one.'

(left) *Doña* Concepción Uribe Reyes at Las Brisas sipping a Coke in front of a photograph of herself (aged seventeen)

(facing page) *Doña* Ana Josefa Vázquez Uribe at Las Brisas, which has been handed down through four generations

(left) *Doña* Ana 'fishing' at the fish market in Champotón, (below) viewing a stingray, and (facing page) enjoying a quiet moment on the pier with her husband, originally from the Canary Islands, whom she met on a dating website

Yucatán: *Maya Wonderland*

The problem with Yucatán is that it is just too rich in culture, history and natural bounty. For the outsider, it is the go-to centre for culinary experiences mixed with historic landmarks and beguiling landscapes. It is also an easy make for film and photography. And for adventurous travellers, splendours abound: different biospheres, fabulous flora and fauna, culinary delights ... No wonder the Maya centred some of their most magnificent cities in Yucatán. Yet its history is one of splendid isolation. As a consequence, the state developed its own unique culture, twice declaring itself an independent republic during the 1800s. It was separated from Campeche and Quintana Roo in the late nineteenth and early twentieth centuries. Nevertheless Yucatecans continue to express pride in their independent culture.

According to historical accounts, the name Yucatán derives from the native word *tectetán*, meaning 'I don't understand you'. It is also said that the Spaniards, when hearing the locals answering questions with '*uh yu ka t'ann*', which in Mayan means 'hear how they talk', decided to go with 'Yucatán'. The conquistador Bernal Díaz del Castillo held that the name derived from *Yucatá*, meaning 'land of yuccas'. The area's rich Maya heritage is reflected in spectacular ancient cities like Chichén Itzá, Izamal, Mayapan and Motul. Mérida, the capital, was itself built on the ruins of Ichcaanzihó.

A spiritual people holding fast to tradition, Yucatecans are known for their shamanistic practices. My first encounter with a shaman was a cleansing ceremony arranged by the authorities in Mérida; it was underwhelming and overplayed. A piratical character with a wicked smile and an obvious appetite for life, the gentleman in question (whose name escapes me despite the fact that we share the same birthday) agreed to perform his ceremony at the base of the Temple of Kukulkán in Chichén Itzá. Entertaining, yes, but a tad *lèse-majesté* given the pre-Columbian structure's magnificence. A real spiritual experience lay in store with the setting of the spring sun, bringing to life the frightful splendour of the Feathered Serpent (carved along the north-west balustrade) as it slithered down the pyramid. Overcome by the moment, I imagined throngs of worshippers murmuring chants as the high priest atop the temple platform raised his head to the cloudless sky. Clever, those Maya: the pyramid's four sides have ninety-one steps each. Add them together, plus the platform at the top, and you have 365 – the number of days in the solar calendar, or Haab, as the Mayans called it.

The experience demanded communion with the spirits, so we set out in search of *Abuelo* Antonio Oxté, guardian of Maya medical traditions and famed in Mexico City for his spiritual counsel. People from all over the country seek him out (if they are lucky) at his small ranch in Sisbichén, two hours' drive from the Temple of Kukulkán. He lives a frugal life of study, writing and contemplation among semi-tropical gardens, several spectacular *cenotes*, chickens and a pet pig. 'Spiritual osmosis' is what I wrote in my notes afterwards. Spiritual filtering to be precise: two men standing together staring into the abyss, a deep turquoise sinkhole with wild creepers reaching down to the water's edge.

David Cetina
Chef, La Tradición, Mérida, Yucatán

Since both of David Cetina's parents worked (his mother was Yucatán's first congresswoman), he was raised primarily by his grandmother, who taught him how to cook. A restaurant owner and solo pianist, she instilled passion and a strong work ethic in her grandson, emphasising the transmission of love through food. Cetina's sense of duty to Yucatecan cuisine goes hand in hand with his belief in family, tradition and authenticity.

Cetina was seventeen when he decided to become a chef. Lacking the resources to pay for a culinary education, he decided to open his own restaurant, La Tradición, in 1991. His primary focus was already on local cuisine. In 1998 he opened Danny's Burger in Mérida, and in 2003, together with business partner Manuel Avila Rodriguez, he reopened La Tradición. Five years later the restaurant's capacity had doubled.

Using traditional ingredients and techniques including charcoal made from aromatic wood, Cetina's team lacks a formal hierarchy. He himself gets up at 5.00 a.m. every day to buy fresh ingredients, returning to start cooking at 10.00 a.m. 'I believe we all have a mission to accomplish,' he explains. 'In the same way that there are extraordinary doctors, extraordinary mechanics, extraordinary inventors, I have that virtue in being a cook. Before being a chef, I am a cook with a duty to my kitchen, with a duty to those extra-sensorial flavours that we make … For me what is most important is that the diner feels ecstatic while eating each dish.'

'It has taken me twenty-five years to be where I am today, to be an icon of good work, of good things,' Cetina muses. 'Yucatecan cuisine has been prostituted, right? Already those in the restaurant business are seen more as business owners than cooks. To me it is not the same to make *poc-chuc* – which in Mayan means "roasted on coals" … on a grill. Why? Obviously the costs are considerably lower when you don't use coals, but the taste is something else.' Musing on the connections between power and gastronomy, between cooking and positivity, he describes a foreign businessman for whom he once cooked a *cochinita*. 'The man was ecstatic with flavour and he gave six hundred beds to a hospital here in Yucatán!' exclaims Cetina. 'That's how food, how flavours, how love that one transmits, can reach someone.' By contrast, 'when one is upset because something happened, the rest of the day will go wrong … You'll even burn the water!'

(previous spread)
The limestone ruins of Casa de las Palomas in Uxmal, a Maya city from between the sixth and tenth centuries AD in Yucatán

(left) **David Cetina preparing *poc-chuc* (marinated pork) in the kitchen at La Tradición (he cooks using two types of fuel: charcoal made from *kin ki che* wood, and aromatic *jabím* logs, the wood preferred by traditional cooks); and** (right) *Longaniza de venado de Valladolid* **(venison sausage from Valladolid)**

(far left) **A woman selling** *chaya* **leaf at Mérida's Mercado Lucas de Gálvez, which Cetina visits regularly;** (left) **Sweet pepper;** (below) **An ice porter at the Mercado Lucas de Gálvez, which is open round the clock; and** (facing page) **Cetina serving Ceiba (a Yucatecan artisanal beer),** *chaya* **margaritas,** *cochinita pibil* **(barbequed pork),** *longaniza de venado* **(venison sausage) and** *queso relleno* **prepared with** *El Gallo Azul* **cheese (originally made in the Netherlands and now produced in Mexico)**

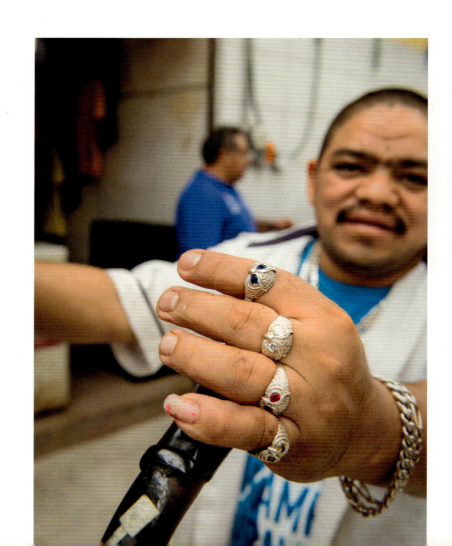

Valladolid, Yucatán

(above) **A vegetable stand;** (left) **A market in Valladolid;** (facing page, left) **The convent in Izamal, built by Franciscan friars atop Maya ruins; and** (facing page, right) **Nuns at the convent in Izamal, whose founder, Fray Diego de Landa, consigned many Maya manuscripts and images to the flames**

Antonia Chulim Noh, 'La Tía'
Cook & Owner, La Tía de Kahua, Kahua, Yucatán

'La Tía' has been making tortillas for sixty of her approximately seventy years (she does not know the year of her birth). She never had any formal education. Her workplace is not so much a restaurant as an area outside her hut where she serves food. She gets up at 4.00 a.m. to start serving passing lorry drivers, only returning to her hammock at midnight; in between, she rarely moves from her cast iron *comal*, or griddle.

The maize *La Tía* cooks with comes from her own *milpa*, a small arable field that is sown and harvested by her husband, who also gathers firewood. Her signature dish, *poc-chuc*, consists of thinly sliced pork marinated in orange and spices and cooked on her *comal* over hot coals. Another favourite is *huevos encamisados* – literally 'eggs in shirts' – which consists of eggs fried between two tortillas. *La Tía* herself is a vegetarian although she occasionally eats meat. Her personal menu includes tortillas, tomatoes, coriander, pumpkin seeds, a bit of *atole* (a hot drink made from maize flour) and black beans.

'When I started working,' *La Tía* remembers, 'no-one knew how to make *empanadas panucho* [stuffed refried tortillas]' – and ingredients were of course much less expensive than they are today. Hurricane season has regularly brought hard times. For example, when Hurricane Gilbert passed through in 1988, there was nothing to eat in the area and *La Tía* wore the same clothes every day for six months. 'From around 3.00 in the morning,' she recalls, 'there were people shouting at the front door: "Tiiiaaa!" "What do you want?" "*Huevo encamisado!*"' Things have improved since then. 'Thanks to God, we are doing very well,' she says. 'We are by no means rich, but there is food on the table. With the little bit that we have, we have enough. That's what I say: I give thanks to God that we have enough to eat, otherwise I cry because there is nothing.' *La Tía* never changes her tried-and-true recipes, reasoning that 'people want it, so I serve it. It's my job. I have to do it.' She is accustomed to working through temporary setbacks: 'On Saturday there was such heat! All of my bones started hurting. But even when I am crying, I am rolling out tortillas.'

(above) *La Tía* prepares her famous tortillas over hot coals on her *comal*; they are served with *poc-chuc* and *frijoles* (beans)

A grandchild at play (left) in the family's communal sleeping quarters

Home is where the hearth is: (above) *La Tia*'s modest house, where she and her large family sleep and eat, serving food daily from 4.00 a.m. to local truckers and itinerant international publishers at her roadside restaurant; (top right) *Frijoles* topped with coriander; and (right) *Pan de espelón* (tamale cooked underground)

Abuelo Antonio Oxté
Spiritual Guide & Healer, Yaadzonot, Sisbichén, Yucatán

Guardian of the Maya medical tradition *Abuelo* Antonio Oxté was born in Tzucacab in the state of Yucatán, where he received his first initiations into midwifery and traditional practices of body, mind and soul. He also obtained a deep knowledge of the elements, plants and sounds, and learned massage and healing from his maternal grandmother. After working for some years in the commercial sphere, *Abuelo* Antonio spent seven years walking across Mexico, acquiring ancient knowledge and sharing his awareness of universal love. He incidentally has a degree in social anthropology and studied accountancy.

Abuelo Antonio's sanctuary, Yaadzonot, is close to the Maya town of Sisbichén ('flower that opens consciousness'). The village preserves ancient Maya wisdom while the not-for-profit ranch is dedicated to sustainability and promotes health as well as economic, cultural and family welfare in the region. The biodiverse gardens are stocked with native flora and fauna, among them medicinal plants, and *Abuelo* Antonio's primary project to date has involved the reforestation of 5 hectares of damaged land.

Abuelo Antonio's beliefs focus on the notion of equality among all individuals. 'We are the same,' he says, 'because we eat, we sleep, we wish, we dream, and we die.' He claims to have had several near-death experiences himself: 'The first one was like everybody says, the tunnel that goes towards the path, but my experience was that

when I reached it, when I arrived, that universe existed the same as here but [without] matter. [It is] holographic – you can see the forms, but it's pure light. You can hear music everywhere with the movement of the air, divine music. It's where the fountain of life is.' Everyday life is, he says, also sacred, 'but it's another thing – matter, density – and the laws are very different from the laws where matter doesn't exist.' His near-death experiences taught *Abuelo* Antonio that he needed to love and enjoy himself wherever he happened to be.

The particular energy present in *Abuelo* Antonio's mind has been present since he was a young child. 'I perceived many things that are not easy to explain,' he recalls, and he was able to understand voices speaking at great distances. Most important, he says, is that human beings 'are part of nature' – this is his 'first principle'. The second principle: 'Understanding our mind, and that through our mind, we can have that connection with all the celestial beings and divine entities that exist in all religions and traditions ... We need to understand that we live on this planet of matter, and we need to work to have something.' When temptation has come his way, he has responded like this: '"Okay, I am going to walk this line for a moment. If it is correct, I'll keep going. If not, I'll divert and follow another route." So I enjoyed everything and said thank you.' He embraces failure 'because everything is good. Nothing is bad. It's just life experience'.

Abuelo Antonio explains that being a spiritual guide 'is a kind of knowledge that the native people have, an understanding that is much better than [that of] others [of] how to live in harmony in nature, to understand the laws of Mother Nature, to not destroy this planet, and to be like brothers and sisters, helping and serving others'. Wisdom, he believes, only comes with time, 'if you wake up the love of God in yourself and others ... This planet needs wise people who love what they are doing'. Food, in this life a question of textures and flavours, is, in the afterlife, a form of music; most important 'in this dimension' are the various flavours of water. As well as being aware of 'sunlight, moonlight, air, wind, air', *Abuelo* Antonio adds, 'we need to pay attention when we are breathing ... When you are breathing, flavours open up.'

Ingredients used in cooking at the ranch are locally sourced and change with the seasons. In the summer, the menu includes tomatoes, avocado, garlic and a spice known as *achiote* (annatto), 'one that they make a lot of dishes with [for example] *cochinita pibil*. They have a very strong red colour ... It's also a medicine. We use it when we have stomach inflammation ... At the same time it is the best purifier for the blood ... And we use it for sun dishes, for *el sagrado platillo*, a sacred dish as an offering to the sun'. Winter, on the other hand, is a time of fasting during which chilli water is drunk 'to warm the blood. This knowledge, this wisdom, comes from the Aztecs and the old Maya people'. In the production and preparation of food, *Abuelo* Antonio (who is currently writing a book about prehispanic cuisine) maintains a deep connection between the past and the present day.

(facing page) ***Abuelo*** **Antonio Oxté at home on his ranch, Yaadzonot, in Sisbichén, and** (left) **helping burn the ranch's** **summer undergrowth near his local** *cenote* **(sinkhole) as a means of natural cleansing and renewal**

(above) *Abuelo* **Antonio with his pet pig Solecita;** (top right) *Abuelo* **Antonio's assistant Anne Marie Domkar helps maintain Yaadzonot with her husband Eduardo;** (right) *Abuelo* **Antonio preparing the evening meal with vegetables from his garden; and** (facing page) **A 'virgin'** *cenote* **(sinkhole) at Yaadzonot. These extraordinary natural phenomena are found on the Yucatán Peninsula**

(previous spread, left) **The bar at Ku'uk; and** (right) **Evia and his business partner Eduardo Rukos reviewing the day's menu with Ku'uk staff members**

(left & below) **A member of Evia's team preparing dishes using regional ingredients, including** *tostadas de mariscos* **(seafood tostadas) and vegan tartar**

(above & right) **Desserts and petits fours, some of the specialities on offer at Ku'uk**

(above) **Salt marshes produce alien waterscapes and colours in Celestún;** (right) **An iguana basking in dappled shade; and** (top right) **Fishermen taking a break**

Luis Eduardo Marrufo Basto
Chef, El Buen Comer, Celestún, Yucatán

Luis Eduardo Marrufo Basto attended secondary school in Celestún before going to Mérida to study accounting. On a return visit to his hometown, he fell instantly in love with the woman who went on to become his partner. Marrufo Basto decided to move back to Celestún. Now he can be found every day working in his restaurant, El Buen Comer, a *cocina economica*, or inexpensive local eatery. He also cooks at local restaurants El Pargo and La Palapa when there are special events.

Marrufo Basto became interested in cooking at a young age, learning at home from his mother. 'One starts with fried eggs, Mexican-style scrambled eggs,' he remembers. 'I started understanding the kitchen. It's like having a gift for cooking because I didn't complete any studies in gastronomy.' His favourite ingredient is a type of prawn sourced from the nearby river. At El Buen Comer he has a small kitchen where he works with his mother and a single employee preparing food for the locals. The working day runs from 8.00 in the morning until 4.00 in the afternoon. 'From there,' he explains, 'I go home to rest with my family, and if there's time we go out for a stroll around the port.' El Buen Comer's menu consists of typical Yucatecan food – *frijol con puerco*, seasoned chicken, *puchero* (a type of stew), sandwiches of steak and pork, chilli *mole* – prepared using mostly local ingredients but also some frozen ones. 'The fishermen are our friends who we have known our whole lives,' the chef explains. 'When we need a fish ... we give them a day's notice.'

Like many chefs, Marrufo Basto finds that the 'everyday routine' of cooking can dampen his own appetite. 'Sometimes I prefer to toss some eggs on the stove and fry them, and that is what I have for lunch with rice and plantain. That is it!' he laughs. 'The truth is that sometimes you spend so many days looking at the same sauces that you don't even want to eat them!' His passion for his local community has to do with the people who live there and the beautiful natural surroundings, including a wetlands reserve. 'Celestún is a very welcoming place to visitors,' he says. 'What more can we ask from life? We have the river, the ocean, the waterhole, the salt ponds, the ruins of Real de Salinas. That is why Celestún is so special: because it has all those precious places.'

(facing page, left) **Luis Eduardo Marrufo Basto preparing** *ceviche* **at La Palapa;** (facing page, right) **Marrufo Basto with his parents, Eroquerio Arufo Suarez and Maria Concepción Basto Pérez, at their local eatery, El Buen Comer, and** (above) **on his way home**

(above) **Carlos Daniel, a seventeen-year-old** *lucha libre* **mask salesman, working a traffic signal in Mérida**

(above) **Maya shaman and leader of the Grand Itza Council of Mayan Priests and Elders Manuel Xijum performing a ceremony at Chichén Itzá**

Roberto Solís
Chef, Néctar, Mérida, Yucatán

Born in 1976, Roberto Solís was only twenty-seven years old, and lacked any formal training, when he opened Néctar in Mérida. A leading authority on molecular gastronomy, Solís' minimalist concept is constantly evolving. Trained at The Fat Duck (UK), Noma (Denmark) and Per Se (New York), among other restaurants, Solís currently works with a chef and two sous-chefs to create a daily menu emphasising the cuisines of Mexico, Chile and Argentina – a genre referred to as 'new Yucatecan cuisine'. Mayan culture and traditional ingredients are at the heart of his approach; typical dishes include poached eggs in a *chaya*, chilli and *queso cotijia* salsa; *tacos de relleno*; and venison in *pipián* sauce with cherry tomatoes, coriander and sweet chillies. The restaurant makes its own preserves and smokes many of its products.

As a colonial city, Mérida once had the greatest concentration of wealth in the world; in the nineteenth century the town's sisal barons hired Parisian architects to build opulent villas there. Less important as a civic centre today, the town has become home to a community of expat American artists and bohemians, among them chef Jeremiah Tower, Alice Waters' partner at Chez Panisse in California. Solís' family owns a construction business. 'I think it was good that I got away and developed myself in a different way,' he jokes. He first opened Néctar in a small rented house, and his early clients were all locals. Back then, he says, nobody ate tuna except from a tin, nor did anyone eat lamb and duck at all, 'so we started with those proteins and offering international food based on books I had read because I didn't know how to cook.' Laughing, he adds, 'Imagine Mérida ten years ago. Putting an ice cream in a salad was like, This guy's fucking crazy! What's he doing!?'

Having studied abroad with such chefs as Heston Blumenthal, Solís developed a kitchen philosophy based on 'a friendly ambience'. 'Talk with everybody,' he says. 'Treat them as your equal, serve them food, and know the people you are working with – privately, I mean closely, not just their name and "Thank you for coming".' It was only after a successful year of running his restaurant that he decided that he 'really wanted to cook' himself. 'I was partners with another guy who was a chef in a hotel,' he explains, 'and the idea originally was for me to have the restaurant and for him to be *in* the restaurant all the time so I could party and travel. But it turned out the other way, so I was like, Okay, now I'm running a restaurant, so I want to learn how to cook professionally ... I decided to start doing courses in the summer and close the restaurant for three or four months, because it is very slow in the summer here.'

About the individuality of Yucatán, Solís observes that in earlier times Mexico 'didn't care about us; we were too far away ... So we developed, because we were so isolated [with] our own stuff, our own ways ... We were extremely rich; people in the haciendas had gold bars instead of money'. In terms of food culture, he adds, 'we don't eat a lot of vegetables. In traditional food you will not see any salads and hardly any vegetables. A lot of pork, heavy sauces, heavy dishes. A difference that we're trying out in the restaurant is the same philosophy of using local ingredients but with lighter versions of some sauces.' Indeed it was his interest in traditional culture that inspired Solís to open a restaurant devoted to Maya 'gastronomy' and inspired by, for example, the colours assigned to the cardinal directions.

'I have moments of inspiration,' Solís says of his method. 'When I have those moments, I translate them with my team into dishes.' Unenthusiastic about today's media spotlight on celebrity chefs and restaurant lists, he believes that 'chefs are losing the reason why they are cooking ... The essence of having a restaurant in the first place is to realise yourself and feed people and make them happy; that should be the only pursuit or objective.' Although earlier in his career he remembers getting carried away by 'travelling a lot, and talking to a lot of magazines, and being in the places you have to be', these days he stays close to his home base. 'If a magazine is interested [they should] come, eat, take pictures if they want. But I'm not going to be in the places I have to be or whatever,' he says firmly.

(facing page) **Roberto Solís on top form, explaining his philosophy of creating a moment: 'A mouthful only lasts a moment, but I get to keep feeding people every day and recreating that moment'; and** (left) **frying eggs on toast**

(facing page) **Solís and Jacob Herrera Mendoza, his sous-chef, planning the day's menu at Néctar.** (right) **Dishes in preparation, including fried eggs on toast with** *béchamel de longaniza* **and** *queso de bola* **(Edam cheese);** (far right) **Venison in** *pipián* **sauce with local coriander, cherry tomatoes and sweet chilli (the latter prepared by Herrera at Hacienda Santo Diego La Cruz); and** (below) **Eggs poached for breakfast in a** *chaya* **(a type of spinach),** *xcatic chile* **and** *queso cotija* **(hard cow's-milk cheese) salsa**

Walther Osorto
President, Yucatán Hairless Pig Association, Mérida, Yucatán

Yucatán hairless pigs were already being raised in Maya times, fed on the fruit and leaves of the *ramón* tree. The breed tolerates extreme tropical heat very well, can move easily over difficult terrain and is resistant to disease. As well as being the main ingredient of slow-roasted *cochinita pibil*, the hairless pig has a ceremonial importance in Maya culture; the Pig Head Dance is performed to summon the rainy season and ensure an abundant grain harvest.

In 1910, 95 per cent of the Yucatecan porcine population were hairless pigs; today they represent less than 1 per cent. The breed is at risk of becoming extinct due to the disappearance of traditional Maya production systems as well as the importation of higher-yielding foreign species, which are better adapted to industrial breeding methods. It was only recently that the Asociación Mexicana Especializada en Cerdos Criollos developed a plan to safeguard the breed, which thrives on such local produce as pumpkin, *Leucaena*, *chaya* and purslane. The association encourages the breeding of the hairless pig in rural indigenous communities and promotes its meat to high-end chefs and restaurants.

Honduras-born Walther Osorto chose to relocate to Mexico to champion the cause of the *cerdo pelón*. 'It is high-quality food,' he says, 'more important than chicken ... It is also an animal that can be produced without as many negative effects on the environment.' Since Mexico consumes between 12 and 20 kilos of pork per person per year, depending on the region, the proper development and controlled production of this historically important meat are critical. The pig was not native to the Americas. As Osorto explains, it constituted 'a resource brought by the conquistadors that has been modified in certain ways, its genetics adapted to our regions'. Experiments with crossbreeding resulted in genotypes that have prevailed for centuries. 'It is that work, that genetic conquest, that we are doing: rescuing the work of the Mayas but in a responsible and more controlled way ... so that this type of pig can continue to be produced sustainably in the future,' Osorto adds. Critical to this enterprise is the support of top chefs, among them Pedro Evia, Roberto Solís and in particular Enrique Olvera. In Osorto's words, 'They show support and aid Mexican products ... It is a great task that they do ... and bit by bit that list of clients is increasing.'

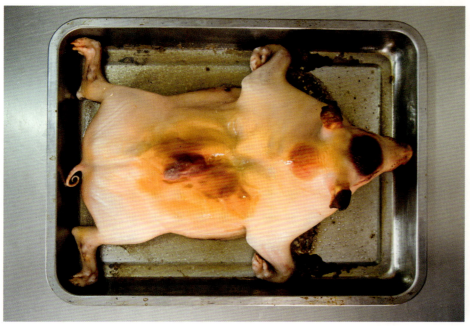

(facing page, left) **Farmhand Jorge Uicab Cuytun taking lunch with his boss Walther Osorto at his hairless-pig farm;** (facing page, right) *Cerdo pelón*, **a much sought-after Yucatecan delicacy;** (left) **A suckling pig being cooked at Osorto's home; and** (above) **Uicab attempting to catch a pig on Osorto's farm. The animals are primarily fed their mothers' milk supplemented with leaves of the** *ramón* **tree (***yaxox*** in Mayan), wild Yucatecan** *leucaena*, *verdolagas* **(purslane), seasonal fruits and squash**

Quintana Roo: *Islands in the Stream*

Quintana Roo and the Riviera Maya are the least developed yet most picturesque of the three states on the Yucatán Peninsula. Quintana Roo was only granted statehood in 1974, making it the country's youngest state, but since then it has developed rapidly as an international tourist destination. Cancún, the largest resort, with some of the charms of the Caribbean (palm trees, sandy beaches, mangrove swamps) but no colonial character, is now a popular package-holiday destination. Vast hotel complexes fill up and empty out each week as charter jets come and go, mostly from North America and Europe.

For most travellers, Quintana Roo and the Yucatán Peninsula are their only Mexico stops, a limited window onto a country offering a kaleidoscope of unique colours and flavours. Viewed through the prism of a pair of swimming goggles and experienced via tequila binges, it makes for poor reflections. In short, nobody gets to see the real Mexico, only the copy-and-paste pastiche of similar experiences packaged worldwide. While Cancún services millions of visitors annually, Tulum, the state's high-end destination replete with rich archaeological heritage, caters to a select clientele, attracting those with deeper pockets who are looking for an environmentally rich experience complete with *Robinson Crusoe*-style boutique hotels and beach huts. A developer's dream, Cancún was built from scratch beginning in 1973 in order to create a tax base for Quintana Roo. Before that, it was just a barrier island, home to nesting seabirds and turtles. Attempts to create a self-sustaining economy with an agricultural base were abandoned due to poor soil and a lack of resources.

Most labour in Quintana Roo is imported from adjoining states and quartered in industrial-scale housing projects at best, rapidly expanding slums at worst. Ecological impact aside, the demographic fallout from the dichotomy of rich tourists serviced by unskilled workers living in barrios is a recipe for trouble. With these scenarios in mind, our project threw up so many interesting characters that one can hardly do them justice. Christian Rodríguez was one of those characters, a nativist chef/cultural activist who likes to 'bring people food made with love'. 'Food,' he adds, 'that does not just fill their stomachs but that fills their souls and fills their dreams.' A man of evident passion, he likes to stir things up, mixing the food experience with street art at Mora Mora, his Cancún café-gallery. Rodríguez trained as a photographer before going to Switzerland to study gastronomy. Why? Because, in his opinion, the education system in Mexico is not good enough: 'It's the perfect way to have a blind country!' Putting words into action, he returned to his homeland to work for the people and his beliefs rather than staying on in Europe.

Or meet another passionate chef, Karla Enciso, in her small eatery selling oodles of character out of a nondescript shopping mall. This former industrial engineer is adamant in claiming Mexican cuisine as a national treasure whose potential has yet to be fully realised. 'I cook with my ears,' Enciso says. 'I cook very well but didn't know how to make money!' I enjoyed listening to Enciso tell of her struggles in the mostly male-dominated world of professional chefs in Mexico. 'My kitchens are like little factories,' she jokes. 'When I'm in the kitchen, I ... forget that time exists.'

Federico López
Chef, Zama Beach Club, Isla Mujeres, Quintana Roo

Forty-six-year-old Federico López claims to have been the first chef to champion Yucatecan food. His particular interests include the global problems surrounding food production and the dangers of overfishing. His main concern where restaurants are concerned is that they offer local, seasonal produce at all times.

López trained in the US at the Culinary Institute of America (CIA) and in Spain, where he spent, by his own account, 'eight months with no salary, no days off, no nothing'. Of his Spanish apprenticeship, he says, 'It was the first time that balsamic vinegar and olive oil were becoming known to the world – herbs, Mediterranean spices, healthy cooking. It was the first time that they put a meat sauce with fish, the first time that you could drink red wine with fish; you were breaking all the rules ... So it was really a time of a lot of changes.'

López describes Zama Beach Club as a 'fine-dining restaurant' rooted in local cuisine. Open every day from 10.00 a.m., its menu features seafood, especially *tacos al pastor*, *ceviche* and shrimp *enchipotlados*. López himself, however, is a vegetarian and believes in 'conscious eating' to help to combat overfishing. In Yucatán, for example, lobster is taken young and out of season since customers prefer it to be smaller and juicier. Worried about the consequences of overfishing, López comments, 'I don't think my kids are going to be sitting when they are my age and eating what we're eating.'

Describing his early experience of working in Yucatán, López says, 'When I arrived here, all the hotels gave you club sandwiches and fajitas. So I wasn't working in my workshop, I was just doing a plate. I had to get out of my workshop and start making what the old chefs made in the kitchen.' Working around the limitations of government-controlled seasonal fishing can be complicated, especially because the policing powers of the coastguard are limited. 'In places like Isla Mujeres, Cozumel, Holbox, Isla Contoy, part of life is the fishermen, so it's a political issue. If you take out the fishermen and pressure them, you're losing votes.' Meanwhile local species have been overtaken by lionfish, whose population originated in a Florida aquarium that was destroyed by Hurricane Katrina in

2005. 'That fish comes from Indonesia in the Indian Ocean,' López observes. 'There is a grouper in the Indian Ocean that eats that fish and controls the ratios. In this part of the world, it doesn't have a predator.' Ironically, a campaign to promote the cooking and eating of lionfish backfired: 'Lionfish doesn't really have a lot of taste, it's really mild ... It's more like a *tiradito* [served raw], maybe in an *empanada* [stuffed pastry], maybe as an appetiser, as *ceviche*, but not really as a main dish. Restaurants don't really like it because it's expensive; it costs 180 pesos a kilo, and only comes like two per kilo. And you have a lot of bones.'

As formative influences López cites French chef Pierre Gagnaire and the CIA's Fritz Sonnenschmidt. But 'the most important, influential chef' for him is Ricardo Muñoz Zurita, 'because Ricardo and I have been working with Mexican cuisine for the past twenty-three years, and this is the end of our work.' He jokes that he would prefer to be playing golf all day: 'In 1996, '97, '98, '99, I belonged to the modern Mexican cuisine "team". I was one of the ones who started making changes to classical Mexican dishes. In the year 2000, I changed caps and became one of the purest and most conservative chefs in the country, with Ricardo Muñoz Zurita, with Alicia Gironella De'Angeli.' This tight-knit group, he says, wants the new generation of chefs 'to make a new presentation; we want them to make new things, to create stylish presentations like the black tostada. But the flavour has to be there, the technique has to be there, the history has to be there, and it also has to belong to the place. So I don't want to do anything. I just want to keep track ...'

'People eat what they used to eat in their childhood,' López believes. 'My clients are not foodies,' he adds. 'I have a family of four. One son doesn't eat anything that has a flower, green vegetables, or anything that is not steak and potatoes. And the other one only eats fruit and vegetables and hardly eats any meat protein ... And my wife is more picky than I am ... So when I go to a restaurant, believe me, I go to the bathroom and wait for them to order because for me it's a pain. That for me is how the common family eats ... '

(previous spread) **Mangrove swamps around Isla Holbox, an unspoiled nature preserve in Quintana Roo**

(facing page) **Federico López cooking grouper *tikin-chic* over hot coals outdoors at Zama Beach Club;** (left) **Grilled octopus with mashed potato; and** (far left) **pork-jowl taco wrapped in *hoja santa* (an aromatic herb)**

Karla Enciso
Chef, Aroma Cilantro, Cancún, Quintana Roo

Trained as an industrial engineer, gutsy mother-of-three Karla Enciso thinks of herself as somewhat resembling the cartoon mouse Ratatouille in that she always cooks 'with her ears'. The owner of Aroma Cilantro and Manyee has taught gastronomy at Cancún's culinary institutes and has also been a moderator for, and organiser of, cooking demos at the annual Wine & Food Festival in Cancún and Riviera Maya.

Enciso was twenty-four when she went to France to train as a chef. 'After two years, I came back to Mexico City and opened a little French restaurant in La Colonia Condesa,' she remembers. 'It was called Los Pequeños Placeres; it was a very nice little restaurant. The only problem was that I cooked very well, but I didn't know how to make money ... So we closed. I came here with my husband and we opened Manyee, which is ... French cuisine with a little Mexican touch.' Her concept restaurant in Playa del Carmen, Aroma Cilantro, now has a branch in a shopping mall in Cancún. All of her recipes are standardised, thus reassuring clients with their consistency.

'My kitchens are like little factories,' jokes Enciso. 'When I'm in the kitchen, I ... forget that time exists.' She especially enjoys creating sauces by combining textures and flavours, for example tamarind sauce and *chile de árbol*. As influences she cites Ferran Adrià, known for his rule-breaking approach to gastronomy, and Federico López, a personal mentor committed to preserving Mexican traditions. She notes that not many chefs manage to distance themselves sufficiently from their restaurants to run them as proper businesses, citing Adrià's decision to close elBulli because it was not profitable. In order to make money, 'you have to become very famous, like Enrique Olvera ... But how many years have passed for him to get to this stage? I don't know exactly, but I think sixteen, eighteen, maybe twenty.'

Enciso's explanation for the lack of business acumen on the part of many chefs is that they like to think of themselves as artists, while successful businesspeople draw on the other side of their brains. 'Here at Aroma Cilantro, my partner and I have just started with ... business coaching,' she notes. 'We realised that after eleven years of having one of the best restaurants in downtown, it is not normal or logical that we haven't had the capacity to grow. So now we're starting ... One of my kids, the ten-year-old, said, "Mum, I don't understand why McDonald's and a lot of not good places just grow, grow, grow, and you just don't grow. Why?"' Enciso cites Roberto Ruiz, who 'has one of the best restaurants in Spain. He is Mexican, and he is the first Mexican restaurant in Europe to have a Michelin star for Mexican cuisine ... He has four restaurants. The main restaurant, the one with the Michelin star, doesn't make any money. It doesn't lose, but it doesn't make money. The three other restaurants make the fourth one possible. He is franchising. For me, it took ten years to realise that being passionate about what you do doesn't take you anywhere. I mean, yes, it has taken me to having Aroma Cilantro and having partners that want to be associated with me, but decision-making hasn't been my strength That's why I started with the business coach ... I am convinced I need to have that skill myself.'

The world of celebrity chefs, Enciso believes, is 'very new', the result of television programmes like 'MasterChef' and 'Top Chef' which have grown in popularity over many seasons of high ratings. 'Before, being a chef was something that fathers did not allow you to study,' she observes. 'It was like, "No! How to be a cook, it's not something you have to do." Then came Ferran Adrià, who for me broke all of the paradigms that you have about the kitchen. Before, the kitchen was only for the French cook, French cuisine ... I don't remember before Enrique Olvera what cooks or chefs we could talk about as "celebrities" [in Mexico] ... And I don't know how many years the "World's 50 Best Restaurants" San Pellegrino list has been going – eight, nine years? Before that list, who talked about chefs as if they were something important?'

(facing page) **Salsas on a table at Karla Enciso's restaurant, Aroma Cilantro;** (right) *Esquite,* **a maize snack for which Aroma Cilantro is famous; and** (below) **Enciso preparing** (right) *tacos de chile relleno* **behind the hatch**

Christian Rodríguez
Chef & Gallery Owner, Mora Mora, Cancún, Quintana Roo

'We like to bring people food made with love, food that does not just fill their stomachs but that fills their souls and fills their dreams, and we like to mix it with street art.' This is how young chef Christian Rodríguez explains the philosophy behind his Cancún café-gallery Mora Mora.

From a middle-class background, Rodríguez became a photographer before going to Switzerland to study gastronomy instead of studying at home. 'If you try to give your kids higher education in Mexico, it's pretty expensive, it's for rich people,' he explains. 'And it's not so good, actually ... This is one of the main problems in Mexico: people don't finish school. They don't have money to go to college ... they don't have knowledge, they don't have education. It's the perfect way to have a blind country. We call it "*ignorante*" – ignorant. It's pretty sad.'

Rodríguez started cooking professionally in his twenties while living in the Basque Country. On returning to Mexico, he opened Mora Mora. His initial aim was to create a community project that would involve local kids and neighbours, and be a place to relax, and a refuge from work, street life, family pressures and financial worries. Early customers were mostly young artists and 'eccentrics'; today the café's fan base includes government workers and politicians. 'They all sit at the same table and eat peacefully,' Rodríguez observes with pleasure. Works on exhibit are by international as well as local practitioners, mainly muralists and street artists. An internship programme has attracted participants from Chile, Germany, the US, Spain and elsewhere in Mexico, while a new project, La Tostada Anarquista, will offer free food in the morning and vegan dishes in the afternoon. 'It is going to break the system,' Rodríguez says, 'because people who come to eat at night are going to feed the people in the morning. So it's going to be a food shelter and, at night, a restaurant.'

Mora Mora's menu combines local ingredients to create international recipes (Spanish, Italian, Basque, Vietnamese, North American) as well as modernised traditional Mexican dishes. Rodríguez uses a lot of Italian bases and changes the menu every six months. A current bestseller, the beef-tongue taco, consists of grass-fed local beef cooked for eighteen hours in dark beer. Aware of the differences that defined each of Mexico's states prior to the arrival of the Spaniards, Rodríguez appreciates the relationship between food and the country's ancient gods. 'It depends on the region where you were born or which kind of tribe you belonged to – Aztecs or Toltecs or Maya ... They all had special gods for different things, for the earth, for growing vegetables, for the moon, for the rain, for the sun. They believed in how they all work together so you can have harmony.' Attempting to honour this ancient respect for natural systems, he describes his own approach as putting 'a few stones on the other side of the balance, to make it more equal'. Perhaps the most important of these 'stones' is passion: 'The passion we try to give is the passion of the heart, so people can open their eyes and see reality, see the real world we are living in, the Mexico we are living in, and the way we can impart something to make it better.'

Before Mora Mora was established, Rodríguez recalls, 'Cancún was focused just on the tourist industry and the hotels ... They forgot about us, about the town, about the people who make everything happen. After I had travelled all around the world, I recognised that we need this – we need a space where people can feel free.' The whole point of Mora Mora, he says, is 'to break the system from the restaurant that just wants to kick you out because they want to sell more; they want you to eat and leave'. His alternative to Cancún's hotel culture of expensive meals is a place with, as he puts it, 'a fair price for everyone'. A number of similar projects have opened up in the intervening four years, capitalising on Mora Mora's successful alternative approach. 'It doesn't matter if you come in a huge, expensive car or if you come on foot or by taxi,' Rodríguez laughs. 'We're gonna treat you the same ... Now the global markets have started to change. It's not just about money; people are searching for something different, something more original, something that was made by locals.' Authenticity is the watchword at Mora Mora.

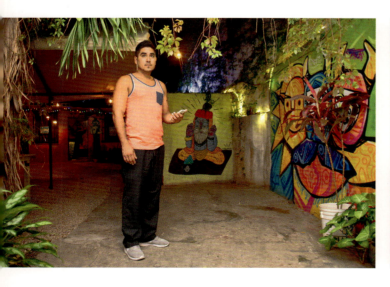

(far left) **Christian Rodríguez at Mora Mora (the name means 'slowly slowly' in Malagasy) in downtown Cancún;** (left) **Rodríguez visiting his favourite eatery, Il Posito, a family-run restaurant in a former garage in Cancún;** and (facing page) **Mora Mora's painterly doors. Rodríguez is deeply involved in the local art scene**

A swimmer in a magical *cenote* (sinkhole) at Tankah, a recreated Maya village in Tulum. *Cenotes* result from the collapse of limestone bedrock that exposes the groundwater underneath. They were used by the Maya for sacrificial offerings

Xavier Pérez Stone & Jonatán Gómez Luna
Chefs, Axiote & Cocina de Autor, Playa del Carmen / Le Chique, Puerto Morelos, Quintana Roo

Mexico City natives Xavier Pérez Stone and Jonatán Gómez Luna, who have both done stints in some of the world's best kitchens (among them el Bulli, Noma and The Fat Duck), have been friends for a decade. Their respective fine-dining restaurants are Cocina de Autor at the Grand Velas Riviera Maya resort in Playa del Carmen and Le Chique in Puerto Morelos. Stone's more casual establishment, Axiote, embodies his personality, he feels, but he is able to do things at Cocina de Autor that he would not be able to do without the backing of a huge kitchen. Luna designed Le Chique's kitchen himself and wanted the chef's table to feel totally interactive. Most evenings there is a steady flow of clients coming through the kitchen.

Stone, who attended culinary school in Mexico, started thinking about becoming a chef when he was still a teenager, because he 'liked to eat everything'. 'Both of my grandmas used to cook a lot in the house, my mum used to cook, my father was a hunter, and I really like that feeling, to kill the animal and clean it, to feel the blood and everything, and then just eat it,' he explains. His father hunted deer, wild boar, pigeon and rabbit. His luxe establishment Cocina de Autor is an offshoot of Biko in Mexico City, one of the world's best restaurants, which was founded by Bruno Oteiza and Mikel Alonso. It was their idea to invite Stone, a former apprentice, to set up in Playa del Carmen and radically alter the dining scene there. The restaurant serves a tasting menu composed of more than twenty dishes that changes every four months; it is the world's only AAA Five Diamond all-inclusive restaurant. 'About 90 per cent of the ingredients we use in the kitchen are from Mexico,' Stone says. 'We try to represent new flavours with classic ingredients ... The ingredients I must always have in the kitchen are coriander, onions, garlic, tomatillos, avocados and limes.' Tuna *crudo* served with a cactus paddle, avocado puree and tomato granita is a typical dish.

Luna, who cut short a career as a footballer to concentrate on becoming a chef, is a graduate of the Centro Culinario Ambrosía. From 2002 until 2008, when he opened his own restaurant, he was Chief of Culinary Development for the Karisma Hotels and Resorts chain. Le Chique takes an avant-garde approach to Mexican food, deconstructing traditional dishes and reinventing them using cutting-edge techniques. Examples include a Yucatecan dish, *panucho*, which is traditionally made with fried tortilla stuffed with refried black beans. Luna's version reimagines *panucho* as a perfectly shaped egg with a surprise black-bean filling.

'Right now,' says Luna, 'chefs around the world are looking at Mexican food.' He credits this interest to Mexico's unique techniques and combinations of ingredients, for example *tatemado*, *recados* and *moles*. His clients are probably 30 per cent local and 70 per cent tourists. 'One dish in Le Chique is six different stops in different parts of Mexico,' he explains. 'You have different preps, different ingredients, and when you arrive at the table, you smell the fog and the breeze from the ocean ... We distil ocean water and use liquid nitrogen ... It's not a show, it is a performance.'

Stone is a perfectionist, evoking the necessity to do his job better every day. 'We have many families – my family, all my cooks have a family – we have to feed them, we have to teach them, we have to be careful about the products, the ingredients, the family, the restaurant,' he muses. 'You have a responsibility not only to the food and the clients.' He sources ingredients from all over the country, emphasising how critical it is to 'travel to see the products, to eat them, to know how to cook them and then to talk to the producers ... You have to go there; it's very important.' His big industrial kitchen located in a grand hotel uses ingredients from around the world because the hotel is able to supply them. The hotel also offers the services of a marketing team to promote Cocina de Autor, although Stone does his own promotion for the much smaller Axiote, travelling to food festivals, for example. Despite the size of a chef's kitchen staff, he emphasises, 'you are the face at the end of the day. You need to travel and show and speak and, in the end, sell your product.' On a personal level, both he and Luna favour 'simple, nice tacos, nice street food'. 'Family-style, cook it at home, with the family, friends. That's it,' says Stone. 'Mexican, Canadian, Israeli, whatever. Feed them and have a good time with family around the table.'

(left) **Friends, colleagues and partners Xavier Pérez Stone and Jonatán Gómez Luna exchanging ideas at the bar of their restaurant Axiote; and** (facing page) **Gómez Luna at work at Le Chique, his own restaurant in Puerto Morelos**

Durango: *Land of the Scorpion*

Durango is the Wild West in every sense of the word, with its magical landscapes, clear blue skies and semi-arid climate. The railroads brought film to the state at the turn of the nineteenth century, and D. W. Griffiths produced *The Life of General Villa* in 1914 based on actual footage made around Pancho Villa's battles during the Mexican Revolution. Hollywood arrived in force in the 1950s, with Durango going on to host more than 130 star-studded films by such luminaries as John Huston (*Unforgiven*) and Sam Peckinpah (*The Wild Bunch*). John Wayne, Kirk Douglas and Jack Nicholson are just some of the screen idols who starred in films made around the village of Chupaderos; Wayne was so enamoured of the place that he bought a ranch there.

Durango is dotted with lakes, waterfalls and gorges used by extreme sports enthusiasts from around the world. It is also known for its scorpions, with the locals referring to themselves as *Alacrán de Durango*, or Durango Scorpions. I ran into one of these natives by the name of Sergio Ávila, a.k.a. *El Rey Alacrán* (The Scorpion King) in Durango city. Ávila is every bit the Hollywood character but in real life, testing the limits of bonhomie by forcing a live scorpion (minus sting) down my throat and washing the taste away with rapid shots of mezcal to ensure the creature drowned before I croaked.

This in a land ravaged for centuries by Comanche and Apache raiders moving across several states, from Sonora, Durango, Chihuahua and Texas down to Jalisco, Colima and Nayarit. Fearsome guerrilla fighters, the Comanche made raids across both sides of the Mexico–US border. Francisco 'Pancho' Villa (born José Doroteo Arango Arámbula), himself an *Alacrán de Durango*, was one of the most visible figures in the Mexican Revolution whose boisterous style and no-holds-barred personality became part of the country's history and mythology. Pancho Villa fashioned his own fame, summoning writers like John Reed to interview him and starring in several biographical films. His raids across the US border and cat-and-mouse game with General John J. Pershing continue to feed the legend.

Villa later joined forces with Emiliano Zapata, another revolutionary figure with both photogenic and populist appeal, to briefly take Mexico City in 1914. The two men met in Xochimilco at the height of the Revolution. Although divergent histories mark distinct social and political differences, there are important parallels between the Mexican fight for freedom and the simultaneous revolution playing itself out in Russia. Following their Hollywood script down to the last detail, both men died heroic deaths, assassinated by rivals. Pancho Villa finally received a hero's send-off in 1975, being interred in Mexico City's Monumento a la Revolución with huge crowds in attendance.

Among the cowboys, Comanches, revolutionary heroes and omnipresent scorpions, imagine my surprise at coming upon a Mennonite community of cheesemakers smack-dab in the middle of the desert. Over twenty thousand Mennonites live in Durango, descendants of German speakers who moved down from Canada at the turn of the last century, having been offered land to settle in the middle of nowhere. Cattle- and sheep-herding is one of Durango's principal economic activities, and the Dutch cheese produced by these shy, self-contained communities is sought after by Mexico's major chefs.

Sergio Ávila, *'El Rey Alacrán'*
Cook, Raíces Comida Mexicana & Dolores Mezcal Bar, Durango, Durango

Sergio Ávila's restaurant and bar are located in his great-grandmother's house in the centre of Durango (the building is more than two hundred years old). Four years ago Ávila decided to start making tacos with scorpions, which are an excellent source of protein and highly sustainable. Various 'collectors' bring him any of the thirty-three local species from the *sierra* of Durango – with one exception. The only species he does not cook with is the 'blue' scorpion, which local people use to treat cancer.

Born and bred in Durango, Ávila studied at the University of Minnesota. His eatery functions half as a restaurant and half as a museum with the purpose of preserving Durango's traditions. His cooking method involves piercing the arachnids with caramelised skewers; their poison is neutralised as they are cooked. He spent a long time finding ways to make their somewhat bitter flavour more palatable.

Ávila believes that 'the gastronomy of the insect is the future ... maybe of the world, and of Mexico too.' Pork and beef he describes as 'toxic to human life, but insects, they do nothing [bad]'. He was about ten years old when he handled a scorpion for the first time; now, he says, 'scorpions are my friends.' (Once stung by a scorpion, a person will die within half an hour – it depends on the variety – if the antidote is not available.) He offers them in the form of food as a way of addressing people's natural fear of them, saying, 'If you eat your fears, you don't think they're bad [any more], you see?'

(previous spread) **Durango's spectacular desert landscape**

(facing page) **Sergio Ávila in the 211-year-old family home that houses Raíces Comida Mexicana & Dolores Mezcal Bar;** (left) **Lightly fried scorpions served on sliced avocado as part of a taco; and** (above) **A baby scorpion in a jar under UV light. Ávila has more than five hundred scorpions of different types at home at any one time**

Paola Mares
Wagyu Beef Farmer, Canatlán & El Mezquital, Durango

Paola Mares is one of very few women running beef-production businesses in Mexico. Born in Guanajuato, Mares, like her parents, was trained as a civil engineer. Her company, De Campo Libre, which she runs with her family, is based at two ranches, one in Canátlan and the other in El Mezquital, both in the state of Durango. Having started breeding in 2012, the company supplies beef to all of Mexico's top chefs, including Enrique Olvera, Lalo García and Jorge Vallejo. The cattle are raised without growth hormones or filler feed and are slaughtered at thirty months, which is twice the age of commercially raised beef. The meat is prized for its unique tenderness and marbling. Wagyu ranching became possible in Mexico in the late 1970s and early 1980s, when embryos and semen were brought to the Americas and cross-breeds were developed with resident Angus cattle.

The family already owned their land and were working it when Mares completed her civil-engineering degree. 'We needed an idea of how the ranch was going to support itself,' she explains. 'A friend of my father said we should look into Wagyu. And when I did my investigation, I just fell completely and madly in love with it.' Although she used to spend three or four days each week travelling long distances to visit the ranches, she now works mainly from her

home in Mexico City, leaving day-to-day responsibilities to the onsite team while she concentrates on acquainting chefs with her top-end product. She describes the chefs as 'very humble; they are very nice. They know what they're looking for and what they want. So when they heard about the project and what we're doing and tasted it, they were convinced'. Mares describes chefs as being 'like rock stars, like leaders of opinion' when it comes to recent major changes in food production and preparation as well as eating. 'I believe there's this movement where we didn't ask ourselves what was on our plate before,' she says. 'Now we do, and we know how important the food going into our system is.'

Wagyu beef, Mares feels, is a healthy option for meat-eaters. 'We have 50 to 60 per cent mono-unsaturated fat, the good fat. That you won't get with any other type of beef ... Secondly, because there is a lot of marbling, it's very juicy, flavourful and soft.' The company's approach involves letting the cows roam free until they are about a year old rather than confining them in covered feed lots for their entire lives, as is done in Japan. Plans for the future include the introduction of pigs, chickens and bees, as well as, Mares hopes, expansion into the export business.

(facing page) **Paola Mares** at her Wagyu beef ranch in Canatlán. With over a thousand head of cattle, she and her team manage the entire process from breeding to raising, finishing and processing; (right) **Mares** riding at her second ranch, Santa Elena, in El Mezquital at the end of the dry season; (below left) **Javier Valenzuela**, one of two vets who help with the day-to-day running of Rancho Santa Elena, preparing beef for a barbeque; and (below right) **Flatiron** steaks being barbequed with fresh artichokes from Heiman Russek's vegetable patch

Heiman Russek
Farmer & Mezcal Producer, Tuitán, Durango

Heiman Russek set up his company Mezcal Minotauro in 2011 with the aim of distilling organic *mezcales* from wild agave plants. Also an organic farmer, Heiman grows artichokes, asparagus, beetroot, coriander and other crops, as well as flowers (including tulips), which he sells locally. Having moved back to Durango after a spell studying viniculture, he plans to start supplying high-end restaurants with heirloom vegetables, and enjoys interacting with, and being inspired by, chefs.

'To me, mezcal represents the biodiversity of the country,' Russek says, citing the variations in landscape, soil, plant types and fermentation processes used in mezcal production. He is proud that Minotauro has played a role in saving species of maguey that were thought to have been lost. The best mezcal is aged for three years and, unlike tequila, must be fermented in glass. Joven, the youngest and freshest mezcal, is best when mixed with other beverages as it lacks a strong flavour. Reposado and Añejo's flavours are more smoky. Madurado is more like a fine scotch than a tequila.

Mezcal was first produced in Durango as a treat for mine workers. In the 1600s, alcohol production was controlled by the Spaniards until the Church became involved. When the central government took over the mezcal business from the Church, things took a commercial turn. A regulatory body established guidelines defining mezcal for the purposes of accurate labelling. For example, the alcohol content must be between 34 and 54 per cent.

Russek, who is of Belarusian descent, defines 'intelligent' farming as a vocation. His father believed that investing in land was a sound business practice, but Russek himself has taken a different tack. While studying Food Engineering at Universidad de Monterrey, he became aware of the problems involved in processing food. 'The first one, and the most common one, is to make food out of junk, products that are not really natural food or don't exist in nature,' he explains. 'The other category that is harmful is making junk out of food. You see all this easy-to-buy fast food, candies, a lot of sugar, a lot of processed ingredients ... In my opinion, it

needs to change.' After all, he goes on, 'food is the most intimate relationship we have with the earth as humans. I believe that in the last couple of decades we've lost all of it; the food industry has lost [sight of] the human balance that sustained it. How could they have values when they are huge corporations?' Russek believes that it is down to individual farmers to preserve biodiversity by not using huge amounts of chemicals just to ensure ever-increasing profits. Education is also key. Where today consumers might prefer to buy Coke and crisps, they could instead be buying 'a kilo of beans, or rice, or vegetables, or fruit ... You start improving people's life through their basic way of seeing'. His intention is 'for every person to have a complete diet within reach. That should be the basis of getting rid of fast food'.

About starting up his mezcal business, Russek says, simply, 'We were looking to make an honest drink.' It came as a big surprise that it was not possible to find a benchmark against which to compare his product: 'We couldn't, not in our category, not with mezcal or any agave-based beverage. I was amazed by that at first ... As soon as I started digging, I found things that made me uncomfortable.' So he said to his partner, 'Let's find the mezcal in Durango that is worth the pain, and find a cute name for it ... We tried to find the right – honest! – distiller. Not so easy! So we found [master distiller] Alejandro ... He had already retired from the world of mezcal.' Nonetheless, Alejandro agreed to work with Russek for a year on a trial basis. 'Mezcal had its own plan,' Russek muses. 'It keeps pulling people and situations to feel out this game that it has set out in life ... Starting that year, we announced that we wouldn't harm the environment or people – our clients. The only way to achieve that was to create a really pure product from the start.'

With mezcal becoming a high-end fashionable drink, the concern now is that there is insufficient agave to meet demand. The fact that it takes an agave plant between eight and fourteen years to reach maturity – essentially the life of a child – puts the challenges of Russek's chosen specialism into daunting perspective.

(left) **Heiman Russek at his organic farm outside Durango city, and** (facing page) **loading flowering artichokes into his truck under the watchful eyes of his Labrador Retriever**

(below) **Russek with Alejandra González Serrano and her grandchildren in her kitchen. The eighty-one-year-old owner of Gorditas** *Doña* **Aleja in Nombre de Dios has been selling** *gorditas* **(stuffed pastries) for more than thirty years; and** (facing page) **Russek and master** *mezcalero Don* **Alejandro Gamiztake in the desert inspecting wild maguey to harvest for their Minotaur-brand mezcal**

Isaac Enns Wall
Manager, Quesos Holanda,
Nuevo Ideal Mennonite Community, Durango

(above) **Isaac Enns Wall visits the home of his cousin, rancher Gerhard Redecop, in the Nuevo Ideal Mennonite Community; and** (facing page) **Redecop with his wife Sara and four of their six children**

The ancestors of the vast majority of Mexican Mennonites settled in the Russian Empire in the late eighteenth and nineteenth centuries, moving on to Canada in due course. When, prior to World War I, some of the Canadian provincial governments passed laws that threatened the Mennonites' way of life and educational preferences, delegates of the community negotiated certain privileges with then Mexican President Álvaro Obregón that made it possible to settle in northern Mexico. There the Mennonites established farms and machine shops. Today they continue to dress conservatively, and intermarriage with outsiders is rare.

About eight thousand Mennonites live in Nuevo Ideal, about 120 kilometres outside the city of Durango. Among them is Isaac Enns Wall, who manages Quesos Holanda, a manufacturer of *queso Chihuahua*, a semi-soft cheese made from cow's milk. The cheese is also called *queso menonita* or *campresino menonita* (the word *campresino* refers to the compression process used to produce this type of cheese, which is similar to cheddar). Unlike Mexican white cheeses, *queso Chihuahua* is pale yellow in colour and has a cheddar-like sharpness.

In speaking about how the Mennonites came to emigrate from Canada to Mexico, Enns Wall explains that in the course of the Revolution, Mexico 'was devastated, so … a decree went out saying that [foreign] agricultural workers were allowed to enter the country. Since our group came from an agrarian class, I guess [the authorities] saw some benefit [in allowing Mennonites to settle in Mexico]'. The group that ended up in Durango 'were the last ones to leave Canada to start a new colony,' he adds. 'They were pioneers who settled in a new place.' He stresses how important it was to the community to be able to retain the religious basis of its education programme, and how religion remains a cornerstone of everyday life. The group's Anabaptist founder Menno Simons 'professed the idea that Christianity did not only have to … be seen in the church but that [the church] should be incorporated into every aspect of Christian life'. Simons' followers adhere to the concept of 'he who doesn't work doesn't eat', 'so the noblest thing we could do,' Enns Wall continues, 'was to work the land that feeds us.'

Today the Mennonites' high ideals are constantly under threat from globalisation and what Enns Wall describes as 'infamous capitalism'. During the early period in Mexico, each Mennonite family had to be self-sufficient, 'so in the orchards next to the houses there was … pretty much everything,' he says. 'You could find cucumbers, carrots, cabbages, squash … pretty much anything edible.' Nowadays, things are different. 'It is as if someone said, "We now have a Walmart, so we might as well go and shop there",' Enns Wall observes sadly.

(facing page) **Enns Wall at the entrance to the community's cheese plant, and** (left) **inspecting semi-soft cheeses made of cow's milk.** (below) **More than thirty households thrive on Nuevo Ideal's large ranch. The community still maintains such Germanic practices as serving soup with cabbage and beef at weddings**

Sinaloa: *Bridging Divides*

Driving along the Durango–Mazatlán highway, the traveller experiences three micro-climate shifts, from desert to pine forest to arid plains, then back again to pine forests. You pass through the longest tunnel in Mexico (the so-called 'Devil's Backbone') and the highest cantilever bridge (Baluarte) in Central and North America, whose midpoint delineates the cross-points of the parallel that marks the northern limit of the Tropic of Cancer.

Road journeys in Mexico are pleasant experiences, the highways and byways generally in good condition and security (federal police or marines) manning checkpoints at strategic intervals along the way. Toll roads are relatively cheap and very well maintained, better in some ways than the highway system of Mexico's giant northern neighbour. Sinaloa surprises the early summer visitor with its agricultural prowess, with fields of maize burnt golden brown by the June sun stretching for kilometres. Contrary to common belief, the state is not so much known for growing marijuana (although its mountain hideaways are ideal for the purpose) as for being the kingdom of Mexican tomato production, yielding massive crops for export to the US.

Given all that one hears and reads about the narcos and their grip on certain sectors of Mexican life, driving to Sinaloa (the home state of Joaquín Archivaldo 'El Chapo' Guzmán, the kingpin of the state's drug cartel now ensconced in a U.S. prison) intrigued this first-time visitor. What lay in store was, surprisingly, no different than travelling the length and breadth of the rest of the country. It felt not unlike New York, London or Paris with their increasingly visible gun-toting security, and Sinaloa's inhabitants were certainly as polite and engaging as most people north or south of the Equator. Kind, generous and humble, ordinary Mexicans are very welcoming, clearly people whose fortitude in the face of adversity, poverty and back-breaking life-problems has been a lesson learned. Yet cartel culture is present to a greater or lesser degree in certain areas of the country. Large numbers of people feed off the production and trafficking of drugs directly or indirectly. The unfortunate truth is that despite violence and hazards to local communities, the cartels create jobs and provide income, a detail lost in the noise of foolish border politics in the US.

There are many theories about the cartels' power base, an issue about which ordinary Mexicans themselves are overly sensitive. Despite thirty-four thousand violent deaths in 2015, many people tend to sweep the subject under the carpet. While US politicians rant about Mexican drugs and gangs, most Mexicans see themselves as victims of America's insatiable demand for drugs, pointing to the influence of the US gun lobby, which allows unlimited numbers of weapons to be smuggled into the country, weapons which are then turned on the local populace. The pattern seems to be that agricultural development and industrialisation bring with them drug use, which in turn brings in the cartels, which then expand their hold while fighting or fending off rivals. The *ranchero* culture underpinning cartel activities pits the individual against society, valuing familial (tribal) fealty above civic law and order. Given varying levels of corruption, incompetence and waste throughout Latin America, hard-pressed local populations are coerced into the economy of the cartels, thus undermining social order. Despite the Mexican government's best (often successful) efforts, the military counter-attack remains stymied.

Manuel Sánchez Villalpando
Chef, El Cuchupetas, Villa Unión, Sinaloa

Originally a cantina, El Cuchupetas has been a popular seafood restaurant since 1987, known especially for its prawn dishes. The original menu offered ceviche, prawn soup, whole prawns and crabs, abalone and scallops. Today El Cuchupetas boasts around fifty covers and is filled on a daily basis with locals, tourists from Mazatlán and visitors from abroad. Sexagenarian founder, owner and enthusiastic raconteur Manuel Sánchez Villalpando cooks with all ages and backgrounds of potential customers in mind, regularly prepares banquets in Mexico City and elsewhere for politicians and businesspeople (sometimes travelling to and from faraway venues in a single day), and has cooked for the President of Mexico on several occasions. Located in a simple two-storey building, his restaurant's main attraction continues to be the best regional seafood (the sea is a mere 8 kilometres away).

Sánchez, who took over the cantina after his father died, describes himself as having been adrenalin-driven and 'very eager to work' when he was younger, and his enthusiasm and energy show no sign of abating. Culinary issues to one side, it is clear that the social aspect of running a restaurant is hugely important to him. He loves to meet new people, saying, 'I imagine that that is the foundation of cooking and of the whole world, right?' When asked to explain his success with customers, many of whom have been returning regularly for nearly thirty years, he replies, 'The food is what attracts them; humour is the other thing.' Also, he says, he has 'never liked to imitate anyone. Everything I eat – I really like seafood and so did my father – I prepare it how I like it. I have never wanted to go around copying other restaurants'.

Sánchez describes the people of the state of Sinaloa as 'very kind, very pretty [and] very good hosts ... There are problems like there are in the rest of the world, with violence and attacks, and that makes us sad because it's only a few and we all get blamed. It is not exclusive to Mexico, it's the whole world ... People shouldn't have to live like that; you have to see terrorists for what they are. It's better to live life and let God bless us, and I hope He doesn't forget me because life is difficult. The best thing we can do is laugh every day to live well [and] entrust ourselves to God and the Virgin of Guadalupe.' His own favourite dishes are the local peel-and-eat shrimp, ceviche and scallops, whose distinct taste he attributes to the estuarine waters from which they come (Villa Unión is located on the Rio Presidio). 'They say that anything that is produced in that water is tastier than what is produced in the deep sea,' Sánchez observes. '[Catches from the] sea are more insipid; they have another type of flavour that is diluted by the water.'

As to the future, Sánchez believes that increased tourism holds the key to the area's growing success as a potential economic magnet. The main occupations include agriculture, fishing, livestock breeding, commerce and industry, with Sinaloan products used both locally and nationally. Sinaloa is one of the country's most prominent states in terms of agriculture and is, additionally, home to the country's second-largest fishing fleet. Significant crops include tomatoes, cotton, beans, maize, wheat, sorghum, potatoes, soybeans, sugarcane, peanuts and squash. Meat, sausages, cheese, milk and sour cream are of equal importance. 'I have helped the town a lot,' Sanchez says of Villa Unión, 'but they need more, and in terms of agriculture, they ... need money ... Here we cater for tourism ... Agriculture sometimes doesn't pay well, but we produce a lot of fish.' And beautifully prepared fish, as he himself has shown, can be a huge draw.

(previous spread) **Maize fields between Mazatlán and Culiacán turned golden brown by the summer heat at the end of the dry season**

(left) **Oyster shells pile up in the kitchen at El Cuchupetas**

(above) **Manuel Sánchez Villalpando, the owner of his namesake restaurant, in front of a mural by one of his employees, Higinio Moreno. The mural depicts famous *sinaloenses* Pedro Infante, Cruz Lizárraga, José Ángel Espinosa '*Ferrusquilla*' and the Cuchupetas. Known widely as '*El Cuchupetas*', Villapando has a larger-than-life reputation, having received presidents and other big-wigs over the years**

(left) **Kitchen staff peeling prawns, a favoured house dish. The shells are used to make stock for their famous prawn soup;** (below) **A lunchtime spread at El Cuchupetas, where Sánchez serves more than fifty covers every day; and** (facing page) **Sánchez preparing a *lubina* (bass) as *pescado sarandeado* (marinated fish which is butterflied and grilled)**

(facing page) **Law-enforcement officers and private security details all carry guns in Sinaloa.** (above) **The chapel of Jesús Malverde in Culiacán. Malverde, member of a criminal gang, has grown a posthumous reputation to which narcos and ordinary citizens pay homage**

Diego Becerra Rodríguez
Chef, El Presidio, Mazatlán & Culiacán, Sinaloa

A self-confessed 'addictive personality', Diego Becerra Rodríguez opened El Presidio in Mazatlán in his great-grandparents' house, which he modernised together with his brother just over three years ago. He was then invited to open a sister restaurant with the same name in an old house in Culiacán. Signature dishes include *chamorro* (pork or beef shank stewed in chilli sauce), oxtail in tomatillo sauce, baked Kumamoto oysters, and *tacos de buche*, a stewed, then fried combination of beef and pork stomach. 'I don't want a chain,' Becerra insists. 'I want three restaurants ... I don't want to grow bigger than that because it's going to lose its soul if you make it big.' His next place, he hopes, will be a 'downscale restaurant on the beach, cooking pigs and surfing every day'. Simplicity is the key to success: 'I don't want my food to be fancy ... I want my clients to come three times a week and eat *chamorro* or ceviche and say, "I'm full ... That was a good meal. I can have a beer, I can drink, and I can relax."'

Becerra's background is somewhat paradoxical; his mother is wealthy, he says, but his father 'never was'. A luxury visit to Europe as a teenager in the company of one of his grandmothers took him to Amsterdam, Venice (where they stayed at the Danieli), Florence, Rome, Nice and Monaco. To this day the chef remembers the calamari he was served in Venice. 'How do you know when you've eaten a good meal?' he asks rhetorically. 'When after a month you still remember the taste exactly.'

Becerra's other grandmother was 'an amazing cook'. In fact, for his entire family, 'food is the most important thing ... Anything that you have to celebrate, it has to be celebrated with a meal.' His father, also a 'great cook' and clearly a huge influence, had 'a lot of culture. He read like crazy; he was very smart; he had everything that a playboy should have except money'. And, says Becerra, his dad had 'this way of making everything look so grand ... He took me to La Côte Basque when it was an important place to eat in New York City ... And he always told the story that when he got his dish and ate it, there was a lot of sauce left on the plate, and he asked for more bread to eat the rest of the sauce. The chef came out to say thank you because that was a compliment'.

Becerra started to cook when he was just seven years old, influenced by one of his grandmothers' cooks, called Ramona. 'She had the worst temper,' he remembers, 'but she loved us deeply ... She taught me to make eggs and other things ... I always had this need to be independent, and I figured I needed to learn how to cook because if I had to wait for somebody else to cook what I liked, I was gonna depend on them to eat well.' In secondary school, he was already cooking for his friends. 'We used to go out and get drunk, sometimes get in fights, 'cause when you're that age, it's like rutting season,' he laughs. Afterwards the crew would go back to his house and he would make them a meal. While in San Francisco for a couple of years, ostensibly to study graphic design, Becerra found that he hated the homework, preferring to party and cook for friends. It was then that he decided to become a chef.

After winning a cooking competition, Becerra was taken to New York City, where he went to Nobu and many other famous eateries, including Maya, where the chef was Richard Sandoval. 'We met him because one of my teachers was studying with him,' Becerra explains, 'and he offered me a job to open the San Francisco Maya.' Becerra was just twenty-five. 'I lasted there for about eight months, and then I came back to Mexico City,' he says. His return to Mazatlán was marked by the establishment of a new business: a small quesadilla stand, which lasted for about a year. 'Then I stopped because I got involved with using hallucinogenic drugs,' reveals the chef. 'After a year of doing it hard-core, I was like, Oh, man! ... I was in this auto-destruction phase, which I also did when I was in San Francisco ... I mean, you have to have these phases, you just have to have them.' A couple more restaurant ventures 'started very well and then went into a nosedive', and then Becerra opened a beach restaurant (now managed by someone else). El Presidio followed, at which point things became 'very different'. The joint venture with his brother also engaged with the family's history. 'My mother wanted that house to come alive again,' the chef explains of the venue. 'So it was a combination of needs that came together.'

(facing page) **Diego Becerra Rodríguez in the garden at El Presidio in Culiacán; and** (right) **The restaurant's cut-glass hallway, mixing modern design with its nineteenth-century interior and exterior brickwork**

(above) **El Presidio in Culiacán is housed at Casa Bon, a former family home built in 1890.** (right) **Becerra worked with architects to integrate new and old architectural styles in the building, which includes a brewery at the back where he and his business partner plan to brew high-quality sake**

  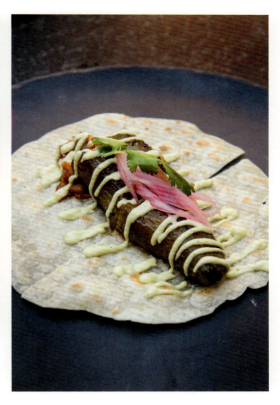

(above left) **Hamachi**, or
Japanese amberjack;
(middle) **Stewed oxtail
in tomatillo sauce; and**
(right) **A** *chile relleno de
marlin* **(marlin-stuffed
pepper) taco**

Miguel Taniyama
Chef & Politician, Tomo, Culiacán, Sinaloa

(left) **Miguel Taniyama prepares a whole octopus at his sushi restaurant Tomo;** (facing page, left) **Octopus cooked in chillis and garlic; and** (facing page, right) **Fruit from the** *pitaya* **cactus. The** *pitaya* **season lasts for just over a month, from the end of April until the beginning of June, and has a festival dedicated to it in Sinaloa**

Japanese immigrants and their descendants have lived and worked in Mexico since the late nineteenth century. In fact, Mexico was the first country to recognise Japanese sovereignty after the end of isolation; an 1888 treaty allowed citizens of both countries to travel between them. Nine years later, Mexico became the first Latin American country to receive Japanese immigrants, most of whom came to work in agriculture and fishing.

Miguel Taniyama's Japanese grandfather arrived in Sinaloa in 1927. An agronomist specialising in vegetables, he had been invited by the Mexican government and stayed on after meeting the woman who was to become Taniyama's grandmother. Taniyama's cooking reflects his family background, utilising as it does a mixture of Mexican and Japanese ingredients. He set up his business in 1997 with the help of his father and brothers. He cites commitment, love and passion as the keys to his success, and sees himself as a social activist as well as a cook. His family restaurant, Tomo, specialises in fish prepared with a Mexican/Japanese fusion twist.

'My story is a curious one,' Taniyama says. 'I had a mother and a grandmother who were excellent cooks of Mexican cuisine, and my father was passionate about food. So as not to lose too many of our Asian – Japanese – traditions, my father always cooked.' After studying industrial engineering, Taniyama took up cooking as a profession. 'I really like to eat, I like it a lot,' he enthuses. 'I am happy cooking … Like life, like therapy, it fills me up.' When asked to encapsulate the difference between true Japanese and fusion cooking, he replies, 'The simplicity. Japanese cuisine is much more simple, much cleaner, with

more defined flavours … Mexican food or fusion is a mix of flavours, spicy, acidic.' He caters for the local Japanese community of about three hundred families (which he describes as well integrated, 'very strong economically' and successful) by using special types of seaweed and sauces. Most of the fish he purchases is fresh and locally sourced, although he does have specialty fish products such as eel, *tobiko* (flying fish roe), *ikura* (salmon roe) and *masago* (capelin roe) flown in from Mexico City or Los Angeles. When asked to explain the difference between his approach and that of the larger Japanese restaurants in Mexico City, he says that they adapt traditional recipes by using local ingredients such as jalapeño or serrano peppers and cilantro, as well as fresh fish from the entire Mexican coastline, including Ensenada, Sinaloa and Oaxaca.

Taniyama is also involved in local politics and ran as an Independent candidate in 2016. Although he lost the election, he is pleased to have participated and is planning to run again in 2018. Defeat, he feels, is less important than the fact that he focused awareness on issues specifically affecting Culiacán. 'When you want to do things honestly and transparently, you have a longer battle,' he observes. 'But that does not mean that the Independent option has suffered a setback. It means that we are playing clean. It means that the fight is totally transparent and honest. We are citizens. We do not have a cartel or a political group … Those of us who are from a culture of hard work, of constant work, we know that it is one step at a time. I will be back in 2018 because the district … belongs to its citizens. It belongs to those who are honest, to those who work.'

Baja California Sur: *Missionary Zeal*

Much of the history of the Viceroyalty of New Spain (colonial Mexico) is entwined with the Catholic Church via its various tentacles, whether political, economic or spiritual. In the history of conquest and colonisation, the role of religious orders has been profoundly important in its socio-economic impact on native peoples and their lands. The Church was the first 'civilising' presence once military pacification had been achieved, building missions as quasi-military redoubts from which to proselytise and convert the indigenous 'heathens'.

The Baja California Peninsula (Las Californias) was first settled in 1697 by Jesuit missionaries, who were expelled in 1767, and were in turn replaced by Dominicans charged with exploring Alta California (today's American state of California). Early fortune hunters, the first one in the guise of the aptly named Fortún Ximénez, had arrived in 1533 to indulge in a bit of rape and pillage, stealing the area's pearls and having their way with the local women. Ximénez was put to death by the locals, but tales of treasure soon brought Hernán Cortés to Baja California's shores. Cortés landed in La Paz (the state's present-day capital) two years after Ximénez, naming the 'island' (as he then thought) as California. The Gulf of California was later changed to the Sea of Cortés in 1539.

Bordered to the north by Baja California, to the west by the Pacific Ocean and to the east by the Sea of Cortés, Baja California Sur is home to the resorts of Cabo San Lucas and San José del Cabo, which benefit from its hot climate and clear azure seas. The narrow peninsula broke off from the mainland some two million years ago due to tectonic-plate activity, leaving the land with nothing more than sun, sea, sandy beaches and few natural resources except for the rich fishing along its coastline. It was in La Paz that I first encountered *Panopea generosa*, the Pacific geoduck (or Gooey Duck as the Chinese call it), a rare (and challenging) clam that can reach over 20 centimetres in length. Far more delicious than it looks, a very large specimen dropped live into boiling water for a late breakfast tasted totally exquisite.

Apart from coming across the (mythical) Hotel California (a song made famous by the Eagles in the late 1970s and played interminably over the quaint hostelry's loudspeakers) in Todos Santos, the only saving grace of our visit was a chance encounter with a goat farmer. Demetrio Flores was the real-deal descendant of a family that has been working the same ranch for the past 150 years. Our goat farmer lived with his relatives in the foothills of the Sierra Madre along with some goats, a few cattle, some sheep and a couple of horses (one of said nags nearly cost me an arm and a leg, but that's another story). A true son of the earth, Flores had two kids slaughtered for our visit. While the women prepared the food, he sat on his porch recounting his life story, his few hopes and minimal aspirations. Wouldn't he rather live in the city in a better house, have more money, be able to afford household appliances? 'No, no, no,' he protested calmly. 'What would I do with all that?' Become a political activist, fight poverty and corruption, do things he felt strongly about? His fear: 'I'd become corrupt myself.'

Pescadería Fish Market
La Paz, Baja California Sur

(previous spread) **The crystal-clear waters of Puerto Balandra, La Paz, Baja California Sur**

(above) **Fishmonger Jorge Armando Pérez at the entrance to Pescadería Marsel, where he works**

(left) **A freshly caught lobster for sale;** (below) **Pérez holding a geoduck clam, one of the world's longest-living creatures, with a lifespan of up to 140 years, and most delicious when cooked;** and (bottom) **Chef Héctor Palacios preparing a geoduck-clam breakfast at Hotel La Concha in La Paz**

Demetrio Flores
Goat Farmer, Rancho Santa Marta, Baja California Sur

Rancho Santa Marta has been owned by the Amao family for 150 years. Today it is managed by Demetrio Flores, his wife Isabel Rochin and their four children. The ranch raises goats (primarily Nubians, Syrians and a few Murcianos); the herd currently numbers between fifty and sixty animals. They are allowed to roam to forage during the day but are brought in at night. The males are sold for meat or butchered and eaten by the ranchers in stews; the females provide milk for drinking and cheese-making.

Flores has raised specialist 'goat dogs' who are left with the goats as puppies before their eyes open and are raised to protect the herd. This is a typical technique in the area as the dogs grow up feeling responsible for their herds. Flores himself has to be careful around the dogs when they are protecting his goats.

Historically in Mexico goat farming was associated with rural poverty. The country's goat population developed from animals brought over by the Spaniards five hundred years ago, but interbreeding was not attempted until relatively recently. In the last forty years, new breeds have been introduced through both private and federal or state governmental efforts. In the 1970s, the federal government, acting through the Agricultural and Livestock Secretary's Office, established a large breeding centre in northern Mexico. The breeds housed there – Alpine, Nubian, Saanen and Toggenberg – provided genetic material with which to improve the local flocks. Private producers have continued to import pure-bred animals with the objective of improving their own flocks, and they sell on animals with high genetic potential to smaller producers. Not all breeds can cope with the often rugged terrain.

Flores distrusts city dwellers and politicians in equal measure, blaming the latter for being corrupt; politicians, he says sadly, 'don't keep their promises'. Life on the ranch suits him completely. He describes seeing goat dogs fight to the death to defend their herds. 'When they feel the herd is threatened – for example, if a calf gets too close to it – they might even kill it. It's happened before that they killed a calf [but if that happens, I do] nothing [to the dog]. I don't hurt him or anything.' If a dog kills a goat, it is muzzled and tied up to prevent it doing further harm to the flock, or it is rehomed.

Flores, who was born in La Paz, has worked at Rancho Santa Marta for fifty years. His parents were cowboys, and this is the profession he hopes his children will follow. 'Opportunities [for them to go to university or work] are very limited now,' he observes. For entertainment he plays cards for five hours at a time in order to relax after a full day tending his flock.

(left) **A herd of goats roaming among cacti and mesquite trees at the Amao family's Rancho Santa Marta; and** (facing page) **Demetrio Flores striking a pose**

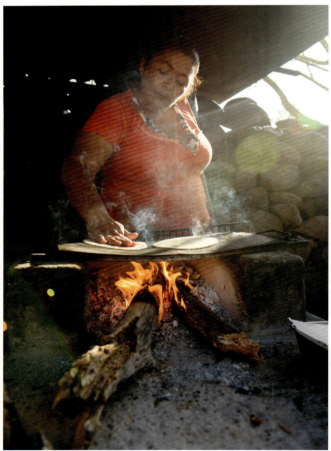

(far left) **Flores' wife, Isabel Rochin, prepares** *cabrito* **(kid stew) with flour tortillas fried in a touch of goat's milk curd;** (left) **The Flores family enjoy stewed kid once a month as a treat. Rochin uses every part of the animal, except for the liver, in her cooking;** (above) **Flores and his wife get up at 5.00 a.m. every day to tend to the goats and look after a small herd of cows; and** (facing page) **Kid on a spit ready for a feast. The female goats are kept for their milk while the males are sold for meat or eaten by the ranchers**

Sonora: *Rawhide Country*

Organisation and logistics are everything when you are travelling with a team bound for unknown climes, always seeking something new, something special. A different bit of Mexico at every turn, unencumbered by the vicissitudes of bureaucracy and story-boards presented by some state or local authorities bent on showing you what they think are the best flavours of their neighbourhood. The extraordinary experience of trying out a place for the first time without any packaged preconceptions about it is both a gamble and a punter's delight. The gamble is that you can fall into the hands of apparatchiks too keen to please, too preening or just plain incompetent. Thank God it didn't often happen, but what is one to do in such circumstances? Say goodbye and look for the next flight out, or grit one's teeth and nod politely?

Then there's the dynamic between team members and the clash of egos accentuated by the limitations of time and resources. There is the irritability that brews from being cooped up inside a working bubble, eating, drinking, debating and arguing greater or lesser points, be they routine or strategic. Too true what they say about getting to know someone while travelling. It is the easiest way to unravel relationships.

All things considered, the team that worked on this book acquitted itself rather well, despite episodes like 'Breakfast at Guaymas'. Not a remake of Audrey Hepburn's classic movie with a similar title but an opportunity to practise all the skills, tested or untried, that such adventures require of someone in charge. Enough said.

Having got that digression off my chest, it is only fair to separate out the wheat from the chaff and talk about our Sonora experience. 'Resourceful and bucolic, sparse and beautiful, cheery and sombre' is how an outsider could describe the state. The people look taller and have fairer complexions than I encountered elsewhere. They say that the inhabitants of northern Mexico are generally distinct from others in the country mostly because of their European ancestry. In some instances, I heard them profess a closer affinity with their northern (American) neighbour than with the rest of Mexico.

One constant in my intrusive experiences of Mexico was the sense of all-round nationalism that pervades the country, trumping tribal or regional loyalties, always on guard in defence of the notion of Mexican-ness. Having said that, the state is the primary arbiter of affiliation and association. More so in states like Sonora, where the character of the people is shaped not only by the sedimentation of history but by climate and geography. Sonora is cattle country, *Rawhide* in the flesh. Divided into the Sierra Madre Occidental to the east, rolling hills and plains in the centre, and the coast facing the Sea of Cortès to the west, the state is mostly arid and semi-arid desert mixed with grain-producing grasslands and irrigation-dependent agriculture in the valleys producing large crops of wheat, maize, cotton, sorghum, alfalfa and fruit. Sonora produces almost half of Mexico's wheat and a sizeable portion of its watermelons. Plus a crop of characterful, beautiful, colourful women as strong and feisty in the saddle as they are in the business world.

Luisa Alejandra Gándara Fernández
Director, Fundación Ganfer & Owner, Aromaz Ranch, Zamora, Sonora

When asked what she thinks of when she sees a cow, Luisa Alejandra Gándara Fernández replies, 'I see an animal that we respect, but it serves a purpose ... We get an income and it feeds us.' On her family's working ranch outside Hermosillo, cattle are allowed open grazing so they fatten up before being exported to the US. Gándara, who has been around horses for as long as she can remember, spends her weekends riding with her family at their larger spread in northern Sonora. This energetic, animated rancher also runs the Fundación Ganfer, set up by her mother twenty-five years ago. The foundation supports disadvantaged Sonoran children and young people, especially those requiring help with bullying and alcohol abuse, via programmes promoting art, music and gastronomy. With the assistance of chef Eloy Aluri, Gándara's intention is to preserve recipes from Sonora's eight different indigenous groups. She has also appeared on cooking shows with such chefs as Dante Ferrero, Angel Vázquez and Javier Plascencia. In essence she is using philanthropy to expand the region's gastronomic profile.

Gándara's family still run the local mill and are currently working on creating a special organic wheat for chef Diego Hernández-Baquedano. Another culinary magnet, the Festival del Chef Sonora, was founded by Gándara in 2014 and is held in Hermosillo each spring. Considered one of the most important gastronomic dates in Mexico's calendar, this fundraising event includes conferences, round-table discussions, wine and beer tastings, and traditional Sonoran bacanora, a type of mezcal. Local exhibitors have a chance to mingle with international visitors.

Sonora's food culture is meat-based; most of the country's beef and pigs are bred there. Chef Aluri, who formerly owned a mini-chain of sandwich and salad shops in Hermosillo, spreads the word via catering and consulting. At the Festival del Chef Sonora, Hermosillo restaurants and confectioners set up stalls in the city's convention centre, and prominent chefs from around the country are flown in to serve samples, give classes and let Sonora's residents know how their agricultural exports are fuelling farm-to-table cuisine in Mexico City, Monterrey and Baja Sur. 'We can show our culture, the beef – and show that we are not all gangsters and cowboys,' Aluri explains.

Gándara's grandparents were both businesspeople. Born in Spain, her grandfather began working in Sonora in 1917, having arrived in Mexico with no money. 'It's a funny story,' she says. 'He got married at forty-two because he wanted to wait until he had enough money, so he dated my grandmother for thirteen years!' One of the founders of Universidad de Sonora, he was essentially the family's first philanthropist. Today its members 'all work together ... in different businesses,' Gándara explains. 'We have tomato greenhouses, we have ranches, we have flour mills, dealerships, Dairy Queen and Papa John's franchises. Each one of us is in charge of a different business'. She calls her own work with Chef Aluri 'gastronomy with a cause', citing the very real difference the foundation's programmes have made in the lives of the children it seeks to help. The promotion of traditional cooking also engages members of the state's eight ethnic groups by inviting them to teach their regional specialities.

There are approximately fifteen hundred head of cattle on Gándara's family's ranches at any one time. Once they achieve their optimum weight, they are trucked across the border for sale. The larger ranch boasts 9,000 hectares and has four families living on it who control the herd and bring the cattle to corrals for marking, branding and vaccinating. 'It's an old-school, traditional ranch,' Gándara says with pride.

(previous spread)
The Pacific Ocean from San Carlos in Guaymas, Sonora

(left) **Roadside fruit vendor Javier Ramirez, nicknamed '*El Matemático Enigmático*', working on a sudoku puzzle while waiting for clients outside Hermosillo;** and (facing page) **Luisa Alejandra Gándara Fernández readying up for herding cattle on her family ranch in Zamora**

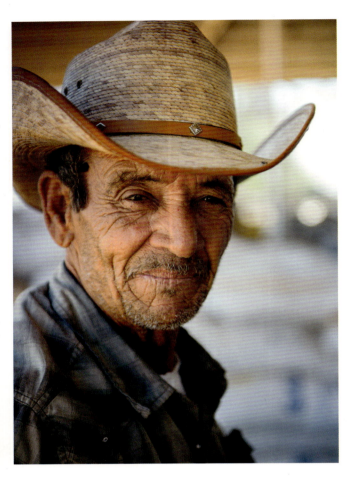

(left) **A ranch hand at Aromaz Ranch in Zamora;** (right) **Clodorimo Celaya, another ranch hand;** (below) **Cattle being rounded up;** and (facing page) **Gándara, a former pupil of a Swiss finishing school, has ridden horses her entire life, here seen herding steers with the ranch hands**

(following spread, left)
Old flour-mill machinery still in use; and (following spread, right) *Tortillas de agua* **(large, thin flour tortillas), a local speciality, ready for sale in a Sonoran bakery**

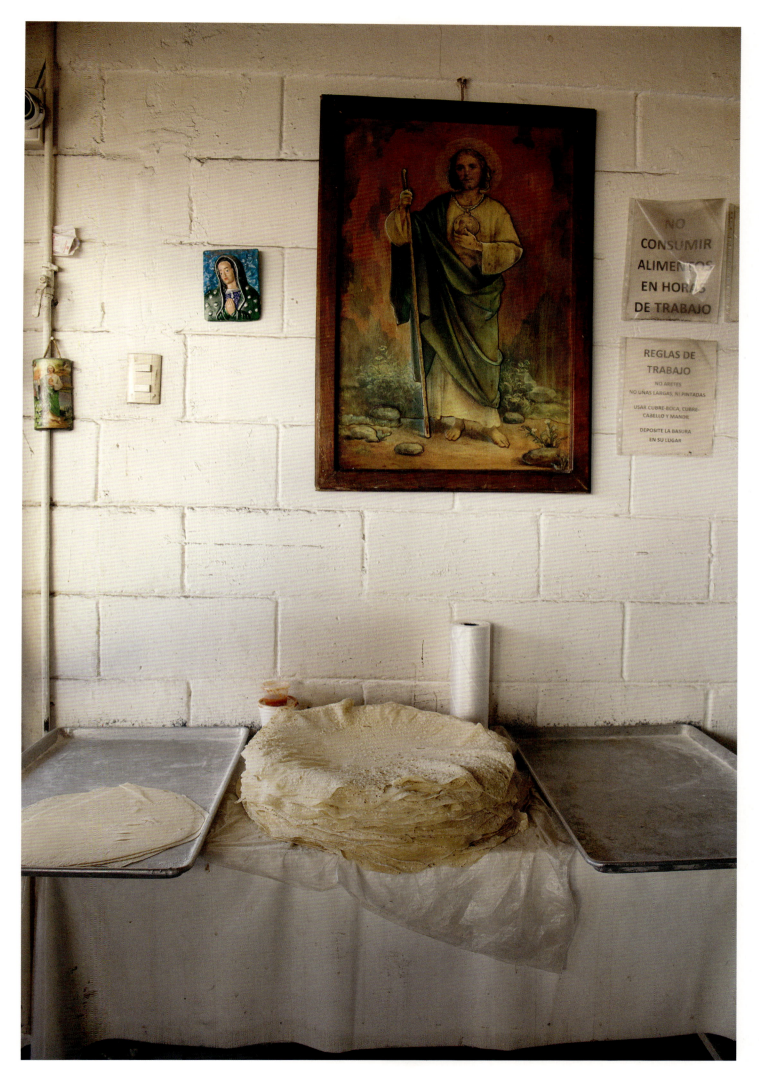

Bahía de Kino
Sonora

(below) **A *pata de mula* ('mule's foot') clam being opened in Bahia de Kino. A local speciality, this type of clam is known for its strong taste;** (right) **Mariscos El Terry in Bahia de Kino; and** (facing page) **Abigail Morales, a member of the Seri tribe, in Bahia de Kino**

Baja California: *Border Crossings*

Nothing challenged my temper more on this Mexican quest than having to confront the Mother of All Walls – 106 kilometres of fencing, razor-wire barricades, lookout towers, and metal and brick obstacles demarcating the border with the US. All this smack-dab in front of a visitor deplaning at Tijuana's airport, with San Diego, California staring back from a distance like a shimmering Shangri-La always and ever beyond reach, except for the few bearing the cross of assimilation into the Land of the Free. The divisiveness of contemporary American politics merely reinforces the shock, a spectacle so overwhelming as to take the edge off any excitement at arriving in one of Mexico's most colourful (and storied) states. History has a long fuse but a short memory; 170 years ago, all of California was Mexican territory, plus Nevada, Utah, New Mexico and portions of Oregon and Colorado; Texas had already seceded in 1836.

A double band of fencing and wall stretches for kilometres across the sprawling city of Tijuana, continuing its climb up and down mountains and finally dipping into the Pacific Ocean. There's a strip of no-man's-land between the bands, a free-fire zone I presume, patrolled by helicopters, drones and border-patrol cars on the US side. Having stood on the American side of Checkpoint Charlie in Berlin before and after the collapse of Communism, this was not an endearing site, especially as I had grown up in the 1950s and '60s, when some of us looked on America as the Shining City on the Hill. This was cruel, a rude reality unbecoming of the America I came to know in younger days. Yes, there are huge problems, but all countervailing arguments pale for a historical second when one is confronted by the reality of this jarring divide.

Politics aside, our spirits began to rise as we headed out of Playas de Tijuana bound for Baja California, an experience all its own. Not just because of the natural beauty of its beaches, forests and deserts but also because of the characterful personalities that populate this pioneering region. One of Mexico's fastest-growing states, Baja California has attracted a great number of enterprising people, whether in the proliferating vineyards, the burgeoning hospitality sector or advanced industry.

It is invigorating to see what climate and geography can deliver to a populace heading for adventure. Take Noel Téllez, for example. A lawyer by profession, Noel and his family decided to turn their conventional vineyard into a biodynamic enterprise producing Mexico's only natural wines without the use of fertilisers or pesticides. There are myriad vintners scattered along the state's valleys and uplands, from large, established wineries to smallholdings. Juan Chiquito's 2-hectare vineyard and orchard represent a labour of love by a working man enjoying his retirement growing his own grapes, selling what he can over the counter, and saving the rest for friends, family and his own pleasure. Then there is Mariscos La Guerrerense, which offers the best street food 'on the planet', according to celebrity chef Anthony Bourdain. *Doña* Sabina Bandera has been manning her food truck on a corner in Ensenada for over fifty years, her seafood tostadas sought after by people who visit the town just to taste her food. A former farm labourer from Guerrero, this street chef has ambitions to open food stalls in New York and elsewhere.

Javier Plascencia
Chef, Misión 19, Tijuana, Baja California

'I don't see myself as a celebrity, I see myself as a creator, a chef that people look up to. I like it that younger people come up to me or write to me, or email or Facebook me, [because] I made a statement that you actually can do it.' So says chef Javier Plascencia, owner of a number of award-winning restaurants in Mexico and the US, among them Misión 19 in Tijuana.

Plascencia studied Culinary Arts at San Diego Mesa College, having previously attended military school after being expelled for planting a cherry-bomb under his teacher's car. An accomplished surfer and golfer, this 'Baja badass' has been an energetic promoter of Tijuana, which has suffered for many years from its reputation as a party destination. He also created Baja Culinary Fest in 2011, has featured in several TV series focusing on food, and been the recipient of numerous awards both at home and in America.

Plascencia trained in hotels and restaurants in Baja California, opening his first eatery, Saverios Mediterráneo (later Casa Plascencia), in 1989 together with his family. It was at Misión 19 that he finally had the freedom to create something of his own, personally supervising the interior design, the kitchen, the menu, and the wine and craft-beer lists. The menu emphasises regional ingredients, with special touches including the use of 'Chinese boxes' to cook meat and of a spherification agent to create jalapeño beads, the addition of charcoal oil to enhance the preparation of beef dishes, and the chef's preference for 'architectural' plating.

Plascencia remembers being taken across the Mexico/US border by his mother to buy groceries in San Diego, California and noticing 'lots of [Mexican] people jumping the fence and running, trying to get over to the other side. We saw many accidents on the freeway; people got run over and were just lying dead … For me it was an everyday thing'. Although cross-border traffic remains a major political issue, the culinary balance between the two countries has shifted in the intervening years, with restaurants now targeting local people rather than American tourists. 'We don't worry as much about needing people to come down from America to make a good living, be profitable or be successful,' Plascencia observes. 'It's not that we don't need the Americans any more, but I think they saw that side where we could make a living without them. And now they appreciate it more.' While Tijuana, he feels, will always be a party town, he notes that now 'a better quality of tourist comes down to Tijuana, people who are interested in the food, the wine, the nature, the art.' Meanwhile local cuisine has both diversified and benefited. 'Back in the '50s and '60s, Tijuana was dominated by French and Italian restaurants for tourists,' the chef remembers. 'There were no Mexican restaurants in Tijuana or in Baja California.' Of his own involvement in the process of change, he adds, 'I never went to school because I wanted to change my city with food or with restaurants. I went to school because I was passionate about it, and I am still very passionate about it. I saw that we could change a city, or at least try to make it better with the quality of tourists coming down … I was, I am, very happy and satisfied with the work I have done.'

(previous spread)
A graffiti-covered section of the Mexico–US border fence at Playas de Tijuana in Tijuana, Baja California

(left) **Javier Plascencia on the roof of the VIA Corporativo building that houses his flagship restaurant, Misión 19, in the heart of Tijuana's Zona Río business district**

(left) **Plascencia reviewing the day's menu while enjoying a glass of local house wine at Misión 19, and** (above) **in a different environment buying** *churros encanelados* **at the border at Playas de Tijuana. Because he owns restaurants on both sides of the fence (Bracero Cocina de Raiz is in San Diego), Plascencia frequently travels back and forth across the border**

(facing page) **The Mexico–US border fence at Playas de Tijuana near Friendship Park. This is the point along the 3,000 kilometres of border where families meet and touch fingertips once a year. The pro-Tijuana graffiti reads:** '*Estas de mi lado? Entijuanarte*' **(Are you on my side? Tijuana-ise yourself), a play on words with the name of a city festival**

Denise Roa & Mariela Manzano
Chefs, Rancho la Puerta & La Cocina Que Canta, Tecate, Baja California

Denise Roa always wanted to be an executive chef. 'Food has given me everything and taken everything away from me,' she says. 'It has not been a simple journey.'

Roa's American mother learned how to cook Mexican food from a book by Diana Kennedy. Roa's teenage years in Florida 'revolved around soccer; food was present in the form of lobster and crabs that we would pull up during our boat rides'. She studied Culinary Arts at Johnson & Wales University in Miami; her first job after graduating was as pastry chef at the Hilton in Torrey Pines, California. Deborah Schneider, who was executive chef there at the time, was a big influence. Roa went on to work at many of San Diego's top restaurants before opening La Trattoria in Santee. When the economy tanked, she had to close her doors. It was while 'healing' from this experience that she was offered a job at Rancho la Puerta.

Roa's approach fuses her own culinary and cultural heritage with the spa cuisine pioneered by Rancho La Puerta's co-founder Deborah Szekely. The ranch is a fitness retreat that follows slow food precepts. The cooking school attached to it, La Cocina Que Canta, celebrates 'the magical results of cooking' with organic ingredients. As well as being executive chef, Roa hosts demonstrations, tastings and dinners; one of the people regularly involved with these events is Mariela Manzano, head chef and owner of El Lugar de Nos in Tecate. The two chefs are friends of Ana-Fernanda Castro Santana, who runs her family's bakery, El Mejor Pan de Tecate, founded in 1969.

'Mexico has everything you could possibly want to have, especially as a chef,' says Roa. 'We have tradition, culture, all the perfect ingredients … but what l like most are the people. Having lived in Miami, lived a very fast life there, being able to come back to Mexico and enjoy the quality of life is what attracted me … In Miami as a chef you know that people go to dinner late. We start late and we finish early, and when you do that for twenty years you miss your whole life. Being somewhere where family is the most important thing … is important [now]. Money is not the driving force of happiness.' That said, she admits to loving the 'instant gratification, the adrenalin' of restaurant cooking. She also loves to teach. 'We forgot where food comes from,' she observes. 'I've always wanted to be outdoors and in nature, so when I came here I felt all the energy. I owe a lot to a wonderful farmer we have here called Salvador. For the first four years that I lived here, I worked with him every day outside … You start realising how the sun affects how things grow, and you notice, when the weather drops, how things change.' Of her vegetarianism she says, 'We are not necessarily at war with meat, but we are in love with vegetables … Diets are a funny thing. We always want to put things in little boxes and say, "This is the best for you." The truth is that we have to start to think about how we feel and how we want to feel. When you eat better, you feel better … Life is about balance … Your body tells you everything, or your mind tells you everything. We don't always listen.'

(facing page) **Mariela Manzano and Denise Roa in the traditional kitchen of Rancho La Puerta, Tecate;** (above left) **Salad of fresh spinach, strawberries, quinoa and pecans; and** (above right) **Roa's award-winning** *causa*, **a Peruvian dish made with pureed yellow Andes potatoes and** *hamachi*

Noel Téllez
Winemaker, Bichi Vineyard, Tecate, Baja California

Lawyer Noel Téllez and his family decided to turn their conventional vineyard into a biodynamic, low-sulphite winery after he and his brother Jair, a chef, encountered natural wines in Europe and the US. The brothers went on to resurrect the old vines on land owned by the family and currently work 8 hectares.

Bichi is Mexico's only natural wine producer. The Mission grape, the oldest known grape in the Americas, was brought over by the conquistadors. Originally tended by monks, it was first used to make sacramental wine and only later as everyday table wine. Bichi's winemaker Levi Diaz's current favourite is the Pet Mex, whose name is a play on the French abbreviation '*pet nat*' (for *pétillant-naturel*). Pet Mex is Mexico's first sparkling wine made using the ancient technique of bottling before primary fermentation is finished, without the addition of yeasts and sugars. All of Bichi's wines are aged in concrete, although there are plans to convert to terracotta amphorae.

Natural wine originated in France in the 1960s, when people began to understand how the heavy use of chemicals was adversely affecting agriculture. Téllez credits his brother with foregrounding the quality of the ingredients in his cooking. In their conversations about food, Jair would ask, 'Why is it that we cooks are putting ... the emphasis on the product and winemakers in Mexico are not?' Téllez freely assigns credit for the evolution of natural wine in Mexico to 'cooks who want a wine product that would go with what they are doing'; the most important thing, he believes, is to 'let the product express itself'.

The brand name Bichi comes from a Yaqui word meaning 'naked', which references Téllez's desire to make his wines 'the most pure ... that you can get'. Financing this kind of project is not necessarily straightforward, he admits, but more important than money is the fact that 'everything starts with emotion. This is the way [the venture] started.' He credits his mother, who creates natural remedies, as a key inspiration, and her mother before her, describing his grandmother as 'a very strong character', adding that once emotion kicks in, 'then you are ready to go for it'. Putting Bichi's achievement into context, he asks, 'How many winemakers or bodegas that make wine can say, "From tomorrow onwards, I will change 100 per cent of my agriculture, biodynamic or organic, whatever, and the way I make wine. Forget about, throw away, all the chemicals ... We are going in this direction. I don't care!"'

(above) **A picnic laid on by Noel Téllez's mother Ana includes local cheeses, olives and bread, as well as dried beef from Sonora. Ana makes her own compost and natural remedies for treating the vines at their vineyard;** (right) **Téllez and winemaker Levi Diaz's early-morning inspection of the vines;** and (facing page) **Téllez chuffed at the taste of his own wine in his cellar, behind him the oak barrels no longer used for ageing Bichi wines**

Tito Cortés
Dairy Farmer, Valle de Guadalupe, Baja California

Tito Cortés makes three types of cheese – Guadalupe, Gouda and oreado – plus several variations on the oreado (with added herbs such as rosemary) on his ranch of more than 300 hectares. His father, a naval officer, acquired the land for his children; the dairy herd now numbers more than a hundred cows, among them Jersey, Montbéliarde, Normandy and Holstein breeds. In addition to cheese and milk, Cortés sells small amounts of beef to restaurants in Valle de Guadalupe, Ensenada, Tijuana, Mexico City, Cabo San Lucas and Cancún. For now, he is not interested in exporting to the US, citing the small scale of his refrigeration facility, which limits the amount of cheese he can store, as an obstacle to expansion, if a temporary one.

Baja California's Mediterranean climate is ideal for growing grapes and olives as well as dairy farming. Cortés grew olives for a time, but around five years ago the entire grove burned and he decided not to replace it, instead using precious water resources to nourish his grapevines. But his priority is clearly his cows, whose company he cannot imagine exchanging for the bright lights of Mexico City. 'I like the cows,' he says. 'And I can produce something good for everybody. I can enjoy them, other people can enjoy them, and I feel proud of what I am making.' His fondness for the Valle de Guadalupe extends to the many outsiders who have come to live there, spurring on development: 'We have people from all over the world here: you have English, you have French, you have some from Holland. Different people have come to the valley with a dream, and if we can realise that dream together, we can make the valley really successful.' Things have changed from when he was a child and his family was producing just 'a little bit of cheese; we didn't make so much because we didn't have a market. Ensenada was smaller, there were many farmers, and in that time we had more beef cattle'. While his business has expanded, he accepts that he needs to build on his small-scale success. 'Our cheese is not cheap,' he explains. 'It's pure milk; it doesn't have added fat in it.' Although he has no local competitors, there is competition from farmers in other places, for example Ojos Negros and Maneadero. 'They produce a lot of cheese, more than us, a lot more than us,' he says. 'But it's different cheese.'

Cortés seems guardedly optimistic about the future, saying, 'There's a market for everybody. It all depends on what you want and what sections of the market you want to be in … The portion of the market we are fighting over is a little higher, possibly the upper middle and upper classes.' For now, his focus is solely on Mexico. 'We need to consolidate this market, and the only way you can consolidate this market is to make a good name for yourself in it.'

(facing page, left) **Curds being stirred and cooked on Tito Cortés' dairy farm;** (facing page, right) **Cortés walking to the sheep pen on the 300-hectare ranch where his family has been making cheese for more than forty-five years, and** (above) **in reflective mood inside his refrigeration facility**

Doña Esthela Martínez Bueno & Diego Hernández Baquedano
Traditional Cook & Chef, La Cocina de *Doña* Esthela & Corazón de Tierra, Valle de Guadalupe, Baja California

Doña Esthela Martínez Bueno, originally from Sinaloa, has lived in Baja California for more than twenty-five years. Five years ago she opened her own eatery, which specialises in *machaca con huevos* (shredded dried beef with eggs) and Sinaloa-style *barbacoa*. In 2015, her machaca dish was named FoodieHub's 'Best Breakfast in the World'. Diego Hernández Baquedano, whose restaurant is located not far from *Doña* Esthela's establishment, received classical culinary training and is a passionate advocate of local, sustainable ingredients. 'I am obsessed with knowing everything about the plants and animals I use,' he asserts, 'because to me, they are not just ingredients but living species ... At Corazón de Tierra, we offer the best of the best. It is beyond organic. We have an emotional, social, economic and cultural impact on the community. To me, that is what food is about.' These two cooks epitomise the opposite poles of Mexican cooking today: the traditional and the modern.

'I was trained in French techniques,' explains Hernández, 'but now we are trying to learn more about our traditional techniques ... and maybe use them in a different way.' *Doña* Esthela, who started out as a baker, opened her own place 'because I really love cooking, to welcome people, to take care of them'. For her, money is not the point of the exercise: 'I would cook without making any. Why? Because cooking is my pleasure, my passion. As a girl, I would cook on Fridays for the farmers who arrived [in town to do] their shopping. They would tie up their animals, horses or mules, and we'd invite them to eat.' It was her mother who taught *Doña* Esthela how to cook; she and her eleven siblings also learned cleaning and ironing. 'I know how to read and write because my mum taught me ... I did not have schooling,' she says, contrasting herself with Hernández, whom she calls 'a professional'.

Despite the differences in their backgrounds and education, Hernández and *Doña* Esthela clearly admire each other. Hernández notes that his 'is a generation that did not learn Mexican cuisine, and that is not right ... That really is something I'm not proud of ... I learned the European style, but Europe is not better than Mexico. Our Mexican cuisine has history ... and we chefs apply foreign techniques to our national ingredients'. When speaking with *Doña* Esthela, he emphasises the importance of mutuality: 'We have more to learn from you and you from us.' She agrees, describing how her customers 'come for the *pozole*, the enchiladas ... I make my *empanadas* every Wednesday. I make them with pumpkin, with pineapple. I make *coricos* [doughnuts], I make *elote* [maize] cakes, and with the seeds I make an *atole* [a hot maize-based drink] for dessert. But I don't know how to make pastry or pie!'

Hernández makes a strong case for the creation of 'a technical glossary of Mexican cuisine ... For example, if you read an old recipe book there are many recipes that tell you to boil a tomato, grind it and then fry it "quietly". What does that mean?' *Doña* Esthela knows, of course: '"To fry quietly" means to cook something over wood at a low heat, slowly.' Another traditional term the two cooks discuss is 'spooning'. *Doña* Esthela saves the day yet again: 'If you just finished cooking something – for instance a sauce – and you leave the spoon in for whatever reason and it boils twice for the same meal, and one time you don't leave the spoon in, but for the other you do, that food won't be any good. Why? Because you bruised it by leaving the metal in the sauce. That is why ... we use wooden spoons ... If you are making an *atole*, you shouldn't leave the spoon in because it will turn into water.'

(facing page, left)
Lunchtime diners at La Cocina de *Doña* Esthela in Valle de Guadalupe; (facing page, right) **Two young cordon bleu-trained chefs, one Swiss and one Italian, learning to cook Mexican food under Diego Hernández Baquedano's guidance at Corazón de Tierra** (above)**; and Hernández visiting *Doña* Esthela's restaurant altar to the Virgin of Guadalupe**

Ezequiel Hernández Zuñiga
Founder, De Garo Ja'Mat & Chemistry Teacher, Sauzal, Ensenada, Baja California

The town of Ensenada – hedonistic Tijuana's cosmopolitan sister – was the capital of Baja from 1882 to 1915. When the capital shifted to Mexicali, Ensenada became a gambling centre until the sport was outlawed by the federal government in the 1930s. Today Baja California is known for so-called 'Baja Med' gastronomy, a fusion of Mexican, Mediterranean and Asian cuisines

Ezequiel Hernández Zuñiga arrived in Ensenada from his native Oaxaca at the age of twenty to study oceanography. Fast-forward to 2002, when his wife Laura founded the Centro Educativo Patria school in outbuildings on their property, having realised that there was no good secondary school in the area for their sons to attend. Both parents are involved in teaching the 180 students alongside a team of other instructors. The school boasts alumni studying at top universities all over the world.

'Oaxaca is a place with a lot of contradictions. Poverty and richness come together, and in a very ugly way,' Hernández says of his native state. 'Since there are those contradictions, there is a lot of political turmoil and political problems.' He fell in love with Ensenada, citing its proximity to the ocean as its main attraction. Instead of going abroad to study at a time of political turmoil in Mexico, he became involved with the local Japanese community through his thesis advisor, whose sister was running a company that worked with Japanese and Korean fishing boats and also processed and exported fish to Japan. 'She opened my path into the fishing business,' Hernández explains. But the ocean signifies more than the sum of its fish. 'So in this Japanese way, the ocean means not only poetry and beauty to me, and immensity; it also is a way to live,' he

says. 'Everything I have, everything you can see, comes from the ocean.' His Japanese colleagues taught him 'to feel respect for the ocean, to feel respect for the fish ... Their philosophy is not only economic'. He finds inspiration in the principles of Buddhism, saying, 'If you can live like the Dalai Lama, if you can live one day without doing any harm to anyone, that is a good day.'

So, as well as teaching chemistry, Hernández is a fish merchant who supplies some of the best restaurants in Mexico. His business philosophy can be summed up this way: 'If you already sacrificed an animal, the least you can do is to respect, to honour and to consume it with pride ... This is something that they don't teach you at school, of course.' Among other things, his company ships live lobsters, as well as several varieties of tuna, to China, Taiwan and Hong Kong. 'The minimum size they get for bluefin is about 10 kilos,' he explains when discussing quotas. 'And they can get 40-, 50-, 60-, 80-kilo tuna. Then they just have to prepare [them] to be ready. When I say "ready", [what I mean] is [for the fish] to have the right amount of fat for Japan.' A straight sale in Japan might gross US$25 or $28 per kilo, though auction prices can reach more than double those amounts. The rich fishing stock present in the Pacific and the Sea of Cortés is down to two factors. 'One: the currents,' Hernández notes. 'There are the cold currents from the north, with a lot of nutrients, a lot of minerals. They come like a river ... and they surge up here ... and with this amount of light and nutrients there is a lot of plankton.' And where a lot of plankton is present, there may not be many species, but there is (this is the second factor) plenty of biomass, and rich pickings to be had as a result – a true sea of plenty.

(left) **Ezequiel Hernández Zuñiga surveying fishing boats in Sauzal's small harbour; and** (facing page) **Laura and Ezequiel at home in Ensenada with their Rottweiler, obtained by Ezequiel in exchange for two wild turkeys**

(above, top right & right) **Laura and Ezequiel at home preparing** *burros* **of** *centolla* **(king crab) over hot coals using their outdoor oven. Crabs are bottom-feeders, eating dead fish and shrimp. 'From dead things come delicious things,' Ezequiel notes;** (bottom right) **Cheese and dessert at the Hernández home. Ezequiel enjoys dried bananas with his cheese; and** (facing page) **A brilliantly coloured, freshly caught** *centolla* **at the marina in Sauzal. King crabs can vary in weight from 2 to 6 kilos**

Alfredo Acosta
Hotelier & Vineyard Owner, Encuentro Guadalupe, Valle de Guadalupe, Baja California

Encuentro Guadalupe – recipient of many awards – consists of fifty-eight 'eco-lofts' built into a hillside along with a restaurant, a swimming pool and an eco-villa, all surrounded by vineyards. In addition to running the hotel, owner Alfredo Acosta and his wife make wine for their own cellar and as gifts for friends, using a blend of Cabernet Sauvignon, Cabernet Franc, Malbec, Nebbiolo, Merlot and Petite Sirah grapes. 'We have dug deep into the soil and have discovered a drinkable wine,' Acosta explains.

The hotel was conceived by Acosta with fellow entrepreneur Juan Yi; the pair drafted in architects and designers from Gracia Studio to realise their concept. Gracia Studio favours the creation of economical architecture by devising flexible modular buildings. Explaining that the hotel's rooms are intentionally small and simple in order to encourage guests to get out and enjoy the valley's natural beauty, Acosta declares: 'The most beautiful things on earth are created by nature, not built by men.' The lofts' luxury decor features clean lines, sharp industrial accents, retro Edison light bulbs and sliding melamine doors, all evocative of on-trend urban decor. Wine tastings can be arranged daily, and the style of cooking is described as resolutely 'anti-resort'. 'We try not to intervene with the natural environment and put all our love into maintaining the land,' Acosta notes. 'I am from Baja, born in Baja, and I'm trying to show Baja to the world in another way.'

Wine-making began in Mexico in the sixteenth century with the arrival of the Spanish, who brought vines with them from Europe; in fact, Mexico is the oldest wine-growing region in the Americas. From the late seventeenth century until Independence, wine-making was either prohibited or pursued on a limited scale, with the exception of production for use in churches. Following Independence, production rose, especially in the late nineteenth and early twentieth centuries, with European immigrants other than the Spanish helping to promote Mexican wine. Since the 1980s, both quality and quantity have increased, although competition from foreign wineries and high taxes make competition difficult. Interest in Mexican wine, especially in major cities and tourist areas, has grown, and various wineries have won international awards. Of the country's three major wine-producing areas, Baja California is the most active, and it is heavily promoted as a destination for oenotourism.

Acosta notes that wine-growing began in the area in part due to the climate, which 'is like the Mediterranean. You need good soil to grow the vines'. He has named each of his vintages after one of his children, explaining that each one is 'blended with the soul of that person' in mind. He is in the wine-making and hospitality game for the long term, prioritising the environment and emphasising the importance of 'thinking globally while starting locally'. 'The wine is the craft of the land here,' he adds. '[We may have] a small production, but you can taste all the little histories, the beautiful histories, of all the producers here.'

(previous page) **Hotel owners Alfredo Acosta and his wife Ana Laura outside their wine cellar at Encuentro Guadalupe,** and (above) **testing wine from their vineyard with chef Omar Valenzuela and winemaker Alejandro Ceceña. The boutique hotel's terrace,** where (right) **bacon and eggs are on offer for breakfast, provides stunning views of the 94-hectare property dotted** (facing page) **with environmentally neutral guest cabins**

Juan Chiquito García
Winemaker, Ejido El Porvenir, Valle de Guadalupe, Baja California

Seventy-year-old Juan Chiquito García, who was born in the Valle de Santiago de Guanajuato, arrived in the Valle de Guadalupe more than forty-five years ago 'looking for life'. Fifteen years ago he bought his 2-hectare property on which he grows grapevines, pomegranates, olives, peaches, pears, guavas and citrus, most of which he gives away. Chiquito produces ten *barricas* of organic wine per year (each barrel makes seven hundred bottles). He has no idea how many bottles he has sold or how much money he has earned.

'I just work,' Chiquito explains. 'I love to grow maize and watermelons, but this year the weather has changed ... The warmth does not want to arrive ... We used to pick the grapes in mid-August. Now [we do it] in September.' Shifts in weather patterns inevitably have an impact on wine-growing areas like Baja California, which produces 90 per cent of Mexico's wine. 'In June, July it is hot ... but now ... it doesn't seem to want to get hot; at night it's very cold,' Chiquito says. He observes the seasons shifting slowly: 'When I first got to the valley, we would press the grapes around August 15th or 20th. Now for some years we have done the pressing ... starting in August and finishing in September.'

Chiquito has about twenty regular clients who come to buy his wine. The small scale of his business seems to suit him perfectly. 'I am getting older,' he notes. 'One becomes calmer. I've always been calm, that's why I lasted ... a long time.' His advice to his eight children: 'Dedicate yourself to the land.'

(facing page) **Juan Chiquito García holding his organic wine up to the light, and** (above) **inspecting his vines. His wine is consumed mostly by friends and family.** (left) **Chiquito and his tractor at his *rancho***

Doña Sabina Bandera, '*La Guerrerense*'
Mariscos La Guerrerense, Ensenada, Baja California

Doña Sabina Bandera has been running her food truck since the 1960s. When the American celebrity chef Anthony Bourdain visited her in Ensenada, he described her menu as 'the best street food on the planet', going on to offer her a place as a vendor in his upcoming Bourdain Market project in New York City.

Doña Sabina's home state of Guerrero bases its economy on agriculture and the raising of livestock, and is known for such dishes as *pozole* (a traditional stew) and *relleno de cerdo*. Before moving to Ensenada, she worked in the fields and had no familiarity with seafood. It was her in-laws who founded Mariscos La Guerrerense; she took over from them later. 'I fell in love with Ensenada,' the street chef says of her adopted town. In addition to seafood tostadas, the menu features a traditional white *pozole*, a savoury red seafood *pozole*, and Ensenada-style fish and shrimp tacos. Vintner Hugo d'Acosta designed three wines to accompany *Doña* Sabina's dishes, a *blanco*, a *tinto* and a *rosado*. Craft beers from Agua Mala are also available, as are sodas and homemade *aguas naturales*.

Doña Sabina's truck is adorned with photographs of her famous customers and surrounded by metal chillers containing fresh clams, octopus, sea urchins, prawns and oysters. Her most popular offering (and her personal favourite because it is packed with protein and contrasts raw with cooked textures) is a sea urchin and Pismo clam tostada, which claimed the Showmanship Prize at the 2011 LA Street Food Fest. Her commitment to seafood extends to using leftover clams as fertiliser for the chillies she grows herself. She buys her seafood 'over the phone' and has it delivered fresh daily, sometimes late at night. 'If I have some shrimp left over, then I slice it and tomorrow I'll make a shrimp *ceviche*,' she explains. 'If I have some octopus left over, I'll leave it for the *ceviche* [too].' When her mother taught *Doña* Sabina to cook, it seems unlikely that she ever imagined her daughter winning third place at the World Street Food Congress in Singapore (2013).

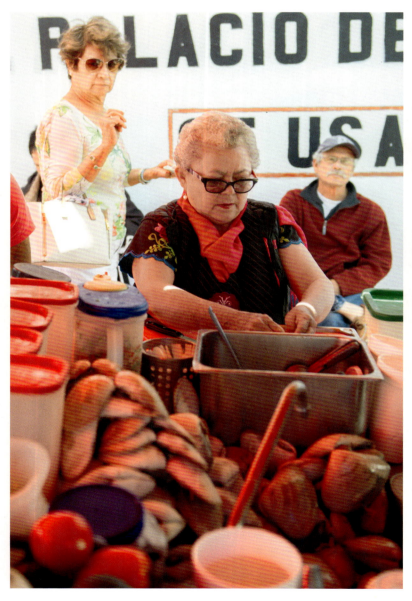

(left) ***Doña* Sabina Banderas preparing one of her world-famous tostadas amid fresh clams and** (facing page) **oysters on her food truck, Mariscos La Guerrerense, and** (above) **her most popular tostada, *erizo con almeja* – sea urchin with clams topped with one of her famous sauces**

Laura Zamora
Oenologist, Santo Tomás Winery, Valle de Santo Tomás, Baja California

'Wine is very jealous,' jokes oenologist Laura Zamora when describing the level of dedication essential to success in her chosen profession. In the course of her nearly forty-year career, she has produced a number of high-quality wines which have received awards both at home and abroad.

The winery is located 50 kilometres from Ensenada, on what is called the 'historic wine route'. 'Grapes arrived in Mexico ... when the Church's possessions were being expropriated,' Zamora explains. 'Around the period of King Philip, a decree banned people from cultivating grapes. They even destroyed many vineyards because they were competing with Spanish wine. Then the friars who came to catechise around Baja California decided to bring grapes and plant them to make the wine they used for Mass ... Vines started to grow in this area during the time of General Abelardo Rodríguez, who supported Russian families that arrived in the Valle de Guadalupe ... He gave them vine shoots ... on the condition that they would sell the grapes in Santo Tomás. That's how grape cultivation was born [here].' Zamora's goal is to be able to compete with the Spanish market, although she notes that 'the amount of wine produced in Mexico is very small. Therefore we are ... competing [on the basis of quality]. We can't compete [when it comes to] volume.'

Zamora began as a lab worker before training with an Argentinian oenologist. Then the winery sent her to Argentina, the Napa Valley and elsewhere to learn more. At the time, she was Latin America's sole female oenologist. Now there are several, and Universidad Autónoma de Baja California offers a certification programme. Asked whether women make better oenologists than men, Zamora refuses to be drawn. 'Women are more interested in aromas ... Maybe we have a little more attention to detail. However, it is not so much a matter of gender but a matter of dedication ... The most important stage is when you harvest the grapes ... It's like having a baby; in the first months, you need to stay by the cradle ... There are procedures, of course, and quality standards that need to be respected. However, there are [also] decisions that you sometimes have to make while you are standing next to the tank.'

People employ all of their senses when tasting wines, even their hearing. 'I always say, "If what the glass is telling you when you see it coincides with what you sense with your nose, and it's backed up by what you taste in your mouth, then the wine is well done. It is a healthy wine,"' Zamora explains. 'If it looks shiny, you usually associate it with more acidity; if it looks too dark, that may indicate a bitter finish ... If all of that adds up, I say, "The wine is well done." Regardless of whether I like it or not, you know that the wine is healthy.' Her own favourite is Barbera, 'usually a fresh wine characterised by acidity. However, it is a long-life wine and very soft. It goes well with Mexican food that is based on earthy flavours like courgette flowers or *huitlacoche* [a fungus that grows on maize].' Pairing food with wine is a task Zamora admits to finding 'very difficult' due to the country's array of regional differences where ingredients and preparation methods are concerned. 'We don't have one representative wine; we have five representative wines,' she concludes.

(left) **The Santo Tomás Winery, which dates from 1888; and** (facing page) **Laura Zamora among French oak barrels of Tempranillo, Cabernet Sauvignon, Syrah, Barbera and Merlot**

Miguel Ángel Guerrero
Chef, Valle de Guadalupe, Baja California

Chef Miguel Ángel Guerrero owns four restaurants, two in Tijuana, one in Valle de Guadalupe and another in Mexicali. In addition to cooking, his passions include hunting, fishing, smoking, drinking and riding a motorcycle. Among his culinary skills he includes menu development, meat and fish butchery, kitchen management and food styling. And he has appeared on television.

Guerrero's family are descendants of Spaniards who arrived in Mexico in the 1500s. They were shepherds in the early days, and the family still have more than ten thousand sheep. 'My grandfather built a big house for the whole family: three daughters, one son and twenty cousins,' the chef says. 'During the two months we were on vacation, we lived there and had motorcycles. We had a couple of ranches where we'd go to see the sheep and cattle. On vacation, my uncles came from Spain and we'd make chorizo, *morcilla*, cheese, butter … We had our own milk. I grew up with a garden filled with vegetables and fruits. That was my beginning.' Guerrero's father took him hunting when he was just five years old, and later on his uncle took him to Baja to fish, dive and hunt for long periods. 'All these things come together in one place: the kitchen,' he explains. 'It came very naturally to me. I like to go where things are, where they're alive, and bring them to the table, to my customers. It's a way of sharing my passion for life … In the kitchen, I share my emotions with my customers.'

Guerrero only became a professional chef twenty-five years ago, however; before that he was a lawyer. 'My mum gave me some land; I was living on that land and I could have done whatever I wanted. I studied law because I was the black sheep and didn't want my mum to be mad at me,' he says. In order to impress his future wife Judith, he would write up menus and send them to her workplace. Having been wined and dined, at one point she observed, 'You know, Miguel Ángel, I see you as a chef and restaurant owner.' It was at this point that Guerrero decided to go to cooking school in Mexico City, where for the first time he encountered people who fully understood his passion for cooking.

Often away hunting or fishing with friends for days at a time, Guerrero is thus continuing a family tradition that goes back many decades. Judith Guerrero describes this hunting ethos as being based,

first of all, on respect for nature and for the times of the year that are designated as hunting season. 'Secondly,' she says, 'whatever you take from nature, you have to use it all! As the hunter, you are responsible for that animal … You are not going to leave anything on the floor. You are going to share it with everybody and bring the best out of each piece.' Her husband hunts mostly in Baja California, his quarry consisting of doves, quails, pheasants, ducks, geese, rabbits, bobcats and wild donkeys – the latter because they become overly possessive of water sources, preventing other animals from drinking.

Guerrero is prepared to cook and eat pretty much anything, being fond of culinary experimentation and the self-proclaimed inventor of the Baja Med style of cookery. 'The produce of Baja is the main actor in this cuisine,' he explains. 'Produce from the sea, from the ground, from the land. Everything that we produce here – it can be abalone or lobster, it can be marlin, it can be tuna, it can be lamb, it can be beef – whatever we produce here is produced the same way … In Baja we have three major influences. First is the Mexican one … Second is the Mediterranean one; we live in a Mediterranean climate here … When I go to Europe, I bring back seeds and plant them. We produce olive oil, vegetables, baby vegetables, all the herbs. Ninety-five per cent of the wine in Mexico comes from Baja … The third influence is Asian. Mexicali is 200 kilometres from here, and there is a big Chinese population there … There are also Japanese with their sushi all over Baja.'

More specifically, Guerrero describes his personal style this way: 'Some [of my dishes] represent myself; some of my dishes have one or two influences. What is always constant is the produce, which has to be from Baja.' Despite being a maverick, or perhaps because of it, he expresses little interest in Michelin stars or other food-industry awards, saying, 'There are too many rules, and I am a man with no rules. They are going to tell me, "You need to do this, this, that." I don't think so.' The best thing about owning a restaurant, he feels, is 'being able to share my emotions with the customers. When I bring things from my garden (I have gardens for my restaurants) – vegetables and spices and herbs and fish, or venison, quails – then try to cook them and share them … For me, there's nothing better.'

(far left) **A 10-kilo grouper from chef Miguel Ángel Guerrero's spear-fishing trip, laid out on his kitchen table; its cheeks, tail, breast and fins will be grilled over mesquite with vegetables. The grouper may feed up to twenty people.** (left) **Guerrero preparing for a hunting trip, with his wife Judith and the family dog; and** (facing page) **Judith picking lavender in their garden**

Lorries transporting an
enormous fishing net
in the port of El Sauzal,
Ensenada

263

Hidalgo: *Bugs & Pasties*

Bugs, Cornishmen and politicians are a few of the high points in the history of this picturesque state. Hidalgo was created in 1869 by Benito Juárez and named after Miguel Hidalgo y Costilla, the initiator of the Mexican War of Independence. Hidalgo's *Grito de Dolores* set in train the movement that culminated in Mexican independence. The cross-currents of history have a way of getting your attention in this vast country; for example, the state of Hidalgo is also famous for its Cornish, Italian and Sephardic Jewish communities, each of which brought their culinary traditions with them. The Cornish community came over in the nineteenth century to work in the region's ancient tin mines, at the time its economic mainstay. *Paste*, or pasties, are an adaptation of their English West Country culinary cousins, Mexicanised with a variety of fillings.

Another early settler was the Jewish conquistador Alonso de Avila. Avila, who was reputed to have worn a star of David hidden under his breastplate, joined forces with Hernán Cortés to escape the Spanish Inquisition and was quickly elevated to the Mayoralty of Veracruz. Jews had first settled in Hidalgo in the sixteenth century, bringing their Iberian expertise in international trade with them along with sheep and livestock, which had not existed before in New Spain. *Barbacoa* is the dish for which the state is noted. A whole lamb is marinated for two days prior to burial in an earthen oven and is left to cook overnight. The ritual is both symbolic and mouth-watering, yet nothing prepares the palate for the tastes in store. Heavy breakfast bowls of marinade broth, sipped together with delectable morsels of tenderised lamb wrapped in a tortilla and garnished with *habanero* salsa, quickly makes you forget the cold, drizzly night before.

My first encounter with *barbacoa* was at El Hidalguense Restaurant in Mexico City, at the very start of this culinary quest. Moisés Rodríguez Vargas, the charming chef and owner, spends half the week on his sheep farm in Hidalgo preparing lambs for kosher slaughter, and the remainder cooking up a storm of tastes in his traditional eatery in Cuauhtémoc. It was there that I was first confronted by plates of *escamoles* (ant eggs) and maguey larvae, expensive delicacies that are an acquired taste for the visitor but much sought after by Mexicans of all stripes, if they can afford them.

Caviar-priced worms, bugs and other creepy-crawlies were a mainstay of Mesoamerican cultures. These protein-rich delicacies are a speciality of Hidalgo, where active 'cultivation' and 'breeding' go on with local expertise acquired before the time of the Aztecs. Entomophagy, according to some nutritionists, is the food salvation for the human race as we race towards the planet's ten-billion population marker. While the rural poor still rely on insects to supplement their diets in Mexico, received opinion in urban areas has opened the way for top-tier restaurants to offer the same delights on their menus. Best get used to eating worms, ants, grasshoppers, locusts and the like. Not only are they extremely good for you, but they are also darned tasty.

Barbacoa Hidalguense
Actopan, Hidalgo

(previous spread) **The former mining town of Real del Monte in Hidalgo, whose architecture was influenced by both Spanish and English settlers**

(above) **Silvestre Santiago and Leonor Mejía preparing lamb** *barbacoa* **in Actopan**

(top left) **Hot coals being prepared for the giant stockpot** (top middle) **that will collect the juices from the meat as it cooks;** (top right) **Lamb laid atop maguey** leaves and then covered (above left)**. The following morning, a delicious broth is revealed** (above middle)**, which is then served together with the lamb** (above right) **at Mejía's restaurant**

(following spread, left) **Empty maize husks; and** (following spread, right) **Paper flowers brightening a table**

Armando Soria
Insect Farmer, Puerto México, San Agustín Tlaxiaca, Hidalgo

The Aztecs and other ancient civilisations flourished for centuries on a diet that routinely included grubs, grasshoppers and other edible invertebrates; some food experts today believe that entomophagy is the key to feeding the world's rapidly growing population. While insects are still eaten (largely out of necessity) in Mexico's poor rural communities, until recently mainstream diners regarded insect-eating with disgust. Now, however, with high-end restaurants exploring the full range of traditional prehispanic foods, top chefs are introducing insects to their menus. High in protein, iron, amino acids, calcium, and omega 3 and 6, insects are also low in calories. Aside from promoting good health, entomophagy is beneficial for the planet due to insects' efficiency when it comes to converting plant into animal protein. But because supplies are irregular and prices high, they remain a delicacy in Mexico. A notable exception are the ubiquitous and inexpensive *chapulines* – grasshoppers or crickets – that are typically sautéed with salt, chilli, lime and garlic and rolled in tacos with guacamole or eaten by the handful. Mexico has as many as 550 species of edible insects, more than any other country in the world. Most are caught wild, not farmed, and then sold at regional markets or trucked into the city.

Armando Soria, who has dedicated his life to the study of insects in the Mezquital Valley (an area that in pre-colonial times had 'no fruit, no animals … so they lived off everything they could find: roots, flowers, insects, snakes'), is one of those who believe that they offer a solution to the problem of world hunger. Hoping to farm *escamoles*, or ant larvae, for use in cooking, in 2013 Soria launched an experiment to transplant larvae intact in their nests while providing them with sufficient food. The difficulty of farming ants is summed up by the fact that nobody knows what an ant eats. 'It's notorious, that thing!' Soria exclaims. 'If we get that knowledge, it will permit us to establish [nests] maybe 10 metres from each other … That moment will be so important for the people in this place, for people to eat.' Although his harvests to date have been modest, he has plans to expand. In the state of Hidalgo, he points out, nests are routinely destroyed by collectors who leave the colonies exposed to the elements after harvesting the larvae. Which, given the nutritional benefits and tastiness of *escamoles*, is extremely unfortunate.

Born in Mexico City, Soria's family moved to Hidalgo, where he has continued to live. He estimates that there are about forty-seven insects in Mexico that can be considered as delicacies. Their flavours, he says, cannot be compared with anything else. Given the choice, he admits that he himself prefers to eat meat, which is 'not good because insects contain a lot of protein [but] meat can combine with other, stronger flavours'. *Escamoles*, for example, contain between 68 and 74 per cent protein compared to beef, which contains only 17 per cent. In fact, they are so high in protein that you can only eat about 150 grams of them per day; any more and the human body becomes unable to process the protein. They possess the alleged added value of acting as aphrodisiacs. The perfect drink to accompany *escamoles* or other insects, Soria notes, is mezcal – completing the ingredients for a tasty and invigorating snack.

(left) **Xahues**, insects used for salsas and eaten fried in season. Armando Soria has been planting *retama* trees, which the *xahues* favour, in order to support the insect population. (facing page) Soria, who has dedicated his life to the study of insects, taking a break at his friend Mauro Vargas Cero's *tinacal* in Puerto México, where Vargas makes pulque and stores saddles

(left) **The Mezquital Valley, where, Soria says, people believe that 'if it moves, eat it';** (below left) **Vargas and Soria enjoying some pulque outside Vargas' home. Vargas learned how to make pulque from his father and regularly finds** *gusanos de maguey* **(maguey worms) among the leaves.** (bottom) **Soria holding a maguey worm, which can be eaten alive but is best when fried** (facing page) **and served in tacos**

Estado de México: *Aztec Crossroads*

The country is called Mexico, Estado de México is called Mexico, and, almost always, Mexico City is referred to as Mexico. To add to the confusion, there is no reference to Mexico City on any map of the country, as it was referred to as Distrito Federal – DF for short. That's until DF was abolished on January 29, 2016! Mexico City is now an autonomous political entity in addition to being the national capital and the most populous state in the country.

Mexico City only became the new country's capital after independence, its territory separated from the state of the same name and later broken up to form another three: Hidalgo, Guerrero and Morelos. Confused? No need, as the denonym for the people of the state is *mexiquense*, as distinct from *mexicano*, actual Mexicans. Everything clear now?

Mexico (*Mēxihco*), the Nahuatl name for the Valley of Mexico where the three cities (Tenochtitlán, Texcoco and Tlatelolco) of Mexica (*Mēxihcah*) of the Triple Alliance were originally located, is mostly in present-day Estado de México. The Mexica founded Tenochtitlán and Tlatelolco on raised islets in Lake Texoco around the thirteenth century, and it is on these lands that present-day Mexico City is situated. Little did the ancients imagine that their cities would be transformed into the monstrous sprawl of today. Scholars and historians differ as to the exact origins of the name Mexico. The accepted derivatives are *metztli* (moon) and *xictla* (navel). *Meshico* was also the name of the Templo Mayor of Tenochtitlán, (Place of the Mexi), a deity that originated as a plant (corn) and then changed into a bird.

Travelling through Mexico is like travelling through time: there is just so much of the old, the traditional and the new, reverentially maintained by both citizenry and government, that its often hard to imagine yourself in the present moment. When you think that the oldest civilisation in Estado de México dates back to 900 BC, with the Pyramids of the Sun and the Moon built around 100 BC, it becomes a bit like a time machine in which you are whisked from one age to another, on and off the country's highways and byways.

Perhaps travel to the charming alpine town of Valle de Bravo, which dates back to the Spaniards, and be mesmerised by the stunning scenery, with the odd environmental knight trying to restore the valley to its pristine origins. You will come upon Dr Dieter le Noir, of German origin with a French-sounding name and every bit a Mexican, determined to renew a broken land (a small parcel of which he bought seventeen years ago and has since rejuvenated through the practice of permaculture) and re-establish its fertility to produce a hundred different species of medicinal plants, which he sells and uses in his Mexico City medical practice. Co-founder of Fundación Valle la Paz, Dr le Noir is dedicated to the development of rural projects to integrate health, agriculture and education. A modern-day missionary of sorts, he believes that Mexico's principal cause of illness is poor nutrition. 'Our whole nature is being destroyed,' he declaims in Teutonic tones. 'Mexico is importing approximately half of all the food they need from the United States and other places, so they are losing their own food culture.' As a consequence, the good doctor believes, the very health of the country is at risk.

Pablo Salas
Chef, Amaranta, Toluca, Estado de México

Pablo Salas is a delegate of the Conservatory of Mexican Gastronomic Culture (CCGM), the agency responsible for the promotion and dissemination of Mexican cuisine as Intangible Cultural Heritage of Humanity by UNESCO. Also a member of the Mexican Cuisine Collective, he gives cooking classes all over the country, and has been a juror and speaker at culinary competitions, conferences and festivals in Mexico, the US and Canada.

Born in Toluca in 1980, Salas fell in love with tattoos and piercings as a teenager before discovering that his 'true passion' involved preparing meals for his family and friends. After studying at the Centro Culinario Ambrosia in Mexico City, in 2002 he opened a pastry shop in Toluca. Over time he discovered a rich local cuisine that had been largely ignored and decided to focus on it, opening Amaranta in 2010. Named one of Latin America's fifty best restaurants in 2014, Amaranta has pork at the heart of its menu. Salas sources his Iberian pigs from a farm in Lerma or from markets in Toluca and Ixtlahuaca. He cultivates vegetables, fruit and herbs on his own plot; in fact, 95 per cent of the products used at Amaranta come from Estado de México. In addition to ensuring freshness, this means that supplies are less costly. 'Today you have to offer what you have, and what you have is a fresh product,' Salas explains. Recent menu changes have included the addition of several vegetarian options and new sauces; Salas tends not to use deep-sea fish as it is not a product of Estado de México, using local fresh-water trout instead. 'I cook what I want to, but I also have to listen to my clients,' he says. 'I have a lot of people from Mexico City that

go to my restaurant. They are reading a lot about what is happening right now in the gastronomy world. They want to see some new things, so I listen to them. I try to read, to change my menu and show something new with my produce.'

Salas has as many as twenty-five cooks working alongside him at any one time, which, given that his restaurant seats fifty, offers an exceptional chef-to-client ratio. 'We have a lot of cooks, and a lot of people are interested in our food,' he explains. 'So this [approach] is growing, and I have a lot of people from other states.' He takes his fame with a pinch of salt. When asked how it feels to be sought after in the sometimes cut-throat culinary world, he replies that he does not particularly notice it, adding, 'I feel like I have to work every day.' His philosophy is 'to first use the best products of our state, then the best products of Mexico, and then the best products of the world, always with a Mexican touch'. Spreading the word to budding culinary students is of critical importance to Salas, who says, 'It's huge, our gastronomy. I don't even know it all in my state ... We have a lot to show the world as a gastronomy, as a culture and as a country.' Everyday routine holds no interest for this young chef: 'To keep doing the same thing all the time, I would be stuck ... I saw the farm-to-table idea growing a lot [but] I don't like to copy those things ... So we are trying to keep moving.' A symbol of change is the absence of televisions in the restaurant. 'We used to have TVs because people used to watch soccer there,' Salas explains. 'Now we don't need the TVs. Our clients changed also. [They used to come] just to see soccer; now people go to Amaranta to eat. That's what I want. It's not a bar.'

(previous spread) **The town of Ocoyoacac, whose Náhuatl name translates roughly as 'where the pines begin'**

(left) **Trainee chefs at Amaranta in Toluca. 'Chefs have to understand tradition before they can begin creating or experimenting,' Pablo Salas notes.** (facing page) **Salas in Amaranta's rooftop herb garden, which primarily supplies the restaurant with garnishes including edible flowers**

(facing page, top left) *Tacos de hueva de carpa* **(fish-egg tacos);** (facing page, top right) *Papada de cerdo* **(pig jowl);** (facing page, bottom left) *Tacos de plaza* **(tacos sold by street vendors); and** (facing page, bottom right) *Croquetas de huauzontle*

(left) **The** *zócalo* **(main square) of Toluca, Mexico's highest city,** (top left) **known for its colonial architecture; and** (above) **Salas eating a** *huarache* **from Tostadas Artesanas La Teresona, made of** *maiz moreno*, *nopales*, **red salsa, beans, cheese, onions and coriander (a** *taco de plaza*)**. The eatery, which opened eighty-five years ago in the centre of Toluca, is run by Cipriano Santa Maria Ortega (standing behind Salas)**

Luis Miguel Torres
Mushroom Enthusiast, Estado de México

(above) **Luis Miguel Torres in the forest of Ocoyoacac in search of wild mushrooms to be sold** (facing page) **at the village market**

Luis Miguel Torres is based near the Velo de la Novia waterfall in Ocoyoacac, Estado de México. As a little boy he would head into the woods to collect mushrooms, cooking them on his return home. Located in the valley of Toluca not far from Mexico City, this forest is the district's most important natural resource, generating revenue through agriculture, livestock and tourism.

Mexicans love mushrooms and consume more of them than any other country in the world with the exception of China and Japan. Seventy-five per cent of the country's mushroom varieties can be found in Estado de México. The state's cool, humid climate and protected woodland provide the perfect conditions for fungi growth. Of the 726 species of mushrooms recognised in Mexico, 256 are suitable for human consumption, although it is said that more than 200,000 undocumented varieties exist in the country.

Mushroom season extends from July into October, coinciding with the rainy or monsoon period in which most of the region's annual precipitation occurs. During the season, many of the state's residents make their living solely by picking mushrooms and selling them to local restaurants and markets. Like Torres, the mushroom hunters' knowledge and expertise are handed down from generation to generation, with many collectors working with the same chefs every year. Often they are sold by older women at weekly markets known as *tianguis*. While these markets mainly attract locals, knowledgeable chefs and expats come to fill their baskets with unique, flavoursome, inexpensive edibles. Farmed mushrooms are also on offer. One of the most renowned stands is Mercado San Juan, no 261, run by Hermelinda Guillén Vargas, who offers farmed porcini and shiitake mushrooms, drying them to ensure year-round availability. When selling wild mushrooms, vendors provide instructions for their preparation which must be followed exactly. They are mostly used in stews with the addition of garlic, tomato, *epazote* and *chile al gusto*, or served as a taco or quesadilla filling. The most commonly sold fungus is the *huitlacoche*, a dark blue-black variety that grows on maize and is similar to a truffle. Usually prepared as a quesadilla filling, it can be made into a sauce for meat or a creamed soup. While such renowned chefs as Eduardo García and Jair Téllez are mushroom enthusiasts, it is unusual to find traditional street vendors using anything but *huitlacoche*.

The ceremonial value of mushrooms in Mexico is said to have been recognised in prehispanic times, when the Mixtec, who worshipped many gods, used entheogen-based plants as part of their rituals and ceremonies. This was first documented in the Vienna Codex – otherwise known as the *Codex Vindobonensis* – from the thirteenth–fifteenth centuries, which is thought to have originated in Tilantongo in the Mixteca Alta of Oaxaca. This codex records over five hundred years of history, using pictographs to describe the mythical origins of the Mixtec universe and the rituals (associated with maize, pulque and mushrooms) that led to the first sunrise of the current era. Gods like Piltzintechuhli are shown holding mushrooms. The Aztecs also saw mushrooms as having ritualistic qualities. Using the psilocybin mushroom, which they called Teonánacatl ('flesh of the gods'), members of the upper class would take *teonanácatl* at festivals with honey or chocolate, having fasted before ingesting this prized sacrament. Although the practice was largely suppressed when the Spaniards arrived, in places such as Ozumba in Estado de México the cultural significance of mushrooms is still alive, helping preserve traditional ethno-biological knowledge.

(left) **A policeman enjoying a waterfall break in the forest of Ocoyoacac; and** (below) **Torres continuing his search** (bottom left)

(left) **Torres and Lucio Guerrero visiting Guerrero's stables on the edge of the forest, and** (top & above) **enjoying a quesadilla at Lupita Sánchez's Miscelánea Las Villas**

(following spread, left) **Colourful *pepitorias* (half-moon wafers with pumpkin seeds and amaranth) are kept together with sticky honey, enticing visitors into a sweet shop in Toluca.** (following spread, right) **Candied papaya attracting some bees**

Dr Dieter le Noir
Physician & Co-founder, Fundación Valle la Paz, Valle de Bravo, Estado de México

Dr Dieter le Noir spends most of his time on his estate except for two days each week, when he sees patients in Mexico City. Having studied integrative medicine in the US, India and Germany, as well as anthroposophic medicine and biodynamic agriculture in Switzerland, Dr le Noir co-founded Sanandi, a company that produces food supplements, herbal remedies and planted-based homeopathic medicines. He is also a co-founder of the Fundación Valle la Paz, which is dedicated to the development of rural projects to integrate health, agriculture and education.

'This land was broken,' Dr le Noir says of his estate, which he purchased sixteen years ago with his brother. 'With the guidance of permaculture, we re-established the fertility of the soil, which had been destroyed by toxic chemicals. This took three, four years ... Now we are growing more than a hundred different species of medicinal plants.' In his practice, his emphasis is on preventative medicine rather than the treating of disease; he believes that in Mexico the main cause of illness is poor nutrition. 'Our whole nature is being destroyed, and Mexican people are eating less and less diverse food,' he points out. 'Mexico is importing approximately half of all the food they need from the United States and other places, so they are losing their own food culture. With this, a big cascade of diseases is coming. What we are trying to do is to give people plant-based medicine which can help them to detox the liver, help the pancreas, help sugar problems and other diseases.' Dr le Noir's ultimate aim is 'to recreate a culture and agriculture based on fertile, healthy soil, and from there to bring medicines and also food – integral foods, real foods – back into the Mexican diet'. He blames the profit motive, big pharma and industrial-scale monoculture for the destruction of the country's traditional agricultural values, insisting that the correct response to 'catastrophic bio-collapse' will never be more chemicals and overproduction.

Although Mexico was always a poor country, Dr le Noir believes that it was a healthy one. 'The rivers were clean, their teeth were perfect, children were strong. Now you see twelve-, thirteen-year-old children with big dental problems and metabolic disorders. These should not occur until you are fifty years old. So you see the pathology ... more and more in young people. That is a consequence of the food system and the destructive forces we are applying to nature.' The country's traditional poly-culture was maize-based, 'the backbone of the Mexican spirit'. Today, however, 'Mexico imports 50 per cent of their corn from the United States, 60 or 70 per cent of which is genetically manipulated, with enormous allergenic problems of which we aren't even aware, because [the whole thing] is an experiment. We don't know the consequences of what we have done. When using biodiversity, you do more than just cultivation. "Cultivate", "culture", come from the same root, which is "cultured", the "culture" of everything. Without culture, we don't have health. That is why you say that agriculture is the beginning of all cultures ... We started from a different grass here in Mexico seven thousand years ago, and we cultivated that grass to give hundreds of species of maize, for all altitudes. We nourished an entire continent. That is "culture" that is "cultivated", and it's what we need to see again: culture and cultivation need to be part of Mexico, not just producing television for the US market.' Modern-day meat production also incurs Dr le Noir's wrath. 'Our meat system is pure torture, is violent from the beginning to the end,' he says, 'and probably very, very toxic to the human body and human consciousness, because we are incorporating a suffering which is much closer to us. As a soul, [an animal] has feelings, and this torture [involves] how we raise them and how we kill them and how we eat them. In the car, in a hamburger! The new culture says, "Eat your hamburger!" You don't even know that tragedy is behind what you eat.'

(right) **A path at the lush Fundación Flor de la Paz winds through medicinal gardens which** (facing page) **Dr Dieter le Noir has spent years cultivating**

(above) **Terraces of plants, the lab, the dryer, the compost and worm farm, and the irrigation system at Rancho La Paz;** (left) **An apiary at the Fundación. Dr le Noir is working with academics to save Mexico's only colony of** *Melipona faciata*, **a species of bee. He also has an apiary for the world's smallest bee.** (below) **Staff at work at a** *parota*-**wood table, packing herbal remedies including loose-leaf teas, oils, balms, herbal extracts and herb-infused honey**

(above) **Dr le Noir's dining room, complete with a wood burner which he lights to read by. He spends three days a week at the ranch but would happily spend all of his time there** (right) **with his dog Bruno**

(left) **Staff picking marigolds, which are used for herbal remedies such as 'Deep Nourishing Cream';** (right) **Felicia Luis carrying part of the harvest in a basket made of** *ocojal* **(Mexican pine);** (below) **María Martínez picking** *cedrón* **(lemon verbena) on one of the terraces; and** (far right) **A field of** *toronjil* **(giant Mexican hyssop), a native plant used as a relaxation aid and to treat digestive problems**

San Luis Potosí: *Peyote Trails*

Some of Mexico's states are just too beautiful to fit into a short description; San Luis Potosí is a keen contender. One of the largest and oldest states, with huge deposits of gold and silver first discovered in 1592, it is also one of the country's richest sectors.

The present-day territory of San Luis Potosí includes the two prehispanic cultural areas of Aridoamerica and Mesoamerica. The early Spanish settlers suffered considerable grief until peace (a euphemism in those parts for the longest time) was established in 1591, thus ending their war with the semi-nomadic Chichimeca. Positioned on the Mexican Plateau, the state is divided between the Sierra Madre Occidental, semi-arid landscapes and fully tropical climates with an abundance of flora and fauna. Though the land is agriculturally unproductive, some 20 per cent of the population are employed to grow maize, beans, sugarcane and coffee, and to harvest *tuna*, the delicious fruit of a cactus plant. The Spaniards first called the state's eponymous capital 'El Gran Tunal' due to the abundance of prickly pear, also known as the Barbary or Indian fig, which had been consumed in the region since before the birth of Christ. The unprepossessing fruit has been used through the ages to treat respiratory conditions, ease diarrhoea, treat wounds and relax aching muscles. Prickly pear cacti are a common ingredient in Mexican cuisine, with the *nopales* (pads) sold fresh, cleansed of their spikes. Sliced *nopales* have a mucilaginous texture yet are delicious in salads or *tacos*. *Tuna* is tasty on its own or in frozen margaritas.

Speaking of which, one of the best margaritas I have ever tasted was in Real de Catorce, an old mining station at an altitude of 2,800 metres, reached (in converted 1940s jeeps!) via some of the hairiest bends on the steepest road anyone's ever driven up. The partially abandoned town is home to a community of Huichol shamans and an increasing number of international hippies in search of spiritual energy, with a little help from the peyote plants found on the arid plains below. The Huichol originated in San Luis Potosí but were pushed west into the Sierra Madre Occidental. From there they travel on foot every year back to Real de Catorce, their spiritual centre, harvesting large crops of hallucinogenic peyote for use in traditional ceremonies during the course of the year. Although peyote is legally banned and a protected plant species in Mexico, the Huichol are permitted to use it.

Edward James, a contemporary acolyte of the spiritual journey, found his Surrealist Shangri-La in Xilitla, tucked away in the Sierra Madre Oriental and home to the Huastecs, indigenous Mesoamericans whose origins can be traced back to 100 BC. Poet, artist, patron and libertine, James was born into money and spent liberally in pursuit of a legendary lifestyle, which included nurturing the Surrealist movement in the late 1930s. Visiting his ghost in Las Pozas – his 30-hectare subtropical garden nestled at 600 metres above sea level complete with pools, waterfalls and follies – would inspire anyone (with or without the help of peyote) to commune with the dead. James passed away in 1984, having created a multi-million-dollar Surrealist sculpture park without compare in the jungle, including a concrete lift to nowhere and a purpose-built steel home for his pet boa constrictor.

The Peyote Trail
Real de Catorce, San Luis Potosí

There are some magical places where a visitor feels a sense of the past and the presence of an inexplicable spiritual force. Real de Catorce is just such a place. An abandoned mining town 2,750 metres above sea level, the only access route is through a 2-kilometre-long tunnel, unless you are adventurous enough to hazard one of the world's ten most dangerous mountain roads.

Today, Real de Catorce is a shadow of its former self. Founded in 1779, the frontier town became one of the New World's greatest silver-mining centres. The Klondike atmosphere attracted all kinds of fortune seekers to a site with no water. With no government either, anarchy ensued among the thousands of get-rich-quick characters, labourers and sundry inhabitants. In its heyday (end of the nineteenth/beginning of the twentieth century), the town boasted a *palenque* for cockfighting as well as a bullring. Fine European wines and the latest fashion items were available in abundance.

The mines were soon exhausted, and the once-bustling town died along with them. Today, some three thousand people cling to an existence born of adventure tourism, international hippies drawn by the desert ambience and the peyote, and Huichol selling handmade trinkets. The Huichol (or Wixárikas, as they prefer to be called) trek back to their spiritual homeland every year, setting out on foot from as far afield as Nayarit, Durango and Jalisco, harvesting peyote along the way, especially around desert scrubland in San Louis Potosí, where the best peyote is found. They then congregate on their sacred mountain, Wirikuta.

Peyote, a small cactus with psychotropic qualities, has been used for the last fifty-five hundred years by the Wixárikas in religious and spiritual rituals. Although banned from cultivation and consumption in Mexico (it is illegal to pick the cactus, let alone consume the plant), peyote use is permitted to the Wixárikas by a legal exemption. Thus they are able to conduct their timeless practices away from prying eyes on the Cerro Quemado, a ceremonial centre where, according to their ancestral beliefs, the birthplace of their Tatewari, or 'grandfather fire', is located. Peyote, the fire that has stoked these psychedelic ceremonies and transcendental experiences, is also used widely for medicinal purposes. *Peyōtl*, as it is known in Nahuatl, can mean 'divine messenger' – hence the attraction of the town to spiritual wanderers. Declared a *Pueblo Mágico* in 2001, Real de Catorce is slowly pulling itself out of the dead zone and seeing its two-hundred-year-old cobblestone streets come alive again to a gabble of strange languages, this time spoken by a different class of piratical adventurer.

(previous spread) **Carlos Kelvin at the side of the tracks as '*La Bestia*' approaches Vanegas, San Luis Potosí. Kelvin, who claimed to be a** *chiapaneco*, **was trying to make his way home after being deported back to Mexico from the US for the second time.** *La Bestia* **(sometimes referred to as the 'Death Train') is known for being very dangerous, as hundreds of migrants lose life or limb in an attempt to hitch a ride atop its carriages**

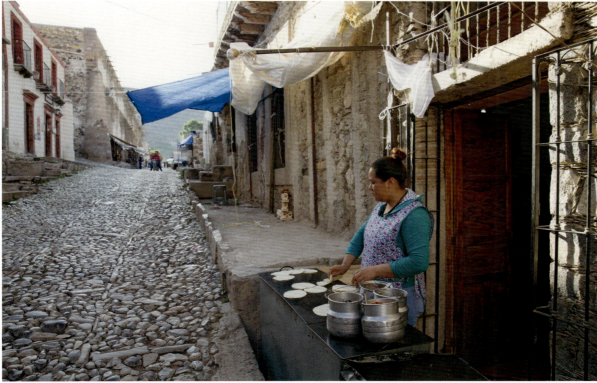

(facing page) **As if untouched by the hand of time, an elderly man carries a bale of hay in what was, until recently, an abandoned town.** (left) **A woman selling tortillas on the street in the early morning in Real de Catorce** (above), a **former mining town and Huichol pilgrimage site**

(left) **Cristino Rodríguez Hernández** eating *biznaga cabuchera*; cactus flowers are often used in cooking in the region. The *cabuche* bud must be cut before flowering as the taste turns bitter later on.
(below) **The famed peyote cactus**

(left) **Two *campesinos* travelling by mule along the dangerously steep road to Real de Catorce, much as they have for centuries.** (above) **The Sierra de Catorce was home to history's greatest silver mines,** and (top) **remains a spiritual and ecological reserve for the Wixárikas, also known as the Huichol**

(above) **Belén Aguirre and her son Marcelino** having *sopa de médula* (bone-marrow soup) for breakfast at Gorditas Doña Coque in Real de Catorce; (top) **Huichol family selling crafts;** and (right) **Two girls in traditional Huichol dress gossiping over a Coke**

(facing page) Descendants of the Aztecs and other more ancient peoples, the striking, colourfully dressed Huichol have lived in the Sierra de Catorce for at least fifteen thousand years

The Cascada de
Tamul, Aquismón, north
of the archaeological site
of Tamtoc, is the state's
biggest, most impressive
waterfall, tumbling from
a height of 105 metres
and reaching a width of
up to 300 metres

Edward James
Surrealist Visionary & Poet, Las Pozas, Xilitla, San Luis Potosí

Salvador Dalí once remarked to Sigmund Freud, 'Edward James is crazier than all the Surrealists put together. They pretend, but he is the real thing.' James (1907–1984), an eccentric English poet, artist and patron of the Surrealist movement, was educated in England and Switzerland. He sponsored Dalí for the whole of 1938; provided practical assistance for artists such as René Magritte; supported *Minotaure*, a Surrealist magazine published in Paris by Albert Skira; and commissioned three ballets from choreographer George Balanchine. James counted among his friends Noël Coward, Aldous Huxley, Humphrey Bogart and Bette Davis. His art collection included works by masters from Hieronymus Bosch, Giorgio de Chirico, Paul Klee and Leonora Carrington to Picasso and Giacometti.

James' first encounter with the mountain paradise of Las Pozas occurred in 1945. While swimming, his companion Roland McKenzie emerged from the water and startled a throng of colourful butterflies which then settled on his body. James interpreted this as a mystical sign. So, the following year, he acquired a coffee plantation near Xilitla, registering it in the name of his friend and guide Plutarco Gastelum, who would later become the foreman and overseer of construction there. Between 1946 and 1960, James had orchids planted and a number of exotic birds and animals took up residence. A frost in 1962 destroyed many of the orchids, so James decided to start building a sculpture garden. The garden's design was inspired by the orchids and other jungle vegetation combined with Surrealist architectural elements.

In the 1970s, James dedicated even more of his resources to his 'Surrealist Xanadu', spending millions of dollars and employing hundreds of masons, artisans and local craftsmen, becoming the biggest employer in the village. He would sketch his ideas on a notepad, and his assistants would carve wooden moulds using machetes, axes and knives. Concrete would then be poured into the moulds. Over the years, the sculptures gradually merged to become a random city, its structures in dialogue with its natural surroundings. Three-dimensional elements include concrete hands and heads, stone snakes and an eye-shaped bathtub in which James used to bathe, surrounded by carp, in 'the white of the eye'. He named some of these structures and had others deliberately left unfinished.

Today, Las Pozas comprises more than 30 semi-tropical hectares on the side of a mountain dotted with nine spring-fed pools – *pozas* – that flow into a small river. James spent an estimated US$5 million on the place (more than US$20 million in today's money). Since 1987 the property has been kept open to the public by the son of James' friend Gastelum. '[James] was an incredible person,' says the younger Plutarco. 'My father was his manager, and although he and my mother complained all the time about how aggravating Uncle Edward was, to me and my three sisters he was our magical uncle, our private Santa.'

(facing page) **The sculpture *Bamboo Palace* in the gardens of Las Pozas, where Edward James (above) built his Surrealist Eden in the jungle and kept wild animals, including a pet boa constrictor corralled in a metal cage beneath his guesthouse**

Xilitla Market
Xilitla, San Luis Potosí

(above) **La Bola Cantina in Xilitla, the small town that supported work on James' Surrealist sculpture garden**

(above) **Anita selling tamales in the plaza where people gather (left) for the market; and** (above left) *Chile piquin* **for those with the courage to try it**

Dr Augusto Visuet Velázquez
Coffee Grower, Xilitla, San Luis Potosí

Dr Augusto Visuet Velázquez is Director General of Development and Promotion of Coffee at the Secretariat of Agricultural Development and Hydraulic Resources in San Luis Potosí, a project aimed at increasing productivity and marketing through technological innovation and an efficient chain of production. By his own admission, he has spent 'thirty years or so practising human medicine … and simultaneously cultivating coffee'. Born in Xilitla, Visuet is the second generation of his family to grow coffee on the same *finca*. 'In my childhood,' he remembers, 'we were sent to the farm to help with the … sowing [and] the harvest. The habit [I developed back then] was, in the end, to do with biology. How does a plant breathe? How does it grow? How does it develop, and how does it reproduce? We call these processes "primary production". Then comes industrialisation … what needs to be done to make the beans taste good, to make [the product] so that the person consuming it finds its flavour to be pleasant, to make sure it doesn't have an unpleasant smell or taste … Those are our main concerns.'

The cultivation of coffee is not simply about coffee, however, as Visuet is quick to point out. It has much wider ramifications for the areas surrounding the *fincas*. 'On a coffee plantation,' he explains, 'shade is created by the plants that is a good place for birds because it creates a microclimate … This generates oxygen and retains carbon dioxide. The coffee plant is not only valuable because it produces beans. It is also important for the environment because it prevents an excess of CO_2 and allows us not to have the problems that we have in large cities. We need to see coffee plantations from this perspective, not only as places providing major harvests of coffee beans (which is our end goal) but also as places providing a better quality of life because we breathe better.'

Visuet accepts the description of himself as a traditionalist, defining his approach to his work this way: 'Our tradition is to have top-quality coffee without, as people often do now, adding anything to it. Ours is pure; that's how we drink it. The younger generations drink a lot of coffee, and we are grateful for that, but it would be terrific if they took the care to consume top-quality coffee.'

(facing page) **Dr Augusto Visuet Velázquez enjoying a coffee at Cafeteria Don Balo (his favourite), which uses locally grown beans,** (left) **enjoying** *enchiladas potosinas* **and coffee served by Claudia Paola Purata Jonguitud at Callos,** and (above) **walking the candy-coloured streets of Xilitla after lunch**

Vicenta Correño de Muñiz
Enchiladas Potosinas, Soledad de Graciano Sánchez, San Luis Potosí

Soledad is nationally famous for its *enchiladas potosinas*. (above) **Tortillas being prepared for the enchiladas by** (top) **grinding maize with chilli to obtain a red dough, and** (right) **adding a filling of chillies and aged cheese**

(above) **The celebrated**
enchiladas potosinas;
and (right) **A statue in
the plaza of Soledad
celebrating the town's
role in inventing
this speciality, which
is shipped all over
the country**

Zacatecas: *Camino Real*

'The best type of gambler is he who does not gamble!'

Along the *Camino Real de Tierra Adentro*, Spain's imperial highway stretching from Mexico City to Santa Fe, New Mexico (USA), you are bound to come across personalities who fit the profiles of both adventurer and renegade. José Luis Bonilla Lizalde seems to walk off the pages of history. A Zacatecan through and through, Bonilla professes historical and familial ties to the state going back several generations. The archetypal Mexican male from a land characterised by several centuries of hard-worn machismo, the moustachioed sixty-eight-year-old has sired twenty-one children with eight different wives over the past five decades; his current spouse is just twenty-eight. In his spare time, he runs a large bull-breeding hacienda famous for its fierce fighting bulls. He is also 'in love' with the Andalusian horse, which he breeds for the heck of it, suffering the financial consequences of his passion. Then there is his other obsession: breeding roosters. His best fighting cocks go for as much as US$25,000.

A jovial, salt-of-the-earth man's man who claims to polish his hair every morning with boot black, Bonilla's worldview has an antiquarian feel. 'In life,' he says, 'you take what you want ... [life] is a path. On that path, you meet different people, different women, and you keep going.' He claims no real attachments except to Rancho El Sauz, a former military garrison on the *Camino Real* that was converted into a ranch for raising fighting bulls in 1932.

Zacatecas is ideal cattle-breeding territory with its semi-arid climate and high (2,300-metre average) altitude. Better known for its rich deposits of silver and other minerals including kaolin, onyx and quartz, the state is home to the largest open-pit gold mine (Peñasquito) in Mexico. By the mid-1500s, the city of Zacatecas had become one of the principal suppliers of silver to the Spanish Crown. As a consequence, the state has had its fair share of conflict, during both Mexico's War of Independence and its Revolution. One of the largest and bloodiest battles of the latter, the Taking of Zacatecas, fought between the armies of Francisco 'Pancho' Villa and Victoriano Huerta, resulted in more than seven thousand dead and five thousand wounded, not counting civilian casualties. One can only imagine the scene looking out across La Bufa and El Grillo, the hills where Huerta's forces, under the command of Gen Medina Barrón, were positioned. Stories of the battle are replete with bravery, savagery and slaughter, and make one wonder why so many men died for the benefit of so few.

A welcome change from history to idyllic scenery came in the form of a young culinary couple picking fresh produce for the table. Hugo and Jessica Soto own Cosecha Taller de Cecina, Zacatecas' newest farm-to-table organic restaurant. This charming young couple's current eatery grew out of their pop-up culinary experiences at their family's hacienda, where they grow their own aubergines, chillies and beans without a battle cry to be heard beside the diners' exclamations of delight.

José Luis Bonilla Lizalde
Bull Breeder & Horse Rancher, Ganadería de Torrecilla, Rancho El Sauz, Saín Alto, Zacatecas

Rancho El Sauz has been home to fighting bulls since 1908, when the Llaguno González family brought six females and two bulls from Spain to start the Torrecillo stud. Before the Revolution, the hacienda served as a garrison. It was burned to the ground in the course of fighting, leaving only the walls standing. In 1912 the family bought ten more animals and kept one bull and sold the other, which was used to breed with thirty local Mexican criollo cows. Today, 95 per cent of Mexican fighting bulls are descended from the Llaguno 'caste'.

Bonilla, who has fathered twenty-one children with eight different women, describes his bulls as being 'like his babies'. Of his many relationships, he says, 'In life you want and you take. It's impossible to say, "No, I don't want to do this." It's already a single path, and you follow the path. On that path, you meet different people, different women, and you keep going.' He claims never to become attached to anything or anyone, whether it be women, bulls or horses. When he goes to bullfights to watch his animals, he takes notes so he can decide whether to repeat the combination of mother and father or swap the mother out for a different one. He currently has 30 *sementales* (stud bulls) and 150 head of cattle in total.

Bonilla's father was a bullfight manager whose job was to arrange fights and select the bulls. Bonilla was just seven when he began to accompany his father on buying trips. As an adult he has travelled extensively, living for a time in the US, England and Spain – but to study horses rather than fighting bulls. 'I've been riding since I was young,' he explains. The Spanish horses he particularly favours are extremely expensive to own and to breed. Horses were introduced to Mexico by the Spaniards, and Mexicans only began riding in earnest once they were given permission to do so by the King of Spain. 'The best way to ride a horse is [still] the way the Spanish ride,' Bonilla claims.

Fighting bulls start their careers around the age of three-and-a-half or four. Bonilla says it bothers him to see one of his bulls killed in the ring. 'I feel bad if it's a bullfight and the stick or sword is stuck in it six or seven times. I feel bad because the bull does not deserve to be slaughtered that way ... [But] I don't say anything ... There's nothing you can say ... I feel bad for any bull, even if it's not mine.' He cannot imagine bullfighting ever being banned in Mexico. 'It's so old and has been part of our culture for so many years that it's hard to take it away ... You can say, "No, I won't do this," but then what are you going to do with the bulls? The bulls are only good for that. With a fighting cock, it's born for [fighting], not good for eating or anything else.' As far as eating is concerned, he adds, bull meat is 'good meat because it's fed just on grass. Whatever it eats is clean, it's organic ... But I never eat it myself ... When you kill a bull, you have to leave it at least fifteen days in refrigeration for it to be soft. And when you cook it, the meat is real tough'. His preferred meat for eating is USDA Choice beef, France and England being America's only competitors when it comes to prime grades for use in the kitchen.

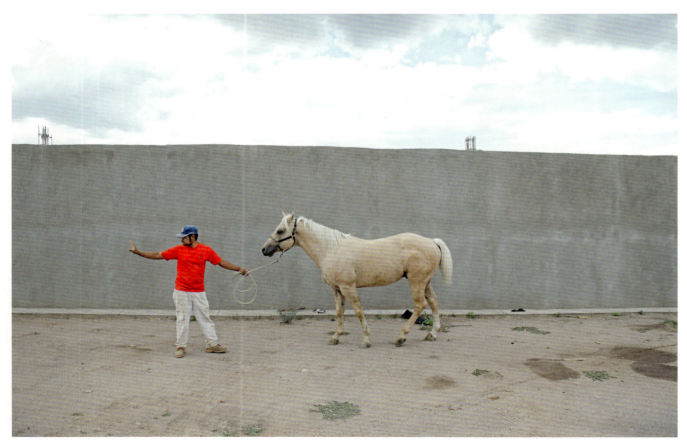

(previous spread) **The World Heritage Site of Zacatecas, the silver-mining town famous for the Battle of Zacatecas during the Mexican Revolution, an event celebrated annually**

(left) **A stable hand leading José Luis Bonilla Lizalde's palomino quarter horse out at Rancho El Sauz in Saín Alto. The ranch's walls are built of *lienzo* stone to keep his fighting bulls separated.** (facing page) ***El Jefe* in front of a *sabino* tree that is more than four hundred years old. 'Even older than I am,' he jokes**

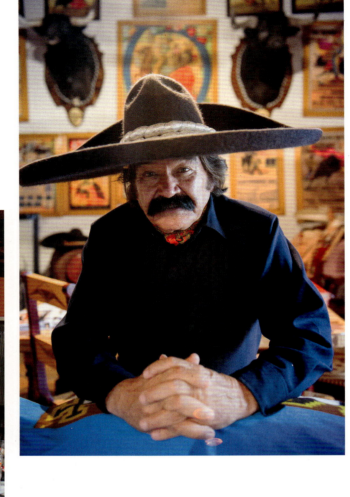

(top) **Bonilla in his living room, donning a** *charro* **hat given to him by singer and actor Antonio Aguilar. Behind him hang the taxidermy heads of bulls that were pardoned or honoured for their bravery and brilliance in combat.** (above) **Bonilla and** *torero* **César Montes eating** *gorditas* (right) **at Gorditas Doña Juanita, not far from his hacienda.** *Doña* **Juanita Rivera Lopez and her family have run the stall for nearly fifty years. Bonilla himself owns fifty 'El Torito' restaurants in the US**

(right) 'The first thing you have to look at with a horse is its ears,' claims Bonilla; (below) His three-year-old fighting bull Jandillo is only used for breeding. Breeding bulls may sell for as much as US$200,000; and (bottom) Bonilla holding one of his prized fighting cocks from the Dominican Republic which sell for up to US$30,000. Though he keeps both fighting and breeding cocks, he never bets himself, saying, 'The only way to be a good gambler is not to bet'

Jerez de García Salinas, Zacatecas

(above) *Charros* Jorge Herrera Juarez, Francisco Javier Bañuelos and Luis Arellano in Jerez de García Salinas, waiting for (right) *escaramuza charras* Beatriz García Márquez, Jocelyn Lucero Sierra Jaramillo and Naqeli Hernández Guerrero

(right) **Faux US visa and passport offices in a town where 60 per cent of the inhabitants live in the US but maintain summer homes in Jerez; and** (below) **Cantina Tizoc, a palm-ceilinged Jerez drinking establishment dating back to 1946**

Hugo & Jessica Soto
Chefs & Owners, Cosecha Taller de Cocina, Zacatecas, Zacatecas

It was while he was working at the Scandinavian restaurant Aska in New York that Hugo Soto found himself inspired by the farm-to-table movement. He decided to recreate this dining experience back in his hometown of Zacatecas. Soto, who studied Gastronomy in Aguascalientes and at the Instituto Argentino de Gastronomía, holds a degree in European Business Administration from the Escuela Superior de Administración de Empresas in Barcelona. His wife Jessica Enríquez also studied business (specifically project management). The menu at their three-year-old restaurant Cosecha Taller de Cocina features vegetables, eggs and cheese from the nearby *rancho* owned by Jessica's family and run by her father. The menu is changed regularly in order to offer diners something different each time they visit. The wine list is designed by the agronomist and winemaker Andrea Pérez Castillo.

Like many other Mexican chefs, Hugo's first memory of cooking was with his family, specifically in his grandmother's kitchen, where 'all the grandchildren helped to cook something, even [just] water.' He spent almost a year in Argentina learning, as he puts it, 'from the bottom [up]'. Then he was offered a placement at Martín Berasategui in Spain, at the time considered to be one of the world's twenty best restaurants. He recalls that 'it was difficult because [restaurant work in] Spain is like [being in] the army ... It was fifty people for fifty guests every service. So all the stress, all the discipline you need, it's a lot. But you learn a lot.' The place where he learned the most about cooking, though, was Chile, where he was taught traditional French cooking based around 'the most beautiful produce'. Fresh local produce became Hugo's mantra 'because in Spain, they have limes from Mexico, vanilla from Mexico, they have things from Africa, from Asia, and these are expensive products, but you didn't realise how important the freshness of the products is. When you work like that, it's good, but it can be better even if it's not caviar or vanilla ... Chile was really eye-opening for me.'

Hugo's eventual return to Zacatecas turned out to be just a matter of timing. 'Now I feel like I'm in my space,' he observes. 'I feel that I have to be here; I have to do this for my marriage, for my family, even for my state. I like it a lot here, both the lifestyle and the produce that is available.' The Sotos' restaurant started life as a pop-up at Jessica's family ranch, where self-sufficiency is a key goal. 'I think we are on the right path, but we need to do more,' Hugo says thoughtfully of the menu. 'We could do something like Italian or Argentinian or French cooking.' Local ingredients continue to inspire experimentation, for example the verbena that grows wild in the area but that is not used in traditional cooking. The Sotos make ice cream with it and include it in salads. Hugo is also a keen champion of local products for export, among them honey. 'I think we need to work more,' he says when discussing current business practice and marketing in the area. 'We need more support. I don't know if it should come from the government; I think it should come from ourselves.'

(left) **Jessica Soto at her father's ranch outside Zacatecas, where** (facing page) **she and her husband Hugo started their pop-up restaurant in the kitchen**

(below) **Hugo and Jessica** gathering vegetables and herbs for their restaurant, including *nopal* cactus, *tuna* and beans; (right) **Hugo** picking *mirasol* peppers with his father-in-law (these become *guajillo chiles* when dried); and (bottom) *Mirasol* peppers waiting to be stuffed with local aged cheese

(top left) **Hugo preparing a tomato salad, fillet of beef from Aguascalientes, courgette blossoms, grilled cabbage heart, stuffed *mirasol* peppers, courgettes stuffed with cheese, and** (above) **a crumble consisting of baked apples from the orchard, local unpasteurised cream and third-season honey (the richest of three local varieties), and decorated with edible flowers from his mother's garden.** (left) **The family relaxing with Solovino the dog, who 'just turned up' one day (and stayed)**

Aguascalientes: *Hidden Charms*

Aguascalientes may have its hidden charms, but they were either well hidden, or I never happened to see anything that would capture an itinerant traveller's fancy. Yet the state capital of the same name, with over a million inhabitants, is one of the most prosperous cities not only in Mexico but in the whole of Latin America. In fact, the OECD recognises the town as having one of the highest business environment standards in the world. So best be careful of what is reflected here, lest I sell the place short.

Among the problems with trying to travel the length and breadth of a country as large and diverse as Mexico are the constraints of time and geographical accessibility, as well as the interplay of logistics and security. The restrictions we encountered were usually born of logistical limitations, conflicting schedules and the ambitious scope of our project. Never short on ambition, we discovered that time and logistical resources are finite propositions despite the best of intentions. There was a wish list to begin with, my map of Mexico dotted with so many crosses and arrows as to make it a work of art. Politics, compliance and (at times) benign silliness marred the journey despite the support we received at many levels. Creative ventures require a degree of reckless adventure. How else could one even contemplate such a grandiose project?

My travels across Mexico were a revelation in many ways, not least because they inspired a recurring question: Why it is that some states (or cities) are more progressive, productive and pro-change than others? Why, for instance, does Aguascalientes differ from Zacatecas? What are the unique attributes of people contributing to better economies, cleaner environments, transparent governance, less corruption, more security and so on? Further contemplation is required to come up with suitable and convincing answers.

Founded in the sixteenth century by the Spaniards as a transit hub on the Camino de la Plata imperial road system linking New Spain's northern and southern dominions, Aguascalientes separated from Zacatecas, its neighbouring state, in 1835 and raced ahead in the realm of economic development. Its hot springs (*aguas calientes*) and enterprising population have made the state a confluence of industry and tradition. Nearly 80 per cent of the population of the capital city of the same name is of European descent, with Spanish and French being the predominant ethnographic mix. Mennonite communities from Germany and the Netherlands also settled in the area, while on average *mestizos* comprise a smaller percentage of the metropolitan area's population. High-tech industry, electronics and advanced automotive plants (Daimler-Benz, Toyota, Nissan) dot the landscape.

The state is located in the central Bajío macro-region with its mostly semi-arid climate, but semi-tropical areas around Calvillo have made Aguascalientes Mexico's leading producer of guavas. The higher elevations comprise oak and pine forests with some fantastic scenery and plenty of game, including pumas and lynxes. It was in Calvillo that I met the 'son of guava', as Saúl Landeros Cardona likes to call himself. A passionate advocate for the state and its inhabitants, Landeros believes that Aguascalientes' promise and products are 'going to conquer the world'. Perhaps it is precisely his brand of can-do enterprise that serves to differentiate the state's population from people in other parts of Mexico.

Saúl Landeros Cardona
Fruit Land Guava Farm, Calvillo, Aguascalientes

Saúl Landeros Cardona, who describes himself as a 'son of guava', founded Fruit Land Guava Farm with his family twenty years ago. Calvillo, where Fruit Land is based, is Mexico's largest producer of guava, and the region is famous for its guava sweets and liqueurs.

Landeros is a passionate advocate for both his town and his business. 'The soil is amazing here, the weather is nice, people are kind and good, you live well, and we make products that are going to conquer the world,' he says. 'We may live here, but we travel the world with our products, making the world a little sweeter.' Every December, Calvillo's farmers celebrate the year's end with a two-week guava fiesta, during which guava liqueurs and other fruit confectionery are sampled. Rich in vitamins A and C, guava is used to make jam and thirst-quenching *agua fresca* as well as sweets. The area is said to produce the country's sweetest guava, 30 per cent of which is exported to the US.

Landeros' parents are descended from Europeans; it was his grandparents and great-grandparents who first settled in Mexico. 'They brought their European customs with them,' he notes, 'mixing their roots with local ones.' This melange, he believes, 'created a certain type of people ... Even if we have European roots, our Mexican roots are present not only in our gastronomy but also in our architecture, in our lifestyle and in our religion'. Guava cultivation developed extensively around Calvillo because it lacked any of the pests that plague trees grown elsewhere. The area is known for its high-altitude dry climate.

With an international array of markets in mind, Landeros explains that he has 'tried to use complementary elements to allow people from around the world to learn to eat guava, which is the queen of fruit because of its levels of vitamin C and fibre. Guava strengthens our stomachs [and] it is very nutritious'. He enumerates a dizzying list of ingredients added to guava at the Fruit Land factory to create a wide range of sweets and treats – 'chilli, cocoa, amaranth, linseed, milk [and] nuts' – emphasising their health-giving benefits. Fruit Land's mouthwatering array of products includes 'a confectionery made with guava jelly, a confectionery made with guava jam, a milk-and-caramel roll, condensed milk with nuts inside, a [type of] chocolate ... amaranth with peanut and guava ... A little cup ... like drinking a glass of milk with some guava inside [is] for people who live far away from producing areas so they can enjoy a bit of guava and a glass of milk! Then there's *queso con ate* (cheese with guava). It's delicious! Excellent, of course!' A health-giving tea is brewed from guava leaves. Clearly marketing is intensely important to Landeros. 'We have built [our business] step by step,' he says. 'We've chosen a product that many people don't know about, so we have to work hard in developing it.'

(previous spread) **Museo José Guadalupe Posada in the Barrio del Encino, Aguascalientes, which served as a convent until it was designated the state's first art museum, and dedicated to the collection of nationally acclaimed engraver, illustrator and caricaturist José Guadalupe Posada**

(left) **Freshly picked guavas; and** (facing page) **Saúl Landeros Cardona plucking a seed from a** *guaje* **tree on his farm in Calvillo. These highly nutritious seeds have been used as energy boosters since prehispanic times and are still used in an array of dishes by indigenous communities**

(above) **Workers at Fruit Land processing guava, which is used to make sweets and liqueurs on the site.**
(far left & left) *Guayaba* **sweets – Cardona has named them after his four daughters Violeta, Noemi, Lucy and Marian.**
(facing page) **Stuffed Aguascalientes-style chilli at the Gran Hotel Alameda**

(following spread, left) **Saddle-making and leatherwork from Calvillo; and** (following spread, right) **The automated Nissan plant in Aguascalientes**

Carnitas Lupillo Restaurante
San Francisco de los Romo, Aguascalientes

Carnitas Lupillo Restaurante is widely thought to produce the most delicious *carnitas* (pork morsels) in Aguascalientes. The restaurant manages the entire process, purchasing whole pigs and using every part of the animal. (above) **Pig skin being air-dried to make crackling; and** (top right) *Carnitas* **frying before being served to customers, usually in tacos**

(above) **Fried trotters, the restaurant's speciality, slow-cooked so the meat falls off the bone;** (top right) **Staff preparing** *carnitas* **for customers who choose the cuts they prefer; and** (right) *Carnitas* **served by the kilo with tortillas and different salsas**

Guanajuato: *History & Colour*

The sheer beauty of Guanajuato, the capital of the state of the same name, is overwhelming. This colourful city with its narrow roads and alleyways, plazas and splendid colonial-era mansions was declared a UNESCO World Heritage Site in 1988. Built cheek-by-jowl with one of history's most prolific silver mines (at the height of its production, La Valenciana produced two-thirds of the world's silver), the city prospered, keeping time with the pretensions of its well-heeled citizenry.

Guanajuato is also the site of the first major battle of Mexico's War of Independence, the moment when insurgents and royalist troops began the eleven-year conflict that ended Spain's suzerainty over New Spain. Led by Miguel Hidalgo y Costilla, a secular priest whose *Grito de Dolores* (Cry of Dolores), shouted from the entrance of the church in Dolores on 15 September 1810, is celebrated as Mexico's Independence Day. Every year Mexican presidents act out the beatified scene by ringing the Dolores liberty bell, now in the Palacio Nacional in Mexico City. Myth and reality have a jarring effect in practice. Seeing the bell-ringer in action did not quite lend itself to the intended high drama of the occasion in my imagination, but Hidalgo lit the fuse that ignited the sentiment of nationalism that still burns fiercely in every Mexican heart. And there was I trying to temper history's moment through a camera lens.

Hidalgo's rise to prominence was one of those quirks of history. A reformist priest inspired by the European Enlightenment, he proved a deft leader and a rousing rebel commander, taking Guanajuato just a fortnight after his call to battle. His ragtag followers, armed only with sticks, stones and machetes, went on to overwhelm the Spanish population holed up in the Alhóndiga de Granaditas. Like all revolutionaries, Hidalgo's forces then proceeded to slaughter the six hundred-odd men, women and children taking refuge in the town's highly fortified granary. And, like all larger-than-life revolutionary leaders the world over, Hidalgo explained away the carnage as a consequence of historical forces bottled up for far too long by the servitude imposed by Spain on its prize colony.

Promoted to generalissimo, Hidalgo declared an end to slavery in New Spain in 1810 (half a century before America did the same). His forces then moved through several other states, the revolutionaries' intentions being to wipe clean three hundred years of servitude under the Spaniards. Atrocities like the Guanajuato incident were repeated in San Miguel de Allende, Celaya and Valladolid by his unruly forces as Hidalgo prepared to march on Mexico City, the capital of New Spain, with an army of a hundred thousand *insurgentes.* Excommunicated by the Catholic Church and relieved of his generalissimo's tunic, he was betrayed (what's new?) and captured in Saltillo by royalist forces in 1811. Refusing a pardon, he was tried and then shot by a firing squad in Chihuahua before being decapitated. His head, along with those of three of his generals, was famously displayed for ten years at the four corners of the Alhóndiga de Granaditas, a grim reminder of the power of insurgent ideas. But Hidalgo seems to have had the last laugh by having a state, and hundreds of towns, named after him, plus myriad national accolades. Today almost deified in Mexico, his parting words to his executioners were: 'Do not pity me. I know it is my last day, my last meal, and that is why I have to enjoy it … tomorrow I will not be here. That is best, I think, since I am old and soon my ailments will sprout … I would rather die this way than in a hospital bed.'

Guanajuato City, Guanajuato

The narrow, winding streets and plazas of Guanajuato city, which boasts colonial mansions and churches built in pink or green sandstone. The city was designated a UNESCO World Heritage Site in 1988 and offers an unimaginable treat for any visitor

(previous spread) **A cactus at El Charco del Ingenio, a 70-hectare nature reserve and botanic garden in San Miguel de Allende. El Charco del Ingenio was designated a 'peace zone' dedicated to nature and free of violence and weapons by the Dalai Lama in 2004**

Doña Alicia Sánchez
Traditional Cook, *Tortillas Ceremoniales*, Comonfort, Guanajuato

The making of tortillas to mark special occasions is a tradition that originated with the Otomies, an indigenous group that occupied the central Mexican plateau. The Otomies worshipped the Moon, and to this day many Otomi communities continue to practise shamanism and adhere to prehispanic beliefs.

Although originally ceremonial tortillas were used in celebrations related to planting and harvesting, now they are prepared for baptisms, first communions, weddings, confirmations and *quinceañeras* (the equivalent of sweet sixteen parties).

The process of making ceremonial tortillas is passed down between women in families, usually from mothers to daughters. The preparation process usually involves three women: one to make the tortilla and set it on the *comal*; a second woman who prepares the mould with dye, prints the image on the tortilla and returns it to the skillet, and a third woman who supervises the cooking, finally removing the tortilla from the *comal* and placing it in a *taxcal* (tortilla basket). The tortillas are normally prepared on a wood-burning stove. On the Feast of the Holy Cross (when the harvest is brought in), the best maize and finest moulds are used.

Dyes are derived from various plants and insects. Dark purple dye comes from *muicle*, a plant found in the wild or grown in the garden and thought to have healing properties. Red or pink comes from the cochineal, an insect. Yellow, bluish purple, pink and green come from sunflowers, another flower, brazilwood and chard respectively. The maize itself can be black, white, purple or blue. Families cherish moulds passed down from generation to generation. Some of them depict Otomi gods, legends, or religious or family symbols. There are also moulds that tell a community's history.

Doña Alicia Sánchez, who was born in 1956, inherited her tortilla moulds from her great-great-grandmother. 'As a little girl I remember looking at the tortilla mould next to the stove,' she says. 'I was curious because it resembled a wheel of chocolate. I waited for my mother and the women who were cooking to become distracted and took it in my hand. It was then that I realised it was a mould.' She has been making ceremonial tortillas for as long as she can remember. 'What I enjoy most is going to fairs and expositions to show people our community traditions,' she says. 'Now two men in the community are making new moulds. The seals of the most antique ones have almost been erased. My favourite mould is the one with the Holy Cross … There are several myths regarding these tortillas. Some say that they were used during the Cristero War [a rebellion in 1926–9 inspired by governmental restrictions on the Catholic Church] to send messages back and forth. This is a tradition that we want to maintain.'

(left) Ceremonial tortillas on a *comal*; and (facing page) *Doña* Alicia Sánchez removing a ceremonial tortilla from her family mould

La Flor de Dolores
Ice Cream Maker, Dolores Hidalgo, Guanajuato

**La Flor de Dolores'
special cactus-
flavoured ice creams**
(far right) **are derived,
for example, from the
fruit of the** *garambullo*
cactus (*Myrtillocactus
geometrizans***)** (right)**.
This cactus, high in
vitamin C, antioxidants
and fibre, has a
long history of use
in Mexico's Otomí
community due to its
medicinal properties.
Since the fruiting season
lasts just one month,
the** *garambullo* **is frozen**
(above) **so that the ice
cream can be made
available out of season**

(above) **Owner Antonio García displaying a couple of the more than fifty prize-winning ice cream flavours available at his shop; and** (left) **Ice lollies made from fresh fruit**

Gorky González Quiñones & Toshiko Ono de Gonzáles
Master Ceramicist & Partner, Guanajuato, Guanajuato

Master ceramist Gorky González Quiñones met his wife Toshiko at a tea ceremony while he was studying in Japan; they have been married for fifty-two years. 'They were inaugurating a new kiln,' Gorky explains, 'and my wife was studying tea ceremonies … The master chose her from among the students to lead the tea ceremony.' When Toshiko first moved to Mexico, there were very few foreigners living there; her family back in Japan thought that Mexicans wore sombreros and rode horses all day.

At a young age Gorky (who was named after the Russian writer) moved to San Miguel de Allende with his father, Rodolfo González, who was a sculptor. After studying at the Instituto Allende, Gorky decided to specialise in majolica, a ceramic style dating back to the colonial period. His work was first shown in New York in 1966, in Tokyo in 1967 and then at Expo 67 in Montreal, and has been exhibited internationally ever since.

In 1965, on the advice of an exchange student from Japan, Gorky obtained a scholarship and support from the Banco de México to study there. He became a disciple of the master Tsuji Seimei, from whom he learned the technique of unglazed *shigaraky*, and of the master Kei Fijiwara, from whom he learned the techniques of *karatzu* (stoneware), *oribe* and *tenmoku* (the latter two are types of tea ware). It was on his return to Mexico that Gorky decided to concentrate on making majolica, whose manufacture had been abandoned in Guanajuato more than eighty years earlier, and about which he had known from some of his father's pieces. He founded a traditional pottery workshop specialising in this technique, which employs a milky-white enamel on both the interior and exterior of ceramic pieces. The enamel serves as a base for colourful decoration in tin, lead and silica.

Gorky is credited with two important innovations in the development of majolica ceramics: firing with gas rather than wood, and the adaptation of enamels and pigments to meet international toxicity standards. He works with a staff of around twenty-five people, among them one of his sons, who provides invaluable support since his father is less able to work now.

(above) **Gorky González Quiñones' studio, with pieces waiting to be decorated with mineral-based colours. Ninety per cent of his works are special orders.** (left) **Toshiko Ono de González preparing lunch with her assistant;** (right) **Gorky and Toshiko in their garden; and** (facing page) **A metal figurine of the Virgin awaiting a client**

Gabriela Noelle Enríquez
Owner, Hacienda Las Amantes, San Miguel Allende, Guanajuato

Gabriela Noelle Enríquez is San Miguel de Allende's youngest hotelier. A chance visit to Hacienda Las Amantes (built in 1877) caused her to fall in love with the place and decide to restore it and open it as a hotel. Built in the colonial style, the hacienda had been a traditional estate with orchards, stables, granaries and a well. A treasure trove hidden under the original stairs included furniture from various periods, artisanal pieces and traditional utensils, all of which were incorporated into the restoration of the building, thus contributing to its bohemian atmosphere. The menu features organic ingredients.

San Miguel de Allende is known for its colonial architecture, cobblestone streets and magical light, all of which are popular with photographers and artists. Once an important stop on the Silver Route (a highway built between Zacatecas and Mexico City to service the country's mining industries), today the town hosts regular festivals, fireworks and parades, and is known for its excellent restaurants and high-class accommodations. In 2008 UNESCO recognised San Miguel de Allende and the Sanctuary of Atotonilco located there as World Heritage Sites, citing the town's religious and civil architecture as a demonstration of the evolution of different styles from the Baroque through to late nineteenth-century Neo-Gothic. Beatniks and artists may have shacked up in San Miguel on a shoestring during the 1940s, but economic growth has left those days behind. Indeed much of the town has been bought up by Americans and Europeans, with few Mexicans able to afford property there and a resulting loss of authentic atmosphere.

'You want to present your town in the best way possible,' says Enríquez, 'and tell the rest of the world: "We are Mexican and we are proud!"' She describes San Miguel as her 'lover', adding, 'I'm its muse.' Behind every door in the town 'there is a universe.' It was never her dream to have a hotel; what she most enjoys is hosting 'interesting guests'. A practising shaman since the age of fifteen, she performs cleansing rituals in a 'cave of origins' located in an outbuilding. On the roof is a garden containing all of Guanajuato's native species of cacti. 'Cactus is on our national flag; we use it for everything,' the young hotelier explains. 'Glue, walls, food, making all sorts of things.' Thus cacti and tourism are critical binding mechanisms for today's Mexican economy.

(left) **Gabriela Noelle Enríquez, owner of Hacienda Las Amantes, outside her 'cave of origins', and** (above) **with her friend Alma Caballero, an event organiser who specialises in table design and floral arrangements, using succulents and greenery from Enríquez's garden**

(above) **San Miguel de Allende from the Hacienda Las Amantes terrace, where Enríquez maintains a cactus garden; and** (right) **A street in a town where every wall is dressed in pastel shades**

Jalisco: *Tequila Sunrise*

'*Jalisco es México*' is how *jaliscienses* describe themselves. The state is one of Mexico's richest, and its capital city, Guadalajara, is the country's second-largest in terms of population. Mariachi, *ranchera* music and tequila all originated there. *Birria*, the spicy local stew made of goat meat or mutton, and the culinary icon of *jaliscienses*, is sold in *birrierias* across Mexico. While variations on the dish exist in other states, in Jalisco the meat is marinated in *adobo* spices. *Birria* is reputedly a hangover cure – something handy to know in the birthplace of tequila.

The state's diverse geography includes all of Mexico's ecosystems, covering semi-arid scrubland, plains, lakes, forests and grasslands with altitudes up to 4,300 metres; its flora and fauna are unmatched by those of any other state. Home (along with other states) to the indigenous Huichol and Nahua peoples, Jalisco also hosts a large population of North American retirees around Lake Chapala, Mexico's largest freshwater lake, and in the resort area of Puerto Vallarta. Both industry and agriculture play major roles in the state's economy. Maize, sugar, barley, tobacco and the agave plant from which tequila is made dominate the landscape. Passing kilometre after kilometre of blue agaves planted in neat rows as far as the eye could see took me back to my first shot of the exotic drink at university. Hardly anyone had heard of it then, yet tequila today is as common a tipple as vodka everywhere in the world.

If Mexican food has conquered America, placing its cultural imprint firmly on the daily lives of Mexico's northern neighbour, tequila has become a daily drink alongside it.

Imagine my surprise when I discovered that tequila is made out of a giant *piña*, or pineapple, which can weigh as much as 25 kilos and is the agave's hidden heart. The *piña* is extracted by trained *jimadores* like Ismael Gama Rodarte, the national face of the Jose Cuervo brand. Wielding sharp machetes, the *jimadores* cut the stems of the agave, then wield equally sharp half-moon-shaped blades (*coas*) resembling hoes, attached to the ends of long handles, to extract the *piña* from beneath the soil. The *piñas* are then collected by truck and hauled to the distillery, where men with even sharper axes cut them into smaller pieces to be loaded onto a conveyor belt. After being washed and mashed, the *piñas*' juice is extracted and piped through various fermentation and distillation stages.

Tequila, which requires a precise determination of origin, is mostly distilled in the region of the same name, which is an hour's drive from Guadalajara, where the red volcanic soil favours the blue agave. An agave takes between eight and twelve years to reach maturity before the *piña* can be harvested; more than three hundred million plants are readied for the plucking every year. The blue agave grown in the highlands (the *piña* twice as heavy as those grown in the valleys) produces a different aroma and taste to that grown in the lowlands, which is fruitier. Drinking six different varieties laid out for a tasting session was an instructive, not to say a daunting, experience. Where was the *birria* fix when I needed it?

Tomás Bermúdez
Chef, La Docena, Guadalajara, Jalisco

Born in Durango, Tomás Bermúdez studied industrial design in Guadalajara before going to Spain to attend cooking school. He trained with Thierry Blouet, owner of Café des Artistes in Puerto Vallarta, and worked at the Michelin-starred Restaurante Martín Berasategui in Spain. Other high-end stops on Bermúdez's culinary journey included Le Chateaubriand in Paris, where he did an internship with Iñaki Aizpitarte. It was in Buenos Aires that he completed his formal training.

Bermúdez's restaurant La Docena (in fact he co-owns it with his business partner Alejandro de la Peña) is known as Mexico's top oyster bar. He also has a café in Guadalajara called Becada, which he established with fellow chef Sergio Meza in order to bring cooking and pastry-making together with the work of local artists. The partners' ultimate aim: to encourage an atmosphere of innovative creativity. (Guadalajara is the cultural centre of western Mexico and the country's second-largest metropolis.) La Docena is known for having brought the flavours of New Orleans to Guadalajara, although Bermúdez's extensive experience in European kitchens decisively influenced his cooking philosophy and methods. The restaurant's atmosphere is relaxed and unhurried – it is a place to go with family and friends.

'All my life I wanted to study cuisine, to cook,' says Bermúdez. 'I liked to see the fire, the food.' By 'fire' he means burning coals, cooking over which results in different tastes and smokier smells than other methods. He likes being his own boss and thoroughly enjoys his work as a chef, in contrast to his studies at school and university, which he never completed. Early each morning he goes to the Mercado del Mar to buy fish, oysters and clams from the Pacific Ocean. He sources his produce from Rancho Villa Cristina, an organic exotic vegetable farm and distribution company (the latter is called X-Picy) supplying all of the top restaurants in Guadalajara and Mexico City. X-Picy's specialities include varieties of chard, chicory, rocket, wasabi, beetroot, daikon and various types of kale. Among their clients are Four Seasons Hotels and Resorts, Quinta Real, St. Regis and Ku'uk restaurant in Mérida. Alvaro Santoscoy farms 180 hectares, and his entire family is involved in different aspects of agriculture. (They also have cattle and sheep.) The original ranch, built many years ago by the Santoscoy family, experienced the vagaries of war and revolution, the diminution of the holding a testament to the changing face of Mexican ranching society. Maria Cristina and her husband Genaro, a gastroenterologist, continue

to work the land that has been in her family for five generations; the hacienda she grew up in had to be demolished when the local river was dammed, thus turning the land it sat on into a lake. She describes the place in its current form as 'not a big ranch but full of love'. The taxidermy ox heads in the patio area are the two oxen originally kept to plough the land.

Alvaro Santoscoy's enterprise has been supported by Bermúdez from the beginning. 'They had this project for three and a half years, and they really changed the mentality of gastronomy in Guadalajara,' the chef says of his friend. 'Every restaurant in Guadalajara makes recipes with vegetables from Alvaro.' The availability of fresh produce contributes 'a hundred per cent' to La Docena's success, influencing every one of its dishes, which change daily to reflect the availability of ingredients. Keynote favourites include the 'volcano' – *dulce de leche* with banana ice cream; the 'bullet', an oyster submerged in a shot glass with vodka, Clamato and salt; Peruvian ceviche chips with tomato, onion, lemon, green pepper and olive oil, and po' boy sandwiches – traditional Louisiana street food which usually consists of meat (sloppy roast beef) or fried seafood (shrimp, crayfish, oysters, crab).

(previous spread) **Sunrise en route from Guadalajara to Tequila, where rows upon rows of blue agave plants stretch to the horizon**

(facing page) **Tomás Bermúdez with Rancho Santoscoy's owner Maria Cristina Padilla Romo; and** (right) **The head of one of two oxen that ploughed the once extensive ranch**

(left) **A Buddha's Hand, or fingered citron; and** (above) **Multi-coloured carrots**

(above) **Bermúdez preparing lunch with** (left) **fresh vegetables; and** (below) **Fresh** *corbina* **being grilled**

351

(left) **Bermúdez preparing** *paella* (below) **over a fire of** *leña,* (bottom) **a difficult feat since the 'rice needs constant attention', as he points out**

(left) Bermúdez's *paella* includes prawns, mussels and dark purple rice from Murcia in Spain, and is garnished with *verdolaga*. (above) Claudia de la Torre and her mother-in-law enjoying *paella* at the family ranch

Maru Toledo
Traditional Cook, Mujeres del Maíz Community Organisation, Rancho El Teuchiteco, Ahualulco de Mercado, Jalisco

Maru Toledo is a researcher, academic and cook dedicated to saving and promoting the culinary traditions and methods of Jalisco. In addition to rescuing the state's prehispanic gastronomy, she has also collected recipes from colonial Mexico. Her organisation Mujeres del Maíz (Women of the Corn) is made up of culinary researchers who collect and document recipes, culinary experiences and flavours from kitchens throughout Jalisco, particularly its rural areas. The first big meal they prepared consisted of 'buried chicken', a recipe from hundreds of years ago that originally involved wrapping wild turkeys in maize husks, coating the husks with a thick layer of clay and then baking the birds underground in hot coals. When the clay casing was cracked open, a lip-smacking aroma filled the air and the meat was unbelievably tender.

Toledo's love for Jalisco and its kitchens, both historic and present-day, is of long standing. 'A long time ago when I wanted to learn more about our cuisine, I realised that much of the information that was written down was inaccurate,' she explains. 'As a young girl I noticed that my mother would cook differently from my grandmothers, and I wanted to know why an *elote* cake was prepared differently by each one and tasted different. That is why I became interested in knowing more about the cuisine of Jalisco.' She notes that Jaliscans 'have the tendency to be interested in the food of other states, of other countries, without ... paying attention to our roots. When I wanted to learn about our roots, I realised that there wasn't a great deal aside from the traditions of our mothers and grandmothers. I wanted to know the origins –

from prehispanic times – of our cuisine'. When asked what value such knowledge adds to modern life, she replies, 'My priority is to study the methods and techniques of food preparation in order to understand our current cuisine. Furthermore, my preoccupation with learning about antique forms of preparation that almost no-one uses had to do with the fact that all this was ending because new generations did not learn them.' She feels an obligation to her own grandchildren but also to other Mexican kids, many of whom suffer from poor nutrition. 'Nowadays [poor nutrition] is an important [social] factor,' she observes. 'It is the reason why many people suffer from obesity, diabetes and many other illnesses. Prehispanic cuisine in the western part of Mexico didn't contain oils or fats – it was very healthy. That is another reason why I am interested in studying it. How was it that they were so well nourished and enjoyed such extraordinary health, as is clear from the archaeological evidence?'

In addition to trying out ancient recipes, Toledo and her team are involved in a range of other activities. 'The first is to generate employment,' she notes. 'Secondly, we do research. We work with older people; we register and document recipes that no-one knows about. I work with them, I teach them, and we cook them and host groups for meals. Sometime groups of people come to take smoke-cooking classes, and we go to exhibitions, events and other places to provide a context for authentic Jaliscan cuisine.' This is how the group makes ends meet: by cooking for visitors, offering cooking classes and furthering the fame of the state in which they work.

(above) **Socorro Martínez** de-seeds chillies while (right) **preparing *salsa verde* in a *metate*, a heavier and wider alternative to the *molcajete*. The *metate* allows Martínez to make large quantities of salsa quickly**

(facing page) **Maru Toledo (on the right) preparing tamales with traditional cooks Francisca 'Panchita' Florez Chocoteco (on the left) and Delgadina Gómez Rodríguez (in the centre), both of whom work with Toledo at her foundation**

Francisco Ruano
Chef, Restaurante Alcalde, Guadalajara, Jalisco

Maverick chef Francisco Ruano grew up and studied in Guadalajara. After completing his studies there, he moved to Puerto Vallarta, where he worked with Thierry Blouet, owner of Café des Artistes. A year later he took a job as a cook on a cruise ship to Alaska and the Caribbean. Travelling to Spain, he studied at the Luis Irizar Cooking School in the Basque Country. Ruano went on to cook in several European restaurants, among them Mugaritz and Akelarre in Spain and Noma in Copenhagen, where he met fellow chef Jorge Vallejo, with whom he worked on his return to Mexico.

Like most Mexican chefs, Ruano attributes his love of gastronomy to the influence of his mother and grandmother, and he favours his country's traditional flavours. 'My mother, when she didn't want to cook, she'd just put bread and cream and avocados on the table and we were very happy with it,' he remembers. Known as a perfectionist, he describes his travels as a 'personal emigration' following which he imported to Mexico the techniques he had learned along the way 'to mix with the food that represents me as a human'. Earning kudos is less important to him than it used to be. 'I opened the restaurant with this idea of success and perfection,' he explains, 'but soon I became really, really unhappy ... So I stopped thinking about that and enjoyed it a little more.' As an antidote to the influence of the global food industry on the Mexican public's eating habits, he believes that 'it's really important for people, including me, to try to communicate and relate with other people.'

Ruano already knew that he wanted to become a cook at a young age. 'I started liking it more when I got into the cooking business and realised that it was a way to relate to people to whom I usually wouldn't speak in other contexts,' he muses. 'It has very personal meaning as a way of telling who I am, through a craft or through hospitality ... It's about how I care for human beings, how we treat you at the table ... Starting from there, it was a life commitment. I realised the power of service.' If he were to lose his culinary skills, he says, he 'wouldn't have any idea what to do in the world. My only function, my only craft, is to cook ... My other passion is music, and I suck as a musician!'

Francisco Ruano in front of the busy kitchen at Restaurante Alcalde

The quality and dedication of his kitchen staff are critical to Ruano. 'I don't want to get crazy about it, but there are certain values of quality and respect for food that are very important and taken care of by the staff and me and the suppliers. I used to get really, really mad about the aesthetic aspect of food or many things that are more about a chef's ego than about food … Now I'm not toying with food on a plate … I just do the best we can and probably have a wider range than other restaurants. We spend very happy times in the kitchen, more than in most restaurants, and for us that is very important. I try to find a balance, enjoying my dream, enjoying what I do, getting better, raising the quality, but in a healthy way.' Today this team effort is if anything more important than ever: 'What we have achieved through our food is to create a beautiful team of people working together, very strong values of kindness and ethics, and we're proud of that.' Ruano believes that he himself is 'just a tiny piece of the puzzle', citing recent time away on a business trip as a period when the restaurant ran 'with special creativity' without his being there. Although he has more years of experience in the kitchen than his most senior staff, he notes that 'everybody's doing excellent work' without him. The reason? 'Because the guys that work here, especially in the kitchen, for 95 per cent of them this is their first job after culinary school. Everything they have learned about quality, they have learned from me. So they are able to reproduce it in the way that I want.'

(facing page, top left) **Green *aguachile* made of prawns with apple, jicama, cucumber and seaweed powder;** (facing page, top right) **Roasted sweetbreads with milk;** (facing page, bottom left) **Deboned, slow-cooked calves' feet in a tostada; and** (facing page, bottom right) **Tapalpa duck served in its own juice**

(top) **Ruano enjoying a *torta ahogada* at Tortas Ahogadas Don José el de la Bicicleta, his favourite street-food stand in Guadalajara;** (above) **Enrique Chávez selling *panza* (cows' bellies) at the Mercado San Juan de Dios from his stall named after the famous comic character Memín Pinguín; and** (left) ***Birria tatemada* (roasted goat) complete with skull for sale at the Mercado**

Michoacán: *Passion in Food*

Passions generally run deep in Mexico, but nothing gets the local and regional talking heads going more than comparisons between one state's culinary history and another's. Time and again I came across chefs, traditional cooks, experts and aficionados extolling the virtues, the very exemplary uniqueness, of their particular cuisine. While bonhomie exists among the rising numbers of chefs skirmishing on culinary battlefields, the prize for who (and what) is best remains an annual enigma.

So whose food is better, best, truly Mexican, unique, exceptional, timeless and so on? Breathless from the attention Mexican cuisine has received in recent years, regional chefs, who mainly end up working in Mexico City, will argue the toss endlessly. Success is determined by the bottom line, but restaurant ratings calibrated by local and international outfits play into individual pride as well as regional prejudice. The culinary scene in Mexico is openly contentious given the high stakes (commerce, tourism, reputations, egos) involved. Especially so as both local and federal governments have shown unprecedented zeal in promoting the country's contemporary global image by tying it to its cuisine.

Mexican food has swept across America, surpassing pizza and burgers in border states like California and Texas. Fast-food chains aside, Mexican cuisine is increasingly in the spotlight, with emerging or established restaurants capturing the attention of critics and foodies alike. While preparing to visit the country, I tucked into numerous Mexican cookbooks, the sheer number of which surprised me, some of them very good. The name that kept popping up was that of Diana Kennedy, holder of both the Order of the Aztec Eagle and the Order of the British Empire.

Kennedy is probably Mexico's most recognised name in international culinary circles. Born Diana Southwood in Essex, England in 1923, she married the *New York Times'* Central America correspondent in the 1950s, and has not stopped travelling the length and breadth of Mexico since then in search of recipes, traditional ingredients, and the intellectual memorabilia that comes with such passion and dedication. Author of several bestselling books on Mexican cuisine, Kennedy has carved out a global reputation as both a tireless activist and an advocate for Mexican culinary culture. Her strong opinions are expressed in both speech and print; the lady has a reputation for straight talking, with no regard for gain or glory. A purist at heart, Kennedy has, she says, travelled to every village, crossed every river, sought out the remotest valleys and climbed the highest sierras in search of the authentic spirit of Mexico via its food. Journeying alone, whether on foot or by bus, car or burro, Kennedy knows more about Mexico and its food than any other living person, Mexican or otherwise.

Since 1976, Kennedy has made Michoacán her home, setting off from her base to explore, never travelling in a straight line, as she likes to say mischievously. The treasury of experience and research which go to make up the Kennedy saga are now of incomparable historic value, as most of the cooks and personalities, many of the recipes and quite a number of the ingredients that she sought out over forty years no longer exist. Were it not for her efforts, much more of this important material would have been lost forever.

Diana Kennedy
Cook & Author, San Francisco Coatepec de Morelos, Zitácuaro, Michoacán

'I have been in every sierra, I've been in villages and stayed there and crossed flowing rivers … in this beautiful country … and of course no-one ever makes money like that!' Now in her nineties, the outspoken Diana Kennedy grew up in England, daughter of a salesman and a schoolteacher. 'I never travel in straight lines,' she says. 'The important discoveries in my life have always happened by chance.' Starting in the 1950s, when she married the *New York Times* Mexico, Central America and Caribbean correspondent Paul Kennedy and then moved to Mexico with him, she made it her business to travel the country's length and breadth, tracking down endless traditional recipes. The author of several bestselling cookbooks, Kennedy received the Order of the Aztec Eagle for her promotion of Mexican food, as well as an MBE for services to Mexican–British relations.

Kennedy has lived at Quinta Diana, her eco-house and organic farm in Michoacán, since 1976, when her husband died. She has done most of her travelling on her own 'because I can't think of anybody else who would have the patience … to go up into the mountains where I go with my sleeping bag and my camp-bed … I never know how long I'm going to stay; it depends on what I find, and people lead me to something else.' Some expeditions have ended in failure: 'I made a special journey to the *sierra de puebla*, and the tree or the bush was bare. They said, "Well, a *manado* of little parrots arrived this morning and ate all the nuts!" … And then trying to see a certain chilli being smoked, and the bridge was down – they were doing a new bridge – and it's like, Come on! … In any case, they said the village where they were doing the smoking … was having a fiesta so everybody was drunk and nobody was working! … All sorts of things happen, so you realise you can't control everything.' Many of the cooks she visited in the early days 'don't exist anymore', she says, 'so many of my reports really amount to an historic part of the gastronomy of Mexico.' These 'reports' originally appeared in magazines accompanied by photographs by a French friend 'who did some lovely stuff'. In due course the book projects unfolded, among them *My Mexico: A Culinary Odyssey with More than 300 Recipes*, first published in 1998.

Kennedy remembers with fondness the markets filled with produce from the countryside 'long before the Chinese stuff came in'. It was this richness and variety that fascinated her. When her husband was dying, they moved back to New York, where Kennedy gave her first Mexican cooking classes: 'Then I was asked to do my first book, so everything just followed in an uncontrollable pattern.' She had 'started cooking very young' while still in England, helping out at Christmas 'and all that sort of thing'; since the family never had much money, they 'used to eat everything from the animal, from the nose to the tail'.

Kennedy was first introduced to Michoacán, where she lives, by a representative of the British auction house Christie's. 'Being a very practical man … he wanted a house in the country and thought 2.5 hours driving from Mexico City was rather enough,' she remembers, 'so he drew a circle on a map … and landed on this place … So many people had gone to the States to work, and it hadn't been spoilt at all … He knew I was dabbling with the idea of finding somewhere in Mexico, as really it would become a culinary centre (but I didn't think of that at the time). So he showed me where he lived … That's how I arrived.' It was difficult to find an ecological engineer who would work comfortably with an architect to build a self-sustaining house for her. The house ended up without a straight line in it and surrounded by rainwater collection tanks.

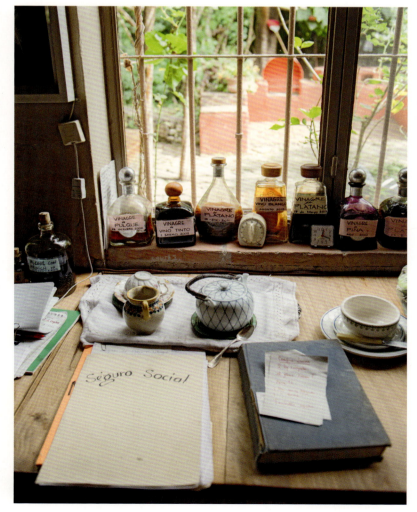

(previous spread) **A lone fisherman in the calm of a Michoacán sunset on Lago de Pátzcuaro. Surrounded by volcanic mountains, the lake is said by indigenous locals to be the point where the barrier between life and death is at its narrowest**

(facing page) **Ninety-three-year-old Diana Kennedy at home in Coatepec de Morelos, where she has lived for the last forty years; and (right) In Kennedy's kitchen, her tidy counter and homemade vinegars on the window sill**

Kennedy's concern for the decreasing biodiversity of her adopted state is very apparent. 'Michoacán has produced more avocados for the world than any other state ... Now, the demands are so great from Japan and China that the biodiversity in this area is being destroyed to plant avocados. It's a very big problem; we have to go right back to unsustainable populations, which nobody wants to talk about, of course. And so many people want the American Dream, to have a house and two cars and use as much water and electricity as they want, and to have enough food to eat and to spare and to waste.' In her own cooking-for-one, nothing is wasted. 'I always like to have some *frijoles* around, beans cooked in the normal way ... I always like to make Mexican rice ... That and a good tortilla and avocado [and] a little *salsa fresca*, and that would be it ... There's one [local] butcher with organic pork, and I go to the market and have a lovely taco of *carnitas*, greasy and wonderful; I always ask for the fat and the skin, the crackling.' She depends on her garden for fresh produce, highlighting the presence of 'a lot of Seville orange trees ... because breakfast for Brits is not breakfast without Seville orange marmalade'.

(facing page) **Objects in Kennedy's self-sufficient home, Quinta Diana, include** (top left) **two scythes for gardening,** (top right) ***barro negro* pottery from Oaxaca,** (bottom left) **reusable and biodegradable scrubbing brushes, and** (bottom right) **a cook's essential ingredient: a string of garlic**

(left) **Stairs at Quinta Diana showcasing some of the two hundred plant species Kennedy has collected on her travels across Mexico; and** (above) **Kennedy with the bitter orange marmalade she makes every year out of 'whatever the plants provide' and then gives to friends**

Benedicta Alejo Vargas
Traditional Cook, Morelia, Michoacán

Traditional cook Benedicta Alejo Vargas is famous for her tricoloured tortillas made from white, red and blue maize, as well as for her unique seven-pointed *colondas de siete picos*, tamales typical of the Uruapan area.

Alejo was raised by her grandmother as her mother had to work to support the family, and it was her grandmother who taught her to cook. She now gives masterclasses at the Taller Zirita in Morelia and has travelled the world, including cooking regional specialities for the Pope at the Vatican as part of a celebration of Mexican regional cuisine. (Among her dishes were *mole de queso* [cheese, tomato and chilli stew], *mole de conejo* [rabbit stew], *atole de tamarindo, atole do ajonjolí* [sesame *atole*] and her special tortillas.) Alejo's students learn to make traditional dishes, cooking outdoors over wood-burning stoves, grinding maize on *metates* and making tortillas from scratch. In interviews she has mentioned that she prays to the Virgin of Guadalupe every time she cooks, adding, 'She helps me to do things because I cannot do them alone.' Alejo,

who always dresses in traditional clothing, recalls being given her first *metate* when she was only three years old. Now her daughter and young granddaughter cook alongside her.

In 2015 Alejo participated in Slow Meat, an event that brought together producers, butchers, and food industry and other leaders to address the conundrum of industrial animal husbandry and celebrate possible alternatives. That year she was named *Maestra Cocinera*. She is also a regular participant in, and winner of, the food festival Encuentro de Cocina Tradicional in Morelia, and won the prize for best rescued dish with her *churipo de carne seca*, a hearty beef soup. One of the main promoters of the rescue of traditional and prehispanic cuisine, her favourite ingredient is *col de árbol* (a variety of cabbage originally from Spain and Portugal). Alejo only works with seasonal, local ingredients and never uses scales or measurements. Other signature dishes include *atapakua de fiesta* (a type of soup) and *tzirita*, a *botana* (appetiser) made of finely ground chilli seeds and other savoury ingredients.

(facing page) **Benedicta Alejo Vargas making her famous tricoloured tortillas at Cynthia Martínez's workshop in Morelia, and** (right) **preparing a** *flor de calabaza* **(squash blossom) salad and the tricoloured** *masa* **used to make her signature tortillas. Tortillas in the area are traditionally made with blue and white maize (representing night and day); Alejo added the red as a tribute to her tribe, the Purépecha.** (below) ***Colondas de siete picos***; **and** (bottom) ***Flor de calabaza***

Esperanza Galván Hernández
Traditional Cook, Zacán, Michoacán

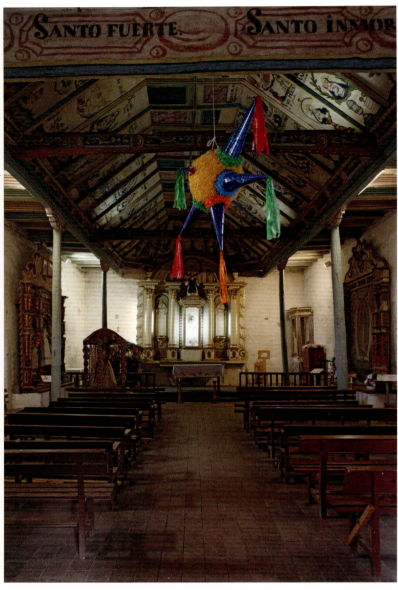

(left) **Esperanza Galván Hernández paying her respects at the family altar at her cousin's home, visiting** (above) **El Templo de San Pedro y la Huatápera de Zacán, a small temple within an old hospital, and** (facing page, top left) **outside the Huatápera**

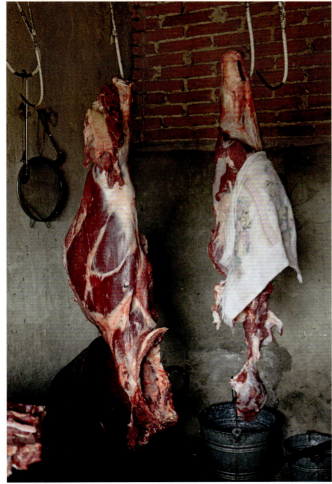

(above) **Zacán's town butcher, Octavio Ramos, at his** (left) *carnicería;* **and** (below) *Maíz azul* **(sweet blue maize) on the cob in Galván's kitchen**

Juana Bravo & Luz Bravo
Traditional Cooks, Angahuan, Michoacán

Traditional cook Juana Bravo was widowed twenty years ago when her husband died in an accident. Her specialities are dishes from Michoacán which she was taught to prepare by her grandmother. Bravo has several children. Her son lives in Maryland and works in construction. He has not been back to Mexico for nearly twenty years, but Bravo now has her papers in order so she can visit him. Her daughters are artisans and traditional cooks. Luz Bravo has recently earned a bachelor's degree in tourism, and is hoping to work with her mother promoting Mexican food worldwide. The two women cook frequently together at events in Mexico and overseas as 'Juana and Luz'.

On her own, Juana Bravo has travelled internationally on behalf of the Mexican government as a champion of traditional cooking methods. In 2005 she went to Paris with a team of cooks who prepared dishes to be considered for UNESCO World Heritage status; she contributed *corundas* (wrapped parcels like tamales but spherical or triangular) and bicoloured tortillas. Five years later she cooked in Nairobi in Kenya at the first Mexican Food Week. Her village, Angahuan, is typical of settlements on the Purhépecha Plateau and is the nearest town to the volcano known as Paricutín, which was active between 1943 and 1952 with disastrous effect. Juana originally trained as a craftswoman. Her father, a tourist guide, would invite visitors to eat at the house since no-one in the community normally prepared food to sell. This is how Juana became a cook. She currently teaches women in the region to preserve and pass on traditional knowledge regarding the gastronomic wealth of Michoacán. She continues to cook and serve food to tourists at her farmhouse. Her signature bicoloured tortillas are half yellow/white and half blue, and are made with two separate doughs, each using different kinds of maize. Other dishes she serves regularly include *atapakuas* (a type of *mole*), *churipos* (beef stew with chillies), *uchepos* (a maize dish) and *corundas* with different fillings. The maize she uses in her cooking comes from her own *milpa* and that of her son-in-law, Luz's husband.

(above) **Luz Bravo looking for *nopales*, and** (left) **harvesting avocados from her family's *milpa*, which also contains blue maize, *manzano* chillies, squash, wild anise, peaches and plums**

(above) **Juana Bravo looking out over San Juan de las Colchas, which was destroyed by lava from the eruption of Paricutín in 1943. Only the church spire is visible today.** (above left) *Flor de Calabaza*; and (left) **Juana preparing a meal at home with** *trompas de puerco* **mushrooms collected by her son**

Tlaxcala: *Bulls & Balls*

There were two fixed points in Mexican life in colonial times, apart from the national culinary obsession: bullfighting and Catholicism. Both came over with the Spaniards in the sixteenth century; both have helped reinforce important qualities of the national character. Today, you can add *fútbol* into the mix with the national hysteria that surrounds it. Although churches outnumber bullrings or football stadiums, it would be interesting to gauge statistical correlations between Mexicans attending the *corrida* and the *estadio* and those who go to church every Sunday.

Mexicans subscribe to an admixture of prehispanic religious traditions and beliefs melded with Catholicism, the most notable expression of which is the worship of the Virgin of Guadalupe, a deity to whom people of every class, level of education and pay grade express varying degrees of fealty. Religiosity makes strict observation of numerous saints' days and other religious festivals a national pastime. The Madonna of Tepeyac in Mexico City is the world's most visited Catholic pilgrimage destination. The site, where a local peasant called Juan Diego first glimpsed the Virgin of Guadalupe in 1531, is today the scene of the greatest religious gatherings anywhere.

Mexico was an early adherent to secular ideals. The 1917 Constitution forbids religious interference in affairs of state; it also codified government intrusion into religious matters; the Church was not permitted to involve itself in public education or to own property. Mexico's population is 80 per-cent Catholic, the remainder mostly Protestants, Mormons and a growing number of other Christian sects. Judaism is practised fractionally, a few of the adherents' ancestors having arrived with the conquistadors.

The urban Mexican's infatuation with bullfighting (*corrida de toros*) is unmatched in South America, or in some parts of Spain come to that. Mexico City's Plaza de Toros México is the world's largest arena, seating up to fifty thousand and bringing the capital to a standstill each time there is a fight. There is nothing like the sound of the thunder produced by spectators at a bullfight. Although most commentators contest bullfighting's description as a sport, the gladiatorial *torero* engages in the most dangerous recreational blood sport in the modern world.

Tlaxcala is known for its cattle ranches and bull-rearing among other things. Meeting José Luis Angelino dressed in his finery at the state's beautiful Plaza de Toros Jorge el Ranchero Aguilar showed me how much history and ritual are involved in the *corrida*. One of Mexico's most famous matadors, Angelino has fought in Madrid, Seville and Colombia, and has the scars to prove it ('a badge of honour', as he calls them). He says he is never as free as when he is standing before a 1-ton bull, as mean a creature as man or nature can breed.

At the other end of the spectrum, José Luis Sánchez Mastranzo is no matador. This slight, gentle Jesuit does not attend bullfights but fights to maintain culinary traditions and artisanal trades in his home state. The soft-spoken Mastranzo is known for his kitchen, which serves the neighbourhood poor and provides employment to traditional cooks from the area. He is a strong believer in the relationship between religion and food in Mexico. 'There's a lot of syncretism, mysticism and magic in the production of food,' he notes. 'The sharing of food is a religious duty.'

José Luis Angelino
Bullfighter, Piedras Negras, Tlaxcala

'You are never as free as when you are in front of a bull,' observes bullfighter José Luis Angelino. 'In the bullring, you live the *hora de la verdad* – the moment of reckoning. You have to respect it, feel it and live it.'

Angelino's native state is known for its many cattle ranches and in particular for the rearing of fighting bulls. The son of professional bullfighter Angelino Joaquín Macías, José Luis is proud of his heritage. As a child he would accompany his father to fights, acting as sword handler from the age of nine and starting to fight in his own right while still a teenager. Esteemed as one of the best matadors in Tlaxcala, he has toured all over Mexico as well as to Madrid, Seville and Zaragoza in Spain. He counts among his bullfighting influences the Colombian master César Rincón, who was born into extreme poverty and left his country to follow his dream in Spain. Angelino describes his own recent goring as a 'badge of honour'.

When asked why he keeps returning to the bullring to look death in the eye, Angelino does not hesitate. 'The truth is that I am very privileged to be a bullfighter,' he explains. 'First, to have been born in this taurine state of Tlaxcala, and second, for being able to wear the suit [of lights] that very few people ... are able to wear ... My dream is to be an important bullfighting figure, a bullfighter who leaves a mark in Mexico, who is remembered. The price I have to pay is very high. I am doing what I love ... It is my way of life, my way of expressing feeling.' And he adds, 'When the bull allows me to express myself as a bullfighter, when a bull gives his life to me and I offer my life to him, the beauty of bullfighting surges, the magic of bullfighting ... I fight in tears. Only my heart fights. I forget the body, I forget technique. Only the heart flows.' Angelino thinks of his matador's suit as a 'sacred' garment. 'With this suit,' he adds, 'I sweat fear.'

Perhaps surprisingly, perhaps not, Angelino's favourite colour is green, the colour of hope and of life – and of his suit of lights. He expects to be able to continue in his chosen profession for 'as long as the bulls continue to respect' him. Boredom is never an issue in the course of his daily routine because 'every day I feed it with training and with hope. One looks to bring things to bullfighting and to keep growing as a bullfighter.' In every fight, of course, either the bull must die or the matador must be wounded or killed; it is important to remember that a fighting bull is an animal whose ferocity is magnified by both anger and speed. 'Imagine 500 kilos from one minute to the next, the speed they can reach,' Angelino muses. 'And he might not kill you by goring you. He could kill you with a hit; you could fall.' On the other hand, there are no words to describe how it feels when Angelino kills a bull. 'I think that it's simply his time,' he reflects. 'Put simply, the bull has given you his life and you have to be able to kill him well.'

Many people, of course, believe that bullfighting is the cruellest, most primitive of sports, that it is inhumane and should be stopped. 'Well, look, above all they should show respect,' says Angelino. 'They should respect what they do not know ... They do not have the background to speak against bullfighting ... What bothers me is that above all I am a human being. I am a bullfighter, and the death of my colleagues in Spain, in Mexico, in Peru ... How is it possible that people laugh at the death of a human being? Above all else we have to respect human beings. Before being bullfighters, we are human beings.' In light of Angelino's admiration for his taurine foes, it is perhaps not surprising that, when asked what creature he would choose to be in another life, he replies without hesitating, 'I would want to be an angry bull, of course!'

(previous spread) **The dormant Iztaccíhuatl volcano seen from the motorway en route from Mexico City to Puebla. Iztaccíhuatl is also called 'White Woman' due to its resemblance to a woman lying on her back and covered with snow**

(left) **José Luis Angelino taking a break in the practice ring at Piedras Negras, and** (facing page) **in his green *toreador* suit at the ring in Tlaxcala. Dating from the early 1700s, the Plaza de Toros Jorge el Ranchero Aguilar, named after a famed bullfighter, is the oldest bullring in continuous use in the Americas**

(above) **Angelino braving wild bulls (in the background), roaming freely within their fenced-off range, and** (right) **resting at Piedras Negras, one of the country's most important fighting-bull ranches and still run by its original breeders, the González family**

(top left) *Agua miel* (honey water) at the heart of a maguey cactus at Piedras Negras hacienda in Tlaxcala. When a maguey is tapped at maturity, it bleeds honey water (essentially unfermented pulque), which needs to be collected three times a day

(above) **Severino, a *tlachiquero*, in the maguey fields at Piedras Negras, and** (left) **stirring some pulque.** (below) **A ranch hand's lunch of squash and pork crackling awaiting a glass of the brew**

Cornelio Hernández Rojas
Anthropologist & Maize Expert, San Juan Ixtenco, Tlaxcala

Cornelio Hernández Rojas, a specialist in Mexico's native maize varieties, lives in the state of Tlaxcala, whose name comes from the Nahuatl word meaning 'place of the maize tortilla'. Archaeologists have found evidence of ancient maize cultivation in Oaxaca, Tamaulipas and Puebla; while Tlaxcala appears not to have been one of the areas where maize originated, its name suggests that it became a centre of diversification over time. Many maize types were discovered more than seven thousand years ago, and ancient peoples experimented in order to improve the quality of their plants.

Hernández was born in Ixtenco, the rural community where he still lives. He grows maize in the traditional way and speaks often in public about the risks of importing genetically modified seeds – a policy supported by national and state governments alike. When he first became interested in maize, it was the range of colours unique to the area's plants that attracted him. 'I began working with various farmers to raise awareness of the importance of rescuing some varieties and preserving others that had not received much attention up until that moment,' he explains. 'Unfortunately, native maize varieties have been threatened in recent years … We know what nature is like. Nature does not respect rules … If I have a transgenic crop plot, it will surely influence the rest of my crops. Pollen will reach them and we will be contaminating our seeds. The other limitation is that in order to plant the native varieties of maize, as farmers we select the best seeds from the best plants. What would happen if these seeds were supplemented by transgenic maize? Each year we would have to buy seeds to plant … If you plant transgenic maize, you have a yearly expenditure. When we plant native varieties, we … do not need to buy them; in the worst cases we exchange them with other producers.' A lifelong advocate and activist for the cause of genetic purity in Mexican corn, Hernández acknowledges the constraints on both sides of the heated global arguments around transgenic mutation.

Hernández continues to rejoice in both the colours and the taste and textural differences between native maize varieties. 'In the '80s, there was a decrease in the sowing of maize of different colours because the politics of commercialisation realised through CONASUPO [the National Company of Popular Subsistence, which played a key role in Mexican agricultural policies, shaping food production, consumption and rural incomes] dictated the buying of white maize, the whiter the better,' he recalls. 'They did not purchase coloured maize, so the market [for it] decreased as well. Fortunately, in the case of Ixtenco our artisans preserved this maize diversity, but in many communities of Tlaxcala, and probably of Mexico, the diversity disappeared since it was not competitive in the market.'

Addressing questions of culinary history and food preparation, he explains that blue maize tortillas are 'sweeter' than white ones, and that red maize, whose taste he finds impossible to describe, is not used as much to make tortillas. Cacahuazintle maize 'is preferred for the crafting of *atoles* [hot drinks] tamales and *pinole* [a mixture of maize, cocoa and other ingredients]. It is also used for *pozole* [traditional soup or stew] because of its porosity … Ixtenco [or] garlic maize is known by agronomists as tunic maize since each kernel has its own covering … It is a variety that for many decades was safeguarded by only two families in Ixtenco: that of *Don* Vicente Hernández Alonso and that of *Don* Catalino Hernández … We rediscovered it and now thankfully many farmers are planting it.' The main point to remember, Hernández notes, is that the process of pollination is impossible to control where maize is concerned. 'It receives all the pollen that comes its way,' he reiterates. 'It's said that maize is one of the most promiscuous plants in nature.'

(left) **Different varieties and colours of native maize were cultivated by Mesoamerican cultures for millennia; some strains are in danger of extinction.** (facing page) **Cornelio Hernández Rojas at work on his** *milpa* **in Ixtenco, under the watchful eye of the inactive La Malinche volcano**

(above) **Hernández among the wildflowers** (above right) **he planted to attract insects away from his maize crop, and** (right) **opening a maize husk. Seven 'races' of maize (and countless 'sub-races') are local to Tlaxcala, which has always been one of the centres of maize diversification. In fact, Tlaxcala means 'place of the maize tortilla' in Nahuatl.** (facing page) **Red-maize** *masa*, **a paste of ground nixtamalised red maize, and the base for the hot drink** *atole agrio*

Francisco Molina
Chef, Evoka Restaurante, Apizaco, Tlaxcala

The young chef Francisco Molina studied in Puebla, France and the US before returning to his native state and opening Evoka Restaurante about five years ago. 'The valley of Tlaxcala is my main influence,' he explains. The tasting menu at Evoka, originally planned with out-of-town visitors in mind, can be described as a walk through that very valley, with every dish 'an ode to local products and tradition'. Sustainability and a revival of the local economy, including nurturing close ties with producers and suppliers, are key aspects of Molina's approach.

The small state of Tlaxcala is located slightly east of Mexico's centre and thus is land-locked. The political heart of the state is its capital, also called Tlaxcala, even though it is not the largest city. Tlaxcala lies at the foot of the north-western slope of the La Malinche volcano and is one of the oldest polities in Mexico, having been an autonomous polity (confederation of *altepeme*) since at least the fourteenth century. The area's economy is still based on the traditional enterprises of agriculture, textile production, and the trading and selling of the products of native peoples such as the Nahua, Otomí and Totonac, especially on market days. Other important cities include Santa Ana Chiautempan, the most populous city in the state, and Apizaco, noted for its textile production as well as being the location of Evoka Restaurante. Most of the state consists of rugged terrain dominated by ridges and deep valleys.

Molina was inspired to open Evoka by the fact that 'there wasn't a single restaurant that was serving good food' in the area. 'Here, a lot of restaurants say, "I'm doing traditional food," but they don't even use local ingredients; they just buy all their ingredients from Walmart,' he notes. Normally on weekends he has a lot of customers who make the long journey from Mexico City and other cities, their numbers growing steadily over the years. 'We are like a destination restaurant,' he says. 'People just come here to eat and they come back. Obviously we cannot base our business on those people because on weekdays we also need to say hi to the locals and they need to come [as well].' Molina's approach to devising dishes

to suit both sets of his clientele has been to constantly tweak all of them so that the gap between the two is becoming less apparent. In this way 'the locals come here more and foreign people come here more, and the difference between the tasting menu and the à la carte menu gets smaller every time.'

Mostly Molina features fish or chicken, but his *moles* and salsas are his 'main product'. What sets Tlaxcaltecan food apart is that it focuses on a few ingredients, perhaps three or four, sometimes as few as two, whereas *moles* made in other states can consist of numerous ingredients from coriander to chocolate. Chillies and maize are critical to the mix as well, as are edible insects and worms. Different-coloured tortillas attest to the varieties of maize that are available in the area, and maize is even used to make ice cream. However, Molina notes that traditional maize varieties are about double the price of non-traditional ones, which are easier to source and thus omnipresent in Mexican cuisine generally.

(above) **Francisco Molina admiring some local produce, a bounty of maize and wild mushrooms. He uses red, blue and yellow maize in his own cooking.** (facing page, left) **Aged rib-eye** *tortas* **(sandwiches) with** *chalupas*, **an upscale take on an Apizaco speciality; and** (facing page, right) **A crab-and-Brussels sprout** *gordita*

Puebla: *Food & Divinity*

Cuetlaxcoapan – 'where serpents change their skin' in Nahuatl – refers to the area where the present-day city of Puebla (capital of the state of the same name) is located. One of the five most important colonial cities in New Spain, and situated between the indigenous settlements of Tlaxcala and Cholula, the Puebla-Tlaxcala metropolis has transformed itself into an industrial powerhouse. Volkswagen has its largest overseas plants there, and Audi's plant in San José Chiapa is the most technologically advanced in the Western Hemisphere. More than three million people live in Puebla, making it Mexico's fourth-largest city. As the principal hub for eastern central Mexico, it has some of the country's best higher-education institutions, and is becoming an artistic centre with the construction of Toyo Ito's Baroque Museum. The Amparo Museum, another world-class institution, is dedicated to Mexican prehispanic, modern and contemporary art.

The city of Puebla has seen its share of historical struggles, having been fought over and occupied by foreign invaders. The American Army arrived in 1847, only leaving after a peace treaty was signed the following year. The French Expeditionary Army (in those days considered one of the world's strongest) was defeated on 5 May 1862 at the Battle of Puebla; annual *Cinco de Mayo* celebrations recall that victory. The French came back the following year and took the city but withdrew for the final time in 1866. Its subsequent architectural splendours are a result of the city's reconstruction.

Poblanos are nothing if not proud of their cuisine, especially their signature dishes. Everywhere you go in Mexico, food talk turns to *mole*, the many-coloured, many-flavoured sauces for which Puebla is famed. And then there is *chiles en nogada*, as near an emblematic national dish as you can get. Both dishes owe their origins to the kitchens of convents that created culinary *mestizaje*. The coexistence of Spanish nuns alongside *mestiza* women helped the transfer of culinary knowledge and the development of uniquely Mexican (as against prehispanic or Spanish) diets. *Mole poblano* is the creation of Puebla's religious orders.

Chef Ángel Vázquez, who is from Puebla, has studied the preparation of *moles* and *chiles en nogada* down to the last detail, whether seated next to his grandmother's *chimenea* or from nuns in the city. *Mole poblano* is composed of thirty different ingredients served over turkey or chicken, while *chiles en nogada* bears the traces of both French and Middle Eastern influences. Made with stuffed green chilli peppers, walnut sauce and pomegranates, it reminded me of a Persian dish, *fesenjan*, that my grandmother used to make with pomegranates, molasses and ground walnuts. It's a small world really. Vázquez is most interested in 'rescuing' the secret recipes that usually go to the grave with their cooks. Recipes are jealously guarded in Mexico, only handed down from one generation to the next within family circles. 'We need to share,' Vázquez says with missionary zeal.

Our own project's missionary zeal took us next to the foothills of Popocatépetl, the ancient volcano just then letting off steam as pickers worked beneath the midday sun to harvest the nutritious *nopal* cactus that is a mainstay of indigenous Mexican cuisine. Having been pricked numerous times by the devilish plant, it felt challenging to eat *nopal* wrapped in a tortilla and mixed with a variety of meats and exotic salsas.

Convent of the Clarisas Capuchinas Sisters
Puebla, Puebla

The Convent of the Clarisas Capuchinas Sisters in Puebla was founded in 1704 by *Doña* Ana Francisca de Zuñiga. Following the Spaniards' arrival, convents became safe havens for women, as well as places where they were taught about Catholicism. As convents metamorphosed into schools and cultural centres, their kitchens became increasingly elaborate. The recipe for one of the most important dishes in Mexican culinary history, *chiles en nogada*, was invented in a convent. Featuring poblano peppers stuffed with pork, beef, fruit and nuts, the dish is covered with a fresh walnut sauce and garnished with pomegranate seeds and fresh parsley.

Convent kitchens were where ingredients and cultural traditions, both indigenous and imported, came together. It could be said that what is thought of today as typically Mexican food had its origins there. Recipes ranged from the simple to the complex. One simple biscuit called a *tlaco* combines pulque and lard. A stovetop pudding, *manjar blanco*, calls for boiling chicken, grinding it until smooth, and then mixing it with sugar, ground rice and milk –

perhaps a distant echo of a recipe perfected in Ottoman Turkey. Butter and cream were rarely included in convent desserts, being too expensive to purchase and too difficult to store. Chocolate only appeared as a beverage. Other specialities included *duraznos prensados* (candied pressed peaches) and *lagrimas de obispo o dulces plateados en dulce de piñon* (bishop's tears or silvered sweets in a pine-nut sauce).

The cooks in convent kitchens were sometimes the nuns themselves and sometimes their servants, who worked to their instructions. The diet of wealthier nuns included a generous meat ration (on days when meat was allowed). The end of the seventeenth century saw them making their chocolate with donkey's milk, which apparently was thought of as being more prestigious than cow's, goat's or sheep's milk. If a nun was unwell, she might drink four cups every day. All convents would sell their sweets to bring in some money. Even the discarded edges of the paper-thin pastry used to make Communion wafers could be purchased by passers-by.

(previous spread) **Street vendors of all ages plying their trade on the streets of Puebla**

(above) **The Convent of the Clarisas Capuchinas in Puebla, where eighteen nuns, including** (facing page) **Sister Cristina Pérez Méndez, live, cook, eat and pray; and** (top right) **Sister Celia Pérez Juarez in the dining room used for receiving visiting**

priests, and (right) **selling tamales made in the convent to visitors and passers-by. The nuns make** *atole, mole verde* **and** *rajas tamales* **to sell to the public. Though their kitchens have been modernised, their recipes are centuries old**

Angélica Moreno Rodríguez
Owner, Talavera de la Reyna, Cholula, Puebla

(above) **Angélica Moreno Rodríguez straightening a Talavera plate in her showroom. She has been instrumental in preserving and modernising the traditional craft of Talavera-making in Puebla**

(right) **Moreno tending her garden in Cholula, where she grows fruit (including forty varieties of fig) to use in the homemade jams and jellies she sells in her restaurant and to friends, and** (below) **her raspberry jam**

Angelíca Moreno Rodríguez, who owns one of the most important Talavera workshops in Puebla, is also the owner of one of the town's top hotels, Casa Puebla. Moreno is celebrated around the world for being the first person to market the region's famous handmade majolica ceramics, turning away from traditional décor and instead featuring contemporary high-end designs. Moreno also makes jam and marmalade from fruit grown in her orchard in Cholula, where she lives. In fact, cooking was her first love. She dreamed of opening a restaurant, instead ending up working for a financial firm. Then she started taking classes with a local artist, moving on to learn from the local masters of Talavera.

Talavera pottery was introduced to Mexico from Spain in the mid-seventeenth century. Moreno is known for recognising that old traditions like pottery-making needed new collaborators and a modern twist to remain relevant. So in the mid-1990s, as Latin American art was rising in prominence, she began recruiting painters, sculptors and graphic designers to create forward-looking ceramics. Since her first show in 1997, Moreno's ceramics company has gone from strength to strength. More than fifty artists have contributed designs or sculpted their own pottery under her supervision, and their work is in constant demand. In 2006, the Mexican government included sixty pieces from Talavera de la Reyna in a display that was part of a cultural exchange with China. Shows in Paris, Barcelona and Madrid followed.

Through both her company and her hotel – with its notable restaurant – Moreno is an ambassador for her town, every aspect of which she believes is 'romantic', right down to the food. Her greatest passion is to remain close to the earth in all that she does, 'because the earth gives us everything. The earth gives us life, food, art, sweets, everything. I love it.'

(below) **The colourful portico at the atrium entrance of** (right) **the Templo de San Francisco Acatepec in Cholula, a Baroque church known for its façade of Talavera mosaics. Legend says that the town has 365 colourful churches (one for each day of the year). In reality there are fewer than half that many**

Ángel Vázquez
Owner & Chef, Intro Restaurant, Puebla, Puebla

Ángel Vázquez grew up around food. 'I got into cooking when I was a kid,' he explains. 'My friends used to have a *taqueria*, a place where they sell *tostadas*, *sopes*, *tlacoyos* – snacks, in other words.' Vázquez attended the Instituto Culianario de México, from which he obtained degrees in Gastronomy and Culinary Management. He also studied in France and Thailand, and has worked in eateries around the world.

Vázquez opened Intro Restaurant in 2003. Its choice menu evokes the flavours he encountered on his travels, but served up with a contemporary, local twist. 'We only have twenty-two dishes on the menu; we change it every six months,' the chef says. 'In the beginning, we started doing one or two plates from Thailand, Vietnam, Scandinavia and Morocco, so more ethnic cuisines; we wanted to offer something that you couldn't get in Puebla [at the time].' After some years of representing the state's culinary heritage at events abroad, he decided to adjust the menu to include some local items.

The state of Puebla, known as the culinary heart of Mexico, is home to many of the country's iconic dishes, among them *mole poblano* and *chiles en nogada*, both of which are served at Intro. Puebla's culinary tradition has its origin in the blending of prehispanic, Spanish, French and Middle Eastern influences. *Mole poblano*, a sauce composed of more than thirty ingredients, is served over turkey or chicken. *Chiles en nogada* – stuffed green chilli peppers with walnut sauce and pomegranate – is only served in the summer. Popular snacks include *chalupas* (fried thick maize tortillas with chicken and salsa), *molotes* (patties made from a mix of fried maize and potato puree, and filled with different stews, cream and salsa) and *escamoles* (fried ants' eggs). Traditional sweets are many and varied, among them *camotes* (flavoured sweet potato), *pepita* sweets (caramel-covered pumpkin seeds), *jamoncillos* (flavoured pumpkin-seed bars) and *macarrones*.

At one time, Puebla's convents were filled with the daughters of the wealthy merchants whose influence and purchasing power brought foreign ingredients and ideas into the city. As a result, traditional cooking was heavily influenced by nuns cooking in convent kitchens with a specialism in the making of sweets. Although this aspect is less apparent in contemporary cuisine, it is one that Vázquez would like to 'rescue', although he has found that local people guard their culinary secrets jealously and do not want to pass them on except perhaps within their own families. Because fewer people these days enjoy complicated cooking, this can present difficulties. 'If you don't love to cook, you're not going to care,' the chef points out. 'They can give you the recipe from maybe a hundred years ago that has been handed down in the family, and maybe now a kid won't care because he doesn't want to make sweets all day.' If this kind of local knowledge is lost, he adds, 'I don't know what will happen. So we need to share.' He convinced his own father to share his family recipe for *chiles en nogada* so that it would not disappear, noting, 'I prefer that someone take the recipe and start doing it so that it will continue. Maybe they'll say, "This recipe was from Ángel, who got it from his dad." I would prefer to have it like that than to not have it at all.'

(above) **Ángel Vázquez reviewing proper knife use with his intern Diana Arizaga in the kitchen at Intro.** (facing page, left) **Raw ingredients used by Vázquez, including whole green poblano peppers, which are soaked and coated in egg batter (*capeado*) after being filled with a mixture of pork, dried fruits and nuts, and then covered in fresh walnut sauce; and** (facing page, right) **The finished dish: *chiles en nogada***

(above) **The Museo Internacional del Barroco in Puebla de Zaragoza, designed by Japanese architect Toyo Ito; and** (facing page) **Puebla from the Casa Reyna hotel**

(above) *Nopal* fields on the outskirts of San Andrés Cholula with Popocatépetl in the background. Well over a hundred species of *nopal* are found in Mexico. (right) José Otilio Toribio preparing *nopal* by scraping off the spines, and (far right) his lunch, a field labourer's royal spread in honour of visiting guests

(above) **Fields of *chiles poblanos* in Puebla.**
(far left) **The ripened red poblano is significantly hotter than** (left) **the less ripe green poblano used for *chiles en nogada***

Tabasco: *Malinche Sauce*

Tabasco is Mexico's wettest state, the year-round rainfall inundating the land, causing periodic catastrophic flooding. As a result, Tabasco is mainly covered in rainforest and provides an ideal climate for the cacao plant that produces the bean that produces the paste that becomes chocolate. Tabasco is also Mexico's largest oil-producing state, with all the attendant problems that mineral riches bring politically and socially. This has bred a laissez-faire attitude to work by *Tabasqueños* – things just don't get done. The state is also the site of La Venta, home to the Olmec civilisation, considered the first of the Mesoamerican cultures that make up present-day Mexico's population. The giant brooding heads one encounters in museums, at archaeological sites or scattered randomly where history abandoned them cast a palpable shadow over people's daily routines.

One of Mexico's principal charms is its ordinary folk, people who welcome you into their homes with a generous dose of hospitality, regardless of means or station. The other consistent theme is the attachment to neighbourhood, tribe and, especially, the modern state. Tabasco's famous daughter, La Malinche, was an offering by the *caciques* (cultural leaders) to Hernán Cortés in 1519. Finding the gift so appealing, the conquistador prohibited his soldiers from bringing women from Spain, thus forcing the mixing of European with indigenous American blood. Born at the turn of the sixteenth century, La Malinche (aka *Doña* Marina, Malinalli or Malintzin) was a Nahua woman who is said to have had an important role as Cortés' lover, consort, interpreter and political intermediary, thus furthering Spain's conquest of Mesoamerica after the defeat of the Aztec Empire. Traitor, slave girl or heroine, she still arouses conflicting passions today. Some view her as the mother of the *mestizos*, the forerunners of today's Mexicans. Others view her as treacherous, an impulse reinforced during the Mexican Revolution when the term '*malinchista*' became synonymous with treachery.

Gabriela Ruiz Lugo is no Malinche, but this young chef, who has recently gained national attention for her work, is a fierce proponent of Tabasco, its food, people, places, even the *pico de paloma* chilli, which she says was 'stolen' by Edmund McIlhenny, the American adventurer-entrepreneur who took the secret of Tabasco sauce and made it world-famous from his manufacturing base in Louisiana. A taste for chillies was probably the only plus for Mexico, as returning soldiers from the Mexican–American War changed dietary tastes in the US. (As an aside, Queen Elizabeth II is a great fan of the hot sauce, with bottles of Tabasco found in the kitchens at Buckingham Palace, Balmoral and Windsor Castle.) 'Food can change your mood,' Ruiz points out. 'It touches the soul, speaks through the senses and can be the perfect cure for what ails you.' To prove her point, we set off on a journey of discovery, the first stop being to see some *pejelagarto*, a prehistoric fish that has remained unchanged for some sixty million years. A species of freshwater gar common to Tabasco's rivers, specimens of this ungainly creature are displayed at most roadside food stalls. Then Ruiz took us to a cacao plantation, the pods in various stages of ripening. Cacao (and its magic elixir, chocolate) is another unique food product which derives from Mexico's deep history.

José Manuel Herrera Sánchez
Pejelagarto Vendor, Comalcalco, Tabasco

Street vendor José Manuel Herrera Sánchez sells eggs, *mojarras* (a common Caribbean fish) and *pejelagartos*, or garfish. Herrera buys his stock from Frontera, which is about 180 kilometres away from his place of business.

Pejelagarto is the large freshwater gar common in south-eastern Mexico, particularly in the state of Tabasco. The fish are notable for their primitive appearance. In fact the family to which they belong, the Lepisosteidae, appeared during the Cretaceous period and have survived to the present day relatively unchanged. They have a snout like an alligator's with long, sharp teeth. Specimens can exceed a metre in length and weigh more than 40 kilos. Grilled *pejelagarto* is a Tabascan speciality dating from prehispanic times; it can be prepared as filling for a simple empanada, in salads or with *chirmol*, a type of salsa or stew made with pumpkin seeds and burnt tortillas.

Mexican street food is often said to be the best in the world; the culture of street vendors dates back to prehispanic times. Fast food prepared in the streets or at market stalls is called *antojitos* ('little cravings') because it is typically not eaten at formal meals, especially not the main meal of the day, which is served in mid-afternoon. Street vendors are usually out in the early morning and evening or late at night. Although the government has tried to control them, many thousands continue to offer their wares illegally all over the country.

(previous spread) **La Venta, an Olmec site now part of the city of Villahermosa, having been transformed into a public park. La Venta originally served as a ceremonial centre with elaborate altars and tombs**

(facing page) **The prehistoric *pejelagarto* (garfish) has such a tough carapace that an axe is required to penetrate it.** (left) ***Pejelagarto* for sale at the side of the road in Comalcalco by José Manuel Herrera Sánchez** (above)

Gabriela Ruiz Lugo
Chef, Gourmet MX, Villahermosa, Tabasco

As far back as Gabriela Ruiz Lugo can remember, she wanted to be a chef. It was her love of local ingredients like cacao that made her decide to go into business in the state where she was born. She started Gourmet MX as a catering business, expanding it into a restaurant, private dining room and cheese shop as demand grew.

'Food can change your mood,' notes Ruiz, who studied at the Escuela Culinaria del Sureste in Mérida, the Instituto Gastronómico D'Gallia in Lima and the Pacific Institute of Culinary Arts in Vancouver. 'It touches the soul, speaks through the senses and can be the perfect cure for what ails you.' Storytelling through food remains a key concept for the young restaurateur, who was nominated as Revelation Chef and Best New Restaurant of Mexico by *Food and Travel Magazine* in 2014, the same year that she opened her second restaurant, Chata Pandal, also in Villahermosa. Now she travels the world sharing the largely unknown cuisine of Tabasco, which is influenced by its intense tropical environment.

Ruiz likes to use seasonal products that she finds in the local farmers' market. She buys lamb raised on an orange farm, as well as smoked cheese with pepper and bay leaves. Her style also celebrates other local products, among them Creole squash, extremely hot amashito chillies and bananas, and she favours such traditional techniques as smoking food over wood with spices. 'At first, my team did not understand my style of cooking,' she remembers. 'They were fascinated by molecular cuisine and ... stylish presentation. It has been a great challenge and a personal growing experience, creating my own style and convincing my team that taste and flavour continue to be the most significant aspect ... Presentation is important, but what I really want to accomplish is a mouthful of taste that leaves you breathless, allowing you to make a connection with a specific moment.' Her 'easy home cooking' aims to heal both body and soul, favouring thick rather than thin tortillas, onions, and lime and sour orange juice. Maize is a less important component of the local diet than elsewhere in Mexico, and Ruiz prefers to use less oil than in other areas. As to the ever-present Tabasco sauce, she recounts the myth behind its invention this way: 'A guy came from the States and picked the "Pico de Paloma" chilli pepper that he found here. He took the chilli pepper out to the States and started to grow [it], so he made this special sauce and put the name on it to remind him of Tabasco.'

Despite the hype and celebrity system developing around chefs internationally, Ruiz is astonished that anyone might recognise her and ask for her autograph, as happened recently in Cuernavaca. The aspect of internationalism that most attracts her is the possibility of discovering ingredients with which she can create tastes that remind her of home. 'For example, I went to Sri Lanka and I brought along this *verde* [sauce],' she says. 'We made this investigation with ... a friend of mine, [chef] Eduardo Plascencia ... and we found some green herbs ... that taste like the ones [at home]. So you are able to make *verde tabasqueño* anywhere in the world.' She seems uninterested in expanding her restaurant enterprise into an urban setting, however, saying, 'I'm very happy living here. You can see it's an adventure every day ... I think I am brave because living here is very complicated because of the weather ... It's hot and humid, but at the same time you have this amazing view, which is like heaven for a cook. It may be called "Green Hell", but it's heaven for a cook.'

(far left) ***Raviolis de platano macho rellenos de frijoles y chicharrón*** (plantain ravioli filled with beans and pork crackling), and (left) ***queso ahumado de Tenosique con miel y pimientos*** (smoked cheese from Tenosique with honey and peppers), prepared by Gabriela Ruiz Lugo at Gourmet MX in Villahermosa; and (facing page) **Ruiz visiting Jesús Maria Hacienda**

Jesús María Hacienda
Cacao Plantation & Chocolate Factory, Comalcalco, Tabasco

The modern history of Jesús María Hacienda dates from its acquisition by *Don* Rutilo Peralta Tejeda in 1917. In 1945 the hacienda was inherited by *Don* Rutilo's daughter *Doña* Rosaura Peralta de Cacep, who in turn handed it on to Juan Cacep Peralta in 1966. After closing the business for a couple of years, Rosa Maria Cacep Peralta reopened it together with her son (the present owner), Vicente Alberto Gutiérrez Cacep. The chocolate factory is known for its cacao derivatives, sweets and other products.

Jesús María Hacienda is dedicated to preserving the traditions of the Chontalpa area, especially the history of cacao production. In addition to cacao plants, chillies, achiote (the lipstick tree), bananas, oranges, guavas, *chicozapote* (a source of chewing gum), cedars, and other trees and shrubs are grown there. One of the workers, *Don* Juan Leyva, describes getting up at 5.30 each morning to cycle to work. *Don* Juan emphasises the pleasure he derives from leading tours around the factory because of 'the beauty of these plantations and the richness of cacao. Here you breathe pure air and you live in peace'. Attached to the house is a kitchen featuring a display of traditional utensils and explanations of traditional methods for making chocolate-based drinks, including *pozol* and *chorote*. *Pozol*, for example, is made by crushing husked roasted cocoa together with Tabasco chilli peppers. They are then mixed with ground maize and cooked.

The hacienda is one of the last plantations of Creole cacao, which only grows naturally in Chontalpa. The cacao is highly regarded internationally because of its high fat content and excellent flavour and aroma, and is purchased by the best European chocolatiers. Cacao is grown by first sowing a seed in a bag with soil. After four months a cut is made to accommodate a graft from an existing plant. The graft is covered with plastic to prevent water or insects from entering the cut. After a fortnight, the graft is checked to make sure it has taken. Then the rest of the plant is cut away so that the nutrients only feed the new one. Production can begin after two and a half years. Various parts of the plant provide a range of edible treats. *Mucílago* is the white coating that covers the cacao seed. Cocoa water and snow or mucilage ice cream are made from it. Jams are made from the seed pulp, while the seeds themselves are used to make butter, pasta and cocoa.

(far left) **The raw fruit of a cacao seed; and** (left) **Cocoa beans roasting in the traditional manner at Jesús María Hacienda.** (facing page) **The hacienda is one of very few to have returned to the farming of** *criollo* **cocoa, the bean most prized by fine chocolatiers but also one of the most disease-prone and difficult to grow**

(right) **A fisherman on Laguna Michoacán transporting fresh oysters, dry palm fronds (for burning) and peppercorn leaves (***hojas de pimienta***) to make** (below) **Tapesco-style oysters, a local speciality served at Chelys Restaurante in El Bellote in Paraíso**

418

Chula Banana Plantation
Teapa, Tabasco

Chula Banana Plantation exports the vast majority of its produce to Russia, Singapore, the US and Europe. Produce that is not good enough for export is sold locally, and the waste is fed to animals. The plantation, which is owned by Gabriela Armengol, produces around thirty-five thousand boxes of bananas, each weighing 20 kilos, per hectare per year – a good yield for the area, which is known for its unpredictable weather.

The banana plant is thought to have originated in southern Asia, possibly in the Mekong Delta. By AD 650, plants had reached the Mediterranean coast. Fifteenth-century Portuguese navigators carried bananas to the Canary Islands, and by the early sixteenth century they had been introduced by Spanish missionaries to Hispaniola in the New World. Bananas reached Mexico in 1554 courtesy of Bishop Vasco de Quiroga of Michoacán, who brought them with him from Europe.

Chiapas and Tabasco are Mexico's largest banana-growing areas. Around Teapa, annual rainfall can average more than 3,000 mm, thus providing ideal conditions. Bananas, which are grown both by small-scale farmers and on commercial plantations, are the world's fourth most important dietary staple after rice, wheat and maize. They are a major source of nutrition for people living in tropical areas. Of the eighty million tons produced globally each year, less than 20 per cent enters international trade; the rest are eaten locally. Banana plants are often used to shade crops such as cacao or coffee.

Each individual plant produces a single stem holding six to nine clusters, or hands, of bananas. A typical plant produces harvestable fruit in between nine and eighteen months. After the fruit is harvested, the stalk dies or is cut down. In its place one or more 'daughter' plants will sprout from the same underground rhizome. In addition to frequent rain, banana plants require rich soil and a lot of sunshine. Fruit can be picked green (unripe) and ripened quickly at its destination. Banana-sorting is done by women. Wielding small, extremely sharp knives, they pull the bananas out of water tanks and, in a matter of seconds, evaluate colour, size and texture, cut the *penca* (the bunch), and decide how many and which ones should be exported and which ones are suitable for the local market. Total concentration is required to perform this hazardous task.

(above) **Chula Banana Plantation in Teapa, where** (right) **bunches of bananas are picked and hung from an elaborate pulley system powered** (far right) **by workers like Constantino García Pastrano and his friend Uciel, who propel the heavy 'hands' along to the sorting and packing shed.** (facing page) **Women sorting bananas for foreign and domestic consumption**

Chiapas: *Glorious Pasts*

Like Tabasco, Chiapas is inundated with water, experiencing up to 4,500 mm of rainfall annually on its borders. Waiting for the skies to clear in order to fly to Tuxtla Gutiérrez, the capital, I could see we were in for a choppy ride. Not just weather-wise but in other ways too, as Chiapas has a reputation for trouble. Home to twelve officially recognised indigenous groups, the state's cycle of rebellion and subjugation dates way back.

Take, for example, Chamula, a *municipio* with a population of eighty thousand folk often seen as unfriendly to outsiders. San Juan Chamula, the main town, has many an apocryphal story around its fiercely independent spirit, especially towards anyone with a camera. We had had to postpone our visit to Chiapas due to troubles caused by radical teachers and students who had decided to take over San Cristóbal de las Casas and other townships, but the wait was well worth it.

To the outsider, it might appear that Mexico has an affinity for insurgency and insurrection. Public spaces throughout the country celebrate revolution, insurgency, patriotism, and not a little death and defiance in their own unique manner through social iconography and political testimonial in the form of statuary and place names. In Chiapas, they relive the insurgent moment every so often. Despite the state's enormous natural potential, the population remains one of the poorest, with the federal government unable to make headway against political and social divisions.

Mexicans generally are a highly cultivated people, with a heritage that no other Central or South American country can match. With an educated citizenry, the country can hold its own in intellectual discourse. It is rare to come across so many universities and institutes of higher learning. Mexico City is home to one of the oldest, largest universities (UNAM) in the Americas, while technical universities like the Instituto Tecnológico y de Estudios Superiores de Monterrey match anything Europe and America has to offer.

Flying over Palenque, the Maya ruins held to be among the wonders of the Western Hemisphere, one can understand Mexicans' attachment to their cultural roots, diverse though they may be. There are too many dead cultures scattered across time for arguments with history, but climbing atop the Temple of Inscriptions and then down into the heart of the pyramid on slippery stone steps worn weary of human feet over thirteen hundred years, you can't help but reflect in awe. This is where they discovered the ruler-priest K'inich Janaab' Pakal (Pacal the Great), who had been buried with his jade finery in AD 683. All this for immortality, or as a tribute to the greatness of human aspirations, little changed over recorded history.

Palenque, along with its great builder-king, was swallowed up by the jungle, taken over by regal mahogany and cedar trees, handed back to the howler monkeys, its rightful owners. Listening to the creatures' crescendo as dusk closed in, I found them menacing and mournful – 'Grave and solemn', which is how the American explorer John Lloyd Stephens, who was responsible for the rediscovery of the Maya civilisation in the 1800s, described them. 'Almost emotionally wounded, as if officiating as the guardians of consecrated ground.'

Marta Zepeda
Chef, Tierra y Cielo, San Cristóbal de las Casas, Chiapas

Marta Zepeda graduated from the Centro de Estudios Superiores de San Ángel in Mexico City with a degree in Gastronomy and Hospitality. In 2007 she opened Tierra y Cielo in order to turn her thesis project on the regional cuisine of Chiapas into reality. Based in what was her grandparents' home, the twelve-room hotel and restaurant celebrate local culinary traditions while supporting local producers and suppliers. The menu features such regional drinks as *pozol* (based on fermented maize), *tascalate* (whose ingredients include maize and chocolate) and chia lemonade, as well as more than forty Mexican wines. For each hotel guest, a donation is made to the conservation fund of the El Triunfo nature reserve, the 'lung of Chiapas'.

'The cultural richness that we have in the communities, the indigenous populations and the large variety of climates in [Chiapas] are what allow us to have very rich and varied ingredients,' explains

Zepeda. 'It is one of the most biodiverse states, and as a result it is one of the states with many ingredients.' Her interest in food developed gradually, in the end focusing on regional specialities and crafts, as well as the best way to support relationships with local producers and nurture a sustainable business approach. Although there were already women working as chefs in Mexico when Zepeda first opened her restaurant, in Chiapas 'women were not expected to become chefs. They could become traditional cooks or housewives who cooked very well ... In fact, when I came to San Cristóbal, there were no chefs in the local restaurants [at all].' Nonetheless, she says, being a woman was not that much of an issue: 'I had the support of my family and the support of local businessmen who liked the work I did and because I started to gain recognition quite quickly. I opened the restaurant in 2007, and in 2008 I already had a national award for regional food, which I received from the former President of the Republic. Instead of being a bad thing and people saying, "She made it because she's a woman," it was a good thing ... Then I received another award for sustainable practice, one for being a female entrepreneur, and then the national award for quality in the tourism sector ... These are awards that no other businessperson from Chiapas has received, regardless of gender ... Nevertheless, of course, when I go to breakfast meetings I am surrounded by men; there are only two or three women [present].'

Zepeda cites the loss of traditional preparation and cooking techniques as 'a very serious issue because we are losing our identity ... and it is something that is occurring right now. If it happens in Chiapas, which is one of the strategic places for indigenous cultures, it is even more evident'. This is the real reason she became interested in showcasing local cuisine. 'My current project is to build a smoke kitchen here to replace the pyramid extractor, so that customers can have this live experience, because I think we are losing it,' she adds. 'If you visit San Cristóbal de las Casas today, there's only a handful of places where you can have a freshly made tortilla ... We no longer see flour mills today ... There are many things that we are gradually losing and that represent [challenges for] our [culinary] profession ... things like working with small producers, having a responsible shopping programme, supervising where we get our produce and how we guarantee that the people we buy from benefit so they can remain in their communities, keep doing what they do best and maintaining their traditions.' Her own customer base includes 'national clients from the central and northern regions of the country, mainly from places that can be reached by plane ... They are clients who value all of this. On the other hand, it hasn't been easy to achieve this with the locals, because they don't want to spend money in a restaurant to eat *mole* if they know that the best *mole* is the one their grandmas make at home ... We have been changing the paradigm that says that the fashionable thing to do is to go out to eat foreign food ... That's what the locals want to try; it's the cool thing to do. I think this will change little by little. The number of people working with traditional food is growing, and people are starting to value the fact that this is done in an innovative way'.

(previous spread)
Palenque's Temple of the Inscriptions in Chiapas, with its early hieroglyphic record of the Maya city's history

(facing page) **Marta Zepeda at Tierra y Cielo in San Cristóbal de las Casas, drinking** *tazcalate* **made from toasted maize, axiote, cinnamon and cacao**

(far left) **Zepeda's** *frijol, maiz y queso de cuadro de Chiapas* **(bean, maize and Chiapas cheese), a play on the three basic ingredients of Mexican cooking; and** (above) *Sopa de chilpilin* **with** *bolitas de maiz* **(soup made from the** *chilpilin* **leaf and maize balls).**
(left) **Zepeda, who regularly visits the local Friday market, enjoying** *tamal de manjar*, **a breakfast tamale made from** *masa colada*. **The** *masa* **(ground maize) is passed through muslin to give the tamales a very soft consistency**

César Aceves
Chef, Mesón de la Cofradía, San Cristóbal de las Casas, Chiapas

César Aceves describes himself as more of a host than a chef, as his small inn aims to 'give guests somewhere homely to stay'. Born in San Cristóbal de las Casas, as were his father and grandfather, Aceves is dedicated to promoting the town's ancient recipes, as well as hosting travellers and chefs from other parts of Mexico.

In addition to cooking, Aceves makes liqueurs, among them *drake*, which can be drunk as an apéritif, as a digestif or during a meal. His version uses herbs and fruit from his own garden. He describes *drake* as the perfect drink for 'when you receive bad news, or good news, and need to calm down'. The herbs, he explains, 'are also used in traditional teas – orange leaf, fennel, lime leaf, basil, rosemary … and of course wormwood, for bitterness'. *Drake* also contains cinnamon, aniseed and clove, and is brewed using aquavit.

An edible insect unique to the region, notes Aceves, is the black *chicatana* (large flying ant), which emerges after it rains. 'It's the stomach of the ant that is most delicious,' he explains. 'It has a buttery flavour because it's basically fat. But it also has a smoky flavour because they are usually toasted over wood.' He collects, cleans and fries grubs from *alcornoque*, or cork oaks; the grubs are the larvae of a nocturnal butterfly which the locals associate with death. Other chef's specialities include crystallised figs and jam made of tiny, nearly extinct green apples. The apples used to grow in orchards in the town, but because almost nobody has orchards any more, they are very, very rare. Aceves buys 50 kilos – the total harvest – from a man who still has an orchard.

Mesón de la Cofradía is a rustic retreat, with brightly tiled bathrooms and a *temazcal* (a sweat lodge of prehispanic origin) for cleansing mind, body and spirit. Bread is baked in a ceramic oven decorated in *trencadís* (broken-tile mosaic). Local cuisine blends indigenous (Tzotzil) and Spanish influences, and is sweet rather than spicy. A favourite flavour profile is based on cinnamon, plantain, prunes and pineapple.

(far left) **Roasted tomatoes; and** (left) ***Gusano zatz* (or *tsats*), the larvae of nocturnal butterflies found on cork trees. The butterflies are unique to the region and believed by locals to be from the underworld.** (above) **César Aceves serving his version of** *drake*, **an ancient drink of the** *coleta* **households of San Cristóbal. This particular brew had fermented for eight years using his family recipe.** (facing page) **Aceves in the kitchen at Mesón de la Cofradía**

(above left) **A family at work in the market of San Cristóbal de las Casas, where** (above) **live turkeys are sold. The wild turkey originated in Mesoamerica and spread to Europe after the Spanish conquest**

(above) *Botil* beans and (above right) fresh rambutans for sale in the market of San Cristóbal de las Casas. The rambutan originated in South-east Asia, and is related to the lychee

Don Gonzalo Villaverde Cancino
Traditional Cook, Acapetahua, Chiapas

Don Gonzalo Villaverde Cancino has been roasting whole pigs in his massive wood-fired clay oven in the small town of Acapetahua for his entire life. An identical oven next to his is used by his wife for her bakery business.

Don Gonzalo is famous for the thin, crispy skin and succulent meat of his roast pigs, which he puts down to the quality of the animals he buys (raised outdoors and fed a diet of vegetable scraps so they do not become too fat) and his signature marinade. He only roasts to order; on weekends his daughters sell tacos to make a bit of extra money. People come from all over the region to enjoy these tacos, which are served with a bit of crackling on the top. Don Gonzalo has been known to send whole roasted pigs all the way to Mexico City on the overnight bus, but always 'accompanied'. 'I think someone would eat them if they went on their own!' he jokes. He purchases pigs from surrounding farms and slaughters them himself.

Don Gonzalo, who has no idea what temperature the pigs are roasted at, says, 'We've never used a thermometer. We just check the heat and eyeball it.' His secret weapon is his marinade, which was perfected by his parents, who had a butcher shop. The ingredients include honey, salt and lime juice. Having begun the marinating process the previous evening, 'early next morning you ... prepare the fire and put [the pig] in the oven ... and give it some time. We estimate the moment when the fire is almost out, and then we clean the pig, we remove all the extra water, and we add some salt and some honey. After the honey, we add the sauce, which is called "salsa de campo" – in fact, it's Chinese sauce! ... Those are the only ingredients. Then you put [the pig] back in the oven and you have to be careful with it. You ... wait five minutes; then you pull it out, you turn it around and put it back in again. Ten, fifteen minutes later, you pull it and push it so it settles where it will be roasted, and then you cover the ears with foil because the ears tend to burn.'

(above) **A pig in mid-roast outside *Don* Gonzalo Villaverde Cancino's wood-fired clay oven. *Don* Gonzalo's roasted pigs average around 50–60 kilos each.** (facing page) ***Don* Gonzalo with family photographs in his bedroom**

431

(above) **An iguana in a bag awaiting its fate: being slaughtered and cooked at Los Almendros, a restaurant owned by Concepción 'Conchita' Salazar Ordoñez in Puerto Arista on the coast of Chiapas; and** (facing page) **Blue Crabs on sale in the local market**

Guerrero: *Loco in Acapulco*

The city of Acapulco, Pancho Villa and Emiliano Zapata were the first Mexican place and people I remember hearing about as a schoolboy. The romance of Villa and Zapata's revolutionaries was far outweighed by my interest in the cinema, however. Memories still linger of *Fun in Acapulco*, Elvis Presley's 1963 film.

It took me more than fifty years to see Acapulco in the flesh. Sadly the resort is now well past its prime, gang violence making it one of Mexico's most violent cities. Whereas in the 1950s and '60s the likes of Johnny Weissmuller, John Wayne and Errol Flynn built grand holiday homes with breath-taking views of Acapulco Bay, the town has gone downhill. Nonetheless, life in this bustling city of nearly a million people goes on without interruption, with major international sporting events, conventions and hundreds of very grand weddings and other corporate shindigs. Today, Acapulco's hotels and restaurants cater more to a Mexican clientele than in its heyday. Given the primacy of tourism for the economy, the decline in visitor numbers has had an impact on employment; Guerrero has one of the highest rates of migration to the US.

The state is named after Vincent Guerrero, a leader in Mexico's War of Independence. Rugged and mountainous, the sea has always been its lifeline, Acapulco becoming a principal trading port after the Spanish conquest. Cuauhtémoc, the last Aztec Emperor, is reputed to have been buried in Ixcateopan in Guerrero, after being hung in Campeche, though historical proof is lacking. Married to Moctezuma's daughter, Cuauhtémoc's short-lived stewardship (1520–21) in the face of the conquistadors had as much to do with smallpox as anything else, the native population of Tenochtitlán (the Aztec seat of power in the Valley of Mexico) being decimated by the disease, brought over by the Spaniards. Cuauhtémoc was captured by Hernán Cortés while fleeing his capital and was shown magnanimity until gold fever overtook such sentiments. Tortured to make him reveal his hidden treasures, his feet were literally held to the fire. He was hung by Cortés in 1525, his legend celebrated among Mexicans today as the embodiment of indigenous nationalism.

Cuauhtémoc means 'Descending Eagle', a title emblematic of the determination and aggressiveness of the region's indigenous peoples. Carlos Gaytán, a son of Guerrero, is no less a worthy descendant of the Aztecs. Rising from very humble origins to become one of Mexico's top chefs, Gaytán's Chicago-based restaurant Mexique was the first Mexican restaurant in the US to receive a Michelin star. Arriving in Chicago in 1991, he started to work his way up by washing dishes. His boss finally let him go because, he said, there was nothing else he could teach his young acolyte. Gaytán remembers hunting with his dad for deer, rabbits and iguanas in order to feed the family. 'We used to ask local landowners if we could pick the leftover vegetables and fruit after the harvest,' he recounts without rancour. That is how he learned to do so much with fresh ingredients. 'When they gave us the Michelin star, I didn't even know what a Michelin star was,' he adds.

The flipside of the Guerrero story is represented by Susana Palazuelos, one of Mexico's top three super-luxury caterers, and someone who has helped to make Acapulco *the* destination for celebrations and ceremonies, especially weddings. Palazuelos started on the culinary ladder by preparing buffets for the Hilton hotel chain, opening her own restaurant a few years later. 'The kitchen,' she says, 'is my life.'

Restaurante El Jaguar
Acapulco, Guerrero

El Jaguar, which has been owned by Fernando Álvarez Aguilar for the last twelve years, is an Acapulco institution. Located on La Costera, the old-town hotel strip, the eatery is named after the enormous taxidermy jaguar displayed on one of its walls. Head chef Maximino Teresa Adame, originally from Quechultenango, Guerrero, has made sure that the menu includes traditional Guerrero staples, such as the famous seven *pozoles*, *relleno de tecpan* (a whole stuffed suckling pig) and coconut tart. The seven *pozoles* include green *pozole* (made with either chicken or prawn as the base protein and a sauce made from *epazote*, tomatillo, coriander and various other ingredients), white *pozole* (traditionally served at weddings and made from a base of squash seeds), *pozole de camagua* (made from a base of black beans and traditionally served with pork), two types of *elopozole* (like a *pozole* but served with sweet corn instead of the larger, chewier

pozole 'hominy' maize), red *pozole* (a base of different chillies served with either pork or seafood) and a vegetarian *pozole* (made from *hojasanta* and wild mushrooms). The preparation of *pozole* varies hugely, not just from town to town in Guerrero but throughout Mexico, where it is common in many states. 'Each household has their particular way of preparing it, and no two recipes will ever be the same,' says Adame.

Álvarez has various other local businesses and runs the online Acapulco virtual museum. He is keen to emphasise the restaurant's family atmosphere and his wish that customers feel as if they are eating at home. He is often at El Jaguar overseeing proceedings with his wife and other members of his family, and is grateful to their loyal base of customers who have never stopped coming to the restaurant, through good times and bad.

(left) **A folkloric dancer at Restaurante El Jaguar in Acapulco; and** (below) **Diners at the restaurant**

(previous spread) **The Island of the Birds, a sanctuary on Coyuca Lagoon in Pie de la Cuesta, between Acapulco and Isla Montosa**

(facing page, left) **Two Guerrero staples served at El Jaguar:** *relleno de Tecpan* **(whole stuffed suckling pig) and** (facing page, right) *pozole* **(stew) with prawns**

Carlos Gaytán
Guest Chef, Muestra Gastronómica de Guerrero, Acapulco, Guerrero

Carlos Gaytán, who was born in Huitzuco, Guerrero, arrived in Chicago, Illinois in 1991. 'I come from a really humble family,' he says. 'With my father I used to go hunting for deer, rabbits, iguanas, quails, pigeons. With my mother I used to … ask the landowners if we could pick the leftover vegetables and fruit after the harvest. We cooked with them, preserved them, and that's how I learned to do a lot of things with ingredients.' Having entered the US illegally with the aim of finding employment at a fast-food outlet, Gaytán worked his way up in the fine-dining world until his boss said to him, 'I don't have anything else to teach you. You are hungry for more. It would be selfish if I kept you here.' After stints at other restaurants and a private club, Gaytán opened Mexique. In 2013, with business drying up and a huge tax bill to pay, he decided to close his doors. The next morning he was awarded a Michelin star. His approach at Mexique – combining French techniques and ingredients with an acknowledgement of his Mexican roots – spawned a revolution.

'When they gave us the Michelin star, I didn't even know what a Michelin star was,' Gaytán jokes on a visit to Acapulco to participate in a food festival and give a masterclass to students from his home state. An aficionado of regional ingredients and tastes, he searches for flavours to introduce in new dishes by distinguishing the appropriate balances. 'If you go to the US, the corn is sweet,' he explains. 'The corn here in Guerrero is not sweet. So I have to incorporate another ingredient to exactly match the flavours that I'm looking for.' In Chicago he visits several markets every day, sourcing fish, meat and produce. 'You get ingredients, you look around, you ask questions' about unfamiliar ingredients. 'You take a couple home and see what they are' – an approach very similar to that of an engineer or chemist.

Gaytán is a great believer in miracles, for example the miracle of the nonexistent ticket. 'When I first opened Mexique, we rented one garbage container for all the garbage,' he recounts. 'What happened was that I filled it all the way up. I wasn't supposed to, but I didn't know that, because I'm not a construction guy, I'm just a cook … An inspector passed by, and he gave me a ticket. I asked, "What did you give me a ticket for?" He said, "You're not supposed to fill it up all the way! There's a line. You have to respect the line." I said, "Can't you give me a break?" He said, "No!" He took pictures, gave me the ticket and sent me to court. In those days I had zero money. I remember the day I had to go to court: I grabbed my car and drove to the courthouse, and on my way I was just praying to God, saying, "You know I didn't do this on purpose! I don't have any money. Can you do something for me so that I can pay this fine?" That was my prayer.

'When I got to the court, the lady asked me for the ticket, looked at it, put it in the computer. She grabbed a stamp and stamped the ticket. She said, "There, you can go now." I said, "But I cannot pay this ticket!" She said, "Your ticket is not in the system. It doesn't exist!" You know what I did? I quickly grabbed the ticket, ran to my car and started crying.' The day he got the Michelin call was similarly miraculous. 'After I hung up, a few minutes later the press from Chicago, from the US, from Mexico, from Japan, started calling me. It was weird! I was like, "Let's see what the Michelin star is going to do for me." Nothing happened on Tuesday. The next day, from it being an empty restaurant, it was a packed restaurant … The One Up There, man, He knows what He's doing … He gives to you and He can take away from you.' When asked about the anti-Hispanic prejudice he experienced in his early days in the US, Gaytán replies, 'I'm not building walls, I'm building bridges. I'm building a bridge that can go from Chicago to Mexico, a bridge that can showcase what we're capable of doing … I can cook, I can showcase, I can educate people in the US about what Mexican gastronomy is right now. I can bring people to Mexico to experience that. I'm building a bridge, not a wall.'

(facing page) **Carlos Gaytán, the only Mexican chef in the US with a Michelin star, returns to Acapulco for lectures and guest appearances, as here at Hotel Elcano. Traditional dishes from Casa de la Cultura in Acapulco include** (right) *fiambre* **(meat stew) from Tixtla and** (far right) *mole rosa de Taxco* **made of beetroot, rose petals and pine nuts**

Cliff Divers
La Quebrada, Acapulco, Guerrero

(left) **Cliff diver Alexis Balanzar in his neighbourhood, the Adobeña barrio of Acapulco, where houses are traditionally made of adobe; and** (below) **Jorge Antonio Ramírez López, a third-generation diver who started out at the age of eleven, praying at the divers' altar to the Virgin of Guadalupe. With the water's depth varying from 2 to 5 metres depending on the waves, timing is critical; there have been many fatalities over the years**

(facing page) **A diver leaping into the Pacific from a height of 40 metres at La Quebrada. Made famous by the Elvis Presley film** *Fun in Acapulco*, **the** *clavadistas* **(cliff divers) have come to symbolise their town, with tourists paying to view up to five performances a day**

Susana Palazuelos
Chef, Author & Caterer, Acapulco, Guerrero

Susana Palazuelos studied Hospitality Management at the Glion Institute of Higher Education in Montreux, Switzerland. 'Preparing a banquet depends on the number of people and the menu to be offered,' she says. 'It can take me up to a week to prepare, but I'm very organised and I have a lot of people to work with.' Known as both a chef and a wedding organiser, Palazuelos has been active in the Acapulco Red Cross even as she has cooked for royalty, including the King of Malaysia and Queen Elizabeth II. She has also dedicated herself to recording her culinary skills as a way of bequeathing 'an inheritance of flavours' to Mexico and the world. Palazuelos has been the recipient of numerous awards and medals, among them the Guerrero National Award in Tourism (Gold & Silver Medal), the Golden Eagle (in recognition of both her work and her involvement in Mexican and international broadcasting media) and tributes at the IV Congress of Gastronomic Heritage and Cultural Tourism in Latin America and the Caribbean.

Palazuelos spent four years working in Puebla, preparing buffets for the Hilton hotel chain. In 1997 she opened her own restaurant, Banquetes Susana Palazuelos, in her native Acapulco.

She has been a tireless promoter of the state of Guerrero and of Mexico generally through her cookbooks, among them *Mexico: The Beautiful Cookbook* (1991), which was translated into several languages and which sold more than eight hundred thousand copies, and *My Favorite Menus* (2015), a compilation of dishes that had been published in *Hello! Magazine*.

A pioneer in promoting Acapulco as one of the world's most spectacular wedding locations, Palazuelos organises up to 120 of these events every year. She has also organised banquets at events attended by the last six presidents of Mexico, as well as for the International Mining Congress and tourism fairs. She has participated in twenty national and thirty-five international culinary festivals. 'I am giving a twist to Mexican food with incredible presentation that does not lose the flavour of traditional cuisine,' she explains. She always insists on using fresh ingredients. 'The kitchen is my life,' she adds. 'It helps me to give a lot of happiness to people. It is done with love, and what people taste is love.' Palazuelos' son Eduardo has followed in his mother's footsteps. As well as being the CEO of Banquetes Susana Palazuelos, he is a chef in his own right with a restaurant in Mexico City.

(left) **Susana Palazuelos handling a local delicacy, *jumiles* (stink bugs);** (above) **A bottle of local Jaguar *mezcal*;** (right) *Agua de bougainvillea*, **a refreshing drink made from bougainvilea flowers; and** (facing page) **Palazuelos checking one of her signature table compositions at her home overlooking Acapulco Bay in Fraccionamiento Las Brisas**

Isla Montosa
Coyuca Lagoon, Acapulco, Guerrero

(above left) **A *mamada*, the seriously alcoholic drink invented at *Doña María Gómez Lubiano*'s restaurant, Doña María; and** (above) ***Sopes***

444

(right) **A shack on Isla Montosa;** (below) **Entrepreneur Eduardo 'Lalo' Palazuelos with his wife Ivette and daughter Emilia, regular visitors to Pie de la Cuesta on Cayuca Lagoon;** and (bottom) **A local boy holding a juvenile crocodile**

Nuevo León: *The Power of Industry*

Nuevo León is one of Mexico's principal industrial and agricultural powerhouses, with Monterrey, its capital, the country's third-largest metropolitan area, and its leading financial centre after Mexico City. Monterrey feels like a version of Dallas, with leading national and international corporations headquartering their Mexican operations there. Iron- and steelworks, heavy industry and tech manufacturing produce everything from beer to advanced electronics. Mostly desert, the state still manages to produce large quantities of maize, wheat, cotton, sugarcane, citrus fruit and vegetables with the aid of the Falcon Dam and reservoir project on the Rio Grande, the river that forms the state's boundary with the US.

Located in the foothills of the Sierra Madre Oriental, Nuevo León has few natural resources. Jews fleeing the Spanish Inquisition began to settle in the area during the sixteenth century and were able to eke out an existence. During the 1800s, generous land deals brought in German, French, Italian and Anglo-American settlers. By dint of hard work and enterprise, the state is today an exemplar of economic success. It is not unknown, though, to hear some people call themselves 'Monterrexans', feeling as they do more akin to their Texan neighbours than to the rest of Mexico. Looking out across Monterrey, a polluted, super-modern metropolis of over four million people, and seeing the enormous agro-industrial estates dotted across Nuevo León's desert landscape, one wonders why some of Mexico's southern states, with all that nature has to offer, remain so far behind a state like Nuevo León with no natural resources – except for human enterprise.

Passing through Monterrey's byways, we stopped for lunch at El Rey del Cabrito, a garish emporium serving up as many as seventy goats daily to a never-ending stream of clients. As a culinary experience, goat is, after all, just goat, the flesh unfamiliar to most palates. But goat really is king in Monterrey (and much of Nuevo León) given that settlers found nothing better to eat there.

Monterrey *is* Nuevo León. Not a place for gourmands, which is surprising given the per-capita income of its inhabitants. Mexicans generally entertain at home, with the weekend extended-family gathering a mainstay of social and culinary traditions. Restaurant culture on a large social scale is a relatively recent trend, and the Mexican kitchen remains the heart of the household, with Grandma the Queen of the Ball. Strong familial bonds are at the centre of the social fabric, so every cook and chef has their stories about jealously guarded recipes handed down over generations by *los abuelos*. The art of cooking is learned at the feet of Mexican grandmothers, great-aunts and family cooks.

Reading *Like Water for Chocolate*, Laura Esquivel's 1989 bestseller, at the beginning of my journey kick-started my imagination around the subject of the Mexican kitchen. Tita de la Garza, the novel's protagonist, is born in the kitchen of a ranch on the Mexico–US border and raised by Nacha, the family cook. Forbidden to marry Pedro (her sweetheart), Tita is condemned to look after her mother and two sisters. But her love for the kitchen, her deep connection to food, strong emotions and lust for Pedro are all mixed into her culinary extravagances, bringing about unimaginable consequences … a little like Mexican food.

Dante Ferrero
Chef, Alodé, Monterrey, Nuevo León

Chef Dante Ferrero was born in Patagonia, Argentina; like him, his father was a restaurateur. Ferrero is famous for #LaVacaEsMía, an event where he cooks an entire cow for about twenty hours to feed several hundred people. This recreation of an Argentine tradition has become a pilgrimage destination for other chefs and has even been written up as a kind of artistic performance. 'You have to watch over it,' Ferrero says of the roasting cow. 'I spend the whole night awake by the fire. It's quite a show and implies a lot of logistics.' He enjoys people's reactions to the spectacle, saying that participants let their 'animal side come out – a nice animal side, I mean. They are all desperate to grab a piece of meat, to eat, and to have me cut a piece and give it to them in their hands. It is very savage, very animalistic, but also very beautiful. It's a group of people who are reunited by eating and enjoying [themselves]'.

Ferrero's approach to cooking is not all about theatrics, however. His father 'loved cooking ... so he made me love everything related to cooking. But ... he hoped that I would pursue [another career]. I went to Buenos Aires to begin a new life studying finance ... I married a Mexican woman and ... we decided to come to Monterrey so she could be closer to her family. I decided to restart my career but as a chef ... As soon as I arrived, I opened a little restaurant'. Ferrero was fortunate to be able to spend time working with Massimo Bottura as well as in such leading restaurants as Pujol in Mexico City and Arzak in Spain, encounters he describes as 'impressive! Those are experiences that broaden your mind a lot'. That said, he adds, 'I don't go to places to learn recipes. I do learn techniques but recipes not so much. What I see is the way they work, the way they think.' When queried about the strengths and weaknesses of contemporary cuisine generally, he quotes Ferran Adrìa: '"Sometimes, innovating means leaving things as they are."'

Ferrero faults some modern chefs for their emphasis on speed, which creates too much pressure in the kitchen and forces them to keep inventing new things. For him, simplicity is key. When cooking meat, for example, he says it can be delicious not because of his cooking but 'because I simply took care of a product that was already good'. His cuisine is 'always related to fire, to a wood oven, to iron, to embers ... I'm not saying it's the best ... No. Each chef has their own style, and if you have to use the most sophisticated modern technique to get the best results, then do it! Just like anything else in life, balance is the key!'

(previous spread) **The stark limestone cliffs in La Huasteca in Monterrey, Nuevo León**

(left) **Dante Ferrero slicing through steak dry-aged between 21 and 45 days in the chiller cabinet at Alodé;** (below) **Grilled Akaushi steak, known for its marbled succulence; and** (facing page) **Ferrero visiting the Carnes Ramos meat-processing plant in Linda Vista, Monterrey, which supplies him with locally sourced beef from traditional European breeds**

Ángel Solís
Head Chef, Pangea Restaurant, Monterrey, Nuevo León

Head Chef at Pangea Restaurant in Monterrey, Nuevo León – Mexico's third-largest city, hosting much of the country's industry and business – Ángel Solís heads up Grupo Pangea, a collection of establishments that includes the French-themed Bistro Bardot, the Asian-influenced Chino Latino, the cantina-style La Félix, La Embajada (contemporary Mexican) and the Italian-style Vasto. Grupo Pangea also manages a catering company and winery. Solís has been at the company for eighteen years, first as a line cook in the pastry department and then rising through the ranks. Solís has been mentored and influenced by Executive Chef and owner Guillermo González Beristaín (considered to be one of the fathers of modern Mexican cooking) since Pangea opened in 1998. Together, González Beristaín and Solís have created the first highly regarded restaurant in north-eastern Mexico and regularly appear in the ranks of Latin America's fifty best restaurants. Friends and colleagues, they collaborate on both tasting menus and à la carte options, offering a menu that mixes traditional Mexican cooking with French influences. Their signature dish is braised meat, most famously ribs, with Bocanegra craft ale. Other specialities include sous-vide duck breast with date *mole*, and grilled octopus with chickpea stew.

(far left) **Deconstructed cheesecake made from guava, mango, *matcha* cream and cream cheese;** (above) **A chocolate financier with beetroot and goat's cheese;** and (left) ***Dulce de leche*, or *leche quemada* as it is called in Nuevo León, with pecans, white chocolate and oregano.** (facing page) **Ángel Solís preparing an *aguachile* dish at Pangea**

Restaurante El Rey del Cabrito
Monterrey, Nuevo León

(above) **Twenty kid goats roasting on spits at El Rey del Cabrito**

(top) **Exterior of the restaurant;** (above) **A typical *cabrito* feast served on a hot plate over grilled onions with tortillas, guacamole, melted cheese, chorizo, salsa and salad; and** (left) **The restaurant's garish décor, including taxidermy and neon lights** (right) **Jesús Alemán earning a living as a fire eater at a traffic signal in Monterrey, a job he has done for nearly twenty years, endangering his lungs and heart, and** (below) **his *Vida Loca* (crazy life) tattoos**

Eugenio Andrés Martínez Ruiz
Orange Grower, Industrias Regules, Montemorelos, Nuevo León

(facing page) **Eugenio Andrés Martínez Ruiz inspecting the orange groves at Industrias Regules in Montemorelos, a place he visited as a boy;** (left) **Pink grapefruits among the oranges, an occasional mishap when young trees get muddled in the nursery;** and (below) **An unripened orange in the rain**

Eugenio Andrés Martínez Ruiz is in charge of production at Industrias Regules in Montemorelos, a town that has been linked with orange growing for centuries due to its moderate climate. Martínez remembers visiting the orchards with his grandfather and says that he has never been ill because of all the vitamin C he consumes.

Oranges are Mexico's most popular fruit. Originally brought over by Christopher Columbus on his second voyage to the New World, orange trees were soon being cultivated by Spanish settlers. They have thrived ever since. Today Mexico is the fourth-largest producer of oranges in the world (behind the US, India and Brazil), responsible for 4.1 million tons each year. The bulk of orange production happens in the state of Veracruz since Montemorelos was hit by a hard frost in 1984, wiping out many orchards. The town has built its production back up since then, however, benefiting from the lack of Mexican fruit flies in the region, which is very dry.

Industrias Regules produces Parson Brown and Valencia oranges, known as 'table fruit' and eaten whole. The other types available in the area include the Albérciga, a green bitter orange, and the Temprana, a sweeter variety.

Juan Carlos Cabada
Master Brewer, Cervecería Heineken Cuauhtémoc Moctezuma, Monterrey, Nuevo León

'Beer is about art and science,' observes Juan Carlos Cabada. 'Actually for thousands of years it was only about art, and now it's a combination of [the two]. It's very interesting [in that] we can measure a lot of things, we can automate and standardise a lot of processes, but it's still up to the master brewer to decide how to tweak and produce the perfect beer.'

Cervecería Heineken Cuauhtémoc Moctezuma owns sixteen beer brands, each with its own identity (Tecate is their best seller.) The brewery's building is 125 years old and originally served as an ice factory. Today it houses Heineken's second-biggest operation after their HQ in the Netherlands. When the brewery was founded in Monterrey, the company brought in a German master brewer to set up operations. The first beer they produced was called Cerveza Carta Blanca. Today hops are imported from Europe and North America as they 'only grow at specific latitudes and need very long days of sunlight – ideally around fourteen hours'. The barley is grown in the highlands of Hidalgo, Guanajuato and Estado de México.

Cabada was born in Veracruz. He moved to Monterrey when he was fifteen after he was offered a scholarship to pursue higher education. He earned a degree in Chemical Engineering from the Instituto Tecnológico y de Estudios Superiores de Monterrey and went on to do a PhD in the same subject at Carnegie Mellon University in the US. He then moved to Boston to do post-doctoral work at Massachusetts Institute of Technology. Before becoming a master brewer, Cabada worked in research and development and as a brewing manager. So it is safe to say that he is familiar with the entire process of making beer.

Cervecería Heineken Cuauhtémoc Moctezuma are currently the second-largest beer producer in Mexico. In addition to the Carta Blanca brand, the brewery originally produced Cerveza Cuauhtémoc and Bohemia. In the 1940s the company acquired Cervecería Tecate; forty years later there was a big merger between Cervecería Cuauhtémoc and Cervecería Moctezuma, a brewery in Veracruz.

Cabada notes that while the Maya and Aztecs did not brew beer, 'they had other types of fermented alcoholic drinks [including] *tepache* and pulque ... Beer came with the colonists.' Today, of course, the drink's popularity is immense almost everywhere in the world. Mexico produces about 35 million hectare litres (1 hectare equals a hundred litres). In terms of international beer consumption, Mexico is not one of the highest-ranking countries; the biggest drinkers live in Germany and the Czech Republic.

Where food is concerned, the master brewer's preferences are not, he says, related to his upbringing. (His mother is from Sonora and his father is from Durango; he describes himself as 'a weird mix of cultures'.) 'I like every type of food actually,' he notes. 'I like *carne asada* a lot, but I also like certain dishes from Veracruz such as *empanadas* and *cochinita pibil*.'

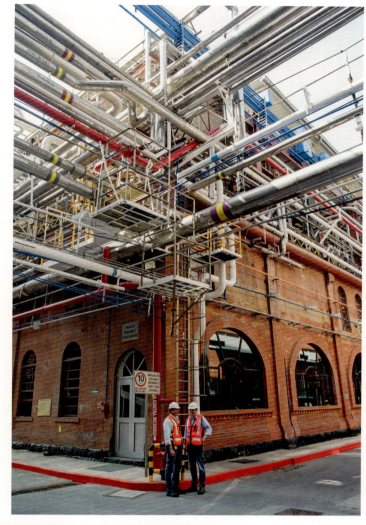

(facing page) **Master brewer Juan Carlos Cabada and brewery Director Isidro Canhisares Neto between two original brew 'kettles' at Cervecería Heineken Cuauhtémoc Moctezuma in Monterrey, and** (above) **in the brewery grounds, whose origin** (left) **dates to 1890.** (far left, bottom) **The canteen at Cervecería Cuauhtémoc, where employees like Osvaldo Gatica Chacón** (far left, top) **prepare and eat their meals**

Lorena Morales Ponce
Horse Breeder, Hacienda Las Morerías, Santiago, Nuevo León

Lorena Morales Ponce was just nine years old when she started riding. Although her first love was showjumping, she became interested in dressage when her father Abelardo Morales, a retired financier, began importing stud horses and breeding Andalusians from Spain and Lusitanos from Portugal. Morales describes dressage as an 'expensive hobby', although her father claims the stud more or less pays for itself – at long last. Thanks to the family's hard work, there are now Mexican-born Andalusian horses competing in dressage events in Spain.

Morales lives close to the stud in Saltillo, Coahuila with her husband, who is a horse-feed producer. 'Horses are our lives,' she says simply. When she is preparing for a competition, she trains every day; in the off-season she rides out three or four times a week. It was after studying industrial engineering that she realised that she wanted to dedicate her time to riding competitively. Her teacher was Portuguese dressage master Joaquín Nunes Cavrela, who has been with the family for twenty-five years, and who still rides every day at the age of eighty.

'My father, since he was little, loved ranches, horses, racing horses and cattle,' Morales explains, 'and after he was introduced to the Andalusian [breed], he fell in love. He decided that he wanted to breed them ... Once you get enthusiastic about horse competitions and breeding, and the little ones become stallions, you get involved. It's part of the family tradition now. It's like a virus. You have it or you don't.' Mexico's first horses were brought by the conquistadors. The so-called '*criollos mexicanos*' represented a cross between the North American mustang and South American criollo horse. After the country's entire equine population was extinguished during the Mexican Revolution, in 1920 the American Quarter Horse was introduced. It was not until 1969 that Mexico had its own breed, the Azteca.

Where Mexico's Andalusians are concerned, Hacienda Las Morerías has been recognised both at home and in the US as 'best breeder' for more than a decade. 'Two years ago,' says Morales, 'we started to take our horses born in Mexico' to compete internationally at Grand Prix dressage level. 'We have an Olympic rider from Spain who joined the team and he was training for the Grand Prix,' she adds – Grand Prix being Europe's top dressage level.

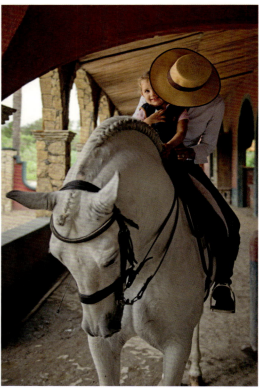

(facing page) **Lorena Morales Ponce at Hacienda Las Morerías, where she trains with her riders** (above) **on Mexican-born Andalusian horses. Horses are important to the entire family, with Lorena's two-year old daughter Roberta** (right) **already comfortable in the saddle**

(above) **Morales and her father Abelardo, owner of the hacienda, talking horses; and** (left) **An Andalusian's mane being plaited along the crest of its neck by a groom in preparation for a show**

(left) A *charro* (horseman) in full regalia showing off his skills at the hacienda; and (below) Abelardo and guests, among them trainer Joaquín Nunes Cavrela, enjoying a lunch of (bottom) *cabrito* cooked *al ataúd* (the 'coffin style' typical of Nuevo León), with *frijoles charros* (beans cooked with lard or bacon) and pork *asado*, plus slices of *chile poblano* cooked in cream and *chile* (*rajas*)

463

Coahuila: *Mysteries of Creation*

Coahuila is Mexico's third-largest state by size but with one of the lowest population densities. Mostly semi-arid, the state's extensive agriculture system, including the growing of cotton, is supported by its rivers. A large proportion of Mexico's milk is produced there. The state has two biospheres. The northern part includes pine and oak forests, while the southern part, including Cuatro Ciénegas, contains springs, lakes, wetlands and some extraordinary, mysterious landscapes that seem to make time stand still.

Coahuila, a big ranching and industrial state, is rich in minerals too. Almost all of Mexico's coal reserves are found there, with strip mining becoming a controversial regional and national issue. Mexico's largest (and Latin America's second-largest) steelworks are located in Monclova, its slurry piped 80 kilometres from pits to plant. Torreón is one of the world's biggest silver producers and the state's second-largest city after Saltillo. Its other claim to fame is its capture by Pancho Villa during the Mexican Revolution.

Situated in the north-central part of the country and possessing the longest border of any Mexican state with its northern neighbour, Coahuila has some spectacular scenery. The Parras district in the south produces some excellent wines; Parras de la Fuente is Mexico's oldest vineyard. Forests provide timber for commercial logging, and the flora and fauna provide spectacular backdrops, with *Pueblos Mágicos* dotting the landscape. The population is mostly made up of descendants of *criollos* and *mestizos*, with a sprinkling of European and North American immigrants but surprisingly few indigenous people.

Coahuila in Nahuatl means 'flying serpent'. The black-tailed rattlesnake, a venomous pit viper whose docility belies its fierce demeanour, is common in the state and across the US border. Snakes are considered a delicacy in Mexico, with restaurants specialising in serving them cooked with various spices. The local speciality that stands out is *cajeta*, a caramel delicacy made with goat's milk (*leche de cabra*), which I watched being prepared in a family's cluttered yard while en route to Cuatro Ciénegas. Grandpa Pedro had to stir the large pot over a wood fire for hours to create the dish's artisanal flavour, while in the kitchen, Milka, the aptly named granddaughter, sucked on a cone of *cajeta*.

Coahuila is also known for its pecan plantations. Mario Zertuche Verduzco, a charming gentleman-farmer who owns a pecan plantation near Cuidad Lamadrid, has worked his estate for thirty-five years, producing 40 tons of pecans annually from fifteen hundred trees planted in neat rows and shipping them to China. The *patrón* recounts how someone told him long ago to honour his trees, to take off his hat and talk to them, to 'tell them that they are beautiful and that you're happy that they're productive, even if it sounds too romantic'.

Mexico's magic is twofold – its people, and its scenery, which is oftentimes exceptional, and at times extraordinary. Seeing Cuatro Ciénegas, a bio-reserve that is one of the weirdest, most wonderful places I have ever visited, made the hair stand up on the back of my neck. The white desert's *pozas* contain a biological soup that is unique on the planet. These *pozas* (clear pools) contain three-billion-year-old stromatolites (morphologies that encode the mysteries of Deep Time) not found anywhere else on Earth. As if that were not enough, the area sports some 150 unique species of flora and fauna, in addition to thirty unique aquatic species.

Mario Zertuche Verduzco
Owner, Pecan Plantation, Ciudad de la Madrid, Coahuila

Coahuila, where pecan farmer Mario Zertuche Verduzco was born, possesses the warm climate that is essential for the successful growing of pecans. After completing his studies in civil engineering, Zertuche set up a construction company in Saltillo. Once he had saved up enough money, he purchased some land together with his father in order to establish a pecan orchard. Pecan trees are very slow to produce. In a decade, all being well, a tree may produce 65 kilos of nuts per year. Zertuche's trees are thirty-five years old now.

'I financed the project and my father supervised the pecan orchard,' Zertuche explains. 'He was in charge of planting the trees … What a blessing.' His father also bred racehorses. 'We would sit down and do the accounts together and share our revenue,' Zertuche remembers. 'My father passed away, so my brother Jesus, who is an agronomy engineer, takes care of the day-to-day [now]. I feel that with the pecan orchard I won the lottery without buying a ticket … Of course there has been a lot of work. Pecan trees need a lot of money, time and care. Otherwise, they don't produce as they should

… But if you tend them and honour them, [they flourish]. Someone once said to me, "Look, *Don* Mario, you have to talk to the trees and remove your hat [while doing so]!" You have to talk to them and tell them that they are beautiful and that you are happy that they are productive, even if it sounds romantic!'

Zertuche's company employs twenty local people 'who are properly paid'. 'If the trees share with me, I like to share with the workers,' he explains. His entire crop is exported to China. The trees are not sprayed with 'anything that will unbalance the environment'. The one serious limitation to the project is the availability of water. Zertuche is fortunate to have two wells on his property.

Zertuche's favourite dish, prepared by his wife, Claudia Garza, comes from a family recipe: chicken in pecan sauce. He describes it as being tasty enough 'to lick your fingers'. The couple also prepare typical northern-style pecan sweets with *dulce de leche*; Zertuche's favourite combines pumpkin with *dulce de leche* and pecans, a dish from his childhood.

(above) **Plantation employees enjoying their lunch hour; and** (left) **Harvesting pecans with a special tractor, shaking the trees to release their fruit into nets – and the owner's hands** (below)**. The plantation includes orange, lemon, lime and pomegranate trees. Mario Zertuche Verduzco** (facing page) **resting on the veranda of his *finca* and enjoying a home-grown pomegranate after a hard day's harvest**

(previous spread) **Dunas de Yeso in Cuatro Ciénegas, Coahuila, an 800-hectare biosphere reserve whose brilliantly white sandy landscape is the result of gypsum residue from drying *pozas* and saltwater lagoons**

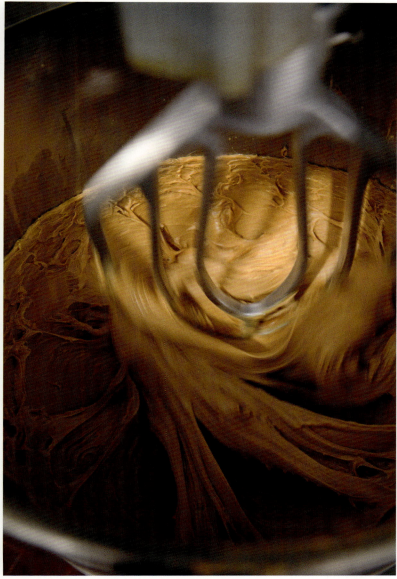

(facing page) **Pecans with *piloncillo***; (above) **Boiling milk and sugar in a copper pan; and** (right) **Whipping *leche quemada* (cooked milk) for *dulce de leche* at Martha's Dulceria in Melchor Múzquiz, Coahuila**

Francisco Rodríguez González
Oenologist, Casa Madero, El Valle de Parras, Coahuila

Casa Madero is 'the oldest winery in Latin America – it was founded in 1597 – and the sixth-oldest [continuously operating] company in the world', says Francisco Rodríguez González with pride. The winery was started when grapes were planted to make brandy and wine at what was then the Hacienda San Lorenzo (now Casa Madero). 'Wine-growing began in the Valle de Parras with the arrival of the conquistadors,' Rodríguez explains. 'Coahuila has a semi-arid climate; this helps to grow grapes of a very high quality, because we don't have problems with excessive humidity, which can lead to fungus.' At 1,500 metres above sea level, the region enjoys warm days and cool nights, and is endowed with an ample supply of water from natural springs and deep wells. The winery's most popular product for the home market is '3V', a mix of Cabernet, Merlot and Tempranillo grapes, but Cabernet Sauvignon continues to be the most popular single grape. Shiraz, adds Rodríguez, 'has the greatest potential in the Valle de Parras [because] Shiraz loves the climate'.

Rodríguez started out as a brandy distiller but became interested in wine-making in the early 1970s. He went to Montpellier in France to study and on his return to Mexico was offered a job at Casa Madero as an oenologist. 'Growing up in Jalisco, my family drank everything but wine,' he jokes; his father was a cattle rancher. He has four other oenologists working with him, one from the local area, one from Zacatecas, one from Chiapas and a fourth, who comes seasonally, from Argentina. Casa Madero grows Chardonnay, Chenin Blanc, Semillon, Gewürtztraminer, Merlot, Cabernet Franc and Malbec grapes, among others. Its Chardonnay, Chenin Blanc and Syrah have all won awards, and its brandies are considered among the best in Mexico.

The year 1997 marked the four-hundredth anniversary of the Casa Madero Foundation. The first harvest of Casa Grande Cabernet Sauvignon was released, and this was the moment when the Shiraz grape began to stand out. In 2008, Casa Madero obtained certification as a manufacturer of wines and distilled beverages, becoming the first winemaker in Mexico to achieve this recognition. Four years later, Casa Madero became a pioneer in organic certification in compliance with the National Organic Program (NOP) standard of the US Food and Drug Administration (FDA). And in 2013, the winery's Casa Madero Chenin Blanc 2012 was named the best white wine in France's most important competition.

(facing page) **Oenologist Francisco Rodríguez González with his German shepherd Polo, and** (above) **testing wine from the cellars of Casa Madero, the oldest winery in the Americas** (below)**, where he has worked for forty-four years**

(facing page, left) *Gorditas* **flattened on a grill with old irons, and** (facing page, right) **filled with** *asado de boda* **(pork stew); and** (right) **Minerva Rodríguez Adriano's granddaughter Chayla enjoying a** *gordita* **at her restaurant, Gorditas La Peri**

Mauricio Garza Montemayor
Steel Worker, Altos Hornos de México SA, Monclova, Coahuila

Mauricio Garza Montemayor has worked for Altos Hornos de México SA for thirty-three years. AHMSA is the country's largest integrated steelworks, operating a vast industrial chain from the extraction of iron ore and coal to the manufacturing of steel. Its two steel plants in Monclova cover 1,200 hectares; the total workforce numbers nineteen thousand. The nation's leader in the production and marketing of flat products – hot rolled coil, wide plate in coils or sheets, cold rolled coil, tinplate and tin-free steel – AHMSA also has production lines for structural shapes for the construction industry. It provides steel for a range of markets including automotive, railroad, machinery and mechanical equipment, piping, wind towers, propane tanks, appliances and public lighting. The company also offers tin plate products for home appliances, tapes and strapping, electronics, containers and lids, and as well as tin-free steel for

sealing and bottle caps. Its main source of iron ore is an AHMSA-owned mine in Hércules, Coahuila, and it prides itself on its philosophy of responsible operation, which has garnered national and international recognition.

Like his co-workers, Garza does long shifts and cooks on site using ingredients brought from home – for example, flour tortillas filled with pork crackling, green sauce, coriander and onion – and heated in a microwave. Cheese with chorizo is another favourite. Staying hydrated is critical. 'We sweat and we need to drink a lot of water and Gatorade,' Garza explains. 'Like 4 litres in eight hours … We work eight hours, we have lunch and then a snack – bread and a banana or an orange.' The three shifts run from 7.00 a.m. to 3.00 p.m., from 3.00 to 11.00 p.m. and from 11.00 to 7.00 a.m. 'We eat and eat,' Garza laughs. 'We need to eat because of the heat.'

(far left) **Mauricio Garza Montemayor preparing flour tortillas for lunch after his morning shift** (facing page) **at one of the open furnaces in the huge AHMSA steel plant in Monclova, and** (left) **gearing up again after lunch**

Etnia Mascogos Comunidad
El Nacimiento, Múzquiz, Coahuila

Escaping from slavery and exploitation in the US, the black Mascogo tribe settled in El Nacimiento 165 years ago. Their exodus began in the early eighteenth century, when slaves working on rice and cotton plantations in Georgia and Louisiana took refuge in Florida, where slavery had been abolished. When the Spaniards gave up Florida, the Mascogos were forced onto reservations in Oklahoma. Led by Wild Cat and John Horse, they fought the American government and in 1850 were granted asylum by the Mexican authorities in return for their help protecting Mexico's northern border from incursions by Apaches and Comanches. As a reward for services rendered, they were granted citizenship and given some land.

Doña Lucía Vázquez Valdes, the community's oldest matriarch at eighty-two, loves to talk about its trials and tribulations. A museum has been built to explain and memorialise its story. 'We wish to preserve and share our culture,' says Dulce Herrera, *Doña* Lucía's grand-daughter, who organises the community's women to prepare traditional meals as a way of generating income. 'We worked up to midnight preparing the *empanadas*,' she explains of a busy day. 'We had to use our mobile phones to see what we were doing, as we do not have electricity. This morning we woke up at 4.00 a.m. to prepare barbequed goat (cooked over hot coals) and make *atole de maíz*, sweet-potato bread, tortillas, beans and potato salad.' The women recently presented their recipes at a congress of traditional cooks.

Herrera is deeply involved in coordinating black communities from Guerrero, Oaxaca and Estado de México to demand constitutional recognition for their members. The Mascogo community comprises approximately seventy families who are engaged in agriculture – particularly the cultivation of beans, maize and wheat – and cattle and goat breeding. Every year on 19 June, they celebrate the Day of the Blacks to commemorate the abolition of slavery in the US. 'We want to progress. We cannot be at ease and at peace if we have too many necessities, like water, daily jobs and health, to worry about. We work together as a community to solve our problems,' explains Herrera.

(facing page, left) *Doña* **Lucia Vázquez Valdés waiting for lunch with her friend** (facing page, right) *Doña* **Margarita González; and** (right) **Claudia González Vázquez preparing food over hot coals** (below)**, including potato salad and barbequed goat. The Mascogo tribe has fought for official recognition as a distinct indigenous group**

Juan Garza Salazar
Kikapú Community, El Nacimiento, Múzquiz, Coahuila

Though they consider Coahuila to be their home, Juan Garza Salazar and his family spend most of the year working in Eagle Pass, Texas, where the Kikapú run a casino business. Originally the tribe was from the Great Lakes area of the US. They began migrating to Coahuila in the mid-nineteenth century; later on, groups settled elsewhere in Mexico and North America. Traditionally hunter-gatherers, in the early twentieth century the Kikapú began switching to agriculture. By the 1930s they had developed a modern system of farming, but due to drought they shifted over to doing migrant work in the US in the 1950s.

'In these modern times you have to make friends with everybody,' Garza replies when asked about working in Texas. 'If some kind of problem comes up, like a justified reason, you can change your mind.' Despite the group's accommodation to modern life, tradition remains important when it comes to their diet. 'As a tribe we still follow the traditional foods of corn, squash and deer meat,' he says. Deer ribs are important in religious ceremonies, while antlers are used to fashion knife handles.

(facing page) **Juan Garza Salazar outside his family's winter home in Múzquiz, where he lives with his son Justin Rodríguez** (above) **and mother Refugia Rodríguez Ponce. The** *wikiup* (far left) **is built out of bent branches and insulated with leaves.** (left) **Kikapú-brand beef jerky**

Chihuahua: *Big Country*

Travelling across a country accompanied by people who know a place or two reveals more things than preparation can conjure. Yet there is always a hidden gem around the corner: an encounter of the stranger kind, spectacular scenery, even a chance meeting with an international concert pianist at his home perched thousands of metres above a valley, an eagle's nest his nearest neighbour.

Romayne Wheeler, an Austrian-American, lives with the Rarámuri, an indigenous group that escaped the ravages of the conquistadors and the encroachment of 'civilisation' by taking refuge ever-higher in the Sierra Madre Occidental. Wheeler, who is also a composer, was moved to seek out the Rarámuri after a chance encounter with a copy of *National Geographic* in a hotel in 1980. Ever since then, he has spent long periods in these mountains out of sight, out of mind and beyond the reach of anybody but these people who are able to run 200 kilometres over two days up steep mountains and down even steeper valleys. Having lived with a family in caves or beneath overhanging cliffs (the long-held practice of Rarámuri in those parts), Wheeler has upgraded to a house perched 2,800 metres up and purpose-built by local craftsmen. A lover of the Alps, he says, 'I always dreamed of having my piano on top of a mountain.' Where, incidentally, there are no roads, tracks or forms of communication but human legs.

You can dream big in Mexico. The Olmecs, Toltecs, Maya and Aztecs dreamed big through monumental architecture and stone figures. The nature of the land demands big vision. Leaving the Rarámuri behind, we came upon the Barrancas del Cobre (Copper Canyon), bigger, longer and in places more magnificent than the Grand Canyon. You are never short on spectacular scenery in Mexico, and Chihuahua has a lot of big thinkers performing economic and social gymnastics, running business empires in a state notorious for gangland violence. Ciudad Juárez was the world's least safe city until recently. A teeming metropolis just across the border from El Paso, Texas, Juárez was the scene of notorious cartel wars in 2008–12.

To see Alejandra de la Vega running the city's most successful football team is therefore arresting. This high-flying executive has not only created an important sporting franchise (Bravos de Juárez FC) but succeeded in bringing differing elements of the violent city together, in order to show how cohesive social environments can positively influence the chaos in parts of Mexico's Badlands along the border with the US.

While the Rarámuri grow all their own foodstuffs in the high sierras (their local delicacy is boiled and fried animal ears), Ciudad Juárez likes its burritos served from food trucks, a practical (and trendy) innovation much in fashion as far away as New York, Los Angeles and Chicago. Same with margaritas, first mixed in the early 1940s at the Kentucky Bar near the Santa Fe Bridge crossing into El Paso. A famous watering-hole during Prohibition in the 1920s, the bar was visited by such luminaries as Al Capone, Marilyn Monroe and Liz Taylor. Just goes to show that times may change, but attitudes and violence, on both sides of the border, kind of remain the same. Especially as this border was set after the US invaded Mexico in 1846.

Romayne Wheeler
Composer & Pianist, Rarámuri Community, Nido del Águila, Sierra Tarahumara, Chihuahua

Romayne Wheeler has lived all over the world, initially because of his father's work, later due to his own career as a musician. Wheeler attended school in Monterey, California, going on to obtain two music degrees in Vienna. In the 1970s, he returned to the US to study indigenous music and dance in Arizona. In 1980, prevented by a blizzard from travelling to the Grand Canyon, his attention was caught by a copy of *National Geographic* in a hotel. The magazine featured photographs of the rugged canyon lands of the Sierra Tarahumara. Wheeler resolved to go there.

Between 1980 and 1992 the pianist spent two months every year studying Tarahumara music and dance while living in a cave. He also composed pieces based on Tarahumara music. He then decided to live permanently in this remote area, even importing a grand piano. On tour for part of the year, he donates most of his income to support the Rarámuri, who live on scattered homesteads and are known for their astonishing long-distance running ability. Runners can make it down to the bottom of the steep canyon near where Wheeler lives in ninety minutes (approximately half the time it would take anyone else), taking just two hours to make it back up to the top. 'They run like deer,' he notes. 'People from Harvard [University] came here last year to measure their pulse rate because they couldn't believe it. It was exactly the same pulse rate when they left the bottom [as when they arrived at the top]. They can run 120 miles in under twenty hours.'

Explaining his improbable decision to settle in such a remote place, Wheeler says, 'When I went to Austria, I went not only for the love of music but because I love the Alps. I always dreamed of having my piano on top of a mountain. But it was a romantic dream … Any piano would be destroyed [by the weather] within a couple of days. Here, suddenly, my dream came true. In spite of the altitude, it is dry and sunny enough [to maintain an instrument in good condition].' The added bonus is the local population, 'some of the kindest people I've ever come across in my life, people who share everything with each other, people who are very low-key and who never raise their voices at each other. (Unless they drink too much maize beer – they are human also!) They never spank their children, they never raise their voices at their children; they punish them with silence and then explain to them as if they were talking to an adult, so the children grow up with a sense of poise that is very special'. He sums up the critical importance of Rarámuri reciprocity this way: 'There's a key word, *kórimar* – 'tomorrow you might help me, today I will help you' … This is how they have been able to survive through the centuries.'

(previous spread) **Barrancas del Cobre (Copper Canyon) in Chihuahua's Sierra Tarahumara Occidental is home to the Tarahumara (or Rarámuri) tribe and a UNESCO World Heritage Site. The walls of the canyon, which is deeper than the Grand Canyon, are copper-coloured**

(right) **Romayne Wheeler with his dogs surveying the Sierra Tarahumara Occidental. His home, which locals call the *pianchi* (piano place), perches 2,800 metres above sea level**

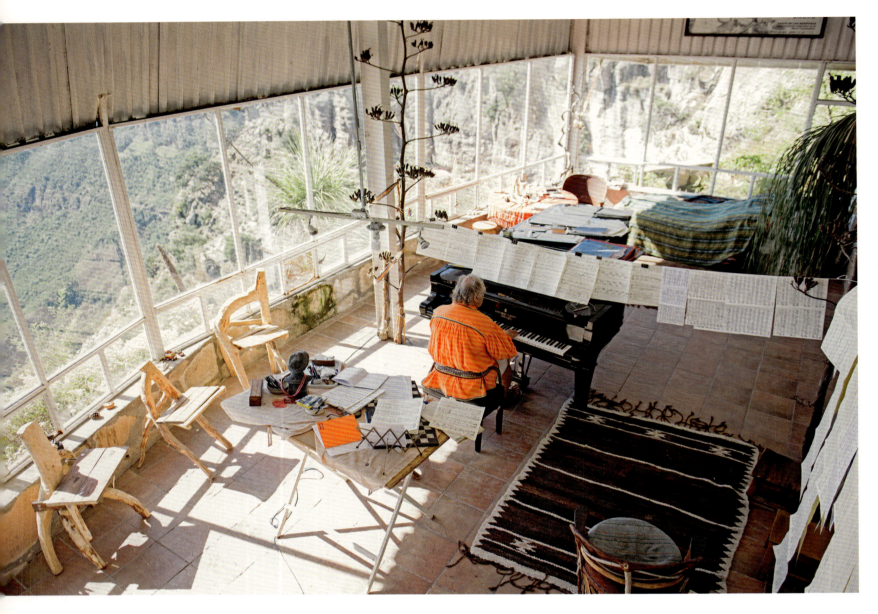

The greatest enemies of the Rarámuri in modern times have been diseases brought in from the outside, among them a range of lung conditions as well as diabetes caused by the soda and un-nutritious food they encounter in towns. 'If they go into a city, they are like a man on the Moon,' says Wheeler of his neighbours. The local diet staples are maize and beans, with some wheat in the winter if there is sufficient rain. Valley residents provide the Rarámuri with fruit, including limes, mangos and oranges. (A runner will race up the mountain with a sack containing three hundred mangos on his back and think nothing of it.) The children of folk who choose to live this sparse, difficult life are educated in primary schools scattered through the mountains, but the small number who wish to study beyond that level have to go further away or attend small government-sponsored *preparatoria*. 'Even here, you can go to college by going into the ruins of the old church and having classes,' Wheeler explains. 'They call it "*telesecundaria*", or "tele-college", because you have the help of TV.'

'To feel free, and that you're not dependent on all the things that try to manoeuvre and manipulate you, is a luxury that is much superior to having all the amenities that we enjoy in cities,' Wheeler stresses. 'I enjoy them when I'm there, but I'm not dependent on them. I can easily stay here and just eat beans and maize so my body is sustained. That's all we really need. I'm rich in all the things I can do without, like Gandhi used to say ... Of the fifty-two countries that I've gotten to know throughout my life, all of them somehow coalesce here. Somehow everything is here in miniature, except for the ocean, which is not very far away ... Earlier this morning, after all that rain that we had last night, the whole valley was a sea of clouds. It was beautiful.' Wheeler claims never to feel lonely. When friends visit from Europe or elsewhere, he asks them to 'adopt' a local child, which is to say to 'help them through school, give them some clothing, befriend the family, so they see that the white man – which for them is everybody "out there" – is not just coming to take advantage of them or take pictures of them. If we take pictures, we always should send them copies, because they say that [otherwise] their soul is sucked away. If they fall sick, it's because of the pictures, because they didn't get any copies!'

(facing page) **Wheeler at his 1917 Steinway, wearing a traditional Tarahumara shirt and huaraches, which he also wears when giving concerts. The piano, which once belonged to Arthur Rubinstein, took eighteen men seventeen hours, fifteen mattresses and four tons of potatoes to transport to Wheeler's eyrie**

(above) **Juan Gutiérrez, Wheeler's friend and father of his star pupil Romeyno Gutiérrez, and Romeyno's mother *Doña* Regina are the composer's mountaintop neighbours.** (right & below) ***Doña* Regina preparing maize for *palomitas* (popcorn) to be roasted in the traditional way**

Barrancas del Cobre (Copper Canyon)
Divisadero, Sierra Tarahumara, Chihuahua

(left) **Heidy Chávez Ramos at the edge of Copper Canyon, contemplating a sheer drop of 3,000 metres without batting an eye; and** (below) **Margarita Ochoa Ceballos and Josefina Moreno Quintero preparing blue-maize tortillas and maize-based** *pinole*

(right) **Chávez watching children at play while** (below) **Rosa Ángela Monarca prepares lunch with** (bottom) **María Monarca on a small Rarámuri ranch inland from Copper Canyon. They are making** *chacales* **(typical of the Sierra Tarahumara), which consist of** *elotes* **cooked in salted water and dried in the sun, as well as** *carne de cerdo* **with** *chile pasado* **(pork with chilli paste),** *nopal* **salad and a dessert of** *torrejas de pinole* **(fritters) with** *piloncillo* **honey (boiled unrefined sugarcane juice)**

Oscar Herrera
Chef, Flor de Nogal, Ciudad Juárez, Chihuahua

Born and bred in Ciudad Juárez, Oscar Herrera opened Flor de Nogal about two years ago in a hacienda he had been using for special events and the occasional pop-up restaurant. Bored by his work in the California telecoms industry, he had switched to professional cooking more than a decade before, opening his first eatery, Maria Chuchena, with his brother. As well as being a committed chef, Herrera is outspoken when it comes to social issues. 'I live in a Third World country full of injustices,' he observes. 'I see politicians full of power and very little wisdom, a country that they have been determined to sack.' Ciudad Juárez, where Flor de Nogal is located, was for a time described as the most violent city in the world due to drug-related crime. In 2008, like many thousands of his neighbours, Herrera fled across the Rio Grande to Texas, where he opened a restaurant that failed due to his own inexperience. Meanwhile, small businesses back home were being attacked and burned to the ground by extortionists; revenues fell by two-thirds at Maria Chuchena. Three years later, even though the daily murder rate was still high, Herrera made the decision to return to Mexico. 'It came to the point where I had to ask myself, "What am I doing for my country?"' he says. 'My position was, "I'm going to take back my city from the charnel house."'

While the bad times are firmly in the past now, Chihuahua's arid climate means that the range of fresh local ingredients available to cooks is inherently limited. Herrera refuses to let this fact prevent him from achieving success as a chef, saying, 'My strength is the adversity in which I live ... I do not have the benefit of reaching out to cut a mango or throw a net and steal some fish from the sea.'

He has been a keen supporter of the gourmet cooking competition Juárez Gastronómica, whose aim is to promote gastronomy as a means of social transformation, and is vocal in his championing of the state where he was born.

Flor de Nogal, considered one of Mexico's 120 best restaurants, is located in a working pecan orchard; deer, sheep, rabbits and chickens raised on the hacienda make Herrera's place 'the first zero-kilometre restaurant in Chihuahua'. Like many other Mexican chefs, he was influenced as a child by the female cooks in his family; his great-grandmother, he remembers fondly, 'made some killer beans'. Discussing his lack of formal training, he admits that his 'entree to [running a] restaurant was through the back door ... When I joined my brother at Maria Chuchena, I took control of purchasing and food costs ... I started to add my own recipes, to take care of all the other recipes, and I put them into this IT program that I had learned how to use'. In effect he learned his trade on the job, although he maintains that 'cooking was something that was always a part of me'. He has seen Ciudad Juárez transform itself from a town of panic, when sundown meant that everyone was safely locked in at home, into a town of hope – and not just for restaurants. Some of his customers come from Texas and off cruise ships, but mainly they are locals. Ever the realist, he says, 'We are not completely auto-sustainable and we don't intend to be, but we do like the exercise of growing our own things.' His close focus, coupled with a wide-ranging sense of social responsibility, are what make Herrera's work unique in Chihuahua.

(above) *Escolar* fish with lentils; (right) Short rib of beef with yellow *mole*; and (far right) Dessert of pumpkin, deconstructed

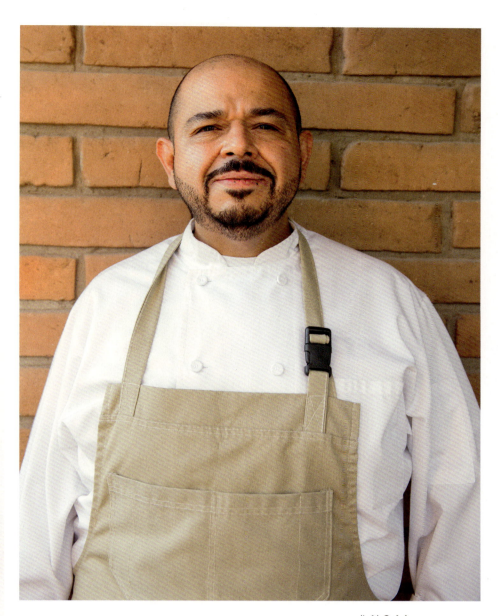

(left) *Calabaza tarahumara* – squash prepared *bichicori*-style, a technique that involves peeling the pumpkin, briefly cooking it, peeling it in one continuous spiral, and then wrapping it and drying it in the sun; and (above) **Chef Oscar Herrera at Flor de Nogal**

Bravos de Juárez FC
Ciudad Juárez, Chihuahua

Founded in 2015 by Alejandra de le Vega, Bravos de Juárez football club is based in Chihuahua's largest city. Their home ground is the Estadio Olímpico Benito Juárez, whose capacity is twenty thousand.

De la Vega is a member of the Vega Group of local businesses, which uses its influence in the service of social improvement. The group sees football as a vehicle to promote the city's growth, and their focus is on offering aspirational models to young people. The guiding principle is that smaller local teams bring people together. Having managed football teams since her twenties, De la Vega is famously remembered as a hero in a brutal match against FC Zacatepec in Morelos where the fans were particularly aggressive towards her and her team, chanting 'Kill the Spaniards!' at her family. The twenty-one-year-old De la Vega ran out onto the pitch under a hail of bottles and cans, demanding that the match be halted until proper security was provided for her players. The team surrounded her to protect her from the crowd, and the match was suspended.

Known as the world's murder capital not too long ago, Ciudad Juárez went through a period of violent social unrest between 2008 and 2010. As the town sits cheek-by-jowl with El Paso's 1.3 million inhabitants, with whom it shares five border crossings into Texas,

it had become Mexico's migrant capital. The economy expanded with the proliferation of *maquiladoras*, low-paying factories run by US and foreign companies. As family ties withered and gangs gravitated to the area, the infrastructure withered as well. Anarchy ensued. The 2008 global financial meltdown amplified the situation, with over ninety thousand jobs lost as the Sinaloa drug cartel took up residence, forging a war with the Juárez cartel. People were scared to leave their homes.

Understanding that 'if locals don't do more for their community, nothing will change', De la Vega used football to access the younger generation, educating a population who knew nothing but street war and violence. 'The team [became] heroes among kids in the poorer communities,' she points out. Players from Ecuador, Argentina and Mexico itself were, and still are, offered a new perspective and social infrastructure, in turn frequently visiting poor neighbourhoods and schools. De la Vega hopes that 'if they have a local team they can really get behind, the community will continue coming together and providing better alternatives for our young people.'

Improvement has been clear over the last few years, with once-unwalkable streets filling again with food trucks, among them Burritos Sarita in Hermanos Escobar, the Bravos team's favourite eatery.

(facing page, left) **Alejandra de la Vega, founder of Bravos de Juárez FC, speaking with captain Leandro Carrijó and players on the practice field. Team members often do community work in Ciudad Juárez.** (facing page, right) **Andrés Mendoza, a star Ecuadorian defender, signing autographs at** Cuauhtémoc primary school, where the players surprised the children with a visit; and (facing page, middle) **The team enjoying burritos from their favourite outlet,** (above) **Burritos Sarita, a food truck in Hermanos Escobar that has been run by two sisters for the past forty-seven years**

Nayarit: *Spiritual Journeys*

The history of Nayarit is written in three parts: by its indigenous tribe, by the Spanish Navy and by the *jején*.

The Huichol recognise the sacred rock of Tatéi Haramura on the Isla del Rey off the port of San Blas as their ancestors' place of origin – the sea. The Huichol see their world as having the shape of a human body, with the feet in San Blas, one arm in Durango and the other arm in Jalisco. The head is in San Luis Potosí, and the heart is in a cave at the base of a hill (almost completely submerged) in the giant lake formed by the Aguamilpa Dam near Tepic, Nayarit's capital.

The Huichol, or Wixáritari (as they prefer to call themselves), originated fifteen thousand years ago in San Luis Potosí and migrated to the Sierra Madre Occidental, settling in Nayarit, Jalisco, Zacatecas and Durango when the conquistadors arrived. The Huichol have vigorously avoided the 'civilising' influences of the last five hundred years. Handsome people with closely held traditions, they worship their ancestors, with some Huichol making annual pilgrimages to Real de Catorce, their ancestral homeland, to perform *mitote* dance ceremonies, having harvested hallucinogenic peyote along the way. Huichol artisans create representations of their roots and customs based on their cosmological beliefs, for example in the four elements of creation: earth, water, air and fire. In ancient times, their ancestors fashioned ritual figurines of deities and sacred animals.

A choppy thirty-minute boat ride from San Blas out into the Pacific brings you to Tatéi Haramura to witness the majesty of nature mixed with the spiritual imaginings of human beings. Made white by multitudes of seabirds, the volcanic outcrop has gained new religious symbolism, with Catholic visitors propping a small statue of the Virgin at its top. San Blas meanwhile is but a shell of its once grand self as the Spanish Navy's principal Pacific port, with ships heading east to load up with spices and others sailing north to explore Alta California. Hardwood forests enabled shipbuilding on the coast, and it was from there that Father Junípero Serra set sail in 1768 to establish missions in Alta California, places which remain as towns and cities today. It was also from there that Juan Manuel de Ayala set sail to found San Francisco in 1775. Oh the paradoxes of history, so often on display in Mexico! The Mexicans were forced to concede California to the US at the end of the Mexican-American War in 1848 for the princely sum of US$15 million.

Meanwhile the Spanish Navy were pushed out of San Blas by no less a force than the merciless *jején*. These mosquitoes rise in waves to attack just as the sun is setting. The semi-tropical coastline has beautiful sandy beaches and mangrove swamps where the wretched *jején* breed, but so do some of the best shrimp in Mexico. Having driven out the Spanish Pacific fleet, the *jején* also managed to depopulate the coast of another northern intruder. Hollywood's glamour kings and queens made the Playa Hermosa Hotel in San Blas a romantic watering hole during the 1950s and '60s. Lee Marvin fished for marlin off the coast, while Jim Morrison fished for the lyrics of 'L.A. Woman' in 1969. Liz Taylor and Richard Burton took refuge there to avoid the press *jején*, and Marilyn Monroe sported natural attire to blend into the landscape.

Mariscos Kika Restaurante
Mexcaltitán de Uribe, Nayarit

(previous spread) **Tatéi Haramara (Isla del Rey), a shrine sacred to the Huichol in the Pacific Ocean near San Blas in Nayarit. Believed to be the dwelling (or earthly form) of the Mother of the Sea, this rocky outcrop is thought of as the source of all life, as well as the boundary between life and death. The Church placed a statue of the Virgin of Guadalupe atop the crag**

(left) **Paola Rivera at Mariscos Kika, which is located on a tiny island off Mexcaltitán. Legend claims that the Aztecs set off from here to found Tenochtitlán.** (below) **Grilled *robalo* with olive oil and salt; and** (bottom left) ***Pescados chicos* preserved in clay in Mexcaltitán**

(above) **The small restaurant founded by Alberto Estrada needs constant propping up to prevent it from sinking into the lagoon, which boasts some of Mexico's best prawns as well as the dreaded** *jején*. (left) **Prawns drying at the restaurant**

(right & below)
La Tovara in San Blas, Nayarit, an extensive estuary system that flows through a lush jungle of *manglar* (mangroves) and ferns, and hosts crocodiles, turtles, ocelots, jaguars and a variety of fish and birds

Abel Pérez Jiménez
Avocado Farmer & Co-operative Member, Xalisco, Nayarit

Having worked harvesting sugarcane, Abel Pérez Jiménez was planning to retire but instead decided to take up avocado farming. As the owner of a large farm, he is deeply involved with his local community as a member of the Rainforest Alliance.

On around 9 hectares Pérez grows sixteen hundred trees which produce between 12 and 14 tons per hectare. He sells his avocados to La Casa de Aguacate, a local co-operative that was founded thirty years ago. The organisation has 130 members, most of whom are local farmers, and who sell to Dubai, Malaysia, Kuwait, the Netherlands, Spain, France and Canada, altogether exporting around 1,600 tons of avocados between August and February every year. Being the only co-operative that transports their goods by plane, they have the ability to harvest in season and provide fresh produce all year round. If they send their daily harvest to the packaging plant by 4.00 p.m., it is packed the next morning and leaves the following day by plane (from Mexico City to serve the European market, and from Guadalajara to serve the Asian one).

Nayarit is primarily mountainous and has a semi-warm climate; the Hass avocado is the most common variety being grown in the area. Xalisco produces a considerable percentage of the world's avocados. Thus they play a pivotal role in the state's economy, with an internal market value of over US$1 billion, covering over 95,000 hectares of agricultural land and producing more than eight hundred thousand units in a single season.

(facing page, top) **Abel Pérez Jiménez tending his avocados during the harvest season; they are packed and then shipped** (facing page, bottom & below) **across the world.** (right) Avocado picker **Alberto Solís Ahumada filling his bag**

(left) **Playa del Amor, a beach hidden in a sun-drenched crater in the Islas Marietas, a group of small uninhabited islands on the Riviera Nayarita; and** (above) **Punta Mita beachfront resort in Nayarit, surrounded on three sides by the Pacific Ocean. The peninsula is home to the early human settlement and ancient observatory of Careyeros Hill**

Huichol Community
Potrero de la Palmita, Del Nayar, Nayarit

Priscilliano Evangelista Eligio and Teodoro Evangelista live in the Huichol community of La Palmita. Other residents include Vicenta López Minjares, her daughter Milka Torres López and Monica Carrillo López (Priscilliano's wife), who make tortillas from locally grown blue maize and cook tilapia farmed in the manmade lake behind the nearby Aguamilpa Dam. They all work at Tawexikta, a tourism centre run by local people who came up with the idea as a way to bring in some extra income.

The Huichol are native Mexicans who live in the Sierra Madre Occidental. They refer to themselves as Wixáritari ('the people'), number approximately thirty-five thousand and are said to be the last tribe in North America to have maintained their pre-Columbian traditions. Once a year, some Huichol journey back to San Luis Potosí, their ancestral homeland, to perform *mitote* ceremonies using peyote. Their religion consists of four principal deities: the trinity of Maize, Blue Deer and Peyote, and the Eagle, all descended from the Sun God, Tao Jreeku. Most retain their traditional beliefs and jealously defend them.

Many Huichol used to work on large tobacco plantations, which proved ruinous to their health. Plantation owners are no longer allowed to use toxic pesticides. Fortunately, the Huichol live near Mazatlán and other tourist meccas, so they are able to sell their crafts as another means of earning income. Their yarn paintings and beaded jaguar heads in psychedelic colours are related to their traditional beliefs and the symbols of their shamanistic culture. Their main crop is maize, but they also grow beans and squash and occasionally raise livestock. The soil is poor and crop yields low, making malnutrition common. The Huichol also hunt, mostly for deer and small animals. The sale of beef provides an important source of income; they also sell timber and excess maize. In summer, when the rains come, they live on farms in tiny hamlets and make cheese out of milk from their cattle, which they slaughter for eating, mostly during celebrations. Marriages are arranged by parents when their children are very young; Huichol usually marry between the ages of fourteen and seventeen.

Each Huichol settlement has a communal kitchen and family shrine. The diet consists of tortillas – made from blue, red, yellow or white maize – beans, rice, pasta, the occasional chicken or pig and chilli peppers, supplemented with wild fruit and vegetables such as *colorines* (coral beans), *ciruelas* (wild plums) and *guayabas* (guavas).

(above) *Flor de Jamaica* growing in a garden in Potrero de la Palmita. Hibiscus is used to make a delicious drink with medicinal properties.
(above, right) **Bartola Carrillo**, wife of the community's shaman, carrying a dish of sliced squash; and (right) **Antonio Carrillo Romero** taking his guard duties seriously

(facing page) **Priscilliano Evangelista Eligio and his wife Monica Carillo López** at their home in Potrero de la Palmita, Del Nayar. Eligio's ceremonial clothing was made by his wife

Colima: *Heartbreak Hotel*

Colima is God's own little country. One of the smallest, richest, safest and cleanest states in Mexico, it is a magnet for inward immigration. The climate is pleasant and the land produces most anything you plant in abundance. In fact, so abundant is nature's bounty that palm trees on municipal streets and highways are 'milked' for the most sugary natural drink I think I've ever come across.

Meet Camilo Bejerano Jiménez, a *tubero*. He is a provider of this nectar of the gods, sapping the coconut palm's juices, climbing dangerously tall palms with only a bucket, a rag over his shoulder, a large, empty cola bottle with its top cut away and some wire. With such rudimentary instruments, he cuts the palm's budding flower before it transforms into a coconut, tethering his unseemly container overnight to catch the sap as it drains from the tree's heart into the bottle.

Colima has many stories to do with the heart and sap of society. It was home to Juan Rulfo, the early twentieth-century writer credited with being the father of Magical Realism, the genre that spawned a generation of Latin American writers who have won international acclaim, even winning Gabriel Garciá Márquez the Nobel Prize for Literature in 1982. Born in Comala, Juan Nepomuceno Carlos Pérez Rulfo Vizcaíno was a poet, writer, screenwriter and photographer with a bit of a dashing reputation. His father was killed when he was only five years old, and the family's troubled existence during the time of the Mexican Revolution, when most of the establishment was disenfranchised, had a profound impact on his writing. Garciá Márquez attributed the main influence for his novel *One Hundred Years of Solitude* to his discovery of Rulfo's only published novel, *Pedro Páramo*, comparing Rulfo's writing to 'pages that come down to us from Sophocles'.

Further to the subject of Colima and romance, in the 1950s Jimmy Goldsmith, the legendary gambler, financier, womaniser and bon vivant, fell madly in love at the age of twenty with Isabel Patiño, the beautiful seventeen-year-old daughter of one of the twentieth century's richest men. Antenor Patiño owned most of Bolivia at the time, as well as the best real estate in the most desirable spots on earth, including Hacienda San Antonio, a run-down former coffee plantation. The beautiful estate was later turned into a mini-Versailles by the same man who was to become Sir James Goldsmith, the mergers-and-acquisitions magnate known for buying companies on the cheap and chopping them up for a huge profit. The inspiration for corporate raider Larry Wildman in Oliver Stone's 1987 film *Wall Street*, Goldsmith in the '50s already knew a good thing when he saw it. The two alpha males went head to head, with Patiño famously quoted as saying, 'We're not in the habit of marrying Jews!' To which Goldsmith is reputed to have replied, 'Well, I'm not in the habit of marrying [Red] Indians!' The matter was resolved unilaterally, with the young couple eloping to France. Jimmy Goldsmith married *Doña* María Isabel Patiño y Borbón in Stockholm in 1954 to the delight of gossip columnists in Paris, London and New York. Romance was overtaken by the death of the young bride while pregnant, forever scarring a man whom Margaret Thatcher described as 'one of the most powerful and dynamic personalities' of his generation.

Gonzalo Mendoza Aguilar
Chef, Hacienda de San Antonio, Comala, Colima

'Hacienda de San Antonio is a privileged place because nearly a hundred of the ingredients [we cook with] are cultivated organically on the property,' explains chef Gonzalo Mendoza Aguilar. 'This is a paradise. As a worker or as a visitor or as a guest, it is a privilege to be here.'

'I started by working at the coalface like all other chefs … learning all the different jobs in a kitchen and ending up a leader,' Mendoza explains. After washing dishes in Tijuana, an early job in a Chinese restaurant was a big influence. Mendoza went on to gain a position at Rancho la Puerta in Tecate (where Denise Roa is now chef, and where the menu was lacto-vegetarian). Stints at Le Cordon Bleu in Mexico City and at the Culinary Institute of America helped him to hone his focus.

Mendoza is deeply committed to his work at Hacienda San Antonio. 'What I do at the restaurant, what we produce, the organic and sustainable approach – all of it is very interesting,' he observes. 'All of the produce is organic; no pesticides or chemicals [are used]. We have twenty varieties of cheese – mature, semi-mature and fresh. My favourite is smoked provolone, also the hard cheeses like manchego and asiago, and goat's cheese as well … We receive our milk in tin containers directly from the cows. We can ask not to have it pasteurised. We also make our own yoghurt (Greek or flavoured), cream and butter. Our pastry is very good … We produce, toast and grind our own coffee.' The occasional rumbling of the nearby volcano provides a certain level of drama, especially 'at night when there are no [other] noises. It sounds like a pressure cooker,' Mendoza jokes.

Asked if his cuisine evidences international influence, the chef characterises it as 'very Mexican', given that the kitchen was designed to cater for the family holidays of British tycoon and politician Jimmy Goldsmith. The hacienda was acquired from descendants of Goldsmith's onetime father-in-law, Bolivian tin king Antenor Patiño, who was famous for his lavish lifestyle. At the age of twenty, Goldsmith had fallen in love with Maria Isabel Patiño, Antenor's daughter, who was even younger. Her parents having declared Goldsmith an unsuitable partner for their daughter, the couple eloped and were married in 1954. Today the hacienda is managed by Alix Goldsmith, one of Jimmy's children, and boasts Mexican and European antiques, endless formal gardens, a pool and a rooftop terrace. Built in the colonial style with arches framing a central courtyard, the main building faces a sweeping lawn and manicured garden paths.

'I do have [knowledge of] international techniques, but what is most important to me, and what I don't wish to change, is respect for food, for every vegetable, for produce, because of the hard labour with which it is harvested,' muses Mendoza. 'We have to respect the hard work that is behind all of our ingredients. Work has to be done in all kinds of conditions.' This commitment grows out of his belief in the slow food movement, a global, grassroots movement linking the pleasure of food with a commitment to community and the environment.

(previous spread) **Pineapple pickers harvesting fruit under the midday sun on a plantation near Tecoman in Colima**

(left) **The colonnade at Hacienda de San Antonio, whose gardens were designed in the style of Versailles; and** (facing page) **Chef Gonzalo Mendoza Aguilar preparing a chicken dish**

Camilo Bejerano Jiménez
Tubero, Colima, Colima

Styling himself after the Spanish singer Camilo Sesto, to whom he bears a striking resemblance, Camilo Bejerano Jiménez has been a *tubero* since he was thirteen. Now fifty-one, he is known for the purity of his product and always serves it fresh on the day of extraction. Camilo is the third generation of his family to climb palm trees across Colima, together with two of his nine brothers. He grows his own palms in his garden, renting others in the region for a small fee. Transporting his palm flowers on his bicycle together with his brother Carlos, who has a motorbike, Camilo has become a local celebrity.

Tubâ is a sweet alcoholic drink often referred to as 'palm wine' and is typical of the region. It is created from the sap of the palm flower. Extracted from a variety of species, including the palmyra, date palm and coconut palm, it is common in parts of Asia, Africa, the Caribbean and South America. Originating in the Philippines, *tubâ* was popularised in Mexico in the sixteenth century, when a trade route was established by a group of Spanish trading ships that set out on voyages twice a year, connecting Mexico to Manila and the Philippines. Through an exchange of commodities and customs, the coconut palm native to the Philippines came to dominate the highway to Colima, and *tubâ* became a local delicacy.

Tubâ sap is extracted by a tapper after making cuts at the top of the tree where the coconuts grow; a container is fastened to the flower stump to collect the sap. This procedure is preferable to the felling of the whole tree, after which a fire is lit at the cut end to allow for the collection of sap. Once collected, the sap begins to ferment because of the natural yeasts present in the air and residual yeasts left in the container. The drink is ready within two hours, and has an alcohol content of 4 per cent and a sweet, aromatic flavour. Left for a day, *tubâ* becomes stronger and more sour, turning to vinegar if left any longer. Bejerano sells mostly to local restaurants, although *tubâ* is also sold on the street and in parks. It is at its sweetest in December.

(above) **Camilo Bejerano Jiménez shinnying up a palm tree to extract nectar from its flowers,** (facing page) **clinging onto a palm (some grow up to 30 metres tall),** and (left) **selling *tubâ* from his bicycle**

(following spread, left) **Kimberly awaiting a *torta* (sandwich) in Cuyutlán, Colima; and** (following spread, right) **Mario Antonio Hernández gathering dried banana leaves to make wreaths for Day of the Dead ceremonies**

Emilio Soto
Owner, Papaya Plantation, Armería, Colima

Papaya, which is native to southern Mexico, was already being cultivated prior to Mesoamerican times. A papaya tree has few branches, large leaves and can grow up to 10 metres in height. While plants can be male, female or hermaphrodite, commercial orchards like that owned by Emilio Soto commonly contain only hermaphrodites as they are self-pollinating and can produce fruit within three years.

Papaya growing is on the increase in Mexico, with the country currently producing 11 per cent of the world's crop and the largest exporter of fresh papayas to the US. Colima's plantations average 2,000 hectares per year, just behind the states of Michoacán and Veracruz. Mexico produces several papaya varieties, including Tainung, Sensation, Intenzza and (the most common) Maradol.

The main reason for Colima's success has been the implementation of the Contamination Risk Reduction System, which focuses on the application of good agricultural and manufacturing practices. In 2011, evidence surfaced of salmonella in Mexican papayas, with approximately a hundred cases found across the US. Even though the source was unclear, the Mexican government and papaya industry took immediate steps to put further food-safety procedures in place throughout the chain of production, processing, distribution and sale.

Another contributing factor is the relative youth of Colima's papaya growers, who have brought a fresh perspective to the industry, seeking to break with long-established paradigms.

In the last decade, Colima's production has grown by 87 per cent. The state is seen as producing the best-quality papayas, as well as being the best organised, most closely consolidated and most self-sustaining group of growers. Colima exports to Baja California, Mexico City, Jalisco, Texas and California, and was the first Mexican state to export fruit to Europe, primarily to Portugal and Germany.

(facing page) **Emilio Soto inspecting a papaya wrapped in newspaper on his plantation in Armería;** (far left) **Rows of papaya trees with their ripening fruit;** (above) **A Mexican papaya; and** (left) **Berries growing wild on the plantation**

Tamaulipas: *Oil Kingdom*

The history of Mexican oil became closely intertwined with the country's sense of nationalism in the course of the twentieth century. Other nationalist drivers have been *Yanqui* imperialism and the historical burden of Mexican–American relations. Oil is both a blessing and a curse, engendering corruption and a false sense of destiny. Mexico is the Western Hemisphere's fourth-largest oil producer (after the US, Canada and Venezuela), and eleventh in the world. Petróleos Mexicanos (PEMEX), the state-owned entity that until recently had dominion over the country's petroleum assets and operations, carried the national flag once oil was nationalised in 1938. Then President Lázaro Cárdenas declared all mineral and oil reserves as government property after an acrimonious and drawn-out confrontation between the oil workers' union and foreign (American and British) oil companies.

The country's first exploratory wells were drilled as far back as 1869 by Mexican and US entrepreneurs, while the existence of oil in the form of tar shales was known well before the arrival of the Spaniards; local tribes used the earth's oleaginous excretions to caulk their canoes. The development of the railways was the spur for the development of Mexico's oil industry, with British and American interests taking charge. Encouraged by then President Porfirio Díaz, Tampico (the state capital) grew to become the country's main oil terminal. Díaz was a great Europhile and brought in British capital to counter America's hold on oil development. (He is famously quoted as saying, 'Poor Mexico, so far from God, and so near to the United States of America!') By the time of nationalisation, all of the companies and capital involved in Mexico's oil production were foreign.

The jury is still out on the economic benefits of nationalisation, but the politics of oil have continued to play a crucial role in the country's affairs. Especially as the government draws nearly a fifth of its revenues from PEMEX taxes, with oil constituting 10 per cent of exports. The dramas of nationalism and nationalisation go hand in glove. Mexico's original oil workers' syndicate was set up in Tampico three years prior to nationalisation. The power of the union was personified in later years through PEMEX boss Joaquín Hernández '*La Quina*' Galicia, a sometimes brutal power broker at the head of a vast army of workers. Hernández 'owned' Tampico; nothing could be done without his sanction. He brooked no dissent, and it was said that he took a slice of every cake in the name of his workers. The petroleum industry suffered as a consequence while Tampico festered with corruption. Hernández was finally brought to heel in 1989 by then President Carlos Salinas de Gortari, who had the union boss thrown into jail on charges of corruption and illegal arms possesion.

The drabness of Tampico was brightened somewhat during our stay by the cheery disposition of Ángel García, the city's leading chef, whose family-owned restaurant, El Porvenir, has sat across from the local cemetery for nearly a century. 'You're better off here than over there!' is an apt motto for the eatery, he likes to joke. The hard-headed García (who once fought off four muggers single-handedly) is passionate about everything Mexican, especially if it has to do with Tamaulipas. He has transformed El Porvenir into a destination eatery specialising in seafood from the area's lagoons and mangrove swamps.

(previous spread) **The Cooperativa Emiliano Gayardo in Las Chacas, Tampico Alto, Veracruz, on the border with Tamaulipas**

(facing page & above)
The port of Tampico in Tamaulipas, one of Mexico's largest oil ports and once the greatest oil port in the world

(right & below) **Félix Hernández** diving for oysters in the Canal de Chijol, a waterway begun in 1901 to connect the oil fields of Tamaulipas with Tuxpan. Hernández, who has been diving for oysters for fifteen years with nothing more than an improvised jerry-can and a small motor boat, harvests up to 150 a day in the high season

Ángel García
Chef, El Porvenir, Tampico, Tamaulipas

Young chef Ángel García studied at the Culinary Institute of America in Hyde Park, New York. In 2013 he organised 'El Porvenir de la Gastronomia', the first international gastronomy congress to take place in north-eastern Mexico, an event that also celebrated his restaurant's ninetieth anniversary.

The story of El Porvenir begins with García's grandfather, who arrived in Mexico from Spain in 1902 'looking for something better'. At the time, Tampico was a boom town due to the growth of the oil industry, and García's grandfather was able to open a general store there. In 1916 he set up a one-table cantina selling wine and tapas. García started working at El Porvenir when he was a child. 'At that time,' he says, 'it was still a cantina where they served a lot of very good seafood. All the recipes came from my dad.' He explains that the high quality of Tampico's seafood is due to its location at the heart of a variety of water-based ecosystems rich in different types of shrimp, crab, molluscs and fish.

García's family's Spanish origins are apparent in El Porvenir's menu today. 'They used to do a potato tortilla, the classic Spanish tortilla,' the chef explains, 'but they were having difficulty getting the potatoes here in Tampico. So my father started adding shrimp and crab and octopus, even eels! ... So he had a seafood tortilla instead of a potato tortilla, and that was one of the biggest hits of the restaurant at that time.' He points to the difference between Pacific Ocean shrimp, which are huge but which taste of iodine, and lagoon shrimp, called 'red legs' by fishermen, which are very sweet. 'You just boil them, just cook them without salt. You don't have to add anything,' he notes. 'The water in the lagoons is like the marinade of the sea; it really changes the flavour. And there is no contamination, no pollution in those lagoons, believe me. The flavours are delicious and unique.'

(above) **Ángel García with the catch of the day, which includes grey mullet and its yellow roe, known as** *hueva de lisa*; **and (right) Fresh** *macabí*

(above) **García enjoying Lágrimas de la Llorona tequila with his father at their restaurant, El Porvenir, in Tampico;** (facing page, left) **Beetroot ice cream; and** (facing page, right) *Filete Nordico* **– smoked** *negrilla* **fish with oysters, octopus and prawns**

(following spread, left) *Hueva de lisa*; **and** (following spread, right) **Freshly caught** *besugo*, *huachinango* **and** *sargo* **kept cool with slushed ice**

Veracruz: *Gold & the True Cross*

Wherever you travel in Mexico, Veracruz is always top of the list when food and culinary traditions are mentioned. Ranked third in population among Mexico's thirty-two states, Veracruz is a mere sliver of land wedged between the Sierra Madre Oriental and the Gulf of Mexico. Despite possessing only 3.7 per cent of the country's landmass, Veracruz packs a big punch both economically and historically. Food apart, its claim to fame is in its variegated climate and biodiversity. The topography changes from north to south, from tropical coastal plains with sandy lagoons to snow-capped high sierras. Mexico's highest peak, Pico de Orizaba (5,636 metres above sea level), is situated in Veracruz. Criss-crossed with rivers and their tributaries, interrupted by scenic waterfalls and lagoons, Veracruz has some of the most varied wildlife in the Western Hemisphere. The state is also rich in agriculture, and its industries play a major part in the national economy.

Rich in history as well, Veracruz was founded in 1519 by Hernán Cortés; the Spaniards called it Villa Rica de la Vera Cruz, the Rich Village of the True Cross. Gold was discovered there and the deep port became the principal entry point into New Spain. La Malinche and Salma Hayek are two famous daughters of the area, Amazons from different times playing to history's audiences, one as Cortés' mistress, the other a Hollywood 'toughie'. La Malinche's story is so vivid and colourful, it almost begs to be scripted for a film starring Hayek.

From tempestuous women to tempestuous political climes, Veracruz has a turbulent reputation. A fun-loving population, both headstrong and stubborn, adds to the combustible mix of beautiful landscapes and colourful history. Archaeological finds date the region's pre-Colombian heritage to twenty-six hundred years ago, with huge Olmec heads a visible presence, like guardians of time randomly dotted around the state. Arriving at El Tajín for the first time can be intoxicating. One of the most important pre-Columbian sites of Mesoamerica, El Tajín was lost to the world for five hundred years. Its rather unromantic rediscovery in 1785 (as jungles had long engulfed the ancient centre) by an itinerant tax inspector is not exactly the stuff of Indiana Jones, perhaps more akin to Rider Haggard's fabulism.

As with many other pre-Columbian sites, differing histories are attributed to El Tajín. Early Spanish maps refer to it as Mictlan, or 'place of the dead', but then most such sites in Mexico are referred to the same way in the absence of archaeological DNA. Having spent a lonely hour sat under gloomy skies at the foot of the Pyramid of the Niches, my money is on the Totonac people's name for the site, 'place of the invisible beings or spirits'. With my affinity with the country growing as we travelled through its Mesoamerican past, juxtaposing time and place, people and historical spaces, I brooded over its present predicaments while considering yesteryear's trials and tribulations.

Tribulations manifested in someone like Raquel Torres, one of Mexico's best-known traditional cooks and an anthropologist who believes that culture is embedded in food, that food is its highest manifestation. Torres is not an academic researcher but rather someone with a talent for tracing traditions and ancient culinary processes, given her emphasis on economics, geography and the division of labour. Precisely what determines the course of history in the *longue durée* sense.

(previous spread)
Honeysuckle in December in Xico, Veracruz

The World Heritage Site of El Tajín in Veracruz, which flourished in the ninth–thirteenth centuries. (above) **The symmetrical Pyramid of the Niches, whose 365 niches represent the solar year; and** (facing page) **Elaborate astronomical carvings and friezes which are unique in Mesoamerica. The complex remained hidden in the jungle until its rediscovery by a local tax collector in 1785**

Martha Soledad Atzin
Traditional Cook, Women of Smoke, Parque Takilhsukut, El Tajin, Veracruz

Martha Soledad Atzin heads up the kitchen and cookery school at Parque Takilhsukut, which aims to teach and preserve Totonacan recipes. In 2016 her work was recognised by the Business Coordinating Council of Northern Veracruz, which described her as 'one of the three most important traditional cooks of Mexico'.

'We Women of Smoke want to share our traditional cuisine and our culture from our hearts,' explains Atzin. 'We call ourselves "Women of Smoke" because we grew up in smoky kitchens, in houses with just one room that was a bedroom, a kitchen, a living room and a dining room all in one, and where women were born, got married, delivered babies and died.' During her thirty years working on behalf of traditional Totonacan gastronomy, Atzin has been at the heart of the Women of Smoke, disseminating traditional cuisine at universities, congresses, workshops and gastronomic meetings.

In the fifteenth century, the Aztecs labelled as Totonacapan the region that extended roughly from Papantla in the north to Cempoala in the south. Totonacapan was largely hot and humid. Along with the normal crops of maize, manioc, squash, beans, pumpkin and chilli peppers, the region was noted for its liquidambar and cotton. Even during the disastrous famine of 1450–54, it remained a reliable agricultural centre. Many Aztecs were forced to sell themselves or family members as slaves to the Totonac in exchange for subsistence maize. The Totonac people's diet consisted of fruit, fish, turtle, venison, armadillo, opossum and frogs. Their main midday meal was based on manioc and bean stew, with the addition of meat sauce for the nobles. Liquor was made from the agave cactus.

When Atzin was growing up, she would stay on her own (in her childhood house; the kitchen was a separate space) while her grandmother got up at 4.00 a.m. to start cooking. 'I would … be afraid,' she recalls, 'so I learned to play with smells with my senses and learned how to feel less lonely. Smoke came in through an opening in the roof tiles. It was a bridge of salvation for me. As a girl I did not think about dolls; I dreamed about being a great cook when I grew up, and that I was going to cook with many women. That's what we've achieved.' She and her colleagues have dedicated themselves to keeping 'uses and customs' alive – 'our communities, our cuisine, our magic, our secrets, all that is implied by a woman's life'.

Atzin notes that in the past, 'we were not used to being hugged and kissed. You did not touch each other. Our greeting was by touching the tips of the fingers. So we could not get close to a grandmother and hug her or kiss her. It was not allowed … In some way I was trying to get closer to my grandmother and feel her closer in my life. So in the afternoons when we talked, I would ask her why she smelled like smoke and why her white hair was a different colour to that of women in the city. She would reply that it was because she was an old woman of smoke … We are the rebel Women of Smoke because we have broken all the locks on the chests that contained the secrets of our grandmothers' recipes. We have shared them with the world so all these secrets would not be kept hidden … Frightened at the beginning, we did not know what to expect without children, without husbands. It was also a way of getting the women out of their homes, of breaking with expectations. Of course our grandmothers would come along so we would not misbehave!'

(facing page) **Martha Soledad Atzin, head of the cooking programme at Parque Takilhsukut, bringing local women together** (above) **to cook traditional Totonacan dishes, including** (right) *bocoles* (*gorditas* **made with maize and pork lard)**

(left) **A parrot surveying the view from atop a pile of cigar boxes in the central plaza of Veracruz; and** (above & facing page) **Tenders and ships amid the city's maritime bustle. Veracruz, a major port on the Gulf of Mexico, was the conquistadors' first port in New Spain; its mix of indigenous, colonial and Afro-Caribbean influences has resulted in unique music and cuisine**

Rosana Ortega Aguilar
Independent Coffee Plantation Owner, Rancho Santa Cruz, Xico, Veracruz

Rosana Ortega Aguilar, who was born in 1965 in Xalapa, studied Business Administration at Universidad Veracruzana. When her husband died recently after a long illness, Ortega inherited about 12 hectares of coffee plantations. 2016 was her first season producing and selling coffee on her own, with the support of *Don* Gonzalo Tlapa, who managed all aspects of coffee production for her husband. Before Ortega met her husband, she knew nothing about coffee. Now a *finca* manager in her own right, she only sells coffee to friends, hoping that her business will grow and become profitable one day.

Ortega's finca produces around 2 tons of coffee per year, depending on the weather. The so-called 'cherries' (i.e. the dried berries) of the coffee are brought to her small house, Rancho Santa Cruz, where they are pulped before being left to ferment, then washed and finally dried in her old swimming pool. (She uses the pool because she does not have sufficient space for conventional drying racks.) Veracruz coffees are known for their pleasant, rounded flavour and warm, cocoa-like quality, with good body and citrus/tropical flavours. The state hosts an abundance of small-to-medium-sized single-owner *fincas*.

'At my age I am still able to work,' muses Ortega, 'and I have a job on my doorstep ... The five people that work for me harvest the coffee ... I only have to supervise them.' She has started to grow her own *café arabigo de altura* plants in a greenhouse and then plant them out on the *finca*. 'I feel so proud of my plants and of what we are doing,' she says. Ortega takes her dried coffee to a local roaster, a less expensive option than buying the machinery herself. She finds it more profitable to sell coffee that has been processed, although it is a challenge to identify sufficient clients, so she is looking to sell to export companies in the near future. She is able to cover her costs and labour expenses with what she sells between October and December.

'My dream is to have a coffee shop,' Ortega confesses. For now, she distributes her coffee under the 'Montecasino' brand name, as yet unregistered. 'I am so busy that work has lifted my spirits in these difficult times,' she adds. 'I am very thankful to my husband for giving me a way of working, not money or property but a way to earn a living.'

(left) **A worker at Rancho Santa Cruz picking coffee cherries to be de-pulped** (above) **and dried in Rosana Ortega Aguilar's** (right) **former swimming pool; and Ortega checking the nursery** (facing page) **at her plantation in Xico**

(right) **Storm clouds threatening coffee pickers returning at day's end to Ortega's small *finca*; and** (below) **One of the ranch's horses snacking on bananas tied to a fence**

(following spread, left) **A vanilla picker at the eco-park in Xanath, Papantla de Olarte, Veracruz.** (following spread, right) **Vanilla originated in Mexico; the Aztecs named the vanilla orchid *tlilxochitl*. Its introduction to Europe in the 1520s resulted in many failed attempts to cultivate it there. Today the vanilla orchid is grown globally, with all modern species deriving from the original Mexican variety**

538

539

Tlacotalpan

(left) **The port of Tlacotalpan, a UNESCO World Heritage Site on the Gulf of Mexico filled with colourful colonial-era architecture, including** (above) **the Parroquia San Cristóbal on the main square**

(right) **A bouquet of pink roses against shades of yellow-orange; and** (below) **A man carrying his shopping through Tlacotalpan's colonnaded streets**

Raquel Torres
Anthropologist & Traditional Cook, Xalapa, Veracruz

'Although I am an anthropologist, I would prefer to be called a cook,' says Raquel Torres, who became a cook not at her mother's or grandmother's knee like many others but 'because of a house' she bought thirty-five years ago. Having learned to prepare Chinese food from an acquaintance whose father-in-law had cooked for the Emperor of China, Torres invited a group of friends round for a meal. When one of them asked whether she was going to turn her new house into a restaurant, she said no, but the question made her think. Inspired by the age of the house, she began to investigate early twentieth-century Mexican recipe books.

When other life plans failed to materialise due to the economic crisis in the '80s, Torres was inspired to start visiting traditional kitchens, mainly indigenous ones, to learn more about cooking. 'I am not an academic anthropologist or a researcher. I love to be with real cooks and get dirty making *mole*,' she says. 'If I smell of onion, it means I have been working ... I tell my writer friends that they should not be reading but living!' She likens her work with traditional cooks to being around 'actors repeating someone else's script', and emphasises that economics, geography and division of labour all contribute to local culinary differences. 'Men bring wood and light the fire, but women decide how to place everything,' she says of traditional Oaxacan kitchens. 'Men and women work together in the kitchen, but it is the woman who is in control. And she makes the man feel as though he is in control.'

Torres believes in the primacy of taste as a way of experiencing the world: 'Yes, you do have eyes, but it is the mouth that makes it possible to feed not just our body but also our spirit, our soul ... Everyone uses a different *sasón* [type of seasoning]. Why does each one of us cook the same recipe and it tastes different? Because our stories are different. One reflects one's own soul when one cooks. It is an extension of energy; that is why I encourage cooks to use their hands. I hate when they use gloves to make food more hygienic!' It was while working with a cook in Sotavento in Veracruz that Torres realised that she should set up a workshop where she could share her knowledge with younger women. 'I had published five or six books [by then], but through books I cannot interact with people,' she explains. 'I prefer doing the cooking workshops to writing books because in the workshops you learn people's stories. I start by asking the attendees who they are and to share their thoughts about how they think the dish we are preparing should be cooked ... We start understanding why each person has a different idea about the preparation of the same dish. At the end of the lesson, we eat what we have cooked and we talk, and it becomes a catharsis. It seems that what I am really doing is therapy through cooking!' Each workshop includes between five and ten pupils and lasts five or six hours. 'One hour of talking with people at the beginning and then one hour at the end when we all cry,' laughs Torres. 'There are so many things that come out! I love it.'

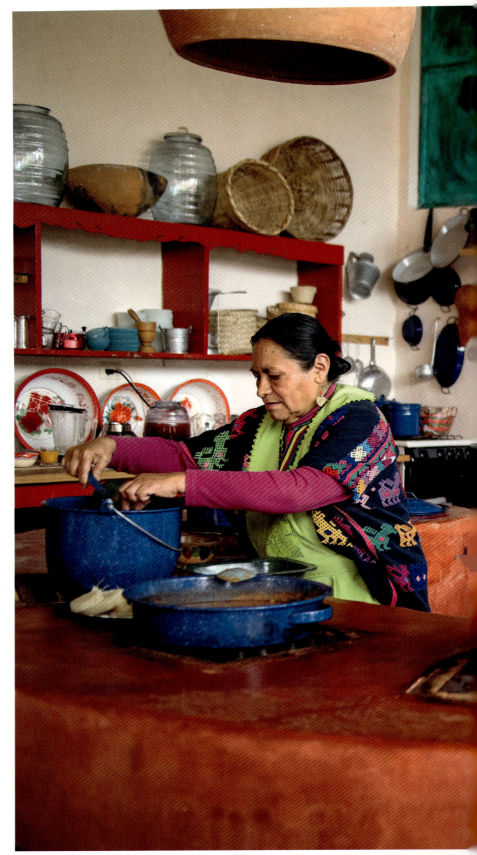

(previous spread)
Anthropologist/ traditional cook Raquel Torres with her assistant in the kitchen of her cookery workshop, preparing *chilatole* **(chicken stew), rabbit in an** *adobe* **stew and a** *pipián verde* **of courgettes**

(left) **Torres visiting the Mercado Leistegui in Xalapa to purchase groceries, including** (below) *chilacayote* **(figleaf gourd), and free-range chicken for making** (far left) *caldo de gallina* **(chicken broth) with** *setas* **(mushrooms) and** *flor de calabaza* **(pumpkin flower).** (facing page, top left) **A live turkey trussed up for sale in the market;** (facing page, top right) **Setas, which grow wild on coffee plantations;** (facing page, bottom left) **Hibiscus petals; and** (facing page, bottom right) **Bags of garden compost**

Morelos: *Viva Zapata!*

The kaleidoscope of Mexican colours has a way of getting under your skin, however many times you determine that it could not get any better. Morelos does that to the visitor. The weather and climate help. Sitting in the back of an open pick-up truck chasing the blues away, one wonders whether this isn't the place to situate the writer's shack at the end of some dirt road going nowhere. Except that reality gets in the way, with security a recurring theme. Cuernavaca, an international bolt-hole for the rich and powerful even before Aztec times, is no longer considered secure. But context is everything in travel, and, truth be told, we never encountered a single dangerous incident during months of travel across Mexico.

Who cares anyway in the face of ripened maize fields stretching towards hilly horizons, random floral outbursts glimpsed between passing trucks en route to refineries and loaded to the brim with cut sugarcane, roadside cantinas painted in bright pastels, and neat little flower displays in planters set next to charming blue and yellow chairs? History tells us that the land has always been thus. The Toltec built the ancient city-state of Xochicalco, the City (or House) of Flowers in Nahuatl. But history stands in silence when one comes face to face with its archaeological wonders. The place was destroyed by fire in AD 900, with site excavations from 1910 revealing personal objects abandoned in haste.

Troubled histories continued in the region from the time of the Olmecs, Toltecs, Mixtecs, Zapotecs and Aztecs right up to the arrival of the Spaniards. The area was incorporated into the Aztec Empire in the late fourteenth century with the marriage of Huitzilihuitl, the second Emperor of Tenochtitlán, to Miahuaxochitl, the Lord of Azcapotzalco's daughter. The union produced a son who went on to become Moctezuma I, the Emperor in whose reign the building of the aqueduct that brought fresh water to Tenochtitlán (where Mexico City is located today) was completed.

Hernán Cortés chose Cuernavaca as his seat of power in 1529, building a fabulous hacienda which today houses a hotel and restaurant set amid lush gardens kept pretty much as he left them – or so the head gardener claims. Further along in history, Father Miguel Hidalgo's call to arms at the start of the 1800s led to an uprising among Morelos' sugarcane plantation workers, their peasant army reaching as far as Estado de México before being repelled by royalist forces. The US occupied Cuernavaca briefly during the Mexican–American War, and Emperor Maximilian I, another invader, chose Cuernavaca for his summer residence in 1865, building a mansion for his mistress, who was known locally as '*La India Bonita*'.

Morelos' citizens have always had a reputation for tilting against the windmills of power. Emiliano Zapata, one of Mexico's most revered (and photogenic) political rebels, hailed from and died there, assassinated in an ambush arranged by Col Jesús Guajardo in 1919. Local mythology has Zapata being shot while eating his favourite stew of *mojarra* (a type of fish) with grasshoppers, tortillas and pulque. The same feast a group of kind citizens prepared for our tasting pleasure. Sitting under the arch where Zapata finally succumbed, I felt a peculiar pang. Too much stew? Too many grasshoppers fried with garlic, and one too many drinks, more like.

Hacienda de Cortés
Jiutepec, Morelos

The heart of the colonial period continues to beat in this sixteenth-century hacienda with all its splendours and contrasts. When Hernán Cortés was awarded the title of Marquis of the Valley of Oaxaca, the Spanish Crown ceded Hacienda San Antonio de Atlacomulco in Jiutepec to him. Surrounded by lush gardens and streams, the hacienda is now a hotel, restaurant and spa. One can imagine how slaves toiled to transform the property into one of the two most important sugar plantations in New Spain, an undertaking critical to the stability of Spain's finances. The house with its imposing stone entrance faces a garden ablaze with purple bougainvillea and red flamboyant; the perfume of orchids fills the air. No surprise, then, that it was used as backdrop in such films as *Butch Cassidy and the Sundance Kid*. It is said that Hollywood star Anthony Quinn wrote in the guestbook: 'Whoever has dreams that aren't fulfilled here ought to leave dreaming alone.'

In its heyday, the hacienda's 1,680-metre-long aqueduct transported water to the increasingly abundant sugarcane fields, and demand for workers increased. Slaves of African origin were brought from the Antilles, giving rise to a new social caste in New Spain. An Indian and black community formed around the hacienda to defend the workers against exploitation. Their organising focused on culinary and crafts practices, most obviously in the production of sweets. It is said that during the Mexican Revolution, the place was temporarily used as Emiliano Zapata's headquarters. After the Revolution, the hacienda's fields were distributed to the local community, whose ancestors had built the hacienda and helped to work the land.

(previous spread) **A truck transporting sugarcane from the December harvest to a refinery in Tlaltizapán, Morelos**

(left) **La Casona restaurant, framed by *amate* trees, at the Hacienda de Cortés** (above)**, originally the conquistador's home and later a sugar plantation**

Posada del Tepozteco
Tepoztlán, Morelos

(above) **The Posada del Tepozteco, a converted 1930s mansion, offers spectacular views of Tepozteco National Park and is renowned as a boutique hotel and for its restaurant, El Sibarita, where** (left) **poached eggs and** (far left) *cecina* **with** *pipián verde* **and** *ayocotes* **are on offer for breakfast**

Early-morning mist lifting in Tepoztlán to reveal the Ex Convento Dominico de la Natividad, a sixteenth-century monastery and church. Legend claims Tepoztlán as the birthplace of Quetzalcoatl, the Aztec feathered-serpent god

'Coyote' Alberto Ruz Buenfil
Spiritual Leader, Huehuecoyotl Commune, Tepoztlán, Morelos

'Much more has been destroyed than has been created. So we are just a flash. That's the beautiful thing about being alive,' observes 'Coyote' Alberto Ruz Buenfil. Born in Mexico, Ruz joined a travelling group of performers, artists and other creatives called the Illuminated Elephants and toured the world looking for a place to settle. Their ecovillage, Huehuecoyotl, established in 1982, is located in the mountains of Tepoztlán. The community tries to be as self-sufficient as possible, with solar-powered houses and rainwater gathered and recycled. Ten different nationalities are represented there.

Ruz studied at the Lycée Franco Mexicain and at UNAM (among other places) before leaving academia in the 1960s to travel the world with his group of like-minded souls. As the founder and coordinator of the Rainbow Caravan for Peace – an itinerant project that covered seven Latin American countries from 1996 to 2009 sowing seeds of change through various educational, experiential and artistic initiatives – Ruz visited dozens of cities and hundreds of rural communities. The project's aim was to create and support community projects and networks of groups and organisations to advance the cause of sustainability. Permaculture, bioconstruction, eco-technology, ecovillage design, conflict resolution, and health nutrition, as well as music, dance, theatre and circus arts made the Caravan a true 'living school'. The author of several books, Ruz has held other posts including Coordinator of the Ecobarrios programme in Mexico City, Director of Environmental Culture for the State of Morelos, and Advisor to the Federal Legislative Assembly for the Law of the Rights of Mother Earth.

'Time is as important as silence,' observes this man of many interests and talents. 'In quantum physics, you start to see that the coincidences that we experience come at random, like electrons. At the same time there is also science in our social relationships.' At the heart of his lifelong project has been respect for nature 'because we *are* nature'. If such respect is abandoned, he asserts, 'we're fucking our future and the future of the next generations as well … Without the Mother [i.e. nature] there are no children. The Mother can continue without us, but we cannot continue without her.' Ruz emphasises nature's neutrality when it comes to being generous with her bounty, saying, 'She doesn't select … It's also because the power that has been developed throughout history has been growing little by little. Maybe there will be a time when the earth will not have those kinds of possibilities.'

Ruz's commune grows coffee as well as bamboo and various types of fruit, including avocados and papaya. 'We are lousy peasants, unfortunately,' he jokes. 'We have our lettuces and potatoes, but we are something besides that. Otherwise, we would not be able to consider intellectual things, political things, spiritual things … Imagine if that part did not exist! Just think about what the world and humanity would be without it, without Jesus Christ and the Buddha and Quetzalcoatl and Che Guevara and Emiliano Zapata and us – what would it be?' In light of these realisations, what is Ruz's mantra? 'Take no more than what you need. Educate. Heal.'

(left) **'*Coyote*' Alberto Ruz Buenfil with the converted Chevrolet Blue Bird school bus used by his troop of troubadours to travel across India, the Middle East and Africa;**

(above) **His home, which was the first to be built on the Huehuecoyotl commune; and** (facing page) **Ruz blowing a sacred conch at the foot of the *amate* tree – the community's spiritual heart**

(left) *Quesadilla de huitlacoche* with *chapulines* (grasshoppers) on offer at the market in Tepoztlán; (above) *Chilacayote*; and (facing page) **A boy leading a mule laden with maize stalks past the wall where Emiliano Zapata, a leader of the Mexican Revolution, was ambushed and shot dead**

Mayordomía de Hueyapan
Santo Domino Hueyapan, Tetela del Volcán, Morelos

On a road that leads to the base of Popocatépetl lies the charming town of Santo Domino Hueyapan, whose name means 'a place with abundant water' in Nahuatl. Founded by the Olmec, today it is a predominantly Nahuatl-speaking community. Every year on 12 December, the community celebrates the Virgin of Guadalupe with a week-long fiesta prepared by the town's *mayordomo* or *mayordoma*, the person in charge of the arrangements. 'The Virgin of Guadalupe illuminates and guides us. She will provide,' explains Reina Maya Rendón, a local inhabitant and *mayordoma* for 2017. Clearly the Virgin does provide, as during the celebration breakfast, lunch and dinner are served to the entire community. It takes a full year to make the necessary preparations.

Why would anyone spend all their resources organising such a grand event? The answers are deep and complex. *Mayordomos* function like essential gears in the community's social life, linking spirituality and ritual to the material necessities of life. Social relationships, political practices and economic solutions all underpin these celebrations. They express the syncretism between indigenous beliefs and the Catholic faith. Essentially *mayordomos* are intermediaries between the saints and the pueblo, the arms and legs of the Virgin, who is the fiesta's principal protagonist. If she is properly attended to, the community will enjoy a favourable natural, social and economic order. This reciprocity between human beings and divinities represents a cycle in which things are given and received throughout the celebration.

At the start of the feast, five images of the Virgin of Guadalupe are taken from the Dominican Ex Convento de Santo Domingo de Guzmán to a specially made altar in the *mayordomo*'s house. From 8 December, the house is kept open to feed everyone who turns up. No-one arrives empty-handed. People bring 50-kilo sacks of beans, rice, sugar, maize oil, wood, and live pigs and chickens. The main ingredients that make up the continuously served *mole* include 100 kilos of chillies and sesame seeds, not to mention cumin, cloves, pepper, cinnamon, almonds, coriander and pumpkin seeds. More than 1,000 kilos of maize are used to make the tortilla dough. Beverages include homemade lemonade, hibiscus water and soft drinks. Alcohol in the form of pulque and beer 'makes men more willing, and happy to help with tough work', says Maya Rendón. They carry the maize to the mill to be ground and shift *mole*-filled casseroles, which can weigh up to 200 kilos. Various 'godparents' pay for decorations and services in the church while others are in charge of candles, fireworks, music and flowers. Community solidarity is expressed through the entire ritual, which also represents a leap of faith.

(above) **The Templo and Ex Convento de Santo Domingo de Guzmán overlooking Hueyapan, Tetela del Volcán, as the town prepares for the annual festival dedicated to the Virgin of Guadalupe by** (far left) **decorating altars; and** (left) **The preparation of tortillas**

Each year, all of the **villagers** (below & right) **help to make the festival a success, including** (above) **a mariachi welcome**

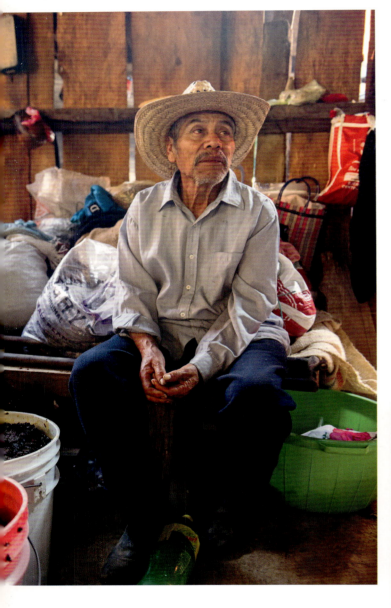

(far left) **Cenaido Soveranes Aragón resting in the kitchen while his wife Katerina Noseda Pérez** (left) **prepares** *mole* **for the festival with Modesta Espinoza Flores** (above)**; and** (facing page, top) **Women gathering to make tamales and** (facing page, bottom) **pluck chickens for the festival's orgy of eating**

Querétaro: *Pueblo Mágico*

Mexico is intoxicating. Its history is dramatic, its people diverse and delightful in most instances. A far cry from the image projected by media and politics north of the border, but you have to seek out the country's hidden and not-so-hidden treasures.

Land-locked Querétaro, among the smallest of states, is one of those treasures. It is situated in north-central Mexico in a region known as the Bajío, and close to Mexico City. Beautifully preserved, its towns and villages have a magical air and an unhurried ambiance as if frozen in time. Yet the state boasts a dynamic economy with a biodiverse mix of agriculture, a thriving industrial sector benefiting from one of Mexico's lowest crime rates, and the highest transparency index on governance. Mining, textiles and advanced manufacturing – mostly born on the back of the North America Free Trade Agreement (NAFTA) – make Querétaro one of the country's richest states. With its rugged landscape, high elevations, steep valleys and dramatic climatic differences (semi-arid desert to semi-tropical), you can visit pine and oak forests in the Sierra Gorda biosphere reserve and follow semi-desert landscapes to Colón (Mexico's only municipality named after Christopher Columbus) and Peñamiller in the same morning. And wander into a bygone era in the *Pueblo Mágico* of San Sebastián Bernal, known to rock-climbing aficionados worldwide as the location of the world's third-largest monolith.

The strangeness of happenstance is the lubricant of all journeys of discovery. Wondering aimlessly, we came upon a parade of horsemen, or *cabalgata*, as if on cue. To see men and women from all walks of life riding their steeds like extras on a film set, showing off their horsemanship and displaying equine finery lovingly polished, was a thrill. The history of the horse in Mexico deserves a book all its own, as Mexicans' love of horses is deeply entrenched, especially among country folk. The hardy Criollos were descendants of Spanish stock introduced by the conquistadors after 1535, as only fifteen horses were originally brought over. The breed was nearly wiped out later during the Revolution, as much fighting was done on horseback.

Querétaro's livestock production and strategic position in relation to its northern neighbour made its capital city of the same name a big player in the history of Mexico. Miguel Hidalgo and his co-conspirators hatched their plot for independence there, while the Mexican government's seat of power was twice moved from its capital to Querétaro city. The short reign of Maximillian I ended in the state, one of the last to remain loyal to the Mexican monarchy. The Emperor's last stand having ended in defeat, he was captured and executed in 1867 along with two of his generals. His last words: 'I forgive everyone, and I ask everyone to forgive me. May my blood which is about to be shed be for the good of the country. *Viva Mexico, viva la independencia*!' I remember seeing Edouard Manet's *Execution of Emperor Maximilian* at London's National Gallery many years ago. I could not help but think of Mexico as a land bounded by irony amid the paradoxes of history as I sat on the steps outside Maximilian's mausoleum in Cerro de las Campanas.

San Sebastián Bernal, Querétaro

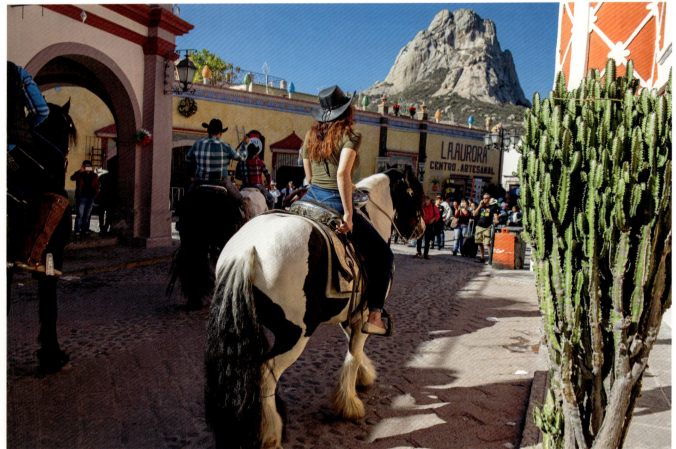

(previous spread) **Flashes of colour amid serenity: an indigenous street vendor hawking her wares in the** *centro historico* **of Querétaro city**

(above) **The queen of the** *cabalgata*, **a traditional procession (left) in the shadow of La Peña de Bernal, the world's third-largest monolith**

(left) **Typical street food: maize** *esquites*, *elotes asados* **(grilled maize) and** (above) *gorditas* **that are prepared and sold to tourists, the town's economic mainstay**

(following spread) **An intricate silver saddle used for the** *cabalgata*. **Horses have been important in the history of Querétaro, and processions on horseback are organised in honour of various saints. For some** *charros*, **the saddle and its finery are more important than their mount**

The General's House
Querétaro, Querétaro

The centre of Querétaro city is filled with houses from different centuries and with many stories to tell. In 1996 UNESCO declared the town's historic centre as a World Heritage Site. Its Baroque and later monuments provide a lively sense of what the place was like during the seventeenth and eighteenth centuries. Most of the splendid *casonas queretanas*, or big houses, date from the 1700s, and cluster around Andador 5 de Mayo, the Plaza de la Independencia and Calle Hidalgo (where the General's House is located).

General Ramón Rodríguez Familiar was born in Querétaro in 1898. Both of his parents were chemists; they amassed sufficient savings to send their son to school. The story goes that the general was born in front of the old Governmental Palace and as a boy became friends with its clerk, José Santiestevan, who allowed him to play in his office. When, one morning, Rodríguez Familiar was found under the Governor's desk, the incident was interpreted as an omen of what he would become. Choosing a military career, he participated in the Mexican Revolution as a follower of the anti-corruption De la Huerta Rebellion. He served under General Abelardo Rodríguez (the two became good friends), Alvaro Obregón and Plutarco Elías Calles, all of whom went on to become presidents of Mexico. In 1935 Rodríguez Familiar became Governor of the state of Querétaro. He married Maria Luisa Fuentes and had three children, the oldest of whom married the daughter of Plutarco Elías Calles, another of Mexico's presidents.

Don Jesús Cruz Cruz, who worked for the general for fifty-five years, describes him as a man of *categoria* (class). 'The general´s term as Governor was preceded by that of a "heretic" called Saturnino Osornio who closed all the churches in Querétaro,' he explains. 'The President asked Governor General Rodríguez Familiar to reopen the churches, saying, "Then you will have the people on your side." The general was good-looking, private, a very good person. He never liked violence.'

It was at the end of his governorship that Rodríguez Familiar purchased the house at Calle Hidalgo 11. The building is said to have been used as a hiding place for nuns during *La Cristiada*, a struggle against the secularist policies of the Mexican government, and has been renovated several times. Because of its architecture, size and the presence of land around it for farming, it has been compared to the missions of California (for example the one in Santa Barbara). The general started breeding racehorses in the 1940s, racing them at the Hipódromo in Mexico City.

(left) **A bedroom being readied; and** (above) **A tea set redolent of more refined times**

(above) **A view of the kitchen, and** (right) **the main dining room in General Ramón Rodríguez Familiar's impeccably restored mansion**

Oaxaca: *Tradition & Art*

Guillermo Olguín Mitchell is a Oaxacan artist and a Mexican in that order. The attachment of Mexicans to their states or indigenous cultures is a constant meme throughout the country, whether rich or poor, rural or urban. When you ask someone in Mexico City where they are from, the answer invariably points in the direction of the state or region in which they were born. Olguín, funnily enough, moved to his adopted state when he was three years old, but he is a tireless advocate for it; he is also someone who puts the 'can' in 'Mexican'. Mindful of the overbearing presence of his country's neighbour to the north, Olguín, like many other intellectuals I came across, feels a strong aversion to the influence the US imposes willy-nilly on his country. 'There are many Mexicans who want to feel that they belong to something to which there's no reason [for them] to belong,' he told me over shots of homemade mezcal. 'The whole direction is trying to copy something.' He angrily bemoans the erosion of pride, as he sees it, in Mexican values and culture.

While much of the country is becoming internationally orientated in terms of taste, Oaxaca is slowly 'trying to say we don't really need the homogeneity that comes with globalisation'. No shrinking violet, Olguín's education included time in Seattle and Budapest. He presently lives between Oaxaca, Mérida and New York, where he has set up one of the city's first *mezcalerías.* Close to his land and its indigenous peoples, the artist has housed his Oaxacan studio-cum-home-cum hostelry on a former goat farm. After painting (which he prefers to do outdoors), Olguín loves food. His open-air oven has pride of place next to a large kitchen with a communal dining table that serves the household and itinerant travellers.

Olguín is an example of Oaxaca's artistic temperament and fiery sense of independence. The state has been a magnet for artists and bohemians for the last few decades. Coming across Francisco Toledo, one of the giants of Mexican modern art, was a coup for us, as the master neither gives interviews nor allows photographs. Toledo is a Oaxacan social, political and artistic activist par excellence. His efforts have led to the founding of Oaxaca's Museum of Contemporary Art among other important cultural landmarks, and he is a tireless advocate for conservation.

Oaxaca is a multicultural state, its unique biodiversity encompassing a wide range of creatures as well as a diverse mix of peoples. The state boasts sixteen local languages apart from Zapotec and Mixtec, the tongues of its original inhabitants. Its history reveals massive bloodletting by the conquistadors and their allies, who managed to kill off 1.5 million indigenous inhabitants through war and disease. The state derives its name from the word *Huāxyacac*, Nahuatl for the *guaje* tree that grows around the capital. One of Mexico's most beautiful states, Oaxaca boasts a long Pacific coastline, impenetrable mountains and archaeological wonders such as the Monte Albán pyramids. Oaxacans have maintained their sense of independence through their native cultures and traditional crafts, as well as their rich and varied cuisine, some of which predates the arrival of the Spaniards. Evidence of human habitation goes back to 11,000 BC; the Guilá Naquitz Cave near Mitla has revealed evidence of the world's earliest known maize cobs.

Guillermo Olguín Mitchell
Artist, Oaxaca, Oaxaca

Born in Mexico City in 1969, artist and mezcal promoter Guillermo Olguín Mitchell studied in Seattle and Budapest; he currently lives and works between Oaxaca, Mérida and New York City. An enthusiastic proponent of Oaxacan culture, he founded Café Central, a space for music, film and visual arts, a decade ago. His interest in native cultures and products inspired him to found Casa Mezcal in New York City.

Although Olguín was not born in Oaxaca himself, one of his grandfathers was, so he considers himself to be Oaxacan 'in many senses'. He cherishes his freedom to be able to 'walk into any hotel in a town, stay there for six days, paint, everything'. He speaks with passion about his perception of Mexico as 'probably one of the most racist countries in the world', where historic multiculturalism has spawned prejudice rather than tolerance, although he cites a commonality of values among a wide range of indigenous peoples as a possible saving grace. What makes Oaxaca special, in fact, is what he terms 'the indigenous factor, the fact that things are still grounded. There is a sense that everything is connected to everything. Everything has a meaning'. These qualities of grounding, interconnectedness and intrinsic meaning form the essence of what Olguín wishes to express in his paintings. 'The symbolism [is] about why things matter, about animals, smells ... It's about the senses,' he explains. In contrast to this quality of being grounded is the admiration many people, both rich and poor, feel for their neighbour to the north: 'There are many Mexicans who want to feel that they belong to something to which there's no reason [for them] to belong ... The whole direction involves trying to copy something.' Olguín blames the ubiquity of television, in particular, for an erosion of pride in Mexican values and culture. While much of the country is becoming internationalised in terms of taste, in Oaxaca, he says, 'slowly, we're trying to say we don't really need [i.e. the homogeneity that comes with] globalisation.'

Setting politics firmly to one side, Olguín believes that food is one of the ultimate defence points of any culture, though in Mexico, as elsewhere, the predominance of supermarkets has heavily eroded the energy and uniqueness of local markets. The only hope, he believes, is for the two types of outlets to coexist. As a fan of good eating, he says, 'I've travelled all over Mexico, and the moment you cross the border from Tabasco, Campeche and so on, things are very limited. It has to do with the number of indigenous people who are doing their own food. Here, if I sit down with a guy from Tabasco

(previous spread) **The Friday *Baratillo* at San Antonino Castillo Velasco. This market is famous for its livestock of every size and shape, including 1.5-ton bullocks the size of pick-up trucks**

(left) **Guillermo Olguín Mitchell in his open-air studio in Oaxaca, a former goat farm**

571

and we're having a little drink and he's talking about tamales, there are sixteen types in this region. There's an abundance. He will hate that I say this is the best place because he comes from Puebla; Puebla has its own gastronomy. But in the end we have to accept that if you stay in Oaxaca for six days, I promise that you will not eat the same dish twice.'

Olguín's *mezcalería* in New York City is located on the Lower East Side; he believes that it is Manhattan's first such establishment. His aim when he opened it was to import authentic Mexican culture by serving proper food rather than Tex-Mex, which depends, he points out, on dry herbs rather than fresh ones. 'It was two years of really searching for proper suppliers to be able to eat what I was eating here,' he remembers. Unfortunately, 'people didn't get it. This was seven years ago. I was doing *tacos de cazuela*, I was making handmade tortillas with maize that I bought here; there were two guys who drove the truck to get it there'. He continues to maintain the place as a symbolic venue, saying, 'It's there. I can go eat my tacos and drink a mezcal.' And, despite the current political situation, he is guardedly optimistic about the future of proper Mexican food and cooking in the US, saying of Americans, 'Those guys can't go one week without Mexican food!' It is possible now to find handmade tortillas in Los Angeles along with herbs grown locally instead of being trucked up from Mexico: 'They're going to have a different flavour because it's a different location, but it's there. So you don't have to have Tex-Mex.'

Olguín's painting 'has to do with food and living. My art is a personal thing, but it also has to do with travelling and looking for *mezcales*, food, rituals, symbolism and everything; it's all interrelated'. He applauds the efforts of younger artists who are producing work that celebrates their own culture. 'I think you can see it, no? It's always been there, but it's been discovered late. Funny, they have a lot more hunger or drive to discover new things ... Here it's always been like this. It matters if you discover it, but it's always been there.'

Olguín, a steadfast gourmand, keeps a traditional kitchen. (top) **The artist making hot chocolate according to his family recipe,** (right) **brewing *café de olla*, and** (above) **sharing his own-brand mezcal with a friend, artist Marcos Tufi from New Zealand**

(facing page) **Olguín likes to paint in the open air, even when it is raining**

Deyanira Aquino Pineda
Traditional Cook & Owner, Restaurant La Teca, Oaxaca, Oaxaca

Deyanira Aquino Pineda's small restaurant has been promoting the traditional recipes of her native region for more than twenty years. Aquino was taught to cook by her grandmother, whose skills were much sought after for weddings and other special occasions. Despite the family being very poor, there was 'always something on the table ... I didn't have plastic dolls or anything, but I always had amazing food'.

The cuisine of the Isthmus of Tehuantepec varies from that found in the centre of the state. 'There are many products that we adapted to our cuisine,' says Aquino. 'The food here is different because of the Chinese, Japanese, Turkish, Lebanese, French and Spanish people who migrated from Veracruz and elsewhere. They stopped in [various] places and brought mustard [for example]; we use a lot of mustard in our cuisine now. They brought [other] ingredients and incorporated them into the food of the Isthmus.'

Aquino takes her vocation very seriously indeed, saying, 'My role is to rescue all those recipes that are being lost. It is [an] urgent [task]. Being a cook is not just about cooking; you have to search, investigate, rescue and document.' She sees herself as part of an historical progression of women who 'have been the ones who have invented, used and recovered ingredients and flavours'. Before opening her restaurant, she worked in education. 'If someone invited me to a meeting, I brought *garnachas* and *moles*,' she remembers. 'Friends ... told me to set up a restaurant.' In 2014, her stews were included as part of a project presenting Oaxaca's cultural riches at the Vatican Museums.

San Francisco Ixhuatán, where Aquino was born, 'is rich in agriculture, fisheries and cattle, but it has some political issues I won't go into,' she says. 'Agriculture has taken a hit, but people are very hardworking.' Her father was a fisherman, and her mother travelled around selling his catch and other items. She has vivid memories of learning to cook together with her siblings. 'I always say that food comes in through the eyes, the nose and the mouth,' she notes. 'The most beautiful memories I have as a child are of the sound of the grinding stone while we played on the patio ... My mother and grandmother made *totopos* and soft tortillas for our meals. My father would bring salt from the beach each year when the lakes dried up.' Women from the area are known for their strong characters. Aquino notes that her mother 'was always the one to keep the money safe, never my father ... It was frowned upon for the man to hold the money .... We are very loving, the women of the Isthmus, but also very strong ... We accept reality and value ourselves'.

(right) **Deyanira Aquino Pineda in traditional dress in the garden of her restaurant, La Teca, in Oaxaca; and** (below) **One of La Teca's specialities,** *relleno de cerdo* **(stuffed pork loin)**

Alejandro Ruíz
Chef, Casa Oaxaca, Oaxaca

'Many chefs will tell you that they are inspired all the time,' says Alejandro Ruíz. 'That is not true, or at least I don't believe it. It is also not true that you cook a dish fifty times before sending it to the table. When you create something, it's a fact of passion, of emotion.' Ruíz, who grew up in the small agricultural community of Raya de Zimatlán de Álvarez as the oldest of several siblings, was given the role of cook's assistant, working alongside his mother. He went on to found El Saber del Sabor, the first Oaxacan festival of gastronomy, and was named Mexican Chef 2016 at the Wine & Food Festival Cancún.

Ruíz may have gained his culinary experience at restaurants in Germany, Spain and Austria, but he speaks of his humble beginnings with a total lack of pretension. 'We used to plant tomatoes, chillies, beans and squash, and my mum was educated to feed her family and to help my father,' he recalls. 'My father was a farmer but also a musician – he played saxophone – and he also built houses … I learned to eat fresh, good food; my mum made fresh tortillas for breakfast, lunch and dinner. She never cooked with gas … She died when she was thirty-one.' Of his father, he says, 'We lost him for twenty years because when my mum died, he tried to drink all the mezcal in Oaxaca. So I had to assume responsibility [for the family] … We continued working the land; we had one cow and three goats.' His mother's early cooking lessons proved invaluable: 'We [would] prepare *salsa de molcajete* at the table; I have done that since I was eight. My mother taught me how to roast the tomatoes and the chilli. I had to do that while she was making tortillas … She gave me directions and helped me to distinguish the different herbs because she also had a small garden.'

Casa Oaxaca features traditional Oaxacan cuisine, but to say that implies a simplicity far removed from reality. The state boasts sixteen ethnic groups and languages, it is divided into eight different regions, and its inhabitants are proud of their complicated family backgrounds. 'We are this mixture of indigenous and Spanish but also Spanish influenced by Arabs, and the Asians are always there,' Ruíz points out. 'So when you talk about Oaxacan food, you talk about these four main influences.' His daily visit to the market invariably results in the discovery of items or products he has never encountered before. This ever-expanding horizon of ingredients, on top of the state's eight different culinary traditions, inspires constant inventions in the kitchen. Ruíz remembers that the first El Saber del Sabor festival was attended by forty-five traditional cooks from the state's eight different regions: 'Those were recipes that we didn't know – and we are Oaxacans, and we are cooks! There were things I'd never seen and of course never tried. It happens to me all the time. I take a shower, go to the market, find things, buy things, come to the kitchen and start doing things.'

Ruíz's approach to cooking remains strongly influenced by his mother's knowledge and methods. 'If we killed a bird, we had to eat it,' he says of his times hunting for the pot with his father. 'There was no killing just for fun. That was my background in terms of palate.' It is clear that he continues to miss her energy. 'A week before she died, she was organising the celebration of the third generation of kids leaving elementary school,' he says. 'I was in that generation. She used to drink mezcal, she used to call my father to play his saxophone with his *compadres* … and she would pull all her friends out onto the dancefloor. Next morning at 5.00 she was washing her *nixtamal* to go to the *molino* to make her tortillas. At 8.00 in the morning, she was the first lady to appear with a *canasta* [food basket] on her head … I learned from her how maize should taste, how herbs should taste and how chicken should taste, tortillas, salsa.' Perhaps it is her particular joy that infuses his cooking still, and that propelled him from the family kitchen to become a restaurateur. 'This is the first goal or idea of being a cook,' he says, 'to make people happy. Then you have to learn how to charge for that. Then you have to organise a team who can run a place. And then you become a businessperson.'

(left) **Casa Oaxaca's patio overlooks the Jardin del Pañuelito, which is bordered on one side by the Templo de Santo Domingo de Guzmán**

(top) **Roberto Solís, his wife, chef Alejandro Ruíz (guarding a bottle of his favourite mezcal), Carlos Gaytán and Gabriela Ruiz Lugo in Oaxaca for El Saber del Sabor, a festival attended by Mexico's leading chefs as well as cooks from around the world.** (above) **The hostess at Casa Oaxaca; and** (left) **A tostada of** *chicatana* **ants,** *gusanos de maguey* **and** *chapulines*

(left) **Cinnamon sticks, roasted cocoa beans and almonds are ground, mixed with granulated sugar in a metal bowl** (above) **and then whipped by hand** (facing page) **at Chocolate Mayordomo in Oaxaca city**

Don Marino Ruiz Rios
Mezcalería Chagoya, Tlacolula, Oaxaca

Don Marino Ruiz Rios is a master *mezcalero*. In charge of looking after the farm at Mezcalería Chagoya, his job is to cultivate and prepare the agave plants. Having lost a hand in a factory accident when he was fifteen, *Don* Marino left Veracruz, where he was born, and went to Oaxaca, where he began working for the Chagoya family, who are still his employers. Back then, he worked cutting agave and transporting it in trailers.

Mezcalería Chagoya is a family business dedicated to the production and export of handmade *mezcales*. Founded in 1893, the business has been handed down through five generations. *Don* Marino has eight children and fifteen grandchildren, but none of his sons have followed him in his profession, which is normally passed down from father to son. Four of his sons live in the US, and *Don* Marino visits them from time to time. Although his own papers are in order, his wife does not have the necessary documents to travel with him, so she stays behind.

'Life on the farm is hard,' *Don* Marino says. 'You sleep very little because you have to … discard the bagasse [the cooked, pulped plant fibres] and change the [distilling] pot … You must also pay attention when the first stream comes down because that is the *punta* [the high-percentage alcohol indicating that the maximum degree of fermentation has been reached]. Then the *shishe* is extracted [this is the liquid obtained from the first distillation]. The *shishe* is distilled again in what we call a *resaque* [a reflux-style alembic still], which is left to boil again in the pot. That comes out as alcohol but in a very small quantity, a maximum of 100 litres … Working with agave is very difficult because the thorns are like nails. So you have to be very careful with it. It hurts a lot if you get stung!' There are upsides to the job, of course. 'Every day I drink two *copas* of mezcal, no more!' says *Don* Marino.

(facing page) **Agave fields belonging to Mezcalería Chagoya in Tlacolula; and** (above) **Mezcal master** *Don* **Marino Ruiz Rios demonstrating the safe handing over of a machete**

(above) **Cooked maguey** *piña* **being pulped down at Mezcalería Chagoya's mill** (left) **by** *Don* **Cornelio Rivera Jiménez and a long-suffering horse**

Adriana Quiroz
Textile Designer, Oaxaca, Oaxaca

Young textile designer Adriana Quiroz's new shop, Mano Madre, sells handmade artisanal items from Mexico and Guatemala. The artisans she represents have in common the fact that they see their mothers as embodying a sacred connection between the spiritual and the everyday worlds – hence the shop's name.

Quiroz started her project about a year and a half ago after studying Textile Design at Universidad Iberoamericana. 'I was always interested in handmade things because I grew up in Oaxaca watching artisans ... but I didn't know I was going to be a designer and work with them,' she explains. The concept behind her shop involves bringing modern garment design together with ancient techniques 'because a lot of [them] are getting lost ... People don't value them or appreciate them the way they should, so artisans stop doing them because they can't make a living ... I want to rescue them'. The shop features contemporary styles to attract young buyers, for example denim or leather jackets, jeans and T-shirts.

Quiroz's mother-in-law is from Juchitán in Oaxaca, a region whose inhabitants 'are very thankful ... to have what they eat, so they have a lot of dances. They dance in their [traditional] clothing before cooking, they have parties and ceremonies where they celebrate food, and they dress in handmade clothes inspired by food and everything around them ... Everything is connected: the food is connected with the ceremonies, and the ceremonies are connected not with gods but with their beliefs, and what they believe is connected with the earth'. The overarching concept is that 'they don't want people to start to lose their essence.' Such ceremonies are invitation-only, and Quiroz feels privileged to have been asked to go along together with her boyfriend, who is an artist.

The central importance of maize in Oaxacan cuisine and culture cannot be overemphasised, so Quiroz worries about the possible negative effects of transgenic crops on both. 'The same thing that is happening with maize is happening with textiles,' she observes, 'because people don't see past the problem. Traditions are being lost ... and people are losing jobs ... They're also losing their health. It's very important to me to find a way to make people aware of everything that is happening in the world, and I choose to do that through my clothing. I tell a story through my clothing; I don't just sell clothes'.

Quiroz's own culinary preference is for 'very strong-flavoured' dishes 'with many ingredients. For example, traditional *mole* has over a hundred ingredients'. In Oaxaca, she notes, 'I'm always finding something new in the way of food. I just tried iguana. I had never tried it before, and it was very interesting. Also armadillo. These are very ancient, special, sacred dishes of the people of Oaxaca.' Interestingly she does not mind that dishes once reserved for special ceremonies are now offered to tourists. 'That's what I love about food,' she says. 'People understand what it means, how it's prepared and that it's a gift from earth, and they don't overexploit it.'

(left) **Adriana Quiroz working on the clothing line which she produces with Oaxacan artisans and sells in her boutique Mano Madre, and** (facing page) **with her mother-in-law-to-be Nereidas Charis Sánchez preparing a colourful** lunch in the garden of Francisco Toledo's archive. (above) **Dishes** include *molito de camaron*, **soup made from a base of squash seeds, tomato and dried prawns, and** *pollo garnachero*

Templo de Santo Domingo de Guzmán
Oaxaca, Oaxaca

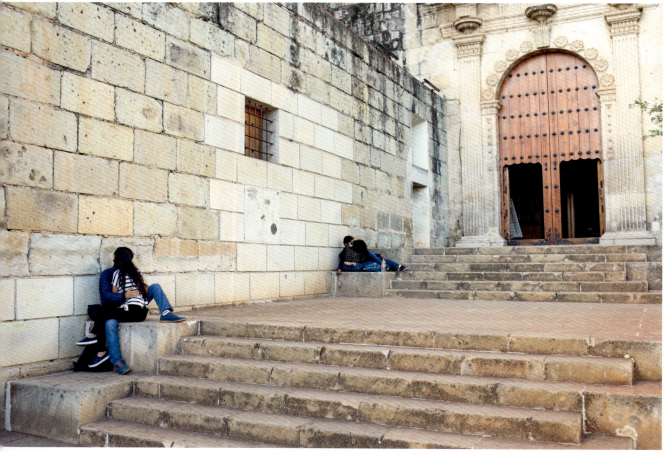

(left) **Entrance to the Templo de Santo Domingo de Guzmán, a rendezvous for young lovers. The Baroque church was founded by Dominicans in 1575, its decorative interior** (above & facing page) **requiring more than sixty thousand sheets of 23.5-carat gold leaf to complete. The former monastery houses the Cultural Centre of Oaxaca, founded and sponsored by artist Francisco Toledo**

Rosa García Hernández
Organic Farmer, San Miguel del Valle, Tlacolula, Oaxaca

Rosa García Hernández, who was born in San Miguel del Valle, went to the US to earn enough money to buy a plot of land back home with her husband. Despite being offered an excellent job and the chance to remain in the States, the optimistic, outgoing García chose to return to Mexico. She initially came into contact with the Fundación Alfredo Harp Helú through a niece who was attending a school at which the foundation was offering nutrition courses. The Oaxaca-born philanthropist Alfredo Harp Helú had set up the foundation in his hometown to support projects to benefit children, the arts and the environment. Seeing an opportunity, García started planting organic vegetables. Now she and her husband cultivate an organic *huerto*, or vegetable garden, together with three other families.

According to the government agency CONAPO (the National Population Council), Oaxaca is the third most economically marginalised state in Mexico. Although the state accounts for 3.3 per cent of the country's population, it only produces 1.5 per cent of the GNP. The main reason for this shortfall is the lack of infrastructure and education, especially in the interior. The vast majority of the state's municipalities do not meet federal minimums for housing and education, as most development projects are planned for the capital and the areas around it. This is why the Harp foundation's work is so important.

'If we want our lives to be healthy, we need to eat healthy food,' observes García. 'We need to teach our children to do so. In our town, children do not have an obesity problem but a nutritional one. Malnutrition is the challenge. We encourage them not only to eat fruit and vegetables but to question what type of fruit and vegetables [they are offered]. If we eat a vegetable that comes from a shop and it was grown with chemicals, we are supporting the [spread of] disease. This means that we will have a shorter life.' Working the *huerto* brings in insufficient funds to live on, so García also does embroidery and makes tortillas to sell in order to beef up the family's income. 'We work every day,' she notes. 'We had said we would rest on Sundays but haven't been able to. We go to the *huerto* to make sure the land is taken care of. At night we check on [everything], and in the morning we check that the rabbits haven't come to eat the produce.' The families harvest broccoli, beetroot, spinach, chard, bok choy, red and green cabbage, turnips, lettuce and radishes which they sell in local markets in Oaxaca.

(facing page) **Rosa García Hernández selling home-grown vegetables at the El Pochote market in Oaxaca city, including** (left) **beetroot from the farm she shares** (above) **in Los Valles Centrales, Oaxaca**

Francisco Toledo
Artist, Oaxaca, Oaxaca

Credited by the modern Mexican master Rufino Tamayo as being the creator of a new school of expression, Francisco Toledo was born in 1940 to Zapotec parents. His father was a shoemaker and tanner. Toledo studied fine and graphic art in Oaxaca and Mexico City, which is where he encountered Tamayo. From 1960 to 1965 he lived in Paris, painting, exhibiting and making editions of graphic work in the studio of the English artist Stanley William Hayter. His return to Mexico coincided with the emergence of the so-called 'Breakaway Generation', a group of artists that included Rodolfo Nieto, Pedro Coronel and Manuel Felguérez. In 1988 Toledo helped to establish a library at the Instituto de Artes Gráficas de Oaxaca, whose holdings include numerous artworks, photographs and books.

Toledo works in various media, including pottery, sculpture, weaving, graphics and painting, and has exhibited around the world. When asked whether cooking can be considered an art, he replies that it might be more accurate to describe painting as a kind of cooking. Regarded by many as Mexico's most important living artist, his compositions feature scatological, humorous and mythical subjects. Although his parents had no books of their own, his father would buy books for the children from travelling salesmen. Thus visual information was important to Toledo from an early age, and he retains his enthusiasm for it (alongside a naughty streak) to this day. 'If there is an image in a magazine,' he explains as an example, 'I'll put some colour on it, moustaches on ladies and things like that; it's just fun, a game ... For a long time, I've been intervening in photographs in magazines or book covers ... They're like a sort of mischief done to an image that is just sitting there quietly.' Although he considers himself a painter 'above all else', he jumps between media as a way of fending off boredom.

Both human and animal figures are important components of his compositions, again a result of childhood experiences. 'When we visited our grandparents ... we went to the river a lot because we didn't have running water in our house,' he recounts. 'We had to bathe in the river; women used to wash clothes; there were wells to draw clean water for drinking. So there was life around the river, and a lot of that is portrayed in my painting: fish, people swimming [and so on].'

Toledo discovered erotic art when he was in Paris. 'A book came out, a collection of erotic art,' he remembers. 'There was prehispanic art, Persian miniatures, [images] from India, Rome, Greece. This opened a whole new world for me. Of course, in ancient Mexico there was a lot of phallic representation; with the gods, everything was sexual.' Another long-term interest is onomatopoeic language, a subject 'that was very close to my father, because when my father spoke Zapotec, he did so in onomatopoeias'. His father's enduring influence is also apparent when Toledo talks about food: 'My father was a big eater, so for breakfast, he would have tortoise eggs (which weren't outlawed back then), armadillo and venison delivered from Oaxaca. He would eat so much for breakfast, like a king, a glutton king! And of course my mother cooked lots of iguana ... The bit [my father] liked the most was the tail, so he would cut it off and give it to me ... It has a lot of tiny bones, but there's also meat in there, and it's completely different from the meat of the rest of the body. So he would give it to me, but I didn't like it.' Toledo's distaste for this delicacy is telling: 'Iguanas were bought alive, so they would be around [the kitchen for a while]. They can live a long time without food or water, so they would be kept for weeks until, well, my dad fancied eating iguana.'

(facing page & right)
Artist Francisco Toledo taking breakfast at Quinta Real in Oaxaca

(following spread)
A pastoral scene near the town of San Bartolo Coyotepec, which is famous for its year-round flower cultivation

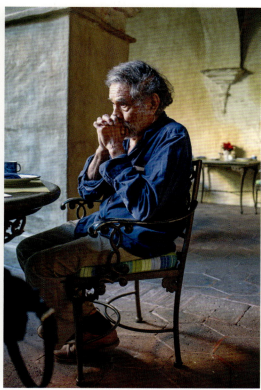

Postscript
Ana Paula Gerard

Our culinary quest began in spring 2016, when my husband, Carlos Salinas, and I first met Hossein Amirsadeghi. Hossein described his intention to create a book that would show an international audience Mexico's 'heart and soul' through its gastronomy. Without a real plan and with a head full of ideas, I threw myself into this thrilling adventure. Mexican cuisine was a fabulous language through which to show the richness of my country's culture and biodiversity. Food is a vehicle to reconnect with our roots, which sustain homeland, community, family and, importantly, personal identity. Throughout the project, I was grateful for the constant enthusiasm and support of my husband Carlos, whose knowledge and expertise of Mexico have informed my experience.

I am hopeful that this book can help to change Mexico's stereotype as a country hijacked and defined by crime. The present is sown with conflict: challenges of insecurity, inequality, poverty, injustice and unacceptable deficiencies of the rule of law. Nevertheless, there are many reasons to trust in another truth that is often forgotten, a reality upheld by millions of hardworking individuals with a profound sense of solidarity and community. People like young Alejandra Carrillo, who with passion and sparkling eyes talks about her hope to bring about social change in her neighbourhood. Carrillo collaborates with Torolab, an organisation located in a shantytown in Tijuana, its modern cement headquarters surrounded by humble homes. Their tireless work to impart music lessons, to teach the cultivation of small domestic *huertos* and to offer cooking and other courses has diminished crime and violence in their community. Or people like Juan Huh, a bricklayer in Mérida, who said to his wife Ana Lilia, 'If we have enough for our two daughters, there will be enough for other underprivileged children.' Their home has been transformed into a diner and classroom for eighty-two kids. The support of innovative chef Pedro Evia has been crucial to this project.

Hossein and I hit the road running, selecting varied characters in one way or another related to food to feature in the book. In achieving this goal, we gathered a diverse and committed team, each member bringing to the enterprise a particular experience of Mexico. Our itinerary was initially planned to cover preselected states and specific places and characters, but these were soon abandoned. How could we not include the bizarre and magical town of Mexcaltitán in Nayarit, famous for its prawns? How could we leave aside *Doña Lucía*, first and foremost a true Mexican matriarch and cook, ready to tell the history of the Mascogos community's escape from slavery in the US and settlement in Coahuila? How not to describe the wisdom and graciousness of the Huichol community, whose rituals are closely linked with food and drink? Our map expanded on the march, given mounting evidence that even in the most remote places, the miracle of a great dish appears.

In the end, our pilgrimage in search of the wealth of Mexico through its aromas and tastes included all the states of the Republic. I found myself sampling the inexhaustible flavours of our cuisine in markets, modest *fondas* and sophisticated restaurants: crunchy red maguey-worm tacos accompanied by guacamole; simple and wonderful moist tamale filled with fried beans; quail in cocoa sauce and honey sprinkled with fried ants, accompanied by a rare drink called 'jaguar blood' in Palenque; *chile en nogada*, proudly composed with the national colours; delicious *huauzontle* (herb) dumplings in a tomato-chilli sauce; the freshness of the *aguachile*, lime-cooked seafood immersed in a mixture of chillies, onion and coriander; delicious grasshopper *tostadas*, a real challenge for the eyes and the palate.

On a warm December morning, while walking to the colourful market in Oaxaca, listening to the melancholy voice of a tamale vendor floating from a distant loudspeaker, I found myself already feeling nostalgic; Oaxaca was the last stop on our pilgrimage full of wonderful, often conflicting experiences. This sense of loss was attenuated by that state's energy and cultural richness. The *Oaxaqueñas* are known for their strength; Rosa García was no exception. We met her in an organic market in Santa Rosa Panzacola. I was drawn to her luminous, contagious smile. Rosa's brightly coloured embroidered apron mirrored the state's character. She displayed her mastery of English, and we discovered that (as for many others) her experience working in the US merely marked an interim before returning to her hometown, San Miguel del Monte. Together with four other women, Rosa farms organic vegetables and has her customers within reach via satellite phone. She passionately believes in the link between food and health, and in respecting the ecological balance of the land. A generous optimist, Rosa is an example of the solidarity of spirit we frequently encountered.

Proust wrote: 'But when from a long-distant past nothing subsists ... after the things are broken and scattered, taste and smell alone, more fragile but more enduring ... remain poised a long time.' Through this book I have travelled in time, back home, to the days of my childhood. The flavours and smells that accompany our childhood carry spiritual and emotional weight: the evocation of some recognisable place or moment, the discovery of unconditional love through food. Recovering an original taste involves the rescue of a forgotten and secret order. Just as I inherited family recipes from my grandmother and mother, I hope to pass them on to my own children.

Traditional cooks of our day – mostly women – and the most renowned chefs – predominantly male – nourish their personal concepts of culinary art via recipes culled from the fabulous metaphorical treasury that shelters family and ancestral knowledge. The language of this book – that of the kitchen – is seeded with codes transmitted through generations. These codes unite and shape us as a society, and define the numerous, well-differentiated ways of harvesting, hunting, breeding or cultivating. We feel part of a community, recognising ourselves as being intertwined by a complex universe of dishes arising from the need, imagination and experimental instinct of our ancestors. The commitment to transmit, preserve and transform that legacy creates intangible bonds of unsuspected strength. A paradigmatic example of this wisdom is Chucho, a modern alchemist at the market in Campeche, an expert in the concoction of *recados*, mixtures of dried herbs and condiments. From his small shop crammed with colourful jars filled with spices, Chucho, with his swift magical hand, opens and closes each container and pours the precise amount of condiments for the dish requested into a plastic bag.

Our gastronomy is nourished by a culture several times millennial. Its basic ingredients are the same ones used by our

(facing page, top)
Ana Paula Gerard at the Pyramid of the Niches in El Tajín, Veracruz.
(facing page, bottom)
Alejandra Carillo playing football with neighbourhood children in Camino Verde, Tijuana;
(left) **Children saying grace before a meal at Nuestro Comedor in the Las Golondrinas barrio, Mexico City; and**
(top right) **Children in class, Fundación Anahí y Celeste AE, Yucatán**

(following spread)
The Maya ruins of Calakmul, Campeche

prehispanic ancestors: maize, beans, chillies and courgettes. From this starting point, combined with the crossbreeding that encouraged the encounter with Hispanic culinary practices (and, soon after, with the cuisines of the world's most diverse regions), has come one of the most nourishing and seductive gastronomic traditions anywhere. Even the technology used for the preparation of food claims the use of our own hands together with traditional tools like the *molcajete* (for sauces), the *metate* (for grinding), the clay pot, the wooden spoon, the wood-fired oven. All this sustains a powerful bond with a social tissue of extraordinary persistence, anchored as we are in our collective unconscious just as the elemental moulding and patting of tortillas is an essential step before casting them onto the *comal*. On our way from Mérida to Chichén Itzá we stopped to have lunch with a Maya woman known as 'La Tía'. In her smoke-filled kitchen, I asked what she was thinking while preparing the tortillas for which she is famous. Surprised by my question, she replied wisely, 'Well, that they come out right.'

Beneath the strong mid-morning sun, sitting in a *trajinera*, floating along the canals of Xochimilco – our first stop on this journey – I could never have re-imagined the extent of the pride I felt for Mexico. Living abroad for the previous few years had provided a new and adventurous perspective. I was irremediably seduced by the taste of the food and its aromas; deeply moved by the people, their generosity, solidarity and strength; and at times overwhelmed by the beauty of the places we visited. The dissonance that I experienced between what I re-witnessed throughout our journey and what I hear on the media about Mexico is disturbing. The country's problems sound loud and clear; our strengths and millennia-old culture need a loudspeaker of their own. It is in this context that we should acknowledge the formidable power of Mexican cuisine.

Acknowledgements

To get to know a country properly means travelling its highways and byways with people who know and love the place. That description exemplifies the seminal role played by Ana Paula Gerard on the quixotic journeys that became *México: A Culinary Quest*. A chance encounter with Ana Paula and her husband Carlos Salinas opened the door to a Mexico that would otherwise have needed far greater preparation and assimilation than was afforded by their knowledge, expertise and devotion to their homeland, its past and its present. Though new to the realm of publishing, Ana Paula's role as Executive Editor and all-round *consigliere* has, without question, made this book a representation of the spirit and soul of Mexico.

Roger Fawcett-Tang, another principal on the project (and a *very* long-time design *consigliere*), needs mention atop the mountain of goodly souls who have made this book what it is. Roger's style and grace under pressure are unique attributes. Andrea Belloli, Consulting Editor, has been on the job from the outset, her authorial and editorial skills a boon to the book. Anne Field, Chief Project Director, has had her skills tested to the limit, and she's come through with honours. Caroline Campkin, Production Manager, and a host of others deserve praise for outliving my tempo and tantrums.

Thames & Hudson have now partnered on my projects for two decades; all manner of kudos to them for their professionalism and efficiency. My thanks to Rolf Grisebach, Sophy Thompson, Christian Frederking, Natalie Evans and her team, Rachel Dewhirst and Isabel Hewitt. XY Digital and Eric Ladd helped turn wonderful photography into a veritable feast for the eyes, while IMAGO and their super-clever staff are thanked for outstanding production and print.

The photography for this book is truly brilliant. For which primary credit goes to Adam Wiseman, whose commissioned work comprises the bulk of the imagery. I chose Adam for the task after a brief encounter based on promise, poise and purpose, on which counts he has surpassed expectations. Carlos Alvarez Montero and Maryam Eisler also made noteworthy contributions with wonderful photography.

Our Mexico City team was itself a colourful weave of characters, none of whom had worked on such a project before, yet each contributing in their own way to make the impossible happen and make a virtue of the possible. Sonia González was my first team pick, a leading documentary filmmaker with a passionate take on her country's culture, society and politics. Her wide experience of Mexico and her organisational skills proved invaluable in her role as Project Director for Culture and Planning. Venetia Thompson, Project Director responsible for the culinary curatorial and editorial side, was a true professional, diligent even under duress. Miriam Tato, the unassuming 'angel' working behind the scenes to fix the unfixable, deserves her due. As does Homero Jimenez, our cameraman, ready to climb any mountain or rickety wall to ensure the best perspectives for the film produced alongside the book. Francisco Mendoza Sánchez deserves very special thanks for keeping the team together and in one piece, and for the gift of a Mexican soldier's friendship. Donato López, our helpful assistant cameraman, deserves our thanks, as do Guadalupe Cervera and Adán Ruiz. My thanks also to Allegra C. di Montezemolo for her help in introducing our Mexico-based photographers and to César Saldívar; to Annuska Angulo for the Spanish translation of the book, and to Eduardo Hurtado Montalvo for work on the Spanish edition. Also to Enrique Martínez Limón for his historical review.

Then there are the project's supporters, without whom this book would not have been feasible, including TV Azteca, Ricardo Salinas and Benjamín Salinas Sada; GBM and Jorge Rojas; and Fundación Alsea, GIA and Nexxus. Pushing us forwards has been the support of Enrique de la Madrid, the Minister of Tourism, and his staff, including José Salvador Sánchez Estrada, Undersecretary of Tourism. To Aeromexico and Andrés Conesa, its CEO, thanks are also owed. As they are to ProMexico and its Director General, Paulo Carreño King, for their enthusiasm.

I would like to thank Margarita de Orellana for her essay contribution to this publication, as well as her assistant Miztli Meléndez. Thanks are also due to our London-based researcher and coordinator Emily Bryson, as well as to assistant researcher Rebecca Gremmo. Also thanks to Melissa Sesana Grajales, Juana Silva and Xaviera Alvarez Nordström (translators), plus Rachel Horsman, Carriona Montgomery (transcriptions) and Liz Jones (proofreading).

Special thanks go to the governments of the states of Aguascalientes, Baja California, Baja California Sur, Campeche, Chiapas, Chihuahua, Coahuila, Colima, Durango, Estado de México, Guanajuato, Guerrero, Hidalgo, Jalisco, Michoacán, Morelos, Nayarit, Oaxaca, San Luis Postosí, Sinaloa, Sonora, Quintana Roo, Tabasco, Tlaxcala, Veracruz, Yucatán and Zacatecas, and their States Ministries of Tourism and Culture, and Public Relations and Communications Ministries.

Where to stop thanking the large numbers of others who've been helpful and supportive in so many ways? We must perforce thank all those profiled in the book. Each one of them took the time to meet us and allow us into their worlds. And to those engaged and not profiled, our gratitude.

The publishers would also like to express their gratitude to the numerous other worthy participants and contributors to the book, including Paulina Abascal, Jordi Abella Armela, Francisco J Acosta Cham, Juan Roberto Acosta Hernández, Marcelino Aguilar García, Belén Aguirre, Armando Ahuatzi, Sandra Albarrán de Calzada, Eloy Aluri, Fernando Álvarez Aguilar, Javier Amao and the Amao Family, Ana Cecilia Amezcua Volante, Alonso Ancira, Carlos Ancira, Claudia Ancira, Luis Arellano, the Arizpe Family, Sara Arnaud, Antonio Baes León, Francisco Javier Bañuelos, Fernando Beltrán, Ericka Blanco, José Blas Gil, Juan Bosco, Christian Bravo, Fernando Bribiesca, José Burela Picazzo, Elsy Caamal Florez, Alma Caballero, Hospicio Cabañas, Jorge Luis Cabrejos Samamé, Eduardo Campuzano, Alejandra Carrillo, Alma Teresa Carrillo, Tobías Carvajal Domínguez, Family Casillas, Rene Delgado Castañeda, Ana Fernanda Castro Santana, Daniel Alejandro Cavick Kantón, Alejandro Ceceña, Enrique Chairez Arellano, Marco Antonio Cisneros, Isabel Coppel, Oscar Cortázar, Guillermina Cruz Solar, Mónica Dafne Ruíz, Anna de la Torre, Nancy de la Torre, Alejandra de la Vega, Guadalupe de la Vega, María Teresa Degollado, Rene Delgado Castañeda, Armando Díaz de la Mora, Federico Díaz de León, Lorenza Dipp, Damaris Disner Lara, Dinorah Diana Disner Lara, María Guadalupe Domínguez, Francisca Domínguez Mendoza, Pamela Dueñas, Oralia Elías Estrada, Francisco Leonardo Esparza Moreno, Mario Espinosa, María Eugenia Rojas, Andrés Eduardo Fernández Samos, Raúl Ferráez, Orchidea Celeste Florez, Angie Florez, Sara Galindo, General Homero Gamboa, Paulina Gárate, Eduardo García, Antonio García, Beatriz García Marquez, Carlos García Travesí Bosch, Bárbara Garza, Mario Agustín Gaspar, Shanuani Gaspar Ortega, Natalia Gil, *Doña* María Gómez Lubianos, Alfonso Gómez Rossi, *Doña* Alejandrina González, Bernardo González, José Carlos González, Gabriela González, Guillermo González Beristáin, Mariana González Foullon, Oli González, Dulce María González Ramírez, Marco Antonio González Villa, Anna Rita González Villa, Vitorio González Morales, Eli de Gortari, Phil Gregory, Lourdes Grobet, Lucio Guerrero, Raíl Guerrero, Renán Guillermo, Zaira

Gutiérrez, Laura Hernández, Alfonso Hernández, Roberto Hernández Báez, José Hernández Castillo, Nayeli Hernández Guerrero, Instituto Nacional de Antropología e Historia, Miriam Hernández Morales, Akim Daniel Hernández Sainz, José Luis Hernández Uribe, Jorge Herrera Juárez, Jessica Marr, Jacob Herrera Mendoza, Victor Hugo García, Dalmacio Jiménez Moncada, Bernardo Juárez Rodríguez, Adriana Kavita, Carlos Kelvín, Felipe Leal, Carlos Leija, Diego López, Margarita López Vergara, Joselin Lucero Sierra, Lourdes Flores Macías, Abram Manzo Murillo, Alfredo Marín, Juan José Martín Pacheco, Cynthia Martínez, Irving Mayett Muciño, Leonor Mejía Gutiérrez, Eric Mendicuti, Paola Mendoza, Roberto Mercado Hernández, Max Mergenthaler, Daniel Milmo, Kalid Mohamed, Benito Molina, Adria Montaño, Héctor Montes, César Montes, Abelardo Morales, Javier Morales Carrizales, Antonino Morán Márquez, Uriel Moreno 'El Zapata', Prometeo Murillo, Solange Muris, Álavaro Navarro, Camila Navarro, Juan Flores Neria, Patricia Nieto de Mayer, Berenice Nieto Olmos, Carlos Núñez Pérez, Sofia Ochoa, Pepe Ochoa, Ivonne Ortega, Noé Fernando Pacheco Villalpando, Paco Padilla, Eduardo Palazuelos, Elena Palomeque Martínez, Walther Pérez Luján, Milena Pezzi de Téllez, Andrea Portal, Leopoldo Pulido, Marcos Ramírez, Juan Bautista Ramírez, María Teresa Ramírez Degollado, Jorge Antonio Ramírez López, Octavio Ramos, Samuel Ramos Martínez, Maya Rasamny, José Carlos Redón, Dulce María Rivas, Jorge Rivera Magallón, María Esthela Rizo, Javier Rodríguez, Moisés Rodríguez Vargas, María Eugenia Rojas, Ana María Romero Mena, Dra Rubi Silva, Eduardo Rukos Dogre, Mateo Salas, Concepción Salazar Ordoñez, Martín Salgado, José Salvador Sánchez Estrada, Cipriano Santa María, Silvestre Santiago Tejeda, The Santoscoy Family, José Guillermo Saucedo, Sergio Guillermo Sauzel Florez, Rogelio Servín Galvá, Jocelyn Lucero Sierra Jaramillo, Javier Solórzano, Juan José Soteno Elías, José-Afonso Soteno Fernández, Lucero Soto, José Soto Acosta, Betzabe Soto del Valle, Alessandro Spagnuolo, Sonia Spinola, Regina Tattersfield, Anna Rita Tazzer, Maximino Teresa Adame, Mauricio Torres Barquet, Pablo Torres Corpus, Berta Torres Valdez, Roselia Trujillo Olivos, Venancio Tuz Chi, Jorge Uicab Cuytún, Carlos David Valdez, María Jesús Valencia Medina, Mauro Vargas Sero, José Luis Vázquez Sanchez, Carlos Vidal, José Emilio and Delia Vieyra, *Don* Manuel Jesús Xijum, María del Rosario Zarate Ruiz and Filiberto Zepeda.

Finally, thanks to *Hoja Santa Magazine*, Villa de Patos in Coahuila, Torolab, Baroque Museum Puebla, Restaurante Bijlum, Restaurante Chelys, Restaurante Doña Lala and Grupo Amanacer del Taller Independiente de Son y Versada.

Hossein Amirsadeghi
London, March 2017